THE
HANDY
ANSWER
BOOK *for*
KIDS
(and Parents)

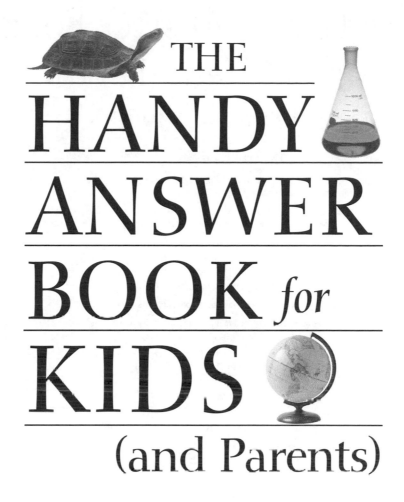

THE HANDY ANSWER BOOK *for* KIDS (and Parents)

Judy Galens and Nancy Pear

VISIBLE INK PRESS

Detroit

The Handy Answer Book™ for Kids (and Parents)

COPYRIGHT © 2002 BY VISIBLE INK PRESS®

Visible Ink Press®
43311 Joy Rd., #414
Canton, MI 48187-2075

Visible Ink Press and The Handy Answer Book are trademarks of Visible Ink Press LLC.

Most Visible Ink Press books are available at special quantity discounts when purchased in bulk by corporations, organizations, or groups. For more information, contact Special Markets Director at (734) 667-3211 or at visibleink.com.

Art Director: Mary Claire Krzewinski
Typesetting: The Graphix Group
ISBN 1-57859-181-3

Library of Congress Cataloging-in-Publication Data

Galens, Judy, 1968-
    The handy answer book for kids (and parents) / Judy Galens
and Nancy Pear.
       p. cm.
Includes index.
    Summary: Answers a variety of questions about such topics as nature, weather, geography, city and country life, technology, family life, death, and disabilities.
    ISBN 1-57859-181-3 (pbk.)
    1. Children's questions and answers. [1. Questions and answers.]
I. Pear, Nancy. II. Title.
    AG195 .G25 2001
    031.02—dc21
                                       2001005608
                                           CIP

About the Authors

With some preliminary experience answering a barrage of *whos*, *wheres*, *whats*, and *whys* coming from her young son Graham, Judy Galens was glad of the opportunity this book gave her to satisfy her own curiosity and prepare for life as the Answer Mom. Judy has worked on a wide array of reference books for kids and adults, covering subjects from world music to food festivals, from hockey to weather. She has edited a multivolume reference work on the Middle Ages, and she recently co-authored a book for young people called *Artists*.

Nancy Pear wishes that she had had some of the information contained in *The Handy Answer Book for Kids* right at her fingertips when she was raising her own very inquisitive child a while back. "He asked so many questions!" she recalls. Nancy has worked as an author and editor of reference books for almost 20 years and has written several works for young people. These include three books on explorers and discoverers and a three-volume set on strange phenomena.

Contents

ODDS AND ENDS . . . 321

Food Trivia . . . Clothing . . . Keeping Track of Time . . . American Symbols and Government . . . Disabilities . . . Substance Abuse and Addiction . . . Environmental Issues . . . Dinosaurs and Fossils . . . Amazing Science

Introduction

Why present information in a question-and-answer format? Because anyone who has ever been a kid, or had a kid, or hung out with a kid knows that asking questions is what kids do. It happens to be a great way to find out about the world around you. Kids have an insatiable hunger for information and a curiosity that winds its way down every road. And it's an adult's job to help satisfy that yearning for learning—by answering questions when you know how or by pointing kids in the direction of a good reference book when you don't.

Written with a child's imagination in mind, *The Handy Answer Book for Kids (and Parents)* is not comprehensive or exhaustive. Naturally we couldn't (and wouldn't want to) anticipate every burning question a kid might have. But it does provide lots of intriguing information on many different topics. Consider *The Handy Answer Book* a starting point, a launching pad that will send an inquisitive mind in many different directions (not all at once, we hope). Or think of it as a fun way to spend a few hours, flipping from page to page and learning new nuggets of trivia with which to impress your friends.

We focus on subjects that are front-and-center in a child's world, things that are parts of kids' daily lives or that spark their imaginations—from the stars twinkling overhead to earthworms burrowing into the earth. By the way, do you know why stars seem to twinkle? Or how big Earth is? Can you answer the ever-popular question, Why is the sky blue? The "Earth, Sky, and Beyond" chapter provides answers to such questions as well as covering weather-related phenomena (What is a hurricane? A tornado? Lightning?) and various features of our planet like rainforests, deserts, oceans, and volcanoes.

"World Tour" takes you on a journey around the globe, delivering answers to intriguing questions like which country is the smallest (Vatican City) and which is the largest (Russia). "World Tour" also gives details about different cultures throughout the world, explaining why we have different religions, why people speak different languages, and which language is spoken by the most people in the world (Mandarin Chinese). You can also compare the starkly different lifestyles of those who live amid the bustle of a city and those who work the land. Speaking of farm life, do you know why so many barns are painted red? Or why horses sleep standing up?

Perhaps the most interesting subject for kids (and adults too) is the sometimes mysterious workings of their own bodies, particularly as they pick their way through the minefield of adolescence. "Me, Myself, and I" addresses the many changes a kid's body goes through and covers the body's basic functions, from how muscles work to why knuckles crack. And we don't shy away from the less appealing (or more appealing, depending on your age and point of view) aspects of the human body, answering questions about sweat, pimples, warts, scabs, vomit, and the crusty bits that sometimes form in the corners of your eyes while you sleep.

From a very young age, children become aware of and fascinated by animals, and for many of us that fascination continues throughout our lives. "Our Animal Neighbors" answers scores of questions about animals of all kinds, from the tiniest insects and bee-sized bats to the largest land animal (the African elephant) and the biggest animal that has ever lived (the blue whale). Sometimes learning one small fact—like why penguins have their unique black-and-white coloring—can inspire us to look around and see things a bit differently. In "Trees, Flowers, and Other Green Stuff," readers will learn that plants are more than just attractive ways to decorate a yard; all animal life (that includes humans!) depends on plants, and their life systems are complex and amazing. Looking for a concise explanation of photosynthesis? Look no further. Do you wonder about the difference between a plant and a weed? Wonder no more. Have you always wanted to know what the biggest flower in the world is? It's a blossom with the lovely name (and equally lovely smell) of stinking corpse lily, and it grows to be nearly three feet wide.

All of us—young and not so young—use numerous high-tech tools and gadgets every day. It's hard to imagine life without cellular phones and e-mail, not to mention airplanes, televisions, and light bulbs. But what miracle of technology makes these items function? The chapter "How Things Work" explains it all. Did you know that a photocopier relies on static electricity to work? And what is static electricity, anyway? Have you ever wondered how an X ray works, or how a submarine can submerge and then rise in the water?

The chapter "Home Life and School Days" addresses such critical questions as, How can I get a bigger allowance? Why do I have to go to school? It answers queries being asked in neighborhoods everywhere: How does a bicycle work? Why do dogs wag their tails? Why do I have to do homework? "My Family and Friends" helps kids define the roles of various family members—siblings, parents, stepparents—and explains the value of things like telling the truth, behaving politely, and being a good sport. That chapter also anticipates some of the more difficult questions children ask about growing old and dying.

And finally, "Odds and Ends" houses the information that doesn't quite fit anywhere else but still is intriguing and important. Do you know why popcorn pops and soda pop fizzes? If you've ever wanted to know why we have times zones and daylight saving time and what the International Date Line is, you can find out here. "Odds and Ends" also covers several topics related to the U.S. government and national symbols, explaining why the Statue of Liberty was built and why the bald eagle is the official American symbol. Here you can learn about various disabilities and how people structure their lives around them. This chapter also covers the difficult subjects of substance abuse and addiction and explores such environmental issues as global warming, acid rain, and fossil fuels. The chapter concludes with discussions about fossils and dinosaurs, answering questions about what dinosaurs ate, which ones were the largest, and why they became extinct.

The Handy Answer Book for Kids explores numerous topics of interest to kids and helps parents provide answers that go beyond "because" and "it just is" and "I don't know." The chapters are divided up into manageable subsections, and a detailed subject index offers an additional avenue for accessing information. The section called "For More Information" provides a list of books and web sites that can help satisfy kids' appetites for knowledge. And more than 120 photographs spread throughout the book illustrate concepts and enliven the text.

It's often said that young children are like sponges, soaking up an amazing array and depth of information at a mind-spinning rate. Part of this rapid learning rate can be explained by physiological developments, but little knowledge would be possible without a sense of wonder and interest. And while those qualities can be found in abundance in most children, they are by no means the exclusive province of the young. If we're lucky, we continue to feel the excitement of learning new things and deepening our understanding for our entire lives.

Acknowledgments

I owe heartfelt thanks to many people who contributed in some way to the completion of this book. Thanks to Rebecca Nelson Ferguson—a person I'm proud to claim as a colleague and more proud to acknowledge as a friend—for suggesting me as a worthy candidate for this job. And thanks to Marty Connors for taking her up on that suggestion. Marty and business partner Roger Janecke also deserve congratulations for the perseverance and downright willfulness that helped raise Visible Ink Press from the ashes. My appreciation goes to the many authors and editors of the other Handy Answer Books, whose works provided interesting information and enlightening explanations as well as an exemplary standard for all Handy Answer Books to come. A special thanks goes to my co-author, Nancy Pear, who unearthed a lot of amazing information for *The Handy Answer Book for Kids (and Parents)* and displayed a gift for presenting complicated concepts in a straightforward, comprehensible, and entertaining way.

Thank you to my friend Jeff Hermann, who wore not one but two hats for this project—that of copy editor and of photo editor. Great job on both counts. Your patience with my last-minute additions was impressive. I'd also like to acknowledge the tremendous contributions of the two sources for this book's photographs: Rebecca Wallace of Corbis and Robert J. Huffman of Field Mark Publications. Thanks are also due to Terri Schell for attentive proofreading, Larry Baker for compulsive indexing, Marco Di Vita for quality typesetting, and Mary Claire Krzewinksi for another beautiful cover design. And thanks to Gonzalo Ferreyra, a dad well-versed in trying to answer juvenile queries, for first suggesting the concept of this book.

I'd like to express my gratitude to and love for my family members, particularly my mother, Jane Galens, whose love, energy, and continual quest for knowledge are inspiring; and my in-laws, Barbara and Bob Narins, who provided (as always) unconditional support, enthusiasm, and a few handy answers. My dear friends offered ideas and sincere interest, and they patiently allowed me to inundate them with things I learned while researching this book. Teacher extraordinaire Amy Goldman was especially generous with advice and insight. Jo-Lynne Rosenstein went the extra mile (as usual), providing me with several bags of books collected over her many years of teaching children (and being a mom). I wish to thank my wonderful husband, Brigham Narins, whose sage advice, unflagging support (technical and otherwise), and editorial acumen have saved the day on many occasions. And finally, I'd like to dedicate my part of this book to my son, Graham Galens Narins, a continual source of wonder and joy (and a master of the unending string of questions).

—Judy Galens

As a twenty-year veteran of the reference book business, I found writing *The Handy Answer Book for Kids (and Parents)* my most challenging project. This was in no small part due to the fact that the book was terminated at one point because of corporate downsizing. Visible Ink Press received its walking papers, and all works-in-progress—even those approaching completion, like *Handy Kids*—were unceremoniously shelved. It would take the great tenacity of Marty Connors to resurrect the imprint and, over time, to bring the project to a happy conclusion.

Handy Kids was also one of the most fun projects I have undertaken, and there are many people connected with it whose contributions I would like to gratefully acknowledge. I would like to thank Rebecca Nelson Ferguson, who suggested me for the job, as well as Julia Furtaw, who got me started on the somewhat daunting task of defining the scope and providing the questions that we thought kids were pondering. I would like to especially thank my editor, Dean Dauphinais, who was calmly supportive throughout the many challenges I encountered, and who was an understanding advocate when the book was unexpectedly scuttled. I am grateful, too, to my many friends, whose suggestions for and interest in the book were unflagging, and who earnestly listened to the mountains of trivia I shared while writing it.

I feel deep and profound gratitude for my talented co-author, Judy Galens. She gamely saw the project through to completion during its second incarnation, when I could not. She enlarged and completed the work and dealt with countless other matters so important to its publication. With *Handy Kids* in her very capable hands, I was able to turn all my attention to one of the sad exigencies of life—the passing of a loved one.

And it is to my loved ones, finally, that I wish to express my greatest thanks: To Brad Pear, my dear husband of more than twenty-five years, who has always been my rock throughout every endeavor, and—at the same time—my soft place to fall. Your gift for finding information over the web proved invaluable during this project. And to my son Winston. The once inquisitive little boy has become a man that I greatly admire, someone who continues to pursue his enthusiasms headlong—and who expects nothing less of his mother.

—Nancy Pear

THE
HANDY
ANSWER
BOOK *for*
KIDS
(and Parents)

EARTH, SKY, AND BEYOND

UP ABOVE THE WORLD SO HIGH

What is **air**?

Air is a mixture of gases that circle Earth, kept in place by gravity. Air makes up Earth's atmosphere. The air we breathe is 78 percent nitrogen gas, 21 percent oxygen, 0.9 percent argon, and 0.03 percent carbon dioxide, along with water vapor—floating molecules of water. Also present are traces of other gases and tiny bits of dust, pollen grains from plants, and other solid particles. As our atmosphere extends higher and higher above Earth, toward outer space, air becomes thinner and the combination of gases in the air changes.

What makes the **wind** blow?

Wind is simply air that moves along Earth's surface. Its speed, or velocity, is measured in miles per hour (mph) or kilometers per hour (kph). The Sun is largely responsible for wind patterns around the world. The pattern begins in the tropics—around the equator—where the Sun heats the air, which becomes lighter and then rises. Cooler air rushes into the area where the warmed air was, and the process is repeated again and again. The heat of the Sun—along with the eastern movement, or rotation, of Earth on its axis—causes this pattern of air movement around the equator. And this pattern, in turn, affects wind patterns all over the world.

Why do **helium-filled balloons** float up in the air?

While it may seem strange, the gases that make up air have weight. A cubic yard of air at sea level (which serves as the starting point from which all measurements of eleva-

1

tion, ocean depth, and atmosphere begin) weighs more than two pounds. When a balloon is filled with a gas like helium, which weighs less than air, it floats.

Could a balloon float into **outer space**? ⌣

The air that makes up Earth's atmosphere becomes thinner and lighter the higher up you go, so a helium-filled balloon would stop rising once the air surrounding it weighed the same as the helium gas inside it. Scientists think that 20 miles (32 kilometers) above Earth is about as far as any balloon could travel.

What is **outer space**? ⌢

Outer space refers to the area that exists beyond Earth's atmosphere. Our atmosphere is divided into several layers based on the temperatures found in each of those layers. The troposphere is the layer closest to Earth; it extends about 5 to 10 miles (8 to 16 kilometers) above the planet's surface. Most of our weather—rain, snow, sleet—comes from the troposphere. Temperatures in the troposphere can fall as low as -112 degrees Fahrenheit (-80 degrees Celsius). The next layer, called the stratosphere, stretches from 11 to 30 miles (17 to 48 kilometers) above Earth's surface. The stratosphere contains the ozone layer, which protects all life on Earth from the Sun's harmful ultraviolet rays. Temperatures gradually rise in the stratosphere, reaching a high of around 28 degrees Fahrenheit (-2 degrees Celsius).

The stratosphere is followed by the mesosphere, which goes to about 50 miles (80 kilometers) above Earth. Temperatures drop well down into the negatives in the mesosphere, but in the next layer, the thermosphere, the Sun's radiation heats the air to around 1,100 degrees Fahrenheit (600 degrees Celsius). The thermosphere ends at about 250 to 300 miles (400 to 480 kilometers) above Earth. The final layer is called the exosphere, and at that level, the atmosphere is so thin as to be virtually nonexistent. There is no line drawn in space marking the end of Earth's atmosphere and the beginning of outer space, but many scientists agree that outer space begins somewhere around 600 miles (960 kilometers) above Earth.

How **old** is Earth? ⌢

Scientists estimate that Earth is between 4.5 and 5 billion years old. They have reached this conclusion by studying Moon rocks and meteorites (rocks that have fallen from space to Earth) that they believe were formed at the same time as our planet.

How **big** is Earth? ⌣

Earth, which is almost round in shape, measures 24,901 miles (39,842 kilometers) around at its widest part, the equator. (The equator is the imaginary line that crosses

Outer space begins about 600 miles (960 kilometers) above Earth.

the planet midway between the North and South Poles.) A measurement through Earth at the equator—in other words, the planet's diameter—reveals that it is 7,926 miles (about 12,700 kilometers) across. Earth's weight, or mass (the amount of matter that makes it), is around 6 sextillion tons. That is 6 with 21 zeros after it! Because Earth cannot be put on an enormous scale to find its weight, scientists use the laws of gravity and mathematical equations to figure this out.

Is it possible to dig deep enough into Earth's surface to **come out on the other side**?

It's a journey that only a superhero could make. Earth is made up of different layers of rock. The outer layer, or crust, is solid layered rock that is about 20 to 30 miles (32 to 48 kilometers) thick under the continents and about 3.5 to 5 miles (5.6 to 8 kilometers) thick beneath the oceans. Earth's mantle, which is made up of a different kind of layered rock, extends for another 1,800 miles (2,880 kilometers) below that. Although scientists cannot penetrate this deep into the planet, they know that the mantle's composition is different from the crust because shock waves from earthquakes travel very differently through it. At the center of Earth is its core, which is more than 2,000 miles (3,200 kilometers) deep. The core consists mostly of melted iron and nickel, with a solid metal center. Rock melts near the center of Earth because the great pressure of so much weight above raises temperatures there to between 5,000 and 7,000 degrees Fahrenheit (2,760 to 3,871 degrees Celsius). The very center of Earth may

The needle of a compass is actually a magnet, and it will always point toward Earth's magnetic North Pole.

reach temperatures as high as 13,000 degrees Fahrenheit (7,000 degrees Celsius). Scientists believe that eruptions of volcanoes, with their hot gases and lava, or melted rock, relieve pressure from Earth's interior; that pressure escapes through the shifting plates of rock that make up Earth's crust.

What is **gravity**?

Gravity, or gravitation, is the force of attraction that exists between any two particles of matter (or any two objects). It is the force that holds planets in their orbits around the Sun, or the Moon in its orbit around Earth. (As the distance between two objects increases, their gravitational attraction decreases.) Gravity is also the force that holds any object to Earth—or to any other heavenly body—instead of allowing it to fly into space. The larger an object, the greater its gravitational pull. That explains why the American astronauts that landed on the Moon could leap about with little effort. With the Moon much smaller than Earth, its gravitational pull is one-sixth as strong as that of our planet.

Gravity also explains why Earth—and other planets and heavenly bodies—are fairly round in shape. When our solar system was formed, gravity drew the dust and gases hurtling through space into lumps. When a great amount of matter is pulled together at one time, it crowds together into the shape of a ball because gravity pulls everything toward a center point. Still, Earth is not perfectly round. As it rotates on its axis, the spinning causes an additional force to pull against gravity, making Earth bulge out a little around its middle.

Why does a **compass needle** always **point north**?

A magnet—made of iron or other special metals that are electrically charged—has two poles, or ends, where its magnetic strength is greatest. Each end has an opposite electrical charge. When two magnets are held near each other, the poles that have the same charges repel each other, while the ends with opposite charges attract. The needle of a compass is a magnet and, believe it or not, so is Earth! Earth's greatest magnetic strength is concentrated at the magnetic North and South Poles (which are different from the geographical North and South Poles). So a compass needle is attracted to the opposite electrical charges of Earth's poles, with the tip of its needle always pointing north and the bottom of its needle always pointing south.

Where is Earth located in the universe?

This is our cosmic address: Earth is the third planet from the Sun in what we call our solar system. The center of the system is our Sun, which is orbited by nine planets, several dozen natural satellites like our Moon, and other heavenly bodies like asteroids, meteoroids, and comets. Our solar system is part of the Milky Way galaxy, a group of some hundred billion stars that are arranged in a vast disk-like shape held together by gravitational forces. Our solar system is located about halfway between one edge of the Milky Way and its center, so all the stars that we can see from Earth belong to our galaxy. But with giant telescopes, scientists have been able to observe many other galaxies in our universe; some scientists believe there are 100 billion other galaxies.

What is the **order of the planets** in our solar system? —

Starting with that closest to the Sun, the order of the planets is: Mercury, Venus, Earth, Mars, Jupiter, Saturn, Uranus, Neptune, Pluto. If you have trouble keeping track of this order, remember this sentence (in which the first letter of each word is also the first letter of a planet): My Very Educated Mother Just Served Us Nine Pizzas.

How did the **planets** get their **names**?

All the planets in our solar system, with the exception of Earth, are named after ancient Greek or Roman gods and goddesses. Gigantic Jupiter, for instance, is named—fittingly—after the Roman king of the gods. The ancient Greeks and Romans believed that their gods and goddesses lived in the heavens. Astronomers of long ago—who thought that Earth was the center of the universe and that the planets and Sun orbited around it—decided to use the names of these mythical heavenly dwellers when they labeled new planets. Because our planet was not considered a part of the heavens it was called Earth, which means "of the ground."

Saturn, one of the four gaseous planets, has bright rings made mostly of ice.

Are any **other planets** in our solar system **like Earth**?

Although scientists believe that all the planets in our solar system were formed at the same time, from the same giant cloud of gas and dust, each is very different from the others. The four planets nearest the Sun—Mercury, Venus, Earth, and Mars—are known as terrestrial planets, because they are made of rock and metal. The next four planets—Jupiter, Saturn, Uranus, and Neptune—are called the gaseous planets, as they are made mostly of such gases as helium and hydrogen; their inner layers are liquids, and they may have rocky cores. Not much is known about Pluto, the farthest planet from the Sun (about 3.66 billion miles away). A small, solid planet, Pluto is thought by some to be made mainly of ice. Some scientists have suggested that Pluto may not be a planet at all; it may simply be a large piece in a band of rocky objects, called the Kuiper belt, that orbits the Sun.

The planets of our solar system vary greatly in size, rotation, and other characteristics. The smallest planet, Pluto, has a diameter (the measurement through its widest part) of 1,430 miles (2,288 kilometers), which makes it smaller than our own Moon. Jupiter, on the other hand, has a diameter of 88,700 miles (141,920 kilometers), which is about 11 times the size of Earth's diameter. If Jupiter were a hollow ball, it would take more than 1,000 Earths to fill it. Jupiter also has the fastest rotation, or spin, on its axis, completing a day and night in just 9 hours, 55 minutes. It takes Jupiter a much longer time than Earth to rotate around the Sun, however: a Jupiter "year" is 4,333 days. Mercury has one of the slowest axis rotations: it takes 59 Earth days for Mercury to make a complete turn on its axis. But Mercury rotates around the Sun much faster than Earth does: it takes only 88 days—a very short year compared to Earth's 365 days. Because Mercury rotates slowly on its own axis and quickly around the Sun, its days—defined as the time from one sunrise to the next—are as long as 176 Earth days.

Saturn is perhaps the most interesting-looking planet, surrounded by seven wide, bright rings made mostly of ice. (Jupiter and Uranus also have rings, though they are harder to see than Saturn's.) Although not closest to the Sun, Venus is the hottest planet because its thick atmosphere of mostly carbon dioxide traps in the heat of the sunlight that reaches the surface of the planet. The average temperature on the surface of Venus is 900 degrees Fahrenheit (481 degrees Celsius). Mars is the planet most like Earth, with a thin atmosphere and a surface that has mountains and valleys, extinct volcanoes, and what looks like dried-up riverbeds. Scientists wonder if some form of life once existed there; they have been trying for years to figure out a way for humans to explore that planet.

Only Earth has liquid water on its surface, which is necessary for life as we know it. Without water, plants could not grow, and without plants, oxygen—the gas essential for animal life—would not be released into the atmosphere.

How was the universe **created**?

There are many ideas about how the universe was formed. The most popular one is called the "big bang" theory. It is thought that at the beginning of time, all the matter and energy in the universe was concentrated in a very small space or volume that exploded. Eventually, the matter left over from the explosion formed galaxies. Within those galaxies came to be stars, one of which is our Sun, and planets, including those in our solar system. The universe as we know it continues to expand, moving away from the center of the big bang.

How **old** is the universe?

No one knows for sure. For a long time, scientists believed that the big bang that formed the universe occurred 15 to 20 billion years ago. This estimate was based on mathematical calculations using the current rate of expansion of the universe. But recent information collected by the Hubble Space Telescope indicates that the universe may be newer—only 8 billion years old.

How **big** is the universe?

Scientists have demonstrated that the universe is expanding in size, with galaxies moving farther from one another (objects within a galaxy, like the planets in our solar system, don't move away from each other, however, because they are held together by gravity). Because distances in space are so huge, scientists often use the measurement of light-years instead of miles to describe them. A light-year is the distance that light can travel through space in one year, which is 5.88 trillion miles (9.46 trillion kilometers). The farthest galaxies that can be seen from Earth are thought to be 12 billion to 14 billion light-years away. That means that the observable universe has a diameter of up to 28 billion light-years. And that's just the galaxies we can see—imagine if we could stand at the edge of one of the farthest galaxies, look through a telescope, and see galaxies extending 14 billion light-years from there. The potential size of the universe is mind-boggling. It is nearly impossible to imagine the distance of one light-year, let alone 14 billion of them!

What causes **day and night**? —

Besides orbiting around the Sun, Earth turns in a circle, or rotates, from west to east on its own axis—an imaginary line running through the center of the planet—spinning like a top. A complete rotation takes about 24 hours, or one day. When the part of Earth on which we live is turned away from the light of the Sun, we have nighttime. At the same time, people on the other side of the world have daytime. As Earth continues its movement, we move toward the Sun's light, and day comes.

If Earth is **moving** all the time, why don't we **feel it**?

Even though Earth rotates at a startling speed (1,036 miles [1,668 kilometers] per hour at the equator) and orbits the Sun even faster (at 67,000 miles [107,000 kilometers] per hour), we don't feel it because the rate of motion is a constant one, never slowing down or speeding up. We can only really feel motion when the speed changes. If you were in a moving car and couldn't see the scenery passing by, couldn't hear the wind blowing, and couldn't feel the car vibrating, you wouldn't be able to tell how fast you were going, or even if you were moving at all. Objects don't fly all over the place when Earth moves because gravity keeps everything firmly in place as the planet orbits and turns.

What causes the **seasons**? —

Earth's complete orbit around the Sun takes about 365 days, or one year. During the course of the orbit, Earth tilts on its axis. When the northern end of Earth tilts toward the Sun, it receives more of the Sun's direct rays. These rays warm the Northern Hemisphere and its summer season arrives. At the same time, winter comes to the Southern Hemisphere, which then receives less-direct solar rays. As Earth continues its orbit through the year, it tilts on its axis in the other direction. Then the winter season comes to the Northern Hemisphere, and the Southern Hemisphere enjoys summer. This tilt of Earth also explains why the length of days varies throughout the year. In the summer, more direct solar rays give us longer days.

What is the **Sun**? —

The Sun is a star, just like the twinkling heavenly bodies we see at night, far off in the dark sky. But the Sun looks different to us because our planet is quite close to it (just 93 million miles [150 million kilometers] away!). The Sun, a sphere or ball made of several layers of gases, gives off tremendous heat and light. It takes about eight minutes for the Sun's rays to cross space and reach Earth. It is believed that the Sun's vast and continuous production of energy is due to nuclear reactions among the atomic particles of hydrogen, one of its gases. The Sun is the center of our solar system, and its gravitational attraction keeps Earth and its neighboring planets in their orbits. The Sun's energy is responsible for Earth's weather—solar heating causes air to move (wind) and also causes rain by contributing to evaporation, a key step in our planet's water cycle. Without solar heat and light, plants could not grow and animal life could not survive on Earth.

How **big** is the Sun? —

The Sun's diameter—its widest measurement across—is estimated at 865,400 miles (1,393,294 kilometers). Its mass is 332,000 times that of Earth. Compared with the billions of stars in the universe, our Sun is considered average in size, with half of the other stars bigger and half smaller.

How hot is the Sun?

The temperature of the Sun's surface is thought to be about 10,000 degrees Fahrenheit (5,500 degrees Celsius). That's more than 50 times the temperature required to boil water. The center of the Sun is much hotter. Scientists have estimated that the center of the Sun is 27 million degrees Fahrenheit (15 million degrees Celsius).

Where does the Sun **go at night**? —

The Sun doesn't go anywhere at night; it is Earth that moves. Earth makes a complete rotation on its axis once every 24 hours. So half of our constantly shifting planet is always turned facing the Sun, experiencing day, while the other half is turned away from the Sun, experiencing night.

Will the Sun ever **burn out**? —

It is believed that the Sun—like all stars—will burn out eventually. As a star uses up the hydrogen that fuels the nuclear reactions that power it, it is thought to die, collapsing in upon itself. But it's unlikely this will happen in the near future: our Sun is expected to shine for at least another five billion years.

Our galaxy, the Milky Way, has some hundred billion stars.

What is a **star**?

Just like our Sun, stars are spheres of gases that give off tremendous energy, light, and heat. While the gases that make them may vary, it is always hydrogen that is responsible for the nuclear reactions that power them. Stars also vary in size and brightness. The largest stars, known as supergiants, are hundreds of times greater in size than our Sun. Other stars—known as white dwarfs—can be as small as Earth. The color of a star is related to its size and surface temperature and can range from red to orange to yellow to white to blue. Red stars have surface temperatures of about 5,400 degrees Fahrenheit (3,000 degrees Celsius), while blue stars have surface temperatures of 18,000 to 90,000 degrees Fahrenheit (10,000 to 50,000 degrees Celsius).

The term scientists use to describe the brightness of stars is magnitude. A star's magnitude can be difficult to determine just by looking at it. A bright star, if it is very far from Earth, may look dim to us simply because its light has so far to travel. A dim star, on the other hand, would appear quite bright if it is very close to our planet. In terms of stars' actual brightness (as opposed to how bright they appear to our eyes), the brightest stars are also the hottest ones—blue stars. Our yellow Sun is a star of medium size and magnitude.

How **many** stars are there?

Stars are arranged in galaxies throughout the universe. Galaxies are very large groups held together in disk-like shapes by gravitational forces. Our own galaxy, the Milky

Way, has some hundred billion stars. With powerful telescopes, scientists have located billions more galaxies in the universe in addition to the Milky Way, and each of these galaxies probably contains many billions of stars. Many more galaxies may exist that scientists have not yet seen. The number of stars in the universe is almost as unimaginable as the vastness of the universe itself.

If there are so many stars all around us, why can we **see them only at night**?

When our Sun shines on us during the day, the light is so bright that we cannot see any other stars in the sky. The Sun is much closer to Earth than are other stars, making it appear even brighter than it is. But at night, when the part of Earth on which we are located is turned away from the Sun, we are able to detect all the stars that are close enough to our planet to be seen—unless clouds get in the way, of course.

What is a **black hole**?

A black hole is an invisible region of space that is thought to have such intense gravity that not even light can escape. Scientists believe that a black hole is created when a giant star collapses in upon itself as it dies. A star lives as long as it can burn fuel. The burning of fuel acts as a counterforce against gravity; without that counterforce, a star's gravity would cause it to collapse in on itself. So when that fuel runs out, gravity takes over and crushes the star. If the star is large enough and has a strong enough force of gravity, it will become a black hole when it collapses.

While the existence of black holes can't be proven by direct observation (because they are invisible), their effects on light and matter—which are pulled inside and disappear—can be seen. Scientists have discovered evidence of several black holes in our galaxy, the Milky Way, and they believe there may be millions more that they haven't yet identified.

Do groups of stars **form pictures** in the sky?

Since ancient times, people have noticed certain bright stars in the sky that are arranged in recognizable groupings. Often a grouping reminded these ancient people of the shape of an animal or an object, or the stars' shapes reminded them of one of their gods. Ancient Greek astronomers gave these groupings—called constellations— many of the names that we still use today: some examples are Leo the Lion, Corona the Crown, and Orion, a character from Greek mythology. Altogether, scientists have identified 88 constellations in the sky, though their visibility varies with the time of the year and the location on Earth of the observer.

11

What is the Big Dipper?

The Big Dipper is part of the constellation Ursa Major, or the Great Bear. It can be easily seen on a clear night in the Northern Hemisphere any time of the year. The seven stars in this group resemble a large water dipper with a long handle. The Big Dipper is useful in locating the nearby Little Dipper, part of the constellation Ursa Minor, or the Little Bear. The Little Dipper, also made of seven stars, includes the important North Star at the end of its handle.

Why is the **North Star** important?

The North Star, also known as Polaris, is important because it is the star toward which the northern axis of Earth points. It appears to shine directly over the North Pole. In ancient times, centuries before the use of navigational equipment, travelers knew that they could count on Polaris to tell them which direction was north.

Why do stars **twinkle**?

The light of stars travels through the many layers of Earth's atmosphere before it reaches our eyes. Along the way, the light rays bump into lots of things—pockets of hot and cold air, for example—and they are refracted, or bent. The crooked path these light rays take makes it look to our eyes as if the stars are twinkling. If we looked at stars from outer space, where the light rays we see are not traveling through (and being bent by) Earth's atmosphere, the stars would not twinkle.

What is a **shooting star**?

A shooting star, or falling star, is not really a star at all. It is actually a meteor, a small piece of matter usually made of stone and iron. Flying through space, a meteor becomes visible when it enters Earth's atmosphere. As it falls toward Earth, it becomes heated from friction with air molecules and becomes incandescent, giving off great light. Most meteors burn up completely before they hit the ground. (If they do make it to Earth, they are called meteorites.)

Can a **wish** made on a **shooting star** come true?

Except for people who watch the skies a lot, like weather specialists or astronomers, it is rare to spot a shooting star. The period of time that meteors are incandescent—heated by friction with Earth's atmosphere and made to glow—usually lasts only a second or two before they burn up. For hundreds of years, when people saw things in the sky that were rare or unusual—like shooting stars or comets—they thought that they were signs from their God or gods predicting events, both good and bad, that would soon occur in their lives.

Even though modern science has now provided us with practical explanations about what occurs in the sky, it can still be fun to believe once in awhile that our lives are connected with what goes on up there. It doesn't hurt to make a wish—sometimes wishing for something helps us come up with ways to turn a wish into a reality. But shooting stars have no special powers that help wishes come true.

What is an **asteroid**?

Sometimes described as "minor planets," asteroids are rocky objects that orbit around the Sun; most of them are located in a belt between Mars and Jupiter. Scientists believe there may be more than 50,000 asteroids in that belt, and perhaps millions more elsewhere in space. They range in size from nearly 600 miles (965 kilometers) in diameter to some that are only about 20 feet (6 meters) across. (While 20 feet seems small compared to 600 miles, the smallest asteroids would still have a pretty impressive impact if they hit Earth.)

Slight changes in asteroids' orbits occasionally cause them to collide with each other, resulting in small fragments breaking off from the whole. Sometimes these small fragments leave their orbit and fall through Earth's atmosphere as meteors (called meteorites if they hit the planet's surface). Some scientists have suggested that it was a huge asteroid's collision with Earth 65 million years ago that caused the massive damage that led to the extinction of dinosaurs.

What is a **comet**?

While asteroids are made mostly of rock and minerals, comets consist of ice, particles of dirt and dust, and gases. They have been compared to gigantic dirty snowballs that orbit the Sun. As these icy bodies get closer to the Sun, the Sun's intense heat turns some of the ice in the comet's nucleus, or center, into gases. These gases, and the dust particles that used to be frozen inside them, fly off the nucleus into space, forming a gaseous outer covering of the comet, called the coma, and a long, glowing tail. While the nucleus of a comet is only a few miles across, the coma can be as big as one million miles (1.6 million kilometers) in diameter, and the tail can extend for millions of miles.

Usually comets can only be seen from Earth with a telescope, but sometimes, when they pass close to the Sun and are at their brightest, comets can be seen just by observing the night sky. The enormous comet Hale-Bopp passed within 122 million miles (197 million kilometers) of Earth in 1997 and could be seen without a telescope. The famous Halley's comet (pronounced "HAL-lee"; also called comet Halley) orbits the Sun once every 76 years (give or take a couple years), becoming visible when it gets close to the Sun. Last seen in 1986, Halley's comet isn't due back until 2061 or

2062. English astronomer Edmond Halley gave the comet its name; he was the first to suggest that comets traveled in regular orbits.

An interesting story about Halley's comet involves the great American author Mark Twain (whose real name was Samuel Clemens). Born in 1835, Twain came into the world in a year when Halley's comet, then a great mystery to scientists, was visible in the sky. Fascinated by the comet's orbit, Twain later predicted that he would die in the year when the comet made its return. This prediction came true—Twain died in 1910, a year when Halley's comet was once again visible in the night sky. When he made the prediction, Twain imagined God saying, "'Now here are these two unaccountable freaks; they came in together, they must go out together.'"

What is the **Moon**? ⏤

The planets of our solar system orbit the Sun, held in their paths by the Sun's gravitational force. Other heavenly bodies in our solar system—called natural satellites or moons—orbit the planets in a similar way. Some planets have many moons (Saturn has 18!), but Earth has just one. Our Moon is an almost-round natural satellite that consists of layers of different rock, similar in structure to Earth. It is believed that both were created at the same time, when our solar system was formed. (Some scientists think that the Moon broke off from Earth after our planet collided with another.) Unlike Earth, however, the Moon has no water or atmosphere, so nothing can live or grow on it. Without an atmosphere, nights (where the Moon is turned away from the Sun) are fiercely cold, and days (where the Moon receives the Sun's full rays) are very hot.

The Moon is located about 240,000 miles (386,400 kilometers) from Earth, close enough for astronauts to make a visit. The Moon's diameter is about 2,160 miles (3,478 kilometers), roughly one-quarter that of Earth, and Earth has about 80 times more mass or weight. The Moon does not shine on its own: the moonlight that we see is simply sunlight reflected off its surface.

Why does the Moon **change shape**? ⏤

The Moon never really changes shape. But the part of the Moon that reflects sunlight—which is the only part of the Moon we see—varies throughout the month. It takes the Moon about 30 days to make a complete orbit around Earth. During that time its position relative to the Sun and Earth changes constantly. These positions are called phases of the Moon. The part of the Moon that faces us can look like a disc (full moon), a half-moon, a slim crescent, or no moon at all (new moon).

Where does the Moon **go during the day**? ⏤

Because Earth makes a complete spin on its axis each day, the spot that we occupy on Earth is generally turned away from the Moon and its reflected sunlight during the

The Moon in its crescent phase.

daytime. When we have daytime, the other side of the world is experiencing night, and the Moon is visible to them. But at certain times of the month, when weather conditions are just right, the Moon can be seen when the Sun is still shining if you look hard enough in the bright sky.

Who is the **"man in the Moon"**?

The surface of the Moon is covered with mountainous highlands and smooth plains and thousands of craters—large round holes or depressions made mostly by meteorites that have hit the Moon's surface. Some of these craters are many miles wide. The plains of the Moon are covered by a thin layer of powdered rock that does not reflect the Sun's rays very well. The highlands of the Moon, however—where most of the craters are located—are covered by rocky rubble that reflects light much better. These conditions make the Moon's surface appear distinctly patterned when viewed from Earth. Some people think that the pattern resembles the face of a man. Because the Moon does not rotate, we always see the same side of it, with the same pattern. So the "man in the Moon" has been watching over us for a very long time! The many craters that can be seen on the Moon's surface remind some people of the holes found in Swiss cheese; in fact, some people used to explain the Moon's strange-looking surface to children by saying that the Moon was actually made of cheese.

What is an **eclipse of the Sun**?

Once in a while the Moon passes directly in front of the Sun as it makes its way around Earth. It temporarily blocks out the Sun, casting a shadow on a portion of Earth that is experiencing day. When this total eclipse of the Sun—a solar eclipse—occurs, the part of Earth affected becomes dark and cold until the Moon passes by. Surrounding areas experience a partial eclipse, where just part of the Sun is temporarily covered by the Moon.

What is an **eclipse of the Moon**?

Once in a while Earth's shadow falls on the Moon, temporarily blocking out the sunlight that causes it to shine. This is called a lunar eclipse. Just as in a solar eclipse, the phenomenon occurs when the Sun, Earth, and the Moon are arranged in a straight line. During a lunar eclipse, which can be seen at night, the Moon will become smaller and smaller—and then disappear—before it emerges bit by bit from Earth's shadow.

Is there **life** in **outer space**?

Despite many reports (over many years) of people seeing alien spacecraft (unidentified flying objects, or UFOs) and of personal encounters with creatures from outer space,

The Moon passing in front of the Sun, creating a total solar eclipse.

there has not yet been any real scientific evidence to indicate that life exists anywhere else in the universe but on planet Earth. The other planets in our solar system cannot support life as we know it—they are too hot or too cold, and they have no water sources. Still, because the universe is so unimaginably vast, the possibility of life existing on a planet elsewhere in the Milky Way or in another galaxy cannot be ruled out for certain.

Since 1960 scientists have been involved in a program called SETI (the Search for Extraterrestrial Intelligence). The scientists who take part in this program look for radio signals emitted in outer space that could indicate the existence of some form of life (assuming these other life forms would have developed radio technology). Radio waves can travel farther than visible light, so such signals could come from places in the universe too far away to be seen with ordinary telescopes. Radio waves are also not blocked or distorted by our atmosphere. In recent years scientists have begun looking for pulses of laser light in addition to radio waves.

Why is the sky **blue**? ―

The white light of the Sun consists of many wavelengths. When seen separately, each wavelength corresponds with a different color. The air molecules and particles of matter that make up our atmosphere scatter some of the Sun's light as it travels to Earth, especially the shorter wavelengths that give us the color blue. Coming to us from all angles in the sky, these light waves make the sky appear blue.

Why is the sky sometimes **red at sunset**? ⌁

At sunset, the Sun is low in the sky, and its light must travel through more of Earth's atmosphere to reach us. The extra air keeps shorter light waves like blue from making their way to Earth. But orange and red, with their longer wavelengths, can travel the distance and are scattered by Earth's atmosphere, becoming visible. They make the Sun and the surrounding sky appear red.

WEATHER BASICS

What is a **cloud**?

Our atmosphere is filled with floating water molecules, or water vapor. This moisture comes from Earth's bodies of water and damp soil; the heat of the Sun evaporates, or turns into vapor, that moisture, and the water vapor rises. When this vapor cools it condenses on microscopic dust and other floating particles and turns into droplets. Groups of these droplets—trillions of them—form clouds, which hang suspended in the air. These cloud droplets are so small it takes one million of them to form a single raindrop. When rain or snow falls to the ground from clouds, most of it eventually ends up back in oceans, lakes, and rivers, where it can again be evaporated by the heat of the sun, starting the process all over again.

What are some of the **different kinds** of clouds?

The different conditions of the atmosphere in which clouds form give them their special characteristics and shapes. The many different cloud types fall into three basic categories: low, middle, and high clouds. Cirrus clouds, which are made of ice crystals, form high in the sky amidst very cold air. They often appear thin and wispy. Stratus clouds form low to the ground. Gray in color, they can often be found in low, coastal areas. White, fluffy cumulus clouds (also found fairly low) dot blue skies during fair weather. Some middle cloud types are altocumulus and altostratus.

Nimbus clouds are storm clouds. They appear dark because the water droplets (or ice crystals) that form them have grown large—large enough for gravity to eventually force them to fall to Earth. (When water droplets are small they reflect light, but when they grow large they absorb light and appear darker.) Rain clouds can be low and flat-looking or high and towering. The towering, anvil-shaped rain clouds are called cumulonimbus, and these clouds are responsible for really bad weather like thunderstorms, hailstorms, and tornadoes.

Condensed water vapor that comes from an airplane's engine makes cloudy streaks in the sky, called contrails.

Can an airplane **fly through** a cloud?

Most of the time, an airplane can fly easily through a cloud, because the water droplets that form it are too small to affect the aircraft's flight in any way. Flying through a cloud is similar to driving through fog—in fact, fog is really a very low cloud. Because his or her vision is obscured, a pilot must rely on navigational equipment to fly through a heavy cloud. Pilots usually try to avoid flying through storm clouds altogether. They often fly above them, because the air currents, rain, hail, or lightning associated with storm clouds can cause bumpy and sometimes dangerous rides.

What are the **cloudy streaks** that airplanes sometimes make **in the sky**?

When an aircraft flies very high in the sky—where the air is cold—the water vapor from the hot exhaust of its engines condenses, leaving a trail of clouds behind, called contrails. These streaks are not the same as skywriting, when pilots use airplanes to write messages in the air. For skywriting, a special machine on a plane creates and blows out white smoke to form letters. A pilot can only skywrite on clear, nonwindy days.

What is **fog**?

Like clouds, fog forms from tiny droplets of water that have evaporated from moist soil or from bodies of water. Fog is basically a low-lying cloud that touches Earth's surface. Water vapor in the air condenses to form fog under many circumstances. On cool mornings, the warm water vapor coming off lakes or ponds meets cold air and forms steam fog. Fog can also appear when a cool front of air meets a warm front. Technically, fog is not fog unless visibility—the distance you can see in front or behind you—is reduced to about one-half mile (or about one kilometer).

Why does it **rain**?

When the water droplets or ice crystals that make up clouds become too large to remain suspended in the air, they fall. Water in any form that falls from clouds—snow, rain, hail—is called precipitation. Many different conditions cause precipitation. In tropical regions of the world, air currents cause the water droplets in a cloud to bump into one another; this bumping forces them together into larger droplets and they fall as rain. If the cloud is high in the sky, and the air the rain passes through is warm and dry, the rain may evaporate before it ever reaches Earth. In colder climates, most rain starts out as snowflakes or ice crystals. Depending on how high the cloud and how warm the air, these crystals will fall to Earth either as rain or as snow (or perhaps as sleet or hail).

What is a **snowflake**?

When droplets of water in a cloud come into contact with tiny particles—specks of dust, tiny pollutants, minuscule pieces of vegetation that have been carried up by wind—they freeze into ice crystals and begin to fall. Traveling through a cloud, these ice crystals may pass by air containing supercooled droplets, which is water that is below the freezing point but remains a liquid. These droplets attach themselves to the sides of the ice crystals, where they freeze, forming snowflakes. When water freezes it forms flat, six-sided ice crystals (though the way the crystals clump together accounts for a number of different snowflake shapes). As these crystals increase in size, they fall to Earth. If the cloud from which they fall is low in the sky, the snowflakes are likely to stay frozen and will fall to the ground as snow.

Although it's hard to imagine, each snowflake does seem to be unique, with a shape or size unlike any other. One American who enjoyed studying the weather, W. A. Bentley, spent nearly 50 years of his life making microphotographs of snowflakes to see if this was true. He never found two snowflakes that were alike.

How much **snow** makes an inch of **rain**?

Ordinarily, 10 inches of snow has about the same amount of water as one inch of rain. But temperature affects this general rule. The dry, fluffy snow we see during very cold weather holds less water—it could take 30 inches of that snow to equal one inch of water. The heavy, wet snow that falls when temperatures are just around freezing contains more moisture—as few as three inches of that kind of snow could melt into one inch of water.

What is **hail**?

A hailstone is a ball made of layers of ice. It starts out as an ice crystal in a cloud, just as a snowflake does. But a hailstone is moved about by drafts or winds in the cloud, rising into cold air and drifting down where the air is warmer, again and again. The process builds up layers of ice and melting snow on the hailstone. While the average size of a hailstone when it finally makes its way to Earth is one-quarter of an inch across, hailstones can become large enough to cause real damage, denting cars and damaging crops. The biggest recorded hailstones weighed well over two pounds! (Fortunately, hailstones don't fall too often and usually only during spring and summer thunderstorms.)

What causes a rainbow?

A rainbow is an arc that shows all the colors, with their different wavelengths, that make up visible light. Seven colors make up a rainbow, and they always appear in the same order: red, with the longest wavelength, is on the top, followed by orange, yellow, green, blue, indigo (a deep reddish-blue that is often difficult to see), and violet, which has the shortest wavelength. (A good way to remember the order of those colors is by taking the first letter of each to spell "ROYGBIV," pronounced "roy-jee-biv.") A rainbow occurs when sunlight passes through water droplets and is refracted or bent by their rounded shape into separate wavelengths. (A specially cut piece of glass, called a prism, can bend light this way, too.) Rainbows can sometimes be spotted in the spray of lawn sprinklers, in the mist of waterfalls, and—most spectacularly—in the sky during a rain shower when the Sun is still shining. A rainbow appears in the part of the sky opposite the Sun. Because the Sun must also be low in the sky, near the horizon, late afternoon is the best time to look for a rainbow if the day has been sunny with a few short rain showers or thunderstorms.

What is a **hurricane**?

A large and fierce storm, a hurricane starts in the tropical areas of the Pacific, North Atlantic, or Indian oceans, where it gathers great quantities of moisture and thermal energy, or heat. It is circular in shape, spiraling inward toward a nearly calm center that is called the eye of the hurricane. A hurricane may blow inland, where its high winds (ranging from 75 to 200 miles [121 to 322 kilometers] per hour) and hard rain can cause terrible damage and coastal flooding. A hurricane might spread over an area up to 600 miles (966 kilometers) wide and last for well over a week. Once a hurricane

Hurricane Elena, as seen from the space shuttle *Discovery* in 1985.

moves over cooler ocean waters or land, though, it begins to lose its strength. In some parts of the world hurricanes are called typhoons.

Why are hurricanes **given names**?

Tropical storms (including hurricanes) that have wind speeds of at least 39 miles (63 kilometers) per hour are given human names to identify them. This way, meteorologists, or weather scientists, can keep track of several tropical storms at once without confusion. Monitoring tropical storms is important for the safety of ships that sail in tropical waters and for people who live along tropical ocean coasts who need to be warned of approaching danger.

The practice of naming hurricanes and tropical storms began in the 1950s. For a long time—until 1979—only women's names were used. The World Meteorological Organization decides which names will be on the list, creating lists for six years at a time. The names begin with all the letters of the alphabet (with the exception of Q, U, X, Y, and Z, because few names begin with these letters). Hurricanes and tropical storms are given names from the list in alphabetical order as they appear, and a name may be reused once six years have passed. But if a storm has caused very great damage, its name will be "retired," which means it cannot be reused for at least 10 years.

What is a **tornado**?

A tornado is a dark, funnel-shaped column of violently twisting air that extends down from a cumulonimbus, or thunderstorm, cloud. It is usually accompanied by thunder, lightning, and heavy rain. Unlike ocean-generated tropical storms and hurricanes, tornadoes begin over land and occur when low, moist, warm winds blowing in one direction meet cooler, higher, drier winds blowing in a different direction. The rotating winds of a tornado can reach up to 300 miles (483 kilometers) per hour, and if it extends close enough to Earth it can destroy anything in its path. While most tornadoes only travel along the ground for a few minutes and a few miles, leaving narrow paths of destruction, others have been known to last for hours, touching down many times and leaving behind hundreds of miles of damage. Despite their small size and short duration, tornadoes do more complete damage than any other kind of weather disaster.

Could a person be **moved safely from one place to another** by a tornado, like Dorothy in the movie *The Wizard of Oz*?

No records show the survival of a person who has traveled long distances in a tornado. It is unlikely that any individual, or the structure in which he or she took shelter, could withstand the fierce sucking winds inside a tornado, which sometimes take objects from the ground and carry them high into the atmosphere for many miles. And remember, such a ride would eventually include a treacherous fall to the ground.

Despite their small size and short duration, tornadoes do more damage than any other kind of weather disaster.

Still, some records exist of nonliving things that have survived wild tornado rides. In the summer of 1953, for instance, a woman in Massachusetts found a wedding gown in her backyard, dirty but in good condition. It had been carried some 50 miles (80 kilometers) by a tornado. In the spring of 1979 people in Tulsa, Oklahoma, saw small slips of paper falling from the sky. These papers were canceled checks coming from a bank struck by a tornado earlier that day. The bank was located in a city in Texas, more than 200 miles (322 kilometers) away!

What can we do to **protect ourselves** if a tornado comes?

Only between 700 and 800 tornadoes occur in the United States each year. And of those, only between one and two percent cause deaths. Communities watch for tornadoes when weather conditions are right and issue warnings to alert people if a tornado has been spotted in the area. In addition to warnings being broadcast on the radio and television, many communities have tornado sirens that can be heard for many miles, signaling that a tornado has been spotted and people should take cover.

The best place to be during a tornado is under the ground, in a storm cellar or basement of a building. Take a radio with you, so that you can keep track of the storm. A flashlight will help you to see if the electricity goes out, and a first-aid kit can help treat any minor injuries that might occur. If you can't go underground, go to an inside room on the lowest floor of a building. Hallways are good places to go, as are bathrooms—the plumbing and pipes in them are strong and could resist violent winds. Get under a stairwell or sturdy piece of furniture, if you can, which will protect you from falling objects. Avoid being near windows; many tornado injuries are caused by flying debris, and sharp objects, like pieces of broken glass, are very dangerous. If you are outside, try to lay as low as possible on the ground—in a ditch, valley, or under a strong bridge. Protect your head with your hands. Don't seek shelter in something that can be lifted into the air by a tornado, like a car or mobile home.

What is **lightning**?

In a large rain cloud, as water droplets bump into each other and increase in size, they become electrically charged. This activity causes electric charges on the ground, too. Sometimes the charges increase until they become so strong (up to 200 million volts!) that electricity runs through the air between the cloud and the ground in the form of a giant spark or lightning bolt.

Sometimes, instead of reaching from clouds to the ground, lightning strikes between two electrically charged clouds, or within a single cloud. This lightning looks like a sudden glow of light in the sky, quite different from the jagged streak of light we think of as forked, or bolt, lightning.

What is **thunder**?

Thunder is the sound made by the gases in the air around lightning, which are quickly heated and expand when a strike occurs. Put simply, thunder is the sound of hot air exploding. Loud thunder may seem frightening, but it is totally harmless.

If **thunder and lightning** happen at the same time, why don't we see and hear them at the same time?

Light from a flash of lightning travels almost immediately to your eyes. That is because light waves move very fast, at a speed of about 186,281 miles (300,000 kilometers) per second (a rate known as the speed of light). Sound waves, on the other hand, travel more slowly: about one-fifth of a mile, or 1,100 feet (335 meters), per second (though this varies with the temperature and medium through which sound is moving). So the sound of thunder reaches your ears a few seconds after you see lightning. Sometimes lightning is so far away that you cannot hear the thunder that goes with it, and sometimes thunder can be heard without seeing lightning, which may be hard to spot if it is deep within a cloud and the day is bright.

A fairly accurate mathematical formula can indicate how far away a lightning strike has occurred. If you count the number of seconds between the flash of lightning and the sound of thunder and divide the number by five, you will know how many miles away the lightning occurred. When thunder seems to follow lightning almost immediately, you know that lightning has struck very close by, and as the amount of time between seeing lightning and hearing thunder increases, you know the storm is moving farther away.

Do people die when **struck by lightning**?

Most people struck by lightning do not die. If lightning, which is about the width of a pencil, does not pass through a person's heart, brain, or spinal chord, interrupting or damaging the electrical-impulse cells that run them, then that person usually survives. While the electrical discharge of a lightning bolt is powerful and hot (up to 54,000 degrees Fahrenheit, or 30,000 degrees Celsius), it is—fortunately—incredibly quick. Survivors often have burn marks on their skin and clothes, especially where the lightning has entered and left their bodies.

While it's possible to survive a lightning strike, it is best to follow safety precautions to avoid testing that possibility. When a thunderstorm approaches, go inside a building or closed car or truck. The vehicle's metal body will offer a safe path for lightning's electrical current to flow to the ground. The exterior of a building will do the same. One thing to remember when you are in a building, however, is to stay off a corded phone and avoid using plumbing fixtures or electrical appliances until the storm passes. Lightning can move through the ground for quite a distance from the place where it strikes, and it may—on rare occasions—travel along water, electrical, or phone lines into your home.

If a thunderstorm approaches so quickly that you can't find shelter, you can still take steps to protect yourself outdoors. Remember that lightning always takes the shortest route to Earth, so avoid being near tall things. You may feel tempted to stand under a tall tree for protection from the rain, but remember that a tree may be struck by lightning. Don't stand on a hilltop; instead, try to find the lowest ground you can—like a ditch or a valley—and crouch there, trying to make yourself as small as possible. Avoid bodies of water (swimming pools, lakes, or even puddles) and metal objects—both water and metal conduct electricity well, and if lightning struck them the electrical current would travel through to everything touching the water or metal.

Why is grass often **wet in the morning** even though it hasn't rained?

Floating water molecules, or water vapor, are always present in the air. The warmer the air is, the more water vapor it can hold. When air cools, it reaches a temperature at which it cannot continue to hold its moisture; this temperature is called the dew point. At this temperature water vapor will condense, becoming a liquid. At night, without the warmth of the Sun, the temperature of the ground and the grass that covers it becomes cooler. If it becomes cooler than the dew point of the air that touches it, condensation will occur. The grass will be covered with droplets of water by morning, even though no rain has fallen during the night. This moisture on the grass is called dew, and it often evaporates in the morning sunlight before we get to see it. (If the temperature at night drops to below freezing, the dew will become frost.) The same thing happens when the glass filled with a cold drink "sweats" on a warm summer day, or when your eyeglasses fog up as you come indoors from the cold.

Why can I "see my breath" when it's cold outdoors?

Sometimes when you breathe outside in cold weather, you can make your own cloud! As the water vapor in your breath mixes with the cold air outside, it starts to condense. The vapor turns into tiny water droplets—its liquid form—and hangs in the air in the form of a small cloud.

Why are there two scales for **measuring temperature**?

Temperature is the amount of heat in a gas, liquid, or solid. Heat results from the kinetic energy, or rate of movement, of the molecules in objects or matter; if the molecules move slowly, the temperature is lower, and if they move quickly, the temperature is higher. Any number of different scales can be used to measure heat: all that is needed to create a scale are two reference temperatures and degrees that mark off intervals in the range of temperatures between them. In the two temperature measurement systems used most often—Celsius (also called centigrade) and Fahrenheit—the two reference points are the boiling and freezing temperatures of water. Celsius is based on the metric system, so 100 intervals or degrees separate these two points (water freezes at 0 degrees Celsius and boils at 100 degrees Celsius). The Fahrenheit scale, widely used in English-speaking countries until recently and still used in the United States today, has 180 units or degrees that separate the freezing and boiling points of water (with 32 degrees Fahrenheit being the freezing point and 212 degrees Fahrenheit being the boiling point).

Other temperature measurement scales include the Kelvin scale, which is used in astronomy and other sciences. One of its reference points is absolute zero, which—in theory—is the lowest possible temperature, the point at which molecules have no kinetic energy or heat. The Celsius, Fahrenheit, and Kelvin scales all got their names from the men who invented them.

Mathematical equations can be used to convert temperature measurements from one scale to another. To convert Fahrenheit to Celsius, subtract 32 from the temperature and then divide by 1.8. To convert Celsius to Fahrenheit, multiply the temperature by 1.8 and then add 32. To convert Celsius to Kelvin, simply add 273.15 to the Celsius temperature.

Why is **mercury** used in **thermometers**?

Mercury—the only common metal that has a liquid form at room temperature—doesn't become a solid until it reaches -38 degrees Fahrenheit (-39 degrees Celsius). Most liquids freeze in temperatures like that. Mercury doesn't boil until 611 degrees Fahrenheit (357 degrees Celsius), and it doesn't stick to glass. So mercury is an ideal material to use in thermometers, which are often needed to record temperatures well below zero and well into the range where most liquids boil. (Colored alcohol is sometimes used in thermometers, but because it boils easily, it is not good for recording high temperatures.) Like all liquids, mercury expands when it is heated and contracts when it is cooled; in a thermometer it moves up and down in a closed tube on which a scale is marked, showing the temperature of the air, liquid, or solid that surrounds it.

A major disadvantage to mercury is that it is extremely poisonous. Some states in the U. S. have banned the sale of mercury thermometers, and others are expected to follow. Mercury thermometers should be handled with care. If a thermometer breaks and mercury spills out, cleanup should be done by an adult wearing rubber gloves. The mercury beads should be scooped up with a piece of stiff cardboard and placed in a container with a lid. Anything that touched the mercury—gloves, cardboard, container—should be sealed in two layers of plastic bags. A local waste disposal agency can advise on how best to dispose of the bag containing the mercury.

Antarctica is a continent completely covered in a sheet of ice that averages 6,500 feet (or 1,982 meters) in thickness.

What is the **coldest temperature** ever recorded on Earth?

The coldest temperature ever recorded on Earth was at the Russian research station Vostok in Antarctica on July 21, 1983. The temperature was -128.6 degrees Fahrenheit (-89.6 degrees Celsius).

Which is colder, the **North Pole** or the **South Pole**?

The Antarctic, the region of the South Pole, is colder than the Arctic, the region of the North Pole. Temperatures are warmer in the Arctic because there is no huge land mass there, and the ice cover in the region sometimes breaks, allowing some of the warmth of the Arctic Ocean into the air. (It's hard to think of the Arctic Ocean as "warm," but it has enough thermal energy, or heat, to raise the air temperature several degrees.) The Antarctic, on the other hand, consists almost entirely of Antarctica, a continent of 5.5 million square miles (8.8 million square kilometers) covered with ice (with an average thickness of 6,500 feet, or 1,982 meters). Winter temperatures in Antarctica can be some 50 degrees Fahrenheit (10 degrees Celsius) colder than those in the Arctic.

What is an **iceberg**?

An iceberg, a large mass of ice that floats in the sea, usually comes from a glacier—a large mass of ice located on land—or from an ice sheet that covers a large expanse of

Only about one-tenth of an iceberg's actual size shows above the waterline.

water. Icebergs are much larger than they appear—only about one-tenth of an iceberg shows above the waterline, a fact that can cause problems for ships. A ship may steer around the visible part of an iceberg only to collide with the wide base hidden beneath the water's surface. The *Titanic,* a luxury ocean liner that set sail across the North Atlantic in 1912, is perhaps the most famous ship to crash into an iceberg and sink, resulting in the deaths of more than 1,500 of its passengers. Modern sonar (sound wave) and radar (radio wave) equipment—used during regular sea and air patrols—have greatly reduced the danger of icebergs for ships today. The largest icebergs can be found in the Antarctic Ocean, near the South Pole. Some large icebergs have been known to reach heights of 328 feet (100 meters) above the water's surface, and one of the largest icebergs ever found was thought to be 170 miles (274 kilometers) long and 25 miles (40 kilometers) wide. The area of that iceberg nearly equals that of the state of Connecticut.

What is **windchill**?

Windchill describes the chilling effect that moving air or wind has on the way we feel different temperatures and on the way our bodies react to them. Two days with the same outdoor temperature will seem quite different if one is very windy and one is not, because the wind carries heat away from the surface of our bodies, making us feel colder. This effect is called the windchill factor. A windchill index or chart has been developed that shows how certain wind speeds or velocities make different temperatures feel. In very cold climates it is important to know the windchill: it tells people who live there how to dress to protect their skin from frostbite, a freezing of the skin that can cause permanent damage.

What is the **hottest temperature** ever recorded on Earth?

The hottest temperature ever recorded on Earth was in the desert settlement of Al Aziziyah, Libya, located in North Africa, on September 13, 1922. That day the temperature reached 136 degrees Fahrenheit (58 degrees Celsius).

Why does **high humidity** make a day feel **warmer**?

Just as the wind affects how we feel and how our bodies react to cold temperatures, humidity, or moisture in the air, affects how we feel and react to warm temperatures. High humidity slows down the evaporation of perspiration, or sweat, which our bodies produce to cool off. So two days with the same outdoor temperature will seem quite different if the humidities vary, with the high-humidity day feeling warmer. The heat index is a chart developed to show how different levels of humidity make various temperatures feel to us, and how our bodies will react. The heat index is important to know because serious health conditions like heat exhaustion and heat stroke can occur on very hot, muggy days if care is not taken.

Can groundhogs predict when spring will come?

Weather experts have found that groundhogs aren't really very good at predicting if the spring season will come early or late—the animals are correct only 28 percent of the time. But the superstition began long ago, when farmers were looking for the appearance of any hibernating animal to signal the end of the long winter. If such an animal emerged on a sunny day—farmers thought—it would be frightened by its shadow and return to its burrow or den for six more weeks of sleep. If the day was cloudy, no shadow would be seen, and the animal would end its hibernation, knowing that spring had arrived. In America farmers chose the groundhog or woodchuck as the animal to watch, and February 2 came to be known as Groundhog Day. Every year certain groundhogs are awakened from their winter's sleep on February 2 and forced outside to see if they cast a shadow. Perhaps America's most famous groundhog is Punxsutawney Phil of Punxsutawney, Pennsylvania, who has predicted spring there for more than a decade.

What is **Indian summer**?

In the United States, the term Indian summer refers to a period of warm, dry weather that sometimes occurs during autumn. Some people say a true Indian summer can

31

only happen if this period of warm weather comes after the first frost, which is when temperatures are cold enough at night for water droplets on grass or car windshields to freeze. Indian summer is so named because it is believed that in past centuries, when such days of unexpected good weather came, Native American Indians would use that time to gather more food for winter storage.

FEATURES OF PLANET EARTH

What is the **equator**?

The equator is the imaginary line that circles Earth at it widest part—around its middle—at an equal distance from both the North and South Poles. It is 24,830 miles (39,952 kilometers) long and runs east and west, separating the Northern and Southern Hemispheres of Earth. On maps the equator is given the coordinate zero degrees latitude, the starting point from which all other latitudes are figured (latitude tells how far north or south a place is located on the globe). Latitude is used along with longitude—which tells how far east or west a place is located in relation to an imaginary line that runs north and south, the prime meridian—to map the exact location of any place on Earth. Because of Earth's round shape, the equator is the part of the world that is always closest to the Sun, receiving its rays most directly. (In other regions, sunlight hits Earth at an angle, and the additional amount of atmosphere through which it travels absorbs more heat, leading to milder climates.) The weather is usually very warm around the equator, regions collectively known as the Tropics.

Why are there **deserts**?

A desert is a land area that receives less than 10 inches of precipitation (rain or snow) a year. As strange as it seems, that definition makes parts of Earth's polar regions—the Arctic and Antarctica—desertlike in their climates. The fierce cold there causes dry air, which allows for little precipitation.

Most of Earth's deserts, however, are dry, rocky, and sandy. And because the greatest of them border the Tropics (North Africa's Sahara is the biggest), many of them are hot. Wind patterns are most responsible for the creation of deserts: most of the world's deserts are located in areas that get a lot of warm, dry wind. That dry air blows through desert regions, robbing them of moisture and reducing the likelihood of cloud formation and rainfall. High temperatures, which cause evaporation, and surrounding mountains—which can stop moist air from approaching—can also help create a desert climate.

Can anything live in a desert?

Plants have developed surprising adaptations to allow them to live in the harsh, dry desert. Many, like cacti, store water in their fleshy stems and have small or no leaves through which water can escape. They have deep, spreading root systems that take advantage of every bit of water, either above or below the ground (some extending down 50 feet). Other desert plants produce seeds that can lie dormant or inactive for years, springing to life when the rare rain storm comes.

Animals, too, have developed habits allowing them to survive in the desert. Many, for example, rest during the hottest part of the day in burrows dug in rocks or sand, becoming active in the early morning and at night when temperatures cool. And people have had a long history of successfully living in the desert: the ancient Egyptians, who lived in the Sahara desert along the Nile River, created one of Earth's great civilizations. A source of water in a desert, like a river or an oasis—where underground water reaches the surface—can be used to water crops and feed livestock, and life can flourish around it.

What Is a **rain forest**?

Rain forests are thick forests of trees and other plants found in the lowland areas of the Tropics around the world. Rain forests exist in parts of Australia, Indochina, India, the Malay Peninsula, the East Indies, in central and west Africa, and in Central and South America. Unlike forests in many other parts of the world, which have been affected by global climate changes like the Ice Age, tropical rain forests have been growing uninterrupted in some places for millions of years. During that time an unimaginable number of different types of plants and animals have evolved to use every food source and live in every spot there. Tropical rain forests have more plant and animal species than the rest of the world combined, and scientists continue to discover new species.

Because tropical rain forests are located near the equator, their climate is warm. The name "rain forest" comes from the fact that they receive a lot of rain—between 160 and 400 inches throughout the year. Plants grow very quickly under such ideal conditions. In order to get the sunlight that they need for photosynthesis (the process by which they—and other green plants—make their own food), rain forest trees grow very tall, up to 130 feet (40 meters) high. Their tops form a huge canopy that shades most of the ground, protecting plants on the ground from excessive sunshine as well as wind. Rain forest trees have very shallow roots, for the soil in which they grow is poor, having long been depleted of nutrients by the needs of thick plant life over millions of years. But the abundant life all around contributes organic matter (the decomposed remains of plants and animals) to the surface of the soil, which is enough to nourish these grand, ancient forests.

33

Why are **rain forests** so important to the **health of our planet**?

In 1800 there were 7.1 billion acres of rain forest in the world. Now, just 200 years later, less than half—3.5 billion acres—remain. Over 100,000 acres of the world's rain forests are destroyed each day, with trees cut down for their valuable wood and land cleared for farming. While covering just two percent of Earth's surface, the dense vegetation of these forests plays an important role in the health of our planet. The destruction of rain forests threatens the health of our planet by reducing the amount of oxygen in our air and increasing carbon dioxide. Too much carbon dioxide in our atmosphere keeps the Sun's heat from radiating back into space, increasing global temperatures (called the greenhouse effect). Global warming, in turn, could bring about major climate changes: melting glaciers and rising sea levels, for example, could cause flooding of coastal regions.

The plants in rain forests produce natural chemicals that fight off destruction by insects, and scientists have learned how to make plant-based insecticides from rain forest plants (without destroying the rain forests) to spray on crops. These natural insecticides are far less toxic than synthetic, or human-made, chemicals. Numerous medicines—as much as one-quarter of all prescription drugs—have been made from materials gathered in rain forests, and many more life-saving medicines may await discovery there. Many products—like natural rubber, essential oils used in cosmetics and perfumes, and rattan, a material weaved together to make furniture—can be taken from rain forests without causing widespread destruction. In addition, rain forests can absorb huge amounts of water. When rain forests are destroyed, the vast amounts of rainfall in those regions cannot be absorbed, resulting in widespread flooding.

Fortunately, international efforts have begun trying to save what remains of the rain forests by helping the people who destroy them find other ways to earn a living. Still, the destruction of these important forests continues at a rapid pace.

What causes **earthquakes**?

An earthquake is a great shaking of Earth's surface. It is caused by the cracking and shifting of the plates of rock that make up the planet's layered crust. As shifting plates suddenly slide past one another, vibrations in the form of waves are released. These shock waves travel through Earth, gradually weakening as they move farther from the spot (or spots) where the quake began, which is called the epicenter. Regions located near faults, places where cracks in Earth's crust are known to exist, are particularly vulnerable to earthquakes.

Earthquakes vary in size and intensity. They may last a few seconds or continue for a few minutes. They may cause no damage, or they could result in widespread destruction and the deaths of thousands of people. Earthquake vibrations can be so violent that they collapse bridges and buildings, destroy highways, cause landslides, and lead to flooding if they occur in shallow water near a coast. When they occur under the ocean, earthquakes can cause a giant wave called a tsunami, which can reach heights of more than 100 feet.

How do scientists measure the **strength of an earthquake**?

A few different scales measure how strong an earthquake is. The best known is the Richter scale, created in 1935, which uses an instrument called a seismograph to measure the size of the ground waves created by an earthquake. An earthquake's size, or magnitude, generally ranges from 1 to 8 on the Richter scale (though the waves of some giant quakes have registered well beyond the top of the scale). The shock waves of an earthquake that registers a magnitude of 1 can only be detected with special instruments, while those with a magnitude of 8 cause massive damage. Every increase of one number means a tenfold increase in the strength of an earthquake; for example, a quake that measures 5 on the scale is 10 times stronger than one that measures 4. Some new methods have been devised to measure earthquakes, including one that measures what is called moment magnitude. This scale examines the size of the fault where the earthquake took place and measures how much Earth's crust has slipped.

The Mercalli scale is also used to measure the strength of an earthquake. This scale works by describing the effect an earthquake has on people and structures. It lists 12 levels of intensity an earthquake can reach. At level 1, for example, only a few people may feel a quake, but at level 6, it is felt by all and damage starts to occur to buildings. A level 12 earthquake would bring about large-scale destruction.

How large was the **biggest earthquake** ever recorded?

Throughout recorded history, numerous giant earthquakes have occurred, each resulting in human losses numbering in the thousands (sometimes several hundred thousand). The most deadly earthquake may have occurred in the summer of 1201 in a region covering part of Egypt and Syria. Historical records show that this quake killed more than one million people there. An earthquake in China on July 27, 1976, is estimated to have killed more than 600,000 people. A giant earthquake occurred in Chile on May 22, 1960. Its shock waves measured 9.6 on the Richter scale. Thousands of people were killed in Chile, and the tsunami, or giant ocean wave, that it produced killed many more people on the islands of Hawaii, Japan, and the Philippines.

It is not always the earthquakes with the biggest shock waves that cause the greatest damage. A large quake that occurs far out in the open ocean, for instance, may cause few problems. Earthquakes that hit cities where a lot of people live, on the other hand, cause the most harm to property and humans.

Volcanic eruptions relieve the enormous heat and pressure that exist deep in Earth's interior.

What is a **volcano**?

A volcano is a natural opening in Earth's crust through which hot molten, or melted, rock, known as lava—as well as gases, steam, and ash (what remains after solid material is completely burned)—escapes, often in a big, noisy eruption or explosion. These eruptions are thought to act like safety valves, relieving the enormous heat and pressure that exist deep in Earth's interior. A volcano is usually a cone-shaped mountain (its sides built up from solidified lava and ash) that has a hole or crater in its center through which it vents. There are several different kinds or stages of eruptions, many causing no damage to the places or people located near the volcano. But a few eruptions are huge and destructive; during these, lava can pour out and run down the volcano into surrounding areas, and enormous suffocating clouds of steam, ash, hot gases, and shooting rock can travel downhill at great speeds, covering many miles. (When Washington's Mount St. Helens exploded in 1980, for instance, such volcanic clouds killed millions of trees.)

One of the most famous and destructive volcanic eruptions occurred in A.D. 79 when Mt. Vesuvius—in what is now Italy—erupted, destroying the important Roman city of Pompeii. The great cloud of cinder and ash that covered the city preserved it remarkably, and much has been learned about ancient Roman times by studying these amazing ruins. Mt. Vesuvius is still an active volcano, which means that volcanic activity still occurs there and eruptions happen from time to time. A volcano may also be described as dormant, which means that no activity has occurred for a long while but conditions still exist for an eruption to take place in the future. An extinct volcano is one that will never erupt again.

Many volcanoes occur near the area where two ridges or plates of Earth's crust meet. Circling the Pacific Ocean—where crust plates meet—is a group of volcanoes known as the "ring of fire." Plate movement in such regions may allow liquid rock (called magma) that is located in chambers in Earth's interior to rise, resulting in volcanic activity. (Such conditions often result in earthquakes as well.) Volcanic activity can take place under the ocean as well as on land, and when this happens the formation of islands sometimes results. The Hawaiian Islands were created by just such volcanic activity some 40 million years ago. Even today, two of the world's most active volcanoes—Mauna Loa and Kilauea—are located on the island of Hawaii. Visitors to Hawaii's Volcanoes National Park can travel to the slopes that surround the great volcanoes.

How do **mountains and valleys** form?

A mountain is an area of high ground that rises 1,000 feet (305 meters) or more above its surroundings. A group of mountains is called a mountain range. Almost all mountains and valleys—the depressions between separate mountains or mountain peaks— are formed when the huge moving plates of rock that make up Earth's crust collide with one another, which forces their edges to break and rise and fold, eventually creating a rising land mass. The process is a slow one, though, taking place over millions of

Mt. Everest rises 29,028 feet (8,848 meters) above sea level.

years. It is also continuous, with new mountains being formed all the time. The age of a mountain can often be determined by its size and shape: newer mountains are high and jagged, while older ones—which have been eroded or worn down by wind and weather over millions of years—are smoother and lower. The movement of rivers or glaciers (large masses of ice on land) through mountains can also create valleys by slowly wearing rock away.

Why are some mountaintops **covered with snow** even throughout summer?

The higher you travel up a mountain, the colder the temperature becomes—and the thinner the air becomes as well (which means there are smaller quantities of the gasses, like oxygen, that make up air). Some mountains are so high that the air at the top is always cold, never warming enough for snow to melt—not even in the summertime. No creatures can live in the highest regions of tall mountains, withstanding the cold, wind, and thin air; beyond a certain height (13,000 feet, or 3,965 meters, in warm regions) even trees cannot grow on mountainsides. To stay alive when climbing the highest peaks, mountain climbers must take along tanks of oxygen to breathe.

What is the **highest place** on Earth?

The highest place on the surface of Earth is the top of Mt. Everest, in the central Himalayas, a mountain system located on the border between Nepal and Tibet in southern Asia. Everest rises to 29,028 feet (8,848 meters) above sea level. On May 28,

1953, New Zealander Sir Edmund Hillary and Nepal native Tenzing Norgay were the first people to successfully make the trip to the top of Everest. Since then many mountain climbers have tried to reach the peak; few have succeeded.

What is the **lowest place** on Earth?

The lowest place on the surface of Earth is believed to be in the Mariana Trench, located deep in the western Pacific Ocean, extending southeast of the island of Guam to northwest of the Mariana Islands. It reaches down 36,198 feet (11,034 meters) below sea level.

How are caves formed?

Caves are hollows in rock, either above or below ground. They are almost always formed when water wears away or dissolves rock, although disturbances in Earth's crust—like earthquakes and volcanoes—can also create caves. When ocean waves crash against rocky cliffs, they carve out caves there over time. When an underground stream or rainwater repeatedly flows across the cracks of soft rock, like limestone—or seeps through it—the rock slowly dissolves, and a cave is formed. The world's deepest cave is at Rousseau Jean Bernard, located in France. It is 5,036 feet (1,535 meters) deep. In Kentucky, at Mammoth Cave National Park, visitors can see the longest cave system (a series of connected caves) in the world. It extends more than 330 miles (530 kilometers).

It would seem that nothing could live or grow in deep caves or long cave systems, so far away from sunlight. But cave explorers have found that this is not true; caves are home to some strange plants and animals that have adapted to their sunless surroundings. Many have no color or pigment, neither of which would serve a purpose in their pitch-black world; some animals are sightless for the same reason.

Caves are fascinating places because they were the first homes of prehistoric men and women, before they learned to build shelters. Caves often hold clues to what life was like when people were in their earliest stages of development. Fossil remains, ancient tools, and even primitive paintings made by cave dwellers can be found in some caves.

What are **stalactites and stalagmites**?

Caves form in huge, thick deposits of rocks like limestone, which dissolves over time when rainwater passes over or seeps through it. As water drips through the roof of a limestone cave, the drips leave bits of mineral behind, causing a stone column called a stalactite to form, which grows down in a cone shape like an icicle. Where the drips hit the cave floor, leaving behind more minerals, a stone column called a stalagmite forms, growing up. One way to remember which word describes which kind of growth is to think of sta-

Stalactites are formed in limestone caves by years and years of mineral buildup.

lac*tites* as holding "tight" to the ceiling; the "g" in stalagmites can stand for the word "ground." Stalactites and stalagmites can become very large, and sometimes they meet in the middle, forming a single column or pillar of stone. The largest stalactite in the world is located in a cavern in County Clare, Ireland; it measures more than 23 feet (7 meters) long. The largest stalagmite known to exist is located near Lozère in southern France. It measures more than 95 feet (29 meters) in length and is still growing.

What is an **island**?

An island is a body of land surrounded by water. While continents are also bodies of land surrounded by water, they are much larger in size. The smallest continent of the world is Australia. It has almost three million square miles (close to eight million square kilometers) of area. That makes it almost four times the size of the world's biggest island—Greenland—which has an area of around 840,000 square miles (2,175,000 square kilometers).

How are islands **made**?

Islands can be created in a couple of ways. Either they are connected (or were once connected) to the continent that they are located near, or they arise through the ocean floor during volcanic activity or other disturbances in Earth's crust. A continental island—as the first kind is called—may be a high part of the continental margin or

Islands are bodies of land surrounded by water.

extension of land that is usually present underwater along a coastline, or may have been separated from its parent continent by a watery passageway carved out by the sea. Great Britain and Japan are examples of continental islands. The islands of Hawaii, on the other hand, are examples of oceanic islands, because they were formed by volcanic activity on the floor of the Pacific Ocean some 40 million years ago.

Where does **dirt** come from?

Dirt, or more accurately, soil, is the surface layer of Earth in which plants can grow. It can be a few inches deep or extend down for several feet. It is made up of tiny pieces of rock of various sizes and shapes, along with air, water, and humus, which is the decomposed remains of plants. (The more humus soil contains, the better it can hold the nutrients and water that plants need to grow.) The different types of rocks that make up soil are usually fine particles of parent rocks that lie farther below Earth's surface; these have been made fine by erosion—worn by wind and water—or by geological occurrences like volcanic eruptions and the movement of glaciers. There are many kinds of rocks—composed of different minerals and formed in different ways—that make up Earth's crust.

Where does **sand** come from?

The rock particles that make up soil come in different sizes and are given different names to show this. Sand, often called a grain, is a piece of rock that measures from

41

.0024 to .08 inches (.06 to 2 millimeters) across. Sand results when larger rocks disintegrate, eroded by water, weather, and glaciers. The two greatest deposits of sand on Earth's surface can be found in deserts and on beaches. When soil consists mostly of sand, its large grains cannot hold the water or nutrients needed for healthy plant growth—one reason you don't see many plants in the desert or on the beach.

When you look closely at a handful of sand, you may find that the grains are really many different colors; this is because sand comes from several different kinds of rocks. Sand may appear brown, yellow, white, or even black (when it comes from certain volcanic rock). The sand of some beaches may also have grains made of organic material—the remains of living creatures, like shells and coral—instead of rock.

What is **quicksand**?

Quicksand is regular sand into which water is forced from below. Usually an underground spring supplies the water that pushes up into a deposit of sand. The extra water makes it so the sand particles don't hold together as well, and they become unstable to walk on. Quicksand is like a thick soup of sand and water—it isn't as watery as a puddle but isn't as firm as regular sand either. A large person or animal that strays into quicksand—which often looks deceptively dry on top—can sink quickly, even disappearing under its surface.

Deposits of quicksand are rare, and they usually aren't very deep. If you do find yourself sinking into the muck, try to hold on to something solid and pull yourself out, or lie on your back with your arms out as if you were floating in water and wait for rescuers to come. It's easy enough to float in quicksand if you stay fairly still; struggling to get out, on the other hand, only makes you sink faster.

How much of **Earth's surface** is covered by **water**?

About 71 percent of Earth's surface is covered by water. Three percent of this supply consists of freshwater, most of which is found in glaciers and ice caps, with a small percentage in rivers, lakes, and streams. The remaining 97 percent of the world's bodies of water is saltwater seas and oceans. (While all bodies of saltwater can be referred to as seas, technically a sea is different from an ocean because it is smaller and at least somewhat surrounded by land.)

How many **oceans** are there?

The world has four oceans: the Pacific, Atlantic, Indian, and Arctic. Sometimes the water that surrounds the continent of Antarctica is called the Antarctic Ocean, which would then bring the total to five. Because all of the oceans are connected to each other, some people consider them to be one gigantic world ocean that is divided into four (or, if the Antarctic waters are regarded separately, five) parts.

The Arctic Ocean is about 5,440,000 square miles (14,103,626 square kilometers) in area. The Antarctic covers 12,450,000 square miles (32,253,886 square kilometers). The Indian Ocean has an area of 28,380,000 square miles (73,523,316 square kilometers), and the Atlantic extends over 41,000,000 square miles (106,217,610 square kilometers). The greatest of the oceans, the Pacific, has an area of 64,186,000 square miles (166,284,970 square kilometers). The Pacific Ocean is by far the deepest: in the Mariana Trench, which extends southeast of the island of Guam to northwest of the Mariana Islands, the ocean floor is 36,198 feet (11,034 meters) down. The tallest underwater mountain—called a seamount—is also located in the Pacific Ocean: Mauna Kea rises from the ocean floor and extends above the water surface in Hawaii. It measures 33,480 feet (10,205 meters) in height, which is even taller than the world's biggest surface peak, Mount Everest (though Mauna Kea's peak is only 13,796 feet, or 4,205 meters, above sea level). The oceans hold 322,280,000 cubic miles (1,347,000,000 cubic kilometers) of saltwater. If you have an aquarium, you know how heavy water can be. Each cubic mile of seawater weighs 4.7 billion tons (that's 9.4 trillion pounds, or 4.3 trillion kilograms).

How **deep** are the oceans?

The ocean floors have shelves, slopes, cliffs, mountains, valleys, and canyons, just like the surface of Earth. So the depth of each ocean varies greatly when measured in different places. The average depth of all the oceans is around 13,124 feet (4,000 meters), though the Arctic Ocean is by far the shallowest.

Along the underwater edges of the continents, in what is called the continental margins, are deep, narrow canyons known as trenches. In these trenches are the oceans' greatest depths. The Pacific Ocean's Mariana Trench extends down 36,198 feet (11,034 meters); the Atlantic's Puerto Rico Trench reaches 28,374 feet (8,648 meters) below sea level; the Indian Ocean's Java Trench descends for 25,344 feet (7,725 meters), and the Arctic's Eurasia Basin reaches 17,881 feet (5,450 meters) in depth.

People can descend to the deepest parts of the oceans only in special vehicles. The deep sea is cold and sunless, and the pressure from the water above is almost crushing. But from ships on the surface, scientists can use sonar, or sound waves, to determine the depth of the seas and the shape of ocean floors. An instrument called an echo sounder sends out sound signals, which travel through water at nearly one mile per second. The signals are reflected back to the ship in echoes that show how far away the ocean floor is; the longer the echoes take to reach the ship, the deeper the water.

Why are the oceans **salty**?

Oceans are salty because the water that fills them contains dissolved salt, just like the kind we use on our food. The amount of salt in ocean water varies from place to place—depending on the different sources of water nearby—but averages about 3.5 percent. Over the course of millions of years, rivers—flowing over salt-containing rocks—have emptied into the oceans, bringing along dissolved salt particles. In addition, salt has leaked from solid salt-containing rocks directly into the seas. Salt can also enter the oceans from volcanic activity on the sea floor.

Why are the oceans **blue**?

Like the blue appearance of the sky, oceans and other bodies of water only *appear* blue, as you know if you've ever scooped some of that water into a clear container and seen that it isn't actually blue. Scientists believe some bodies of water appear to be blue because of the same principle that makes the sky look blue. When sunlight (which is white light consisting of many wavelengths that each correspond to a different color) hits seawater, some of its wavelengths are absorbed. Others—especially the wavelengths that give us the color blue—are scattered after colliding with water molecules and reflected back to us. So if water is clear (without too much dirt, algae, or other material floating in it) and at least 10 feet deep, it will appear blue to us. Water that has a lot of dirt or other floating particles can appear brown, green, or gray.

What causes **waves**?

The wind blowing across water causes most waves. The size of a wave depends on the strength of the wind, how long it blows, and the distance over which it travels. Strong winds and great distances create big waves. Waves occur when the wind forces the surface of water up as it tries to pull it along, and gravity pulls it back down again. These push and pull forces cause the up and down movement of waves. (The tops of waves are known as crests, and their bottoms are called troughs.) Although wavy water looks like it's traveling along, it really doesn't move much, other than up and down. The water droplets that make up that wave travel in a kind of circle, propelled by the energy of the wind, with the top of the circle being the crest of the wave. A seagull floating in the water will move up and down with the swelling of a wave, but it won't move forward toward the shore. When waves reach a shoreline, though, their action is affected by the shallow ocean floor, and they are said to "break" on the shore. There water moves forward with some force, up onto a beach or against rocks. Wave crests that break into white foam are called whitecaps.

What is a **tidal wave**?

Tidal waves are giant waves that hit the shore and cause coastal flooding and great damage. The name is inaccurate, however, because these waves have nothing to do with tides, the daily rise and fall of water levels of the world's great bodies of water. The cause of almost all tidal waves are earthquakes that occur beneath the ocean floor.

Strong winds and great distances create big waves.

The quake causes a deep, long wave that moves very quickly—up to 500 miles (805 kilometers) an hour. When it approaches shallow water and a coastline, the water builds up into an enormous wave that can reach up to 100 feet (30.5 meters) in height. When it crashes ashore, it destroys everything in its path. A tidal wave is also known as a tsunami, which is a Japanese word meaning giant wave.

Why does a **beach** get **bigger and smaller** at different times of the day?

Throughout the day and night the level of water in the world's oceans and other large bodies of water rises and falls. This change is due to tides, which are caused by the gravitational pull of the Moon on Earth as our planet rotates on its axis. Water on the part of Earth directly facing the Moon bulges as the Moon's gravity pulls it, creating high tide, or high water levels. On the opposite side of Earth a secondary, smaller high tide occurs, again related to the gravitational pull of the Moon. So at any given time during the day or night—as the planet rotates—there are two high tides, and two low tides (and all the levels in between) in the large bodies of water that cover Earth. High tides occur every 12 hours and 26 minutes, which is a bit more than half the time it takes Earth to make a complete turn on its axis. (That extra 26 minutes comes from the fact that the Moon is moving as well; it rotates around Earth once every 30 days or so.)

While the pull of the Moon's gravity is only strong enough to change the levels of the oceans about two feet, tides can make a bigger difference near a coast. At low tide

45

(when water levels are least affected by the gravity of the Moon) you may be able to walk far out on a beach, while at high tide, the beach may be almost completely covered by water. The Bay of Fundy, located in Canada, has the biggest difference in water levels between high and low tides—more than 40 feet.

How is a **lake** different from a **sea or ocean**?

A lake is different from a sea or ocean because it is completely surrounded by land. It is situated in a basin or hollow on Earth's surface and is usually shallow compared to a sea or ocean. Most lakes contain freshwater, though some—especially those located in dry areas—are filled with saltwater. Lakes may get their water supply from rivers that empty into them, or from underground springs, or from rain or melted snow. Lake Superior, located on the border between the United States and Canada, is the largest freshwater lake in the world, covering 31,700 square miles (82,103 square kilometers). Lake Baikal, located in Russia, is the deepest freshwater lake, reaching down 6,365 feet (1,940 meters).

Why is it easier to **float in saltwater** than in freshwater?

It is easier to float in saltwater because the salt makes the water heavier than freshwater: if you had two gallon jugs, one filled with saltwater and one with freshwater, the one with the saltwater would weigh slightly more. And the denser (heavier) the water, the easier it is for people and objects to float in it.

An object can float in a liquid when that object's weight equals the weight of the water it displaces, or pushes away (the water is displaced in order to make room for the object). Here's another way of looking at it: when you sit in a bathtub, you can see the water level rise. If you removed the amount of water that was pushed up by your body, it would weigh the same as your body does. When the water is dense, like saltwater is, less of it is displaced by your body (it takes less water to equal your body's weight), and you float higher than you would in freshwater.

Where do **rivers** come from?

Some rivers start as underground streams, making their way to Earth's surface from layers of rock beneath the ground. Others get their water supply from melting glaciers (ice masses located on land). But most get their start from rain or snow that falls in high, steep country; that water then runs down in little streams that join together, making bigger streams and eventually rivers. (And some rivers may join together to form even greater rivers.) Over time, the flowing water of a river cuts a path into the rock over which it passes, creating a valley. Most rivers flow downhill, making their way from their high-country source to lower, flatter land, where they broaden, curve, and move more slowly. Eventually rivers join the ocean. There, at the place where a river enters the ocean—called the mouth of the river—it may deposit much of the sediment or dirt that it has been carrying, creating an area of rich land and many water channels known as a delta.

Rivers have played an important role in human history. They allowed people to settle inland, away from the oceans and other large bodies of water. Before people built roads, they used rivers to travel from one place to another. Towns, cities, and even great civilizations grew up around rivers, which provided the water necessary for raising livestock, farming, and other advanced human activities.

What is the **longest river** in the world?

The longest river in the world is the Nile River, located in Africa. From its source in the country of Burundi to its mouth on the Mediterranean Sea, it extends for 4,145 miles (6,670 kilometers). But the world's second longest river, the Amazon (4,007 miles, or 6,451 kilometers), which is located in South America, is really the world's biggest river. It has more than 1,000 tributaries, or branches, and carries far more water than the Nile.

How do **waterfalls** form?

Over time, a river flows across rocks and carves out a riverbed as it descends from its highland source. If some of these rocks are soft and quickly erode, or wear away, the river valley may slope steeply, causing the river to rush wildly downhill in rapids or even a waterfall.

What is the world's **highest waterfall**?

It isn't easy to measure the height of waterfalls because they usually descend in a series of falls instead of in one big drop. The world's highest waterfall, Angel Falls (named after the man who discovered it), is located in Venezuela, on the Carrao River. It has the largest single drop of any waterfall at 2,648 feet (807 meters). The total height of Angel Falls is 3,212 feet (979 meters). You can see North America's highest waterfall, Yosemite Falls (2,425 feet, or 739 meters), when you visit Yosemite National Park in California.

Yosemite Falls is North America's highest waterfall at 2,425 feet, or 739 meters.

WORLD TOUR

GEOGRAPHY FACTS

What are the **continents**?

The land masses on Earth are divided into seven continents. They are, from largest to smallest: Asia, Africa, North America, South America, Europe, Antarctica, and Australia. Some people group Europe and Asia together into a single continent called Eurasia. At 17,226,000 square miles (44,614,000 square kilometers), Asia covers about 30 percent of the world's area. Australia, at the other end of the size spectrum, is three million square miles (eight million square kilometers). Australia is not only a continent—it's a country, too. And while it ranks as the smallest continent, Australia is one of the largest countries in the world.

What's the difference between a **continent** and a **country**?

A continent is a land mass that is generally (except in the cases of Australia and Antarctica) home to a number of countries. Continental boundaries are determined by geography rather than politics. Canada and the United States, for example, are part of the North American continent because they occupy the same land mass, not because they share a political system. A country, on the other hand, is a defined territory that governs itself and is recognized by the international community. A country's citizens live under the rule of their government and according to the nation's laws.

How many **countries** are there in the world?

There are about 191 countries in the world today. But because the political world is constantly changing, that number never stays the same for very long. For example, in

Canada and the United States are part of North America.

the Federal Republic of Yugoslavia, fighting ethnic groups have declared the regions of Serbia and Montenegro separate countries. But until the United States and other nations accept their independence and national borders, the regions will not officially become countries.

Which country is the **largest**?

Russia is the largest country in the world, with 6,592,812 square miles (17,075,383 square kilometers) of area. It stretches across two continents, Europe and Asia. It is far bigger than the next largest country in the world, Canada, which has 3,851,809 square miles (9,976,185 square kilometers) of area.

Which country is the **smallest**?

The smallest country in the world is Vatican City. It is located on 108.7 acres (or 44 hectares, which is not even half a square mile) in the city of Rome, Italy. Vatican City is where the central government of the Roman Catholic Church is located. The home of the pope—who is leader of the Church—is also located there. About 850 people are citizens of Vatican City, which is ruled by the pope, though a governor and a council actually run it. Vatican City has its own money, postage stamps, flag, and diplomatic corps. Monaco, which is less than one square mile (around 2 square kilometers) in area, is the second smallest country in the world.

How is it decided **where** a country will be?

Sometimes the size and shape of countries are dictated by the geography of the land around them. Mountain ranges, large bodies of water, deserts, and other features often provide natural boundaries that separate one country from another. The location of borders are often agreed upon by the countries that share them and recognized by other nations in the world. (Border and territory disputes can be the source of conflict—and even war—between countries.)

How are countries **formed**?

Often it is a group of people with something in common—whose members identify with one another—that makes up a country. It may be a shared race, religion, language, history, or culture that makes people feel that they belong together as a nation. Because of its uniqueness, the group feels that it should govern itself as an independent country. This feeling of shared identity and loyalty to the group is frequently behind the rise of nations. Some countries are so large and have such complicated histories of war and conquest that they are home to many different groups of people who have their own separate beliefs, languages, and customs. The differences between these groups sometimes make it difficult for them to get along. A nation is weakened by such groups if they put their own interests ahead of those of their country. But a population of many different groups can also enrich a country with diverse ideas and cultures if a spirit of acceptance and cooperation exists.

How many people are there in the world?

When the ancient Romans ruled much of the known world—around A.D. 100—there were an estimated 250 million people on Earth. It took nearly 16 centuries for that population to double, to about 500 million people. By the mid-1800s the Industrial Revolution had brought about such improvements in living conditions, as well as in food production and distribution, that the world's population doubled again, to one billion people. By 1930 that number had reached two billion.

By 2000 the number of people on Earth exceeded six billion. The world's population is increasing as never before, due to scientific advances in medicine and technology and continued improvements in health care, living conditions, and food production around the world. Most countries no longer have the high death rates that were once unavoidable because of hunger and disease, and high birth rates continue in many parts of the world, contributing to our rapid population growth.

Which country has the **most people**?

With one and one-quarter billion citizens, the People's Republic of China is the most populous country in the world. India ranks second, with a population of just over one billion.

Which country has the **fewest people**?

Once again, Vatican City wins a "smallest" award. In addition to being the smallest in area, Vatican City also, not surprisingly, has the smallest population—about 850 people. The country with the second smallest population is Tuvalu (formerly called Ellice Islands). Home to fewer than 10,000 people, Tuvalu consists of a string of nine coral atolls (which are like doughnut-shaped islands—rings of coral with lagoons in the center) located in a region in the South Pacific called Polynesia.

Why do people speak **different languages**?

While some animals have demonstrated the ability to communicate with other animals and with humans, people are the only creatures on Earth who communicate through language, which is a system of vocal symbols. Scientist don't know exactly when humans first spoke, though they know that it happened a very long time ago, in prehistoric times. Different languages arose when groups of people—separated by things like deserts, mountains, or great oceans—developed their own systems of communicating that reflected their unique ways of life. These new languages were passed on when children learned to speak the same way the people around them did.

As groups of people spread out to settle different parts of the world, they took their languages with them. They began to pronounce some words differently as time passed and had to add words to describe the new things and situations they found in distant lands. Languages gradually changed from their parent languages, though they still shared some characteristics. Today, English and French are languages that seem very different from one another, but they came from the same parent language (Indo-European) a long time ago. All languages that share a parent language belong to the same "family." There are 13 large language families in the world today, from which most languages have descended.

How many **different languages** are there?

There are more than 4,000 languages spoken in the world today. In some large countries, several languages are spoken. (India has more than 800!) In other large countries, different versions or dialects of the same language are spoken in different areas. In both cases, an "official" language is usually chosen for the country. That language is used in schools, by the mass media (like television), and by the government.

Many languages have no written form. Tribal languages like some spoken in Africa and Australia, for example, have been passed on orally, by word of mouth. Such unrecorded native languages often disappear when their speakers learn and use the official languages of the countries in which they live. In fact, one reason that languages like Spanish and English are spoken in so many different parts of the world is

Mandarin Chinese is the native language of nearly 900 million people.

because people who spoke them conquered and colonized many foreign lands, replacing native cultures and languages with their own.

For a long time people have been trying to invent a world language that everyone can speak and understand, attempting to remove the barriers that different languages create. The best known of these is Esperanto, invented by a Polish man named Ludwig L. Zamenhof in the late nineteenth century. This and other international languages have not been very successful. Universal pictures, signs, and symbols have actually been the most effective way of communicating worldwide.

Another way to break the language barrier is to study a second language like French or Spanish; many people in the world know at least two languages very well. Such people are considered bilingual, or multilingual if they know more than two languages.

Which language is the most **widely spoken**?

It is not surprising that Chinese—the language spoken in the world's most populous country—is the world's most widely spoken language. Although many different versions or dialects of Chinese are spoken in the country, the standard or official language—Mandarin Chinese—is spoken in its northern and central regions. It is the native language of nearly 900 million people. Spanish is the second most widely spoken language, and English is third. English is the most common international language (spoken in more places around the world than any other).

53

Who decides how a **country is run**?

A country is run by its government. Countries around the world are run by many different kinds of governments. In some countries, a written law called a constitution states what kind of government will be used: it outlines the government's powers and duties, along with rights of the people governed by it. A constitution is agreed upon at the time a country is founded or is adopted at a later date by a country's leaders. Sometimes rules about how a country is governed are not written down but are commonly known and followed, becoming long-standing traditions. Many monarchies, for instance, in which a king or queen rules and another member of the royal family takes the throne after he or she dies, are examples of this. In such countries, the rules about who will inherit the throne are not written down as law but are decided amongst the royals.

In many nations, government leaders get their authority to rule from the citizens of their countries. This authority is granted when people vote leaders into office during elections. Rulers chosen in this way are usually called presidents or prime ministers, and their governments are considered democracies because the power to govern is granted to the leader by the majority of their citizenry. If the citizens of a democracy feel that their leader is doing a poor job running the country, they can remove him or her from office in another election. Many people think that a democracy is the best form of government because citizens have some control over their lives and their country through their government representatives. There are other forms of government in which the authority to lead is given to an individual by just a few powerful citizens or is inherited for life. A government that is lead by one person who has complete, or absolute, power over the citizens is called a dictatorship. Some dictators—known as tyrants—take charge of the country by force rather than by being appointed. Such rulers generally run governments that disregard the needs of their people because they aren't required by law to answer to their people's needs. They can only be removed from their positions of power by others like them who possess greater force. When such rulers and their governments are overthrown, the process is often violent and bloody.

Why do people and countries **go to war** with one another?

Wars have taken place since the beginning of recorded history, and they surely occurred before that as well. A war begins when one group of people (the aggressors) tries to force its will on another group of people, and those people fight back. War frequently springs from the differences between people, or from the desire of one group to increase its power or wealth by taking control of another group's land. Often the aggressors feel that they are superior to the group they want to dominate: they believe that their religion, culture, or even race is better than that of the people they wish to defeat. This sense of superiority makes them feel that it is acceptable to fight to take the land, possessions, and even lives of the "inferior" group, or to force their ways on the dominated people so that they resemble their conquerors. When Europeans settled

North America, for example, the Native Americans who lived there fought a series of wars with them for the next 250 years, trying to keep their land and preserve their way of life. They eventually lost the battle and were forced to either live like their European conquerors or relocate to parcels of land set aside for them called reservations.

Civil wars take place between groups of people within a single country, and international wars occur between nations. Because countries can be very different from one another in government, religion, customs, and ideology (ways of thinking), it is not surprising that nations disagree on many things. But great efforts are usually made to settle the disagreements—through discussion and negotiation, a process called diplomacy—before they result in anything as destructive as a war. War usually occurs when diplomacy fails. Because science and technology have allowed us to create such powerful and destructive weapons that can result in such devastating wars, we now have international organizations that work all the time to try to keep peace among nations.

What is the **United Nations**?

The United Nations (or UN) is an international organization that works to maintain peace and cooperation among nations. Headquartered in New York City, the UN was formed in 1945, right after World War II. (The war was the largest and most costly in human history, involving most of the world and killing tens of millions of people.) The countries that founded the organization wanted to make sure that no such war ever happened again by creating a place where all nations of the world could meet and peaceably solve their problems. Representatives of more than 180 countries join together in regular sessions (though special sessions can be called) to vote on political, economic, and humanitarian matters taking place around the world. A special Security Council is responsible for preserving peace among nations by resolving disagreements between countries or taking actions to stop situations that threaten world peace.

In addition to resolving conflicts, the United Nations also oversees other agencies that help provide the world's citizens with health care, environmental protection, legal aid, and many other services.

Why are there **different religions**?

From our earliest days, many people have believed in a power or powers greater than themselves. This belief is known as religion. In ancient times, it was a way to make sense of the mysteries of the natural world; evil spirits were thought to be responsible for bad weather and disease, for instance. Ancient peoples felt that they had a measure of control over their lives when they made offerings and prayed to friendly spirits, whom they believed could help them win battles or grow better crops. Even today, when people know the scientific explanations for such things as thunder or the eruption of volcanoes, many look to religion to explain some of the other hard-to-under-

55

Muslims praying in Africa.

stand things that we experience as humans—things like the purpose of life or the reasons for tragedies. People look to religion and powers beyond themselves for direction about the best way to lead their lives and for the meaning behind them.

While most religions spring from the same basic human need to believe in a great power or powers, the ideas, practices, and traditions that religions involve can be very different. Long ago, groups of people—separated by things like deserts, mountains, or great oceans—developed special religious beliefs and forms of worship that fit their unique ways of life. Some, like the ancient Greeks, built their religions around the belief in several gods (a practice called polytheism), while others, like the Jews, believed in a single god (monotheism). Great temples, shrines, and churches were built to honor these gods, and believers showed their faith through ceremonies, sacred writings, prayers, and other forms of worship. As civilizations developed and ways of traveling long distances improved, different religions were spread by explorers, traders, settlers, and missionaries to other parts of the world. As religions spread, they were frequently changed and adapted into different forms that better fit the conditions and people of various lands. All the major religions of the world—Judaism, Christianity, and Islam in the Middle East; Buddhism, Hinduism, and Sikhism in India; Taoism and Confucianism in China; and Shinto in Japan—began in Asia before they gradually spread to other parts of the world. Christianity—which is based on the teachings of Jesus Christ, who preached in Palestine about 2,000 years ago—is the most widely practiced religion in the world today.

Why do people **work**?

People usually work to get the things that they need to live. The most basic needs are food, clothing, and shelter. In some places, people grow their own food, make their own clothes, and build their own shelters, living much as their ancestors have for thousands of years. In other places people earn money to buy those things. Work in industrialized, or developed, nations frequently takes place in office buildings or factories, while some people still make their livings as farmers. The economies of such countries are based on advanced technologies and large-scale manufacturing, which create products and services that earn workers more money than people can make in the less industrial, or developing, countries of the world, where farming is the main industry (and most farmers can barely grow enough food for their own families). People who live in industrialized nations—like the United States, Canada, Japan, Australia, and many countries in Europe—are able to buy far more than the basic things they need to live. They are able to make their lives easier and safer by paying for clean water, electricity, good medical care, reliable transportation, and much more. Those who live in developing countries, located mainly in Africa, Asia, and Latin America, still struggle to acquire the most basic necessities. It may be hard to believe, but it's nonetheless true that half of the world's people are malnourished (don't have enough of the right foods to be healthy) and 80 percent live in substandard housing (homes that are not clean and safe).

LIFE IN THE BIG CITY

What is a **city**?

A city is a town that has grown very large. In a city, a lot of people live and work in a very small area. Cities are usually centers of manufacturing, business, government, and culture. They offer a variety of jobs and activities that attract people from farms and small villages and towns, as well as from many different places around the world. Before the industrial revolution (beginning in the 1800s in the United States), most people lived and worked on farms. Now, with modern methods of agriculture that include complex machinery, scientific breeding, and chemical pesticides, farms require far fewer workers. On the other hand, the need for city workers has grown. In the past 40 years the number of people in the world who live in cities has doubled, to nearly two-thirds of Earth's population. In Africa, Asia, and Latin America most people are still farmers. But as the countries located there develop more modern industries, their cities will grow and fewer people will live off the land.

What is the biggest city in the world?

Because most big cities spread out, over time, into the land that surrounds them, it is often hard to say where a city begins and ends. When describing the size of a city—which generally refers to its population, or the number of people that live there—sometimes a distinction is made between the city itself (city proper) and the built-up areas around it (urban agglomeration). Another problem in finding the largest city in the world is that censuses—official counts of populations—are such big and difficult projects that they are only done every decade or so, and a lot of people can come and go in 10 years.

According to a 1997 United Nations count, Seoul, the capital city of South Korea in east Asia, is the most populous city in the world. Nearly 10.25 million people live there. When their surrounding urban areas are included in a population count, some of the world's other largest cities are Tokyo, Japan; New York City, United States; Mexico City, Mexico; and Bombay, India. Mexico City is also one of the world's fastest growing cities.

Why are most big cities **located near water**?

Most large cities got their starts in the days before trains, airplanes, or cars. Land travel back then consisted of riding horses, bumping along rough roads in animal-drawn wagons or carriages, or making one's way by foot. In those days, the easiest way to travel long distances was by ship.

So towns with good harbors that were located on oceans, lakes, and rivers became gathering places. Travelers got on and off ships there, sometimes bringing goods from faraway places (called importing). Such towns became trading centers, developing their own businesses to make goods to ship away, or export. Workers moved into these towns to fill the growing numbers of jobs, and others came to provide services for the increasing populations—building lodging, banks, and stores. Being located near water allowed many towns to prosper, growing into cities.

Where do people **live** in cities?

Big cities have a lot of things to offer residents and visitors, but one thing they don't have is space. The people who live in a city can't spread out—but they can spread up. City dwellers usually make their homes in apartment buildings or condominiums that are several stories high. These allow a large number of people to be housed on a little bit of land. Some of these buildings have hundreds of residents.

High-rise homes have actually been around for centuries. In ancient Rome, poor people lived in multistory apartments. In Yemen, a country in southwest Asia, high-rise

City dwellers usually make their homes in apartment buildings or condominiums that are several stories high, like these in Chicago, Illinois.

homes made of mud bricks have been used for more than a thousand years. Without modern building materials like steel and concrete, though, multistory buildings can't rise very high, because they become too heavy to be supported by their foundations.

What is a **skyscraper**?

A skyscraper is a building of great height that has an iron or steel frame inside that supports its floors and walls. Before builders figured out how to make such frames, stone or brick walls had to bear the weight of structures, which could not stand up if they were made too high. And tall stone or brick buildings had to have very thick walls on lower floors to bear the weight of the walls and floors above them. These thick walls wasted a lot of useful space.

Because cities have limited land, builders experimented with materials and construction methods in an effort to construct taller buildings that were more practical. Finally, in 1885, William Le Baron Jenny built the first modern skyscraper, in Chicago, Illinois. While just 10 stories high, which seems short by today's standards, the Home Insurance Company Building was the first structure to have an internal steel skeleton bear all of its weight. From that point on, tall buildings began to soar into the air, scraping the sky. Just 30 years after the first skyscraper was built, buildings were erected that reached 60 stories high. Today, the Sears Tower in Chicago has the most stories of any skyscraper at 110. Of course, none of these great heights would have been practical if the electric elevator had not been invented.

Skyscrapers, though, presented a unique set of problems. The buildings had to have a certain amount of flexibility so that strong winds and bad weather would not damage them. (The Sears Tower is always swaying, averaging about six inches from its true center!) Too many skyscrapers built close together also blocked out light and reduced air flow to the buildings and the streets below, creating unhealthy conditions. And fires were a special concern in skyscrapers because a small blaze on lower floors could quickly be sucked up elevator shafts and stairways, creating a deadly inferno. So builders learned to use fire-resistant construction materials, as well as safety features like smoke detectors, water sprinklers, metal fire doors, and fire escapes.

What is the **tallest building** in the world?

For many years the Sears Tower in Chicago was the tallest building in the world. Following two years of construction, the skyscraper was completed in 1973. Its 110 stories reach 1,450 feet (442 meters) into the sky, and twin antennae towers on top add another 250 or so feet (about 76 meters). With a foundation extending 100 feet into the ground, the great building weighs 222,500 tons (445 million pounds, or about 200 million kilograms). About 12,000 people work in its many offices. And about 1.5 million people visit its observation Skydeck each year, from which they can see four states (Indiana, Illinois, Michigan, and Wisconsin) on a clear day.

In 1998, though, a taller structure called the Petronas Towers was completed in Kuala Lumpur, the capital city of Malaysia. While just 88 stories high, 241-foot pinnacles (slender peaks) on the building's top bring its height to 1,482 feet, 8 inches (about 452 meters). Not to be outdone, however, builders in Chicago are already at work on plans for another skyscraper that will be taller still.

How do people **get around** in cities?

Because there are so many people gathered in such a limited area in a city, residents frequently use public or mass transportation like buses, trolleys, and trains. If all the people in a city drove their own cars, the streets would be impossibly congested, there would never be enough parking spaces, and the pollution from car exhaust would be unbearable. With mass transportation, large numbers of passengers share the same vehicle, which is kept in constant use throughout the day. Buses and trains can move more people from one place to another using less energy—and producing less pollution—than if private cars were used. Because mass transit vehicles usually travel set routes, they require less land space than cars. And subway trains are ultimate space savers, because they travel in tunnels underground. These electric railways are usually quick-moving as they don't have to contend with other traffic. Passengers get on and off at underground stations that connect to streets above. Actually, a lot of activities take place below the ground in cities, because surface space is so limited.

While mass transportation has many advantages, it can also be somewhat inconvenient. Because buses and subways travel set routes, they usually can't drop passengers off directly at their destinations. People also have to make travel plans that fit the schedules of the vehicles. So some people in cities do own and drive cars, and—because space is so limited—usually pay to keep them in long-term parking spots when they're not in use. And even when car owners drive to places in the city and park temporarily, they almost always have to pay a fee. Taxicabs, however, offer the convenience of a car without the expensive care: People can hire cabs to take them directly to their destinations. Passengers pay according to the distance traveled, which is measured by a taximeter. Taxicabs are similar to mass transit vehicles because they are in constant use throughout the day, moving many people from one place to another. The cheapest and most environmentally friendly way to get around a city (and the best way to see its sights) is to walk.

Why are there **traffic lights**?

Traffic lights were invented to control the safe flow of traffic on streets. They came into widespread use after the invention of the automobile. Until then, people generally didn't require formal traffic rules and control devices, relying instead on polite behavior and common sense when they traveled. But when fast and noisy motor vehicles began to fill the streets, it became clear that traffic control was needed. Lights that

61

stopped some drivers, while allowing others to proceed, was one way to protect both cars and pedestrians (people on foot) from collisions and to avoid traffic buildups.

The first traffic light was erected in 1868 in downtown London, England. This red-and green-tinted gas lantern, hung on a tall iron pole, could be turned in one direction or another by a handle at its base. Of course, at the time, automobiles had not yet been invented. But the number of steam-engine vehicles, animal-drawn wagons and carriages, and pedestrians had become so plentiful at the busy corner (at Parliament Square) that a traffic light was needed to prevent accidents.

The electric traffic signal was invented by Garrett Morgan, an African American businessman and inventor, in Cleveland, Ohio. After buying his first automobile, Morgan realized the need for some traffic control at intersections. He invented a traffic light based on the signals used at railroad crossings; he received a patent for it (that is, he registered the invention as his with the government) in 1923. Some early traffic signals had red and green lights and a warning buzzer that sounded as the color changed. But as automobile traffic and noise increased, people thought that a visual warning between going and stopping would work better than one that was heard. An amber or yellow light was added to traffic signals to warn drivers to prepare to stop.

Why are there **parking meters**?

Finding a place to park in a big city is usually a problem because land space is so limited. In fact, one of the reasons that most big cities have mass transportation systems is because they don't have enough space for all the people who live, work, and visit there to use and park cars. Parking meters—first used in Oklahoma City, Oklahoma, in 1935—were invented to help solve the traffic and parking problems of big cities. By charging drivers for parking spaces and limiting their time there, parking meters encourage people to leave more quickly, which allows other drivers to use the spaces. The devices also encourage people to use public transportation to and from and within a city because parking is so expensive. This, in turn, reduces the number of cars on city streets, cutting down on traffic, noise, and pollution. Another benefit of parking meters is that the money they bring in can be used for city needs.

Why is it so **noisy** in big cities?

Big cities are so noisy because a lot of people and activities are confined to a relatively small space. Think about the activities that happen in a small neighborhood—people talking, car motors running, ambulance sirens blaring—and multiply that several times over. Because cities are usually centers of manufacturing, business, government, and culture, they attract large numbers of people who live and work there. Cities are also home to lots of cars and mass transportation vehicles like buses and trains, all of which produce tremendous noise. And noises in a city often seem louder because the sound waves bounce back and forth between the many tall buildings.

Why do we **use money**?

We use money as payment for goods or services. Today people use coins, banknotes (bills), checks, credit cards, and debit cards (the cards used at automatic teller machines, or ATMs) to pay for things. Before money was invented, you could only get something from another person by bartering or trading something else for it. It was hard to make even trades and the deal had to be made on the spot. The introduction of money offered people greater flexibility when trying to get goods or services: it made it possible to put standard values on things, and money could be saved and used for future purchases.

A great variety of objects have served as money for different people around the world. Anything considered valuable by a group and important to its way of life can be used as money. Shells and feathers, furs and cloth, salt and cattle have all been used at one time or another as money, setting the standard by which the value of all other things were measured. From earliest times, precious metals like gold and silver were used as money because they were durable materials that could be easily handled and divided, and they were considered valuable by many groups of people. Carefully weighed amounts of these metals were used as money, a practice that led to the invention of coins in the seventh century B.C. in the kingdom of Lydia—what is now Turkey. Early metal coins were stamped with designs that showed their weight and value, similar to the coins we use today.

Money bills or banknotes came into use around the tenth century in China. Because Chinese coins were so heavy, people started to leave them with merchants, who gave them written receipts that were sometimes used to buy things. The Chinese government soon took over the job of printing receipts that people could use as money. While they are just pieces of paper and not valuable themselves, banknotes became money because they *represented* valuable things—like gold and silver—kept in other places. Coins, too, eventually became symbols of value rather than actually being worth something—the coins that were once made of silver and other precious metals are now made of combinations of inexpensive metals. The bills, checks, and credit cards that we use today are likewise representative money used because of their convenience.

How does money **circulate**?

After new money is printed at the Bureau of Engraving and Printing, the United States Treasury Department ships it to the 12 Federal Reserve Banks that are spread throughout the country. The Reserve Banks then distribute the cash to commercial banks and other institutions where people keep their money. Customers withdraw cash from banks and spend it on gas, food, books, and so on. Eventually the stores deposit the bills back at the bank, and the process begins again.

DOWN ON THE FARM

Where does our **food** come from?

People in industrialized nations like the United States eat food that comes from all over the world. Such countries have the wealth to buy food products that are brought by plane or ship from far away. A wide variety of canned and packaged foods are available from every corner of the globe. And even fresh foods like fruits, vegetables, fish, and meats can now be sped across oceans in refrigerated boats. So foods that were once rare treats are now available at nearly every time of the year, arriving from places with different climates and seasons. That means that the asparagus and strawberries you eat may be grown nearby—or halfway across the world! Today, when you look in your cupboards, it is like taking a trip around the world: you will see tea from India, coffee from Brazil, olive oil from Italy, and much more.

In the past, people ate only the food that they could produce on their farms or find at their local markets. That is still true of many people who live in developing nations.

Why are there so many **big trucks** on the road?

The purpose of most trucks is to transport goods. Trucks carry materials and parts for manufacturing, finished goods, and food items from the places where they are produced to the places where they are needed. Everything that you see in a store got there by truck. No wonder there are so many trucks on the road! The bigger the truck, the more goods it can carry during a single trip. But for safety reasons, the length of trucks—as well as the amount of weight that they are allowed to carry—is often regulated.

Even things produced overseas eventually make their way to you by truck. Either flown over by cargo plane or shipped by boat, the goods eventually make their way into trucks as they start their overland journey. Not too long ago, though, most goods were transported—especially over long distances—by railroad (some still are). But trucks gradually took over the job as roadways expanded and improved; trucks were preferable because they could take goods directly to their destinations while trains could only travel between stations. When you look at how many abandoned railroad yards and tracks there are around the country, it helps you realize the important role they once played in transporting goods.

How do farmers **grow food**?

Raising crops involves a few simple principles. Although farming has been around for about 10,000 years—a vast sweep of time in which tools and methods have changed a great deal—the basic principles remain the same. The first step in farming involves preparing the land for planting. The second step involves planting the seeds (or cuttings or seedlings). The third step involves helping the seeds to grow. The fourth step involves harvesting the mature plants—and often processing them so that they can be used as food. (Fruit-growing and raising livestock for milk and meat are other types of farming.)

Preparing land for planting involves breaking up the soil with a plow. Early plows were heavy pointed sticks that people pushed through the earth. Later, the points of plows were made of iron, and their shape became broader and flatter. (Plow blades are called shares.) These plows sliced bigger furrows (big grooves) into the soil and flipped it over as well. While first powered by people, plows were soon designed to be pulled by animals because they had to be heavy to cut through hard ground. Usually a team of oxen or horses pulled a plow while a farmer guided and pushed it from behind. Today, powerful tractors pull plows that dig up several furrows at a time. After plowing, early farmers pulled heavy rollers and harrows—flat rake-like devices—over the broken soil to make it even finer and ready for planting. Today, cultivators—with rows of pointed metal prongs—are pulled behind tractors to do the same job.

Before planting machines, farmers sowed seeds by hand. It was a wasteful process because the wind blew seeds away as they were scattered and hungry birds ate them before they could be covered up by dirt. But in the early eighteenth century an English farmer named Jethro Tull greatly improved the sowing process by inventing the seed drill. It was a machine that cut several grooves into the soil and then dropped small amounts of seeds—held in a compartment called a hopper—down tubes or chutes into the neat rows. Crops could be grown in straight lines then, which made weeding easier; special hoeing machines were made with blades that fit between rows

Modern combine harvester machines save farmers lots of time and energy—they can process five acres of wheat in less than an hour.

of crops to uproot weeds. Like a plow, the seed drill was usually pulled by horses and guided by a farmer who walked behind it. Today, of course, tractors provide the power that pulls similar sowing machines.

There was not a lot that early farmers could do to help seeds grow once they were in the ground. At that point, it was really up to nature to provide the things that were needed for growth—like warmth, sunlight, and water—in the right amounts. Early farmers could add natural fertilizers (like manure) to enrich soil, and they could pull weeds that competed with growing plants. They knew about the benefits of rotating crops (growing different plants in different fields each year to keep the soil fertile and free of diseases and pests). In dry areas, early farmers even developed irrigation systems that delivered water to crops. But modern science has given today's farmers many more reliable tools to help seeds grow. Chemical insecticides, for example, kill pests that threaten crops and selective herbicides kill weeds without damaging growing plants; other chemicals called fungicides help eliminate plant diseases. In addition, genetically altered plants and chemical fertilizers have allowed modern farmers to grow more plants than ever before.

Before modern machinery, harvesting crops was a painstaking process. Gathering and removing mature plants from the field had to be done by hand. Farm workers used sharp bladed, long-handled scythes and curved sickles to cut down cereal crops like wheat. Even the fastest reaper could only clear about a third of an acre a day. Because rain could ruin harvested wheat, workers called sheaf-makers quickly tied it into bundles, so that it could be safely stored if the weather turned stormy. During the long winter months farm workers used jointed wooden tools called flails to thresh or beat the dried wheat in order to separate its edible grain seeds from its stalks. But in 1786 a machine that threshed wheat by rubbing it between rollers was invented, replacing human threshers. And around 1840 a reaping machine—whose revolving wheel pressed grain stalks against a sharp blade that cut them down—replaced human harvesters. Today, farm machines called combine harvesters do this work in much the same way. These machines are very efficient and combine all three jobs of cutting, collecting, and threshing a crop. A single combine harvester can process five acres of wheat in less than an hour!

What is **organic farming**?

While most large farms today use chemicals to control weeds and insects and to produce increased amounts of vegetables, milk, or eggs, some farmers have chosen to run their farms without chemicals. Organic farmers believe that the chemicals many farmers use can be damaging to the environment and to the people that eat the food grown on such farms. They feel that natural fertilizers and pest-control methods are just as effective and far healthier.

67

A British farmer and scientist named Albert Howard began the practice of organic farming as an alternative to modern chemical-based methods in the 1930s. His ideas have spread all over the world, taking hold in the United States in the late 1940s. A basic principle of organic farming is to focus on keeping the soil rich with nutrients by feeding it natural fertilizers like cow manure. Such fertile soil can help create stronger plants that are better able to resist disease and insects. Organic farmers also prevent insect damage by putting up insect traps or by bringing in beneficial insects that feed on the harmful ones that are causing the problem. In extreme cases, they need to use pesticides, but to continue being certified as organic farmers in the United States, such farmers need to use botanical pesticides (those that are made from plants) rather than synthetic, or man-made, chemicals.

Organic farmers also try to do more tasks using human power rather than gas-powered vehicles, thereby using less fuel and cutting down on pollution. Organic farms that raise livestock like dairy cows or chickens feed the animals with natural food, avoiding chemicals and growth hormones that make cows produce more milk and chickens produce more eggs. Some organic farmers also allow their animals to roam in a large area (such animals are described as "free range") rather than keeping them in small, climate-controlled pens for their entire lives.

While organic farming began in a small way—in experimental gardens and small, family-run farms—it has grown into a huge industry. As more and more people looked for organically grown fruits and vegetables in their grocery stores, more and more companies began producing "certified organic" foods. At the beginning of the twenty-first century, organic farming was a $7.7 billion-dollar-per-year industry in the United States—a small but significant percentage of the entire food-selling industry.

How do farmers keep animals from **eating their crops**?

Farmers keep animals away from their crops in a number of ways. Birds are probably the biggest wildlife pests because they feed on seeds before they have a chance to grow, and they eat developing food plants. Because loud noises and the presence of predators and people frighten birds, farmers have used things like scarecrows and models of bird predators like hawks—hung from poles or trees—to try to keep hungry creatures away. Devices called "bird scarers," which make repeated, loud, shotgun-like bangs, are also used. But before scarers were invented, it was usually the job of farm children to stand in fields, in all kinds of weather, using wooden clappers, rattles, and other noisemakers to keep birds away from crops.

Other crop enemies in the animal world are insects. Sometimes insect damage can be controlled by introducing beneficial insects that eat the bugs causing the problem. But generally farmers take stronger measures, like spraying chemical insecticides that poison the pests. Sprayers pulled by tractors are usually used, though airplanes ("crop dusters") can spray a large field very quickly.

What are **barns** used for?

Today, the huge, airy farm structures we know as barns are used mostly to store modern farm machinery and house farm animals. But before modern farming, they had a greater number of important uses. Before the invention of threshing machines (which separate cereal grains like wheat from their stalks), the grain harvest had to be stored in barns, where it would await threshing or pounding by hand during winter months. The structures had to be large and drafty for the process of winnowing, which separated straw dust from the grains after threshing.

Before farmers began to raise special crops to feed their livestock during the winter, they used hay, which is dried grass (grown wild or taken from the stalks of cereal crops). Huge amounts—enough to last several months—had to be stored away. Hay was usually kept in barn lofts located above the main floor, where farm animals spent the winter. This high storage place allowed air to circulate around the hay, keeping it from rotting. It was convenient, too, because hay could be pulled down as needed to feed the livestock.

Because farmers had to store their harvest crops in barns, they wisely cut entrance holes near their roofs, inviting barn owls to make nests there. The birds would hunt the rats and mice that liked to feed on the grain.

Why are barns usually **painted red**?

Paint coats wood, protecting it from sunlight and rain damage and making it last longer. When early farmers had enough money to paint their barns, they usually used inexpensive paint because the structures were so large. Ferrous oxide, a chemical powder that gives paint its red color, was readily available and cost little. Thrifty farmers in New England, New York, and the upper Midwest region painted their barns red. In those places, red barns remain a tradition.

But there are plenty of barns in other parts of the country that are not red. Early farmers that were poor—especially in regions like Appalachia and the South—left their barns unpainted because they did not have the money to do the job. Unpainted wood usually weathers to a soft gray color. And in places like Pennsylvania, Maryland, and some southern Midwestern states, the most frequently seen barn color is white. Some people think that white barns grew popular when dairy farming became more important after the Civil War; white suggests cleanliness and purity, desirable qualities to be associated with milk production. Special farms where fancy horses or prize livestock were raised sometimes had barns painted unusual colors, like yellow, green, or black.

What is a **silo**?

The tall, cylinder-shaped farm structures known as silos are used to store silage, which is animal feed. Silage is moist feed made from green crops that ferment when stored in an airtight place. This fermentation process preserves the feed, which is used along with or instead of hay (dried grasses) to feed livestock like horses, cattle, and sheep during the winter when they cannot feed in green pastures. Silage gives farm animals needed nutrients.

Before farmers started to raise food crops to feed their livestock (during the eighteenth century), they had to kill most of their animals when winter approached, because grass in pasturelands stopped growing and the creatures faced starvation. But herds of livestock could be kept year-round once farmers began to grow crops for winter feed. Root crops like turnips, as well as leafy crops, were sometimes used. Today, corn is the crop most often used for silage.

What do **farmers** do in the **winter**?

Some farmers are lucky enough to live in places where the winters are mild and crops can be grown throughout the year. But many farmers live in regions where the winters are cold and snowy, during which time crops can't be grown. In such places, farmers usually plant crops in the spring, tend to them all summer long, and harvest them in the fall. The winter gives farmers the opportunity to do some things they may not have had time for during the busy growing and harvesting seasons. They can work on their barns or homes, repair their tractors and other machinery, and work out a plan for the following year's crops. Some farmers spend time in the winter promoting and publicizing the products they grow and sell. Many farmers find a second job off the farm during the winter to bring in some extra money.

For farmers with lots of animals, or livestock, the work continues right through the winter. The animals must be fed and their pens must be cleaned. Eggs must be gathered from chicken coops and dairy cows need to be milked several times a day. Field work may be suspended for a few months during the winter, but livestock farmers keep busy year-round.

Why does a **rooster crow** when the Sun comes up?

A farm rooster is an adult male chicken. Long ago, when chickens had not yet been tamed or domesticated by people and lived in the wild, roosters crowed to call female chickens to mate. This loud crowing caused problems for roosters, though, because it attracted predators as well as female chickens. So to avoid being eaten, roosters began to do most of their crowing when they couldn't be easily seen, like at dawn or at nightfall, when light was dim. Today's roosters continue the habit, crowing mostly in the early morning or early evening. But it is usually most noticeable at dawn because there aren't a lot of other activities and noises to distract your attention.

How many **eggs** can a chicken lay?

Today, certain breeds of chickens are raised to be eaten because they grow quickly and have a lot of flesh. Other breeds are good egg layers and are raised for that purpose. The best kind of laying hen can produce one or more eggs every day of its adult life (which lasts about a year). A hen that lays large eggs—like the popular Leghorn breed—is desirable because more money can be charged for larger eggs.

Roosters crow mostly in the early morning or early evening.

Before modern farming, chickens were kept in special houses called coops, where they had nests and laid their eggs, which were later gathered by hand by farm members. They were fed kitchen scraps and spare grain, and they spent their days pecking away in farmyards, looking for insects or seeds or any other food they could find. At night they were shut into their coops, warm and safe from hungry wild animals like foxes. Only small numbers of chickens were kept and only limited numbers of eggs were produced.

Today—to keep up with the world's growing need for food and to maximize profits—most chicken farmers keep the birds in huge, mechanized, indoor structures that house more than 100,000 birds at a time. Growing conditions like temperature and light are carefully controlled, and scientifically developed feed is used to cause quick growth and rapid egg production. Laying hens never leave their cages and their eggs are collected automatically, by machine.

How can cows make **so much milk**?

A cow, like all mammals, produces milk to feed its young. If its calf nurses regularly, the mother cow's mammary glands will produce enough milk to give the baby animal all the food it needs. Gradually a calf will nurse less as grass and other feed makes up more of its diet. A mother cow, in turn, will produce less milk until it is no longer needed.

But by milking the cows regularly—two or three times a day—dairy farmers can cause the cows to continue producing milk. Certain breeds of cows are particularly good at milk-making, producing 18–27 pints (around 2–3 gallons, or 10–15 liters) each day. A cow's large, round udder, located on its underside, has four nipples, or teats, that are squeezed to release stored milk. While once done by hand, milking is done on modern dairy farms by machines with suction hoses, which do the job more quickly and cheaply. Tank trucks collect milk from farms daily and take it to processing plants where it is pasteurized (made germ-free) and used to make dairy products like cheese, butter, and ice cream.

While 90 percent of the world's milk today comes from cows, that was not always the case. Goats and sheep—which could graze on vegetation that grew in lands too dry for cows—were long used as important sources of milk and dairy products. Their milk, and the milk of other animals like camels, buffalo, yaks, llamas, and reindeer, is still used today, though in small quantities compared to cow's milk. Every mammal makes milk that is a different from that of other mammals, milk that is especially suited to its young and to the environment in which its babies must grow. Reindeer milk, for instance, has four times the fat of cow milk because reindeer live in colder climates, and more calories are required for living in wintry surroundings. But all animals' milk shares many basic qualities and is full of vital nutrients.

Why do cows stand around in fields eating all day?

In order to produce four or more gallons of milk each day, dairy cows have to eat a lot. Producing milk requires additional calories in the form of extra food. A large dairy cow may eat up to 150 pounds (about 68 kilograms) of grass each day, and all that munching takes time!

Cows have special stomachs, too, that make eating a slow process. Instead of having one chamber like a human's, a cow's stomach has four. When a cow takes a bite of grass it swallows it right away without chewing it. The food goes into the first chamber of its stomach, called the rumen (animals that have such stomachs are called ruminants), where it mixes with fluid to form a soft mass. The mushy grass is regurgitated or brought back up again later, when the cow is resting. This "cud" is thoroughly chewed, swallowed, and digested as it passes through all the other chambers of the stomach. A cow spends nearly nine hours each day chewing its cud. Scientists think that when animals like cows lived in the wild they had to snatch grass in a hurry before predators attacked them. Their special stomachs allowed them to store food for later chewing and digestion once they were hidden and out of danger. Goats, sheep, camels, and antelope are other examples of ruminants.

Why do horses **sleep standing up**?

Almost all horses sleep standing up because of the unique way they are built. The bones and ligaments (elastic bands that connect bones at joints) in a horse's legs lock together in a unique way, allowing its muscles to become completely relaxed while it remains standing. So the weight of a horse's body is safely suspended on its specially locked legs while it sleeps.

Lying down while sleeping probably wouldn't be comfortable for a horse anyway. Horses are heavy animals with big muscles, but their bones are surprisingly delicate. Lying in one position for a long time could very likely injure a horse.

Scientists thinks that horses developed their habit of sleeping upright as a defense mechanism, a way of protecting themselves against predators. Their speed is their main defense in the wild, and a standing position keeps a horse in a constant state of readiness to race away if danger should approach. Rising from a laying position takes the leggy beasts more time than most animals.

How is a **pony** different from a **horse**?

A pony is exactly like any other horse. The only difference is its size. Officially, a pony is any small horse that measures under 14.2 hands (about 57 inches or 145 centimeters) high at the withers—the ridge between the shoulder bones. (The "hand" is the standard unit used to measure a horse's height; it equals four inches.) Most ponies, however, are only around 26 inches (65 centimeters) high.

Beginning about 5,000 years ago, people began to tame or domesticate wild horses. Over time, they bred the animals to serve certain purposes. This selective breeding was done by mating male and female horses with special characteristics—like size or speed—that would then appear in their offspring. Some horses were bred to be large and strong. These were used to carry knights in heavy armor or as work horses to pull heavy carts or farm equipment. Some horses were bred to be swift and were used for hunting or racing. Ponies were mostly bred in the British Isles, where pastureland was scarce—smaller horses have smaller appetites and don't require as much land for grazing. Despite their small size, ponies were bred to be sturdy and hardworking. They were sometimes used to pull carts filled with ore (the natural materials from which metals are made) through the small tunnels in mines. They were also bred to have gentle natures. This feature, along with their size, make them ideal for children to ride.

How are **clothes** made from a **sheep's coat**?

Wild sheep were tamed or domesticated about 7,000 years ago. But for a long time they were raised mostly for the milk that the females (called "ewes") produced, for their meat, and for their skins. It was not until much later that people figured out how to use the long, curly hair, or fleece, of some sheep to make thread and weave it into cloth. Early on, men and women learned that they did not need to kill sheep to use their woolly coats; if they sheared, or removed, the fleece once a year, it would grow back time and again.

Today, some breeds of sheep are raised for their meat, while others—with long, soft hair—are raised for their fleece. In about a minute, a shearer can remove the entire coat of a sheep with electric clippers. The fleece from a single sheep can weigh

73

The long, curly hair, or fleece, of some sheep is used to make thread, which is then weaved into cloth.

up to 20 pounds (or about 9 kilograms). After the fleece is removed, it is cleaned and combed so that all of its fibers are arranged in the same direction. Next, the fibers are overlapped and twisted together into long threads that can be woven in a crisscross pattern on a loom to make fabric. The woolen cloth is then cut into pieces and sewn together to make clothes.

Why are **pigs** so dirty?

Because pigs will eat almost anything, they have traditionally been fed with farm left-overs and waste. This unappealing diet—commonly known as slop—may contain food waste from a farm household or the unusable by-products of the manufacturing processes for things like butter and cheese and even beer brewing. Pigs are natural foragers, frequently using their snouts to dig up roots or grubs for food when they are in the wild. On farms they are fed from low troughs, but their big snouts and foraging habits still make them very messy eaters. Adding to the dirty reputation of pigs is the fact that they have usually been kept in pens, or sties, close to farm buildings to make their feeding quick and easy. They—and their messes—have been confined to small spaces, unlike cows and sheep, which are free to roam pastureland.

Because pigs are raised mainly for their meat and fat, they are given a lot of food and spend most of their time eating. Piglets that weigh only a few pounds at birth can reach more than 200 pounds (90 kilograms) in less than half a year.

Where does **meat** come from?

Meat is the flesh of any animal that is used for food. It is usually the muscle and connective tissue of an animal, though organs like the liver and heart are also eaten. Cattle, sheep, and pigs provide most of the meat that people eat. People in different parts of the world usually eat more of one kind of meat than another, usually because certain animals are easier to raise in particular environments. In the Middle East, for instance, sheep thrive on land that is too dry for cattle; therefore, lamb and mutton (flesh from mature sheep) are the main meats eaten there. Cattle—the source of beef—are raised in big herds and need a lot of grazing room. So large countries that have a lot of pastureland—like Argentina, Australia, Canada, New Zealand, and the United States—raise the most cattle and eat the most beef.

Wild cattle were tamed or domesticated about 9,000 years ago. They were valued as much for the work that they did—carrying and pulling heavy loads—as for the milk and meat that they provided. Over time, farmers developed breeds that were meant only to provide meat. Looking quite different from slim, long-legged dairy cows, beef cattle have wide fleshy bodies and short legs.

Today, livestock animals that are ready for market are usually shipped from the farms or ranches on which they're raised to big meat-processing centers near large

75

cities, where the food they provide is most needed. After they are slaughtered, their meat is packaged and sent to markets near and far, with the help of refrigerated trucks, trains, and ships. Other animal body parts—like hides, hoofs, and bones—are also put to good use, making leather goods, fertilizers, and other products.

What is a **vegetarian**?

A vegetarian is a person that does not eat any animal flesh, including meat, poultry, or seafood. A vegetarian diet can consist of fruits, vegetables, breads, nuts, and pasta as well as dairy products like cheese and milk. Some vegetarians, known as vegans (VEE-ghens), do not eat anything produced by an animal, so they eliminate all dairy—and products made with eggs—from their diets as well. Vegetarians have existed since ancient times, when certain religious or ethnic groups advocated the special diet for religious reasons or health concerns, or on moral grounds, believing that killing any living creature for food was wrong. The reasons people choose to be vegetarians today are much the same as they once were, with health concerns playing a large role. Many people believe that a vegetarian diet—rich in fiber and low in fat, as opposed to the higher fat quantities found in meat-heavy diets—reduces the risk of heart disease and some forms of cancer.

ME, MYSELF, AND I

GROWING UP

How did my **life begin**?

All living things are made up of cells. They are so small that you need a microscope to see them. Your body contains trillions and trillions of cells. Each part of your body is made up of different kinds of cells: bone cells, brain cells, blood cells, and more.

Each person begins life as a single fertilized cell. This single cell contains all the information needed for a new human being to grow and live. The information—coded chemical instructions known as genes—is found on 23 pairs of chromosomes in the nucleus, or control center, of the cell.

That special fertilized cell began with a single egg cell from your mother. Each month a woman releases a mature, or ripe, egg cell from reproductive organs called ovaries. This egg contains half the genes needed to create a new life.

A man produces millions of sperm cells in reproductive organs called testes. Each sperm cell contains half the genes needed to create a new life. When a sperm cell from your father joined with and fertilized the released egg cell inside your mother's body, the cell that would become you was complete. It had all the coded instructions it needed to begin dividing and growing into a baby.

Within a few hours, the fertilized cell that was you split into two complete cells, each with a full set of genes inside. Before long the cells divided again. After five or six days a ball of hundreds of cells existed. The size of the head of a pin, this ball of cells attached to the lining of your mother's uterus, or womb, the reproductive organ in which babies grow. There, in the nourishing lining of the uterus, the cells continued to multiply. Gradually the cells began to specialize, turning into nerve cells, muscle cells, and so on. A tiny baby began to take shape.

77

As you grew, you received nutrients and oxygen from your mother's blood through a special tube that was attached to your abdomen called the umbilical cord. After 40 weeks (between nine and ten months), all of your organs and body systems were developed enough to work on their own, and you were ready to enter the world. Then you made your grand entrance and were born!

What is my **belly button**?

Your belly button, or navel, is a scar where your umbilical cord once was. The tube-like cord connected you to your mother when you were inside her uterus, growing into a baby. It carried oxygen and nourishment to you from the placenta, an organ that develops in the uterus during pregnancy, connecting you to your mother's blood supply. (It also carried away waste products from your blood.) Once you were born, the umbilical cord was no longer needed, because you began to breathe and eat on your own. The cord was clamped off and cut, and what was left of it withered and dropped off about a week after your birth.

How do I grow?

Just as the tiny fertilized egg cell from which you began divided again and again to become a baby, the trillions of cells now making up your body continue to divide as you grow. The more cells you have, the bigger you become. Some cells divide to replace worn out cells and others divide to increase the size and change the shape of your body as you mature. Hormones—chemicals that are produced by glands and circulate in your blood—help direct the growth of cells in your body during the process of growing up. Usually people are fully grown by the time they reach the age of 20 (although men take a little longer than women). By the time a person is 30, however, the rate at which body cells renew themselves begins to slow down, and signs of aging appear. As time goes on, certain body cells—like those of the brain and nerves—are not replaced when they wear out and die.

What causes **"growing pains"**?

"Growing pains" usually refers to the aches and pains that children feel in their legs at night when they are lying in bed. Kids seem to get them during growth spurts, times when they are growing a lot. Doctors think that the tendons—the tough elastic straps, or bands, that attach muscles to bones—of affected children do not grow quite as fast as their bones do. The tendons eventually catch up, but in the meantime this condition puts muscles under extra stress during an active day and causes them to ache and even spasm (contract abnormally) when they are finally at rest at night. Growing pains are not dangerous. They don't bother children during the day, and they usually come and go at nighttime. Regular stretching exercises—keeping the muscles and

After 40 weeks (between nine and ten months) in the mother's uterus, a baby's organs and body systems are developed enough to work on their own. Then the baby is ready to enter the world.

tendons relaxed—often solve the problem for good. But if the pains are very bad and continue for a long time, a doctor should be seen. In rare cases, an infection, disease, injury, or unnoticed malformation of the legs is causing the problem.

How **big** will I become?

Several different factors determine how big a person will grow. The most important one is heredity, the passing of physical traits from parents to children. When you began as a single fertilized cell, your mother and father each contributed half the genes—coded chemical information—needed for you to live and grow. These genes are responsible for your physical traits, like the color of your eyes and hair, how your body will be shaped, and how tall you will become. That is why children look a lot like their parents, or even their grandparents: they have inherited family characteristics that may have been passed on for several generations. If your parents are big or tall, chances are good that you will be big or tall, too. The average height of a woman in the United States is about five feet, four inches (1.6 meters), and the average height for an American man is five feet, nine inches (1.75 meters).

In spite of genetic coding, certain conditions can keep people from growing as large as their genes say they should. Bad nutrition keeps a body from reaching its maximum size. Poor health and disease do the same. That is why people who lived in generations before us, when food was sometimes scarce and health care was poor, were quite a bit smaller than we are today. Taking good care of your body, then, helps it become the best it can be.

What is **puberty**?

Puberty is a time of tremendous change—physical and emotional—that everyone experiences on his or her way to becoming an adult. After the many changes of puberty, people are physically able to reproduce, or have children, though it takes many more years to develop the emotional maturity required for such a decision. While there are many common elements, every person experiences puberty a little bit differently, and kids go through the changes of puberty at all different paces. Some develop early, others late. Girls experience different changes than boys. Puberty can be exciting, but it can also be confusing, scary, and lonely.

The changes associated with puberty are triggered by the release of certain hormones (primarily estrogen for girls and testosterone for boys) that signal the body to grow and change. Puberty usually starts between the ages of 8 and 13 for girls and between 10 and 15 for boys, though it's normal for some kids to develop later. During puberty kids' bodies will not only grow taller, they will also change their basic shapes. Hair that was formerly soft and downy—in places like the armpits, genital area, and, for boys, the face—begins to grow in thicker and darker.

During puberty, girls develop breasts, their waists get narrower, and their hips broaden. Some girls are alarmed to notice that they gain weight, or "fill out," during puberty, but this change is normal and healthy. It's not a good idea to try to counteract the normal growth of puberty with dieting. The female hormones released at puberty eventually trigger menstruation. During each menstrual cycle, which is usually about a month long, an egg is released from one of two ovaries in a girl or woman's body. If the egg were fertilized by sperm, it would implant in the uterus, or womb, and eventually grow into a baby. The uterus prepares for pregnancy each cycle by creating a lining of extra tissue and blood that would nourish a growing fetus. If the egg is unfertilized, that lining is expelled through the vagina. A "missed" period could be a normal occurrence (many women have irregular cycles), or it may be a sign of pregnancy.

Boys' bodies change in different ways during puberty: they get broader shoulders, more developed muscles, and larger penises and testes. Their faces change to look more adult, and their voices deepen as well.

Kids going through puberty often notice emotional changes that accompany the physical transformation. Part of the emotional roller coaster of puberty comes from the hormones coursing through your body, and part of it is just confusion and fear about changing from a kid to an adult. It's important to remember, though, that everyone goes through it, and often it can really help to talk about these feelings with a friend or a trusted adult.

When will I be a grown-up?

In the United States you are considered a grown-up when you reach the age of 18. You are no longer legally connected with your parents, and you are entitled to the rights—and expected to fulfill the duties—of an adult American citizen. (You may vote and be called for military service, for instance.)

There is a good chance, though, that when you are 18 your body has not yet reached full maturity. Many people continue to grow for a few more years. Most are fully grown—at least in height—by the time they are 20 years old, though boys may keep on growing until they are 23.

How **long** will I **live**?

Because medical science has eliminated or brought under control many of the diseases that once kept people from reaching old age, it is likely that you will live a very long time. Today, the average life expectancy of a man living in the Unites States is around 74 years; the average American woman will reach the age of 80. Just 100 years ago, the average life span was more than 25 years shorter. And because medical science continues to improve health care—and is studying old age and trying to find ways to slow it—people are expected to live even longer.

Many factors contribute to a long life. Usually people live longer in Western Europe and North America (and in Japan) than in Latin America, Asia, or Africa. Average life spans are longer in wealthier, developed, politically stable countries where safe and hygienic housing, healthy diets, and good medical care are common. Another important factor that determines long life is the genetic information you inherit from your parents, which give you certain physical and health characteristics. If your great-grandparents and grandparents reached old age, for instance, you have a good chance of reaching it yourself. But even if they didn't, don't be concerned. You can overcome a lot of inherited traits simply by following a healthy lifestyle. Eating a good diet, getting regular medical care, and keeping physically active all contribute to a longer life.

Why does everyone **look different**?

Genes inherited from your parents decide how you look. They determine the color of your eyes, skin, hair, and so much more! They decide how your face will look, how your body will be shaped, and how tall you will grow. There are thousands and thousands of these influential genes inside each one of us.

When you first began, a sperm cell from your father—carrying half the genes that you would inherit—fertilized an egg cell from your mother, which had the other half. These two sets of genes contained all the information needed to create a new human being. So the genes you inherited from your mother gave you some of your features, while the genes you got from your father gave you others. Or their genes may have combined to give you traits that are controlled by many genes. The random mix of genes explains why you may resemble your parents but still have a special look all your own, and it also explains why brothers and sisters can look so different from each other.

People from all over the world may look very different from one another, too. Some have very dark skin and curly hair. Others have almond-shaped eyes and dark, straight hair. Still others have light skin, hair, and eyes. The ancestors of these people came from different parts of the world, where distinct genes—not shared by other people—were inherited and passed on. Still, the number of genes that make people of the world look different is very small compared to the huge number that we all share as human beings.

THE BRAIN

What is the **most important organ** in my body?

While many of our organs are vital, meaning we could not live without them, the brain is the most complex and the most important part of our bodies. The brain is the body's command center; everything we do—eating, talking, walking, thinking, remembering, sleeping—is controlled and processed by the brain. Our brain tells us what's going on outside our bodies (whether we are cold or hot, for instance, or whether the person we see coming toward us is a friend or a stranger) as well as what's going on inside our bodies (whether we have an infection or a broken bone, or whether we feel happy or sad).

The key to the body's nervous system, the brain contains billions (between 10 billion and 100 billion) of nerve cells, or neurons. Neurons combine to form the body's nerves, thin cords that spread from head to toe and all parts in between. Neurons take in and send out electrical signals, called impulses, that control or respond to everything your body does and feels. The brain is like a very busy, high-speed post office, constantly receiving messages and sending them out all the time; it handles millions of nerve impulses every second. (An interesting fact about the brain: While it is responsible for receiving and transmitting all messages of pain for the whole body, the brain itself does not have pain receptors. That means that, if you could somehow gain access to another person's brain, you could poke it or pinch it and that person wouldn't feel the pain.)

The human brain is divided into three main parts: the cerebrum, the cerebellum, and the brain stem. The largest part of the brain (about 85 percent of its total weight), the cerebrum, controls emotions, thought, memory, and speech. It is divided into a right and left side, called hemispheres, and each side is divided further into parts called lobes. Its thick outer covering, called the cortex, is made up of a type of tissue called gray matter. The cerebellum coordinates the kinds of movements we don't usually think about: it helps us walk upright and in a straight line, it keeps us balanced so we don't tip over, and it gives us coordination so we can run and play. The brain stem connects the brain with the spinal cord. It controls our body's vital processes, like breathing, digestion, and heart rate.

What does the brain **look like**?

The pinkish-gray spongy tissue that makes up most of the brain's outer covering is folded over many times onto itself, forming numerous ridges. These folds allow the brain to have a larger surface area—and more room for lots of nerve cells—than it would have if it were smooth. The brain is one of the largest organs in the human body. From about age six onward, the brain weighs about three pounds (1.4 kilograms). While that's only about two percent of an average person's body weight, the brain uses about 20 percent of the body's oxygen. And if it's deprived of that oxygen for longer than a few minutes, it can become seriously damaged.

Why are people **right-handed or left-handed**?

The way your brain works determines whether you are right- or left-handed. The left half of your brain controls the right side of your body, and the right side of your brain

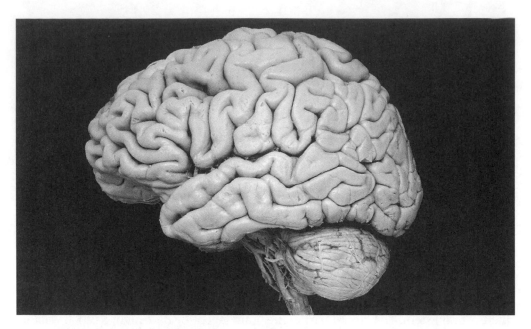

Many of our organs are vital, but the brain is the most complex and the most important part of our bodies.

controls the left side of your body. Because one side of the brain is always stronger or more dominant, there is one side of the body that is more developed and skilled, too. For most people (about 90 percent; more females than males) it is the left side of the brain that is dominant, making them right-handed (and right-footed, too!).

Scientists don't know why the brains of left-handed people develop in a reverse way. But it makes absolutely no difference. In fact, because left-handed people have to get along in a right-handed world, using tools, machines, and instruments designed for right-handers, they are often pretty skilled with their nondominant hand, too. Scientists think that may be why left-handed baseball players are better hitters than those who are right-handed! There are also a few people who are ambidextrous, which means that they can do a task equally well with either hand. And some people are mixed-handed, performing some tasks better with the left hand and some with the right.

BONES AND MUSCLES

How many **bones** do I have?

Babies are born with about 330 bones, but many of them join together during the process of growing up, creating fewer, larger bones. Adults have 206 bones. Some people end up with a few extra bones, though, in the arches of their feet or as an extra set of ribs in their rib cage.

Many bones are shaped to protect and support soft body parts. The curved bones of your skull, for instance, enclose and protect your brain, your body's command center. The ribs form a cage that protects your heart and lungs. Your wrists, hands, ankles, and feet contain more than half the bones of your body. Usually the more bones, joints, and muscles you have in a spot, the more flexible it is. That is why you can make such small, precise movements with your hands and feet, like tying a bow or balancing on your tiptoes.

What keeps the **bones** of my skeleton **together**?

Your skeleton makes up the hard, strong framework of your body. Your skeleton can move easily because it consists of many bones connected by flexible joints. Joints are kept together by elastic straps called ligaments and by a smooth, flexible tissue called cartilage, which covers and joins the ends of bones. Muscles are usually attached to bones by other tough elastic straps, or bands, called tendons. During movement, when muscles contract, it is the ropelike tendons that pull bones into their new positions.

What is the **biggest bone** in my body?

The longest and strongest bone in the human body is the thighbone, or femur. In a man six feet (1.8 meters) tall, the femur would measure about 20 inches (51 centimeters) in length. Leg bones are very strong because they have to carry the weight of the body and move it from one place to another.

What is the **smallest bone** in my body?

The smallest bone in your body is the stirrup, located in the middle ear. It is about the size of a grain of rice. It is named that because it looks just like a tiny stirrup, the part on a horse's saddle on which you rest your foot. When sound waves enter your ear canal they vibrate your eardrum. The three tiny bones behind it also vibrate, increasing the strength of the sound as it passes through the middle ear. The stirrup, along with the hammer and the anvil—bones also named for their shapes—transfer their vibrations to the inner ear, where they become nerve impulses and travel to your brain.

How do I know if I've **broken a bone**?

Bones break when too much stress is applied by physical forces. Breaks usually occur when a person is injured playing sports, or when he or she is involved in an accident. Bone diseases can also cause breaks. With serious breaks—called compound frac-

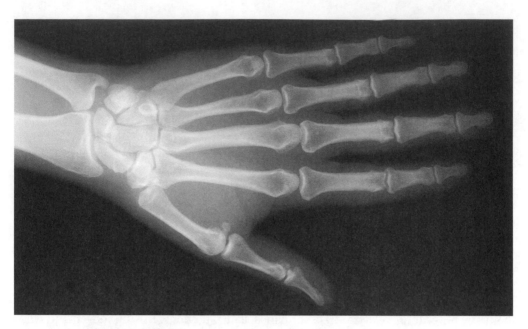

Your wrists, hands, ankles, and feet contain more than half the bones of your body.

tures—you know something is wrong because the bone sticks out through the skin, and muscles and other tissue are damaged around it. But a lot of bone breaks are simple fractures, where the bone has broken cleanly instead of splintering, and it doesn't push out through the skin. In such cases it is hard to know if you have broken a bone, or if the pain you're feeling is caused by a pulled muscle or a sprained joint.

A fractured bone usually causes a lot of pain, and the injured area may look swollen or be shaped funny. Still, the only way to tell if you have a broken bone for sure is to have it X-rayed. X rays, short-wave radiation that can pass through flesh but not bone (leaving a picture on photographic film or plates), can detect a break in a bone.

If your bone is broken, the pieces will have to be held together in the right position in order to heal properly, growing back together as before. Sometimes a hard cast or splint is used to keep the injured body part from moving for a few weeks. Some broken bones are held together naturally, by the muscles that surround them. And in serious cases, metal screws, nails, and plates keep the ends of broken bones in place as they heal. Healing time depends on the bone broken and the age of the injured person. The bones of children heal very quickly.

What is the **"funny bone"**?

The funny bone is not really a bone. It is actually a big nerve that runs through your forearm to the back of your elbow. When you hit that nerve in your elbow on something hard, it really hurts and sometimes causes tingling or temporary numbness in your arm. What's so funny about that? The funny bone got its name from the bone located above it, the humerus (sounds like "humorous") bone in the upper arm.

What makes my **knuckles crack**?

There are tiny amounts of fluid around your joints (the place where two or more bones meet) that keeps them lubricated so they can move easily. When you stretch your fingers quickly, the pressure in the fluid around your finger joints changes, and empty spaces are created. As fluid rushes back to fill the spots, it produces the cracking noises you hear. Other joints—knees, ankles, neck—may crack sometimes when you change their positions, too.

How many **muscles** do I have?

Scientists can't agree about how many muscles the human body has. Depending on whether certain muscles are counted separately or considered part of a larger muscle, the numbers range from 656 to 850. Muscles make up almost half of a person's body weight. Every movement your body makes depends on muscles. Voluntary muscles, which you control with conscious thought, move the skeletal muscles on the outside of your body. When you raise your hand or chew your food, for example, you are using skeletal muscles. Involuntary muscles, on the other hand, move things inside your body, usually without you thinking about them at all. Your heart pumps blood and your stomach and intestines move food through your digestive system, for instance, without your conscious thought.

How do muscles **work**?

Your brain tells your skeletal muscles to move by sending signals through your nervous system. Nerves in your muscles receive the message and make the muscles contract, making them shorter and thicker. Contracting causes the muscles to pull the bones to which they are attached. But muscles cannot push, so usually a second muscle, following a second message from the brain, has to pull the bone back. A lot of muscles work that way—in pairs.

What is the **biggest muscle** in my body?

The largest muscle in the human body is the gluteus maximus. That's the big muscle that makes up most of your bottom. The muscle is large because it has a big job to do: it moves the thighbone or femur, the largest bone in the body. Some of the smallest muscles in the human body are those that move the eyeball.

What is the **strongest muscle** in my body?

The strongest muscles in the human body are the jaw muscles. Working together, they can close your back teeth (molars) with a force of 200 pounds (90.7 kilograms) or more. Muscles become stronger the more they are used, and jaw muscles get a lot of exercise when you talk and eat. (The body's most active muscles, however, are those that move the eyes.)

Do people use more muscles when they **smile,** or when they **frown**?

Yes, what your parents tell you is true: It takes far more muscles to frown than it does to smile. Smiling only uses 17 muscles, while frowning requires 43.

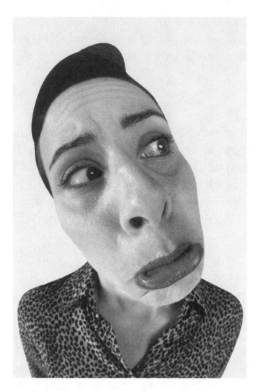
You use more than twice as many muscles when you frown compared to when you smile.

Why can I sometimes **feel my heart beating**?

You usually only notice your heart beating when it is working faster than usual. When you are resting, your heart usually beats about 85 times per minute (slower in adults). But when you are active, your muscles need more oxygen and nutrients. It's your heart's job to increase the amount of blood that flows through your body—delivering what your muscles need—by pumping faster. After a real workout, your heart can be beating twice as fast, and it may feel like it's pounding in your chest.

When you become frightened or excited, a similar thing occurs. The hormone adrenaline, which prepares the body for emergency action, is released into your blood from glands. (Along with your brain and nervous system, hormones—chemical messengers that circulate in the blood—help control body processes.) Adrenaline tells your heart to pump faster in an instant "fight or flight" response that has helped people survive dangers from the beginning of time. Your heart makes sure your muscles are ready to fight or run from the thing that has frightened or excited you.

HAIR TODAY, GONE TOMORROW

Why do we have **hair**?

Prehistoric human beings were covered with a coat of heavy hair that protected them from the cold and from other threats in the environment like attacking animals and rugged terrain. The fine hair that covers our bodies now is probably a remnant of our prehistoric days. Today we have less need for a thick coat of hair on our bodies: we wear clothes to keep warm, and few things in our world threaten to seriously damage our skin. Yet we still have heavy hair on certain areas of our bodies for protective purposes. Our eyelashes and eyebrows, for instance, keep dirt and sweat out of our eyes. And the hair on our heads helps to keep our brains warm in cold temperatures.

Why is some hair **curly** and other hair **straight**?

Hair grows from tiny holes in the skin called follicles. Follicles can have different shapes and sizes. Hair type is determined by the shape and size of the follicles from which they grow. Large follicles mean you'll have thick hair, while narrow follicles result in fine hair. Straight hair comes from round follicles, wavy hair from those that are oval, and curly hair grows from follicles that look like flattened ovals.

Why is **genital hair curly** even on people who have straight hair on their heads?

As with the hair on our heads, genital, or pubic, hair is curly and kinky because of the shape of the follicles (and that hair is thick and coarse because of the larger size of the follicles). When we go through puberty, many of the changes in our bodies result from the presence of certain hormones, which are chemicals that control body processes. We have hair follicles all over our bodies, and the hormone androgen affects follicles in several places—the genital area, underarms, and facial hair—changing those follicles during puberty to produce a thick, curly kind of hair. (Men have much more androgen than women, which explains why women don't usually have coarse facial hair like men do.)

How **many hairs** do I have on my **head**?

The average person has about 100,000 hairs on his or her head. People with red hair have less than this (around 90,000) and blonds have more (around 140,000). People with brown or black hair fall in between. Most people lose between 50 and 100 head hairs each day, but new hairs are usually ready to replace them.

How **fast** does hair **grow**?

Human head hair grows about six inches (15 centimeters) every year. During the summertime it grows a little faster, because warm weather causes more blood to reach the scalp, which gives hair cells extra nourishment. In cold weather, less blood travels to the surface of the body—to skin and hair cells—because it is more important that the internal organs that run the body are kept warm.

Why does head hair grow longer than other hair on the body?

All hairs have a particular life span before they fall out. With a life span of about two to five years, head hair grows longer than other hair on your body. (Eyebrow hairs, on the other hand, have a life span of just three to five months.) If you stopped cutting the hair on your head, you could get it to grow to about your waist before hairs would start to fall out (and new hairs began to grow to replace them). A few people, however, can grow their hair much longer than that. A woman in India holds the record for the longest hair: 13 feet, 10.5 inches.

Why doesn't it **hurt** when I have my **hair or nails cut**?

The hair that shows above your skin is composed of dead cells made up of a tough protein called keratin; toenails and fingernails are also made of keratin. So hair and nails have no feeling above the surface of your skin. They are alive below the skin, though, where their roots are attached to nerves. That is why it hurts when someone pulls your hair: they are tugging at live roots. But having your hair and nails cut doesn't hurt at all.

Why do some people **lose the hair on their heads**?

Scientists have been trying to figure out why some people—mostly men—begin to lose their hair as they grow older. It is believed that a certain hormone (hormones are chemicals that are produced by glands and control different body processes) causes hair follicles to shrink, and they begin to produce shorter, thinner hairs. The tendency to lose hair or be bald runs in families, meaning that it is an inherited trait. In rare cases, diseases can also cause people to lose their hair. Sometimes hair loss happens as a result of chemotherapy treatments for cancer—anticancer drugs affect some healthy cells as well, including those that cause hair growth. Hair loss due to chemotherapy is reversible, however—hair will usually begin growing back once the treatments are over.

Why does hair **turn gray or white** when a person gets old?

A pigment called melanin is responsible for hair color (as well as for skin and eye color). The darker the hair of a person, the more melanin in that person's hair. As people age, the supply of melanin to their hair may stop (pigment-containing cells live and ordinarily multiply in the hair root). While an aging person's hair still grows, the lack of melanin in it makes it gray or white.

THE SKIN I'M IN

Why does my skin **turn red or brown** if I stay out in the Sun for a long time?

A sunburn occurs when your skin is overexposed to the rays of the Sun. Too much sunlight inflames surface skin and the tissues beneath it—just like a regular burn from touching something hot—causing redness, hotness, tenderness, and swelling. In bad cases, blisters may even appear as the body begins to form and protect new skin to replace the skin damaged by sunburn.

Usually people who have fair, or light, skin get sunburns. Such people have less melanin in their skin—the pigment that determines skin color (as well as hair and eye color). Melanin is made in special cells called melanocytes; people with light skin have fewer of these. Sun exposure makes melanocytes produce more melanin in an effort to darken skin—protecting it from damage by "shading" its deeper layers. This process creates what we know as a suntan. Dark-skinned people can produce a lot of melanin fast—tanning quickly—when they are in the sun, but light-skinned people usually get burned before their melanocytes can produce the amount of melanin needed for protection. Fair people can get tans only if they do it very slowly, exposing themselves to the Sun a little bit at a time.

Scientists think that various groups of people around the world developed different skin colors because of where their ancestors once lived. In hot, sunny places, people developed dark skin for protection. In cooler places, where sunlight was not as strong, people developed lighter skin.

What are **freckles**?

Freckles are little spots of color that have more melanin—the pigment responsible for skin, hair, and eye color—than surrounding skin. They are usually seen in people who are fair, because the color contrast between freckles and the rest of the skin is strong. Did you ever notice how being out in the Sun seems to make more freckles appear? Faint freckles become more noticeable when they are exposed to sunlight because skin with more melanin tans quickly.

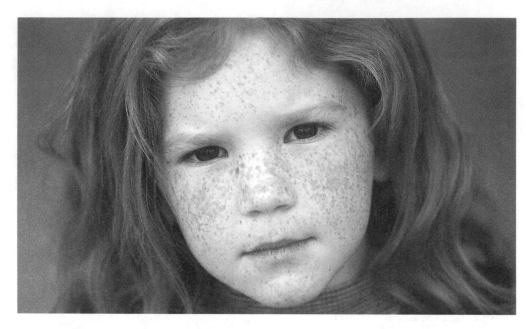

Little spots with high concentrations of melanin, the pigment in skin, are responsible for freckles.

Why do I have to wear **sunscreen**?

If you are going to be out in the Sun for a long time you need to wear a sunscreen or sunblock. These lotions contain chemicals that absorb certain harmful rays of the Sun (ultraviolet rays), keeping them from penetrating your skin. This protection is important because these rays can hurt you, causing painful sunburns that damage the tissues beneath the surface of your skin. Damaging your skin's deep elastic layer makes it look old and wrinkled a lot earlier than it should.

But the most important thing to avoid when you're out in the Sun is cell damage that causes skin cancer. Doctors have found that being in strong sunlight a lot (especially if you are fair) and having many sunburns—particularly when you are young—can cause real problems many years later. Skin cancers can develop and, when not treated quickly, spread to other parts of the body and be extremely dangerous. Because sunscreens can't protect you from all of the sun's harmful rays, it is also wise to use clothing, hats, and sunglasses to cover up when sunlight is strong. In addition, it is a good idea to limit outdoor activities between the hours of 10 A.M. and 3 P.M., when the rays of the Sun are most intense.

Why do a lot of old people have **wrinkled skin**?

Skin is made up of two layers. The thin surface layer is called the epidermis. The thicker layer underneath—the dermis—contains sweat glands and hair follicles. New skin cells are made in the dermis, which gives your skin its firm and elastic, or stretchy, feel.

When people get older, the fibers that make up skin become thinner and lose their elasticity. Places where skin is repeatedly stretched and folded—from smiling or frowning, for example—no longer snap back into place, and lines and wrinkles form there. Constant exposure to the Sun (and cigarette smoking) do serious damage to the dermis, speeding up the normal changes that occur in skin as people get older.

What is a **pimple**?

Almost every part of your body is covered with hair, most of it so fine that it is invisible. Hair grows from tiny holes in the skin called follicles, which also contain glands. These sebaceous (sih-BAY-shus) glands produce oils that make the surface of your skin soft and flexible and keep it from drying out. Sometimes a gland makes too much oil, though, and that extra oil becomes trapped in its follicle. At that point bacteria—which are always present on the skin—may infect the blocked follicle. As your body tries to fight the infection, redness, swelling, and pus may appear at the spot, causing what we know as a pimple. Usually squeezing and picking at a pimple only spreads the tiny infection into surrounding tissue, making the problem worse. Pimples that are very infected may take many weeks to heal and leave small scars in the skin.

Usually when girls and boys (especially boys) become adolescents, they start to have trouble with pimples. Pimples flare up at this time because certain hormones—chemicals made by glands that control different body processes—increase as kids approach sexual maturity; some of those hormones increase the production of oil in the skin. When a person has a lot of pimples, over a long period of time, the condition is called acne. The best thing to do for acne is to keep your skin clean, washing with soap twice a day. If it gets too bad, a dermatologist, or skin doctor, can help. Just try to remember that your acne is normal, it won't last forever, and it is probably more noticeable to you than to anyone else.

What causes **warts**?

Warts are caused by certain viruses that invade skin cells and cause them to reproduce faster than normal, creating a hard bump. Warts can be spread by touch—or by contact with skin shed by warts—but most people are resistant to the different viruses that cause them and will not get warts even after contact. Although warts may not look very nice, they are not harmful, and they usually go away by themselves within a few months. Chemicals are available in drugstores that remove warts by destroying the abnormal skin cells that make them, or doctors can remove warts by freezing, burning, or scraping them off.

What causes an **itch**?

Under the surface of your skin are millions of tiny sensors that detect touch, pressure, pain, heat, and cold. When you have an itch the sensors send a message to your brain that something is on your skin that usually isn't there. It may be an insect, or a piece of fuzz, or a strand of fallen hair. Dry skin is often itchy because you have flakes of dead skin cells on a surface that is usually kept smooth and supple by the oil from skin glands. Sometimes when you eat or touch something that you are allergic to, your immune system—whose mission it is to protect you—releases irritating chemicals that may cause itching on your skin. Why does scratching help quiet an itch? Scientists think that scratching gives your touch sensors a stronger feeling to focus on, and the itch is ignored, at least temporarily.

Why do I **laugh** when someone **tickles** me?

The millions of tiny sensors under your skin—which detect touch, pain, and temperature—send information to your brain about your surroundings, and your brain tells you how to react. When someone tickles you, your touch sensors are overloaded with messages, and your brain puts your body on alert, making your muscles tense to help you escape. During tickling, you always yell "Stop!" and try to get away, right? It's not exactly relaxing! You laugh because it is a way for your body to release tension if you can't stop the tickler. Exercise and laughter are good tension-releasers for the body; both make you feel better afterwards.

What causes **goose bumps**?

Goose bumps or goose pimples are little bumps on your skin that appear when you are cold or afraid. They are named that because they look like the bumpy flesh of a goose that's had its feathers plucked. When you are cold the muscles in your skin raise the hairs on your body so that they can trap a thicker layer of air next to your skin, which may keep you a bit warmer. And, as with all muscular activity, this contraction of the skin muscles also produces heat.

When you are afraid, the same process occurs, but for a different reason. At such times your body produces a chemical called adrenaline, which prepares you for emergency action. It makes your heart beat faster and your muscles tense, and that raises your hair. In animals with fur, raised hair makes them look bigger and may scare predators away. Scientists think that long ago, when people were covered with coats of heavy hair, goose bumps helped protect them in the same way from their predators.

Why do I **shiver** when I'm **cold**?

When your brain receives the signal that you are cold, it sets off a series of reactions. One of these reactions causes your muscles to repeatedly and quickly contract, or tighten, and relax. Muscle movement uses energy and produces heat (that is why people become warm when they exercise). In other words, when you feel cold, your body starts working on its own to make some extra heat to warm you up.

Why do I sweat when I'm hot?

When you get hot, your body has a couple of ways to cool down. The blood vessels in your skin expand, allowing more blood to flow through them; the heat the blood carries then escapes through your skin. When you are hot you also produce more sweat, or perspiration, fluid made in sweat glands (millions of them!) that cover your body, located deep in your skin. Sweat carries body heat to the surface of your skin through pores, or tiny holes, where the moisture evaporates into the air and cools you off. When you sweat faster than it can evaporate, you can get pretty soggy! It is important to remember to drink plenty of water when you are doing a lot of sweating so that you don't dehydrate, or lose bodily fluids. About 62 percent of a person's body weight is water—a lot of fluid is necessary to keep body processes running smoothly. Under extremely hot conditions, a person can lose up to 20 quarts of perspiration a day, which can lead to serious health problems if those fluids aren't replaced.

You've probably noticed that your body doesn't do much to cool you off on very humid, sticky days. Sweat needs to evaporate, or turn into water vapor, in order to make you feel cooler. But on humid days, the air has so much water vapor in it already that it can't hold any more. When the air is nearly saturated like that, the sweat on your skin cannot evaporate fast enough to give you any relief. Sweat will evaporate better off your skin if you wear cotton clothing, which lets your skin "breathe," rather than synthetic fibers like nylon, spandex, or polyester.

Why do people **sweat** when they're **nervous**?

Feelings of nervousness or excitement trigger certain responses in your nervous system, including the production of certain hormones that activate sweat glands. The sweat glands most likely to respond to such hormones are those in your armpits and the palms of your hands. Many people refer to sweating in these conditions as "breaking out in a cold sweat."

Why do people sometimes **smell bad** after they sweat?

You may be surprised to learn that it's not the sweat itself that smells bad. Sweat is mostly water and salt with small concentrations of various waste products. The odor comes from the bacteria living on your skin; when those bacteria begin working to break down your sweat, they produce an unpleasant odor. Fortunately, the smelly results can be washed away with soap and water in the shower or bath.

95

There are actually two different kinds of sweat glands, eccrine glands and apocrine glands. Eccrine glands are found all over your body, while apocrine glands are concentrated mostly in your armpits and groin area. Apocrine glands get especially active when you hit puberty, thanks to the extra hormones released in your body during that time. And, as an added bonus, apocrine glands produce a different kind of sweat, with proteins and fatty acids, that has a particularly foul smell—referred to as body odor—when it combines with the bacteria on your skin.

Kids who haven't reached puberty yet can sweat a lot without getting too stinky—much of their sweat is coming from the eccrine glands, rather than the more potent apocrine glands, which don't really develop until puberty. The high concentration of apocrine glands in the armpits explains why people put deodorant or antiperspirant there and not elsewhere. By the way, deodorant doesn't stop you from sweating, but it neutralizes the bacteria that make sweat smell. Antiperspirant actually blocks pores in your skin, preventing you from sweating. While many people prefer anti-perspirants, wishing to control the wetness as well as the odor of sweat, some experts believe it's better to let the sweat, which carries some waste products out of your body, leave naturally instead of being blocked.

Why does the **skin on my fingers and toes wrinkle** when I'm in water for a long time?

The wrinkles that you see on your fingers and toes when you've been in water a long time may make you think that your skin is shriveling and shrinking, just like a raisin. But actually the opposite reaction is taking place—your skin is expanding. The tough outer layer of skin is thickest on your hands and feet (because those parts get the most wear). This outer layer absorbs water easily once the oily coating on your skin gets washed away in the bath or while swimming. The skin on your fingers and toes soaks up water and expands. Once the water is no longer under your skin, that expanded skin wrinkles up. But those wrinkles don't last long once you get out of the water.

BLOOD MATTERS

What is **blood**?

Blood acts as your body's transportation system. Pumped along by your heart, blood brings oxygen from the air you breathe and nutrients from the food you eat to all the cells of your body. It also keeps cells clean and healthy by taking waste products away after the nutrients and oxygen have been used for processes like growth and repair. In addition, blood transports hormones—chemicals made in glands that control a variety of processes—throughout your body. Blood also carries heat throughout your body.

More than half of your blood is a watery liquid called plasma. Plasma contains things like nutrients and waste products, along with chemicals and matter needed for clotting, or sealing a wound before too much blood escapes. The rest of blood is made of tiny cells. Most are red blood cells, which distribute oxygen throughout your body and carry away the waste gas carbon dioxide, which is released from your lungs. The remain-

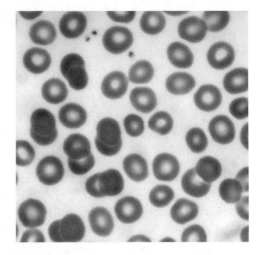

Red blood cells are the smallest cells in your body.

ing cells are white blood cells, which protect you from infections by attacking and destroying disease-causing germs that enter your body.

Red blood cells are the smallest cells in your body. But what they lack in size they make up for in number: in a drop of blood the size of the head of a pin there are five million red blood cells. In that same drop are 10,000 white blood cells and 250,000 platelets, small ovals of matter that gather wherever a blood vessel is injured to plug the hole and help form a clot.

What makes blood **red**?

Blood contains a protein called hemoglobin. Hemoglobin, which contains iron, is found in red blood cells and is the ingredient that makes blood red. Hemoglobin transports oxygen from the lungs to wherever it's needed throughout your body. You've probably noticed that sometimes blood is bright red, while other times it is dark red. The difference in color comes from the changing amounts of oxygen in the blood. Arteries, a type of blood vessel, carry blood away from the lungs and heart to the rest of your body. That blood is rich in oxygen, which joins with hemoglobin to give the blood its bright red color. Tiny blood vessels called capillaries, which have narrow walls through which tiny substances can pass, distribute oxygen and nutrients to all of your body's cells.

One of the waste products produced by your body's cells is the gas carbon dioxide, which enters your bloodstream by slipping through the capillary walls. The capillaries take that oxygen-poor, carbon dioxide-filled blood to the veins, another type of blood vessel, which carry the blood back to the lungs and heart. The lack of oxygen in this blood gives it a dark red, almost purplish color. When that blood reaches the lungs, the carbon dioxide in it is transferred to your lungs. When your brain receives a signal that carbon dioxide is building up in your lungs, it causes you to exhale, or breathe out, expelling all that carbon dioxide into the air. You then inhale, or breathe in, oxygen, which goes to your lungs, and the process begins again.

Why do my **lips turn blue** when I'm in cold water too long?

Your red, fleshy lips are full of blood vessels. When you are in cold surroundings, the blood vessels in your skin become narrower. This narrowing reduces the amount of heat lost through your skin and channels more blood to the internal organs that run your body. When the blood vessels in your skin contract, it loses its usual pinkish color—a color that comes from the regular supply of red blood flowing through it—and you appear pale. Your lips lose their rosy color, too. You resemble a person who has cyanosis, a condition caused by a lack of oxygen in the blood that makes the lips and skin appear blue or gray. Even though you have enough oxygen in your blood when you are in cold water, most of that blood is directed inward. After you leave the water and warm up, your blood begins to circulate normally through your skin again, and your red lip color returns.

Why do I sometimes get a **headache** when I eat **ice cream**?

You may have heard people call it a brain freeze, or an ice cream headache. You're gulping down some ice cream or a slush on a hot summer day, and all of a sudden you have a pain in your head that feels like you ran into a wall forehead first. Why does this happen, and more important, how can you make it go away so you can keep eating?

Everything you eat passes over the roof of your mouth, also called the palate. When something very cold touches the back of the palate, it affects a nerve center there that controls how much blood flows to your head. Depending on the circumstances, the nerve impulses can constrict, or narrow, blood vessels, or it can dilate, or widen, them. Scientists have not devoted much time to studying the cause of ice cream headaches, mostly because they pass quickly and are not serious. But doctors believe that the cold sensation on your palate may send a signal to the nerves there that your head needs warming up. Blood vessels open, allowing more blood (and more warmth) to flow through. This rapid dilation causes a buildup of fluid in your tissues that can't immediately drain; the extra fluid causes slight swelling, which results in the shooting pain you feel in the front of your head.

Ice cream headaches rarely last more than a minute, but the pain can be intense enough to make you want to avoid them altogether. Try eating your ice cream or drinking your milkshake more slowly, and try not to let the cold stuff linger on the roof of your mouth—hold the food more in the front or on the sides of your mouth before swallowing. Also, you can warm up your palate by placing your tongue there for a few seconds.

What happens when my **hand or foot "falls asleep"**?

When a lot of weight is on your arm or leg for a certain amount of time, it goes numb (along with your hand or foot). Your limb has "fallen asleep." Normally, blood flows freely through your arm or leg, bringing it oxygen and nutrients and taking away waste products. The pressure on your limb restricts blood flow. This restriction makes your cells work less efficiently there, especially your nerve cells, which are connected to the touch sensors in your skin. That's why a "sleeping" limb feels numb.

When the pressure is removed from your arm or leg, full blood flow and function gradually return. That's when you have that funny, prickly feeling called "pins and needles." Your nerve cells—irritated by the waste build-up in your body tissues—are finally able to send regular messages to your brain, telling it that something is wrong with your circulation. But by that time your limb is already on its way to working normally again. The annoying prickly feeling soon disappears as full circulation returns and your nerves are no longer alarmed.

If I hurt myself and bleed a lot, can I run out of blood?

An average-sized adult has between five and six quarts (about five liters) of blood in his or her body. Larger people have more, and smaller people—like children—have less. The arteries, veins, and capillaries through which blood travels are so numerous and cover so vast an area that they would measure 60,000 miles (96,500 kilometers) if laid out end to end! With all these blood vessels, then, the likelihood of injuring them is high. But blood contains special clotting elements that quickly take care of broken vessels, preventing any significant blood loss on the inside and the outside of the body. So your chances of running out of blood from a common injury are very, very low. And new blood is soon made to replace that which you have lost.

But during a rare, serious accident in which a large artery is injured, the situation can be dangerous. Arteries carry oxygen-rich blood that is pumped away from the heart under strong pressure. When an artery is injured, then, blood that runs through it doesn't have time to clot before it leaves the body. If a quart or more of blood is lost, a person goes into shock, a condition where blood circulation and other important body functions slow dangerously, leading to death in extreme cases. But if the injured person is close to a hospital, blood transfusions can be given, saving his or her life. Transfusions are collections of blood taken from healthy people, stored, and later used to help the injured and the sick.

What is a **bruise**?

When a bump or fall breaks blood vessels under your skin's surface, a bruise might appear. The blood that seeps out of the vessels and into your tissues changes color over several days—usually from red, to purple and blue, to brown and yellow—before it fades away. Bruises are not harmful unless they are very severe. Bruises on your shin and head, where bones are located just beneath the skin, can swell a lot (like with a "black eye"). A cold, wet cloth or ice can reduce the swelling.

When I cut or scrape myself, why do I get a **scab**?

When you get a cut or a scratch, you break blood vessels in, and sometimes below, your skin. Blood begins to leak out of them then, and platelets—small ovals of special matter in the blood—start to gather and stick together at the area of broken skin. Special chemicals also cause blood to thicken there, forming webs that trap blood cells and keep them from escaping. As more blood cells are trapped, a clot forms. As it hardens, it becomes a scab, a shield that keeps outside germs from entering the damaged skin. Beneath the scab, the body can repair the tissues. The scab shrinks over time as the skin around it heals, and it falls off when all repair work is done.

Why shouldn't I **pick** at **scabs**?

It's hard not to pick at scabs, which sometimes itch and pull and are annoying. But they are there for a good reason. They keep a cut or scrape protected from outside germs while it is healing. New skin cells form on the bottom of a wound first, working their way up to the surface. So the top of a cut or scrape is the last part to be repaired—and the scab will be shed when it is no longer needed. When you pull off a scab before the healing process is done you may expose the wound to germs again. In addition, you may disrupt the repair process and cause more damage to tissues before the cut or scrape is fully healed, leaving you with an unnecessary scar.

Should I **pop** a **blister**?

Just like scabs, blisters appear for good reasons. When skin is injured by burns or irritating chemicals (like poison ivy) or friction (from the repeated rubbing of stiff new shoes on your feet, for instance), your body produces a cushion of fluid under the damaged area to protect the new skin cells that are growing below to repair the spot. So popping or removing a blister takes this protective covering away. It is better to leave a blister alone and keep the damaged skin clean. (A Band-Aid can be used to cushion the spot.) A blister may break on its own; if not, the fluid will be absorbed back into the body once it's no longer needed.

Why do some **wounds** have to be **stitched up**?

Usually wounds that are deep or that have edges that don't naturally stay together need to be stitched up by a doctor. Blood carries dirt and germs out of most wounds, but deep wounds don't bleed much. For that reason, it is very important that deep wounds be cleaned well and closed up, preventing an infection from developing in deep body tissues, where it can cause real problems. Wounds with jagged edges that gap are also stitched up, to keep germs out and to prevent extra scarring. Wounds on the face are often given special attention, too, because scars there are so noticeable and can affect a person's appearance.

Why do some wounds cause **scars**?

Skin cells are some of the busiest cells in your body. They are constantly reproducing, creating new cells to replace those that make up the hard top layer of your skin—the epidermis—which wears off in bits and pieces throughout the day. In fact, the surface of your skin is completely renewed every 28 days!

Because your skin is so efficient at repairs, cuts and scrapes heal amazing well. But sometimes, when a wound is large and extends deep into the inner layer of skin—the dermis—and into other tissues, the damaged areas are replaced by special repair cells called scar tissue. Thick and pale, this tissue doesn't have the flexibility of the skin or muscle it replaces, and it doesn't wear off or renew itself. In other words, while some scars fade a bit over time, they don't go away completely.

HEARING, SEEING, AND SMELLING

Why are **loud** noises and music **bad for my ears**?

Too many loud sounds can damage the tiny hair cells inside your ears. These cells line the fluid-filled cochlea, a part of your inner ear, and change sound vibrations in the fluid into nerve impulses. These impulses then travel to your brain, where they are recognized as sound. Listening to loud sounds causes strong vibrations that flatten the hairs of the inner ear. Too much flattening keeps the hairs from springing back—just like blades of grass that have been walked on too much—and they eventually die. There is no way to fix or replace the hairs, and hearing is damaged forever. So the louder the noise and the longer you listen to it, the more harm can be done.

Sound is measured in units called decibels. People talking normally measures about 60 decibels on the scale. Any noise that registers above 70 decibels can be dangerous. Rock music at a concert usually produces about 110 decibels of sound.

Why do I get **dizzy** when I turn around in circles?

The inner ear, also known as the labyrinth because it resembles a maze, is made of three fluid-filled tubes bent in half-circles. As you move your head, the liquid in these tubes moves, too, stirring tiny hair cells inside that send messages to your brain, telling it what you are doing. The brain takes this information, along with messages from your eyes and the muscles of your body, and tells you what movements you need to make to keep your balance. When you spin around quickly, the fluid in these tubes moves too fast, and your brain gets more messages than it can process at one time. You may get dizzy, lose your balance, and even fall down before your brain catches up, making you steady again.

Why do my **ears pop** when I'm traveling in an **airplane**?

Your eardrum is a thin, stretched membrane that separates your outer and middle ear. When sound waves hit it, it vibrates, just like the head of a drum. Your eardrum transfers sound vibrations to tiny bones in your middle ear, whose own vibrations increase the strength of the sound. The eustachian tube, which connects your middle ear with your throat, is responsible for keeping the air pressure in the back of your eardrum—in the middle ear—the same as it is in front of it.

If air pressure is less behind your eardrums than in front, they are stretched backward and cannot do their job as well. Your ears feel blocked or stuffy and sometimes even hurt. This pressure change happens when you move quickly between high and low places, like in an airplane. Sometimes swallowing hard or yawning can stretch open the eustachian tube, forcing more air into your middle ear. Your ears will pop, then, which is a sign that air pressure is equalized in your ear and that your eardrums have snapped back into place. After your ears pop you should be able to hear normally.

Why is there **wax** in my ears?

Located in the one-inch passageway, or canal, of your outer ear are 4,000 special glands that make wax. Because it's sticky, earwax catches dust, dirt, and other things before they can travel farther into the ear. As you chew and talk, the muscles of your face move the lining of the ear canal, and old wax eventually works its way out of the ear. It is not a good idea to clean your ears with a stick or swab, because that can push earwax against the eardrum and cause damage. A few people produce too much earwax, which causes blockages that reduce hearing; when this happens, a doctor should remove it.

Why do some people have to wear **eyeglasses**?

Some people have to wear eyeglasses because their eyeballs are shaped a little differently than normal: either their eyeballs are a little too long from front to back or a little too short. When light rays enter the dark center of the eye, called the pupil, a lens focuses them onto the back of the eyeball—the retina. There special nerve cells send signals through the optic nerve to the brain, where these signals combine to make a visual picture. In an eyeball that is too long, images of distant objects are focused *in front* of the retina (instead of *on* the retina) and are blurred. People who have this condition are said to be nearsighted, or myopic, which means they can clearly see things that are nearby, but faraway things are fuzzy. About 20 percent of the population has to wear eyeglasses for this condition, which seems to be inherited.

In an eyeball that is too short, images of objects are focused *behind* the retina, blurring things that are close by. A person who has this condition is said to be farsighted. In both cases, eyeglasses are used to correct the problem. The extra lenses of eyeglasses correct what a person's own eyeball lenses can't do, which is to focus light rays directly on the retina, where they belong. Different shaped lenses are used to correct nearsightedness and farsightedness.

As people get older—beginning in their 40s—they often find that they need to wear eyeglasses to see close objects well even if they've never had a problem seeing before. Eyeglasses to correct this condition are frequently referred to as "reading glasses" because a close activity like reading often becomes impossible without them. The lens of the eyeball can be thickened or narrowed to some degree by eye muscles (though not enough to correct near- or farsightedness) to help it focus on objects. But with age, the lens of the eye hardens, and its ability to change shape to focus on close objects is reduced.

What's wrong with your eyes if you're **color blind**?

The back of your eye—the retina—is lined with two special types of nerve cells, both named because of their shapes. Rods see black and white and work well in poor light, while cones see colors and fine details, but only in bright light. When you see an object, each rod and cone cell sends a signal to the brain's sight center, where information about color, form, shading, and light combine to create a visual image.

Cones contain substances that respond separately to each of the colors red, green, or blue (which combine to make other colors). When a person is color blind, he or she is usually missing some of these substances in his or her cones. (It is very rare that someone has none of these substances and sees everything in shades of black, white, and gray.) The most common form of color blindness is the inability to see the difference among some shades of green and some shades of red. The condition usually doesn't cause many problems in everyday life, though it is important to learn if a child has the defect as soon as possible because the color red is often used as a danger signal (as in traffic lights, for example). Many more males than females are color blind, and the condition is inherited.

What are **eyebrows and eyelashes** for?

Eyebrows and eyelashes protect the eyes, which are fairly delicate. Protecting the eyes is important because people rely far more on sight to get information about their   103

Tears help express deeply felt emotions and often release stress from the body.

world than on any of their other senses. (We don't have the keen sense of smell that a dog has, for instance, or the excellent hearing of a cat.) Eyebrows keep sweat and dust and dirt from reaching our eyes. Eyelashes do the same, protecting the delicate surface of the eyeball.

What are **tears** for?

Tears keep the delicate surface of the eyeball clean and wet. Tears are produced in glands (called lacrimal) above the outer corner of the eye. They spread across the eye surface with each blink. A blink takes about a third of a second, and most people blink about every six seconds; when you add it up you spend more than half an hour each day blinking! Tears that wash across the eye usually evaporate into the air or drain into tear ducts, two tiny canals located at the inner corner of each eyelid. From there they pass down into the nose, where they keep nasal tissues moist. (That's why you have to blow your nose when you've been crying.) When you cry or get something in your eyes, you may produce more tears than the system ordinarily handles, and they may spill out onto your face.

Why do I **cry** when I'm unhappy or hurt myself?

Scientists don't really know why we cry when we're unhappy or hurt (or sometimes, even joyful). But tears help express deeply felt emotions and often release stress and tension from the body. From our earliest days, when we were babies and could not yet communicate through language, crying let the people around us know that we needed something. Frequently, even after we become older, crying still serves as a wordless signal that something—help or comfort—is needed. In places all over the world, no matter what language is spoken, crying expresses emotions that are easily understood by all.

What is the crispy stuff in the corners of my eyes when I wake up in the morning?

Tears—made of water, salt, mucus, and other substances—help the eye stay wet and clean. During sleep your closed eyelids keep your eyes wet, and you may have extra tears that gather in the corners of your eyes. The tears dry out, and what's left is dried mucus, which you might find when you awake in the morning.

How long can a person **hold** his or her **breath**?

You usually don't have to think much about your breathing because your brain controls it automatically. When you have a lot of carbon dioxide—the waste gas produced by body processes—in your blood, your brain gets the message and tells your lungs to exhale and get rid of it. This action then causes you to inhale, drawing in air that eventually delivers oxygen to every cell in your body. This carefully regulated exhaling and inhaling takes place about 10 to 14 times each minute when you are breathing calmly.

When you need more oxygen than usual, your brain takes care of that, too. When you're exercising or working hard, your brain tells you to breathe more quickly, taking in 15 to 20 times more air. If that still doesn't deliver all the oxygen that your muscles need, you may "run out of breath," which forces you to rest. You will still breathe hard at that point— every second or so— until your muscles are able to work again.

So you can see that trying to stop the automatic way that your brain controls your breathing is nearly impossible. When you hold your breath, carbon dioxide builds up in your blood, unable to exit through your lungs. Not long after that—in less than a minute—your brain will force you to take a deep breath, as hard as you try not to. You may be able to hold your breath a little longer than a minute if you prepare your lungs first, taking several deep breaths to fill them with as much air as possible before you start. With a lot of practice and physical training, some people have been able to hold their breath for a few minutes. Be careful testing your breath-holding limits, because at some point the lack of oxygen could make you faint.

What causes a **yawn**?

When you are bored or tired you sometimes give a big yawn. Yawning happens because you are not breathing deeply enough. Oxygen, the gas needed to run body processes, and carbon dioxide, the waste gas produced by these processes, travel in your bloodstream and enter and exit your body through your lungs. When you don't breathe deeply enough, too much carbon dioxide builds up in your body and your brain gets the message, telling you to breathe more deeply to fix the problem. A yawn is a great big breath that clears carbon dioxide from your lungs and forces you to take in fresh, oxygen-rich air. Sometimes a series of yawns is required. Scientists don't know why yawning seems to be contagious, but it usually is: when one person yawns, others often start yawning, too.

Why can I **smell things better** when I **sniff hard**?

The air that you breathe through your nose passes into your nasal cavity, making its way to your throat and lungs. Located on the top of your nasal cavity is your olfactory, or smell, center. There, scent particles from the air you breathe are caught in a thick batch of olfactory hairs that send nerve impulses, via the olfactory nerve, to your brain, which recognizes them as smells.

When you breathe normally, the air that you take in is not usually directed toward your olfactory center. But when you sniff hard, you take in a lot more air, and it travels toward the top of your nasal cavity. You can detect smells more easily then. When you "hold your nose" to keep from smelling a bad scent, you breathe through your mouth, which keeps most of the incoming air from reaching in your olfactory hairs.

Why can't I **taste** anything when I have a **cold**?

Even though your mouth has thousands of taste buds (most of them located on your tongue), the way food smells greatly affects your sense of taste. Your tongue can only sense four flavors: sweet, salty, sour, and bitter; it is the different smells of foods that allow you to experience a wide variety of tastes. When you have a head cold, the lining of your nose is swollen and produces extra, thick mucus. This mucus keeps the scent particles of food from getting to your olfactory center, located on top of your nasal cavity. These scent particles cannot reach the thick batch of hairs there that send smell impulses to your brain.

Why do certain **smells** trigger **vivid memories**?

You're at a school fair, and you walk past the cotton candy machine, getting a whiff of the sweet smell. Suddenly you have a strong, clear memory of the trip you took last summer to an amusement park—the memory's so vivid it feels like you're actually there. Why do certain smells have such powerful links to our memories?

Memory is important when it comes to identifying a smell—we are not born knowing what different scents mean. We have to learn to associate the smell of freshly baked cookies with something we like to eat, or to link the smell of burning wood with a nearby fire. But the link between memory and smell goes beyond identifying what that smell is—sometimes a scent can bring back a memory very powerfully, even a memory that was buried deeply. Scientists aren't sure why this happens, but they do know that the scent organs are connected to the limbic system, the part of the brain that controls memory and emotions. Some experts believe that the memories recalled by scent (as opposed to those recalled by seeing a familiar face or hearing music, for example) seem stronger because they are linked to emotions. Studies have shown that people who are exposed to a certain scent while feeling especially happy or nervous will notice a return of those feelings when they smell that scent at a later date.

Related studies have shown that when people learn something—studying for an exam, for instance—while smelling a specific aroma, they can remember more of what they learned when they smell that same aroma later.

What causes a **drippy nose**?

Several conditions can cause a drippy nose. When your eyes have an extra amount of tears in them—either from crying or from getting something in your eyes—some of the excess tears empty into ducts located at their inside corners and travel down into your nose. A head cold—a virus that can infect your eyes, nose, and throat—often causes swelling and fluid and mucus production in the lining of the nose as your body tries to fight the infection; this mucus then drips out of your nose. Cold weather can also make your nose run. When you first breathe cold air into your nose, it "shocks" the delicate lining, which constricts and then expands, producing protective fluid and mucus. Your nose eventually adjusts to the cold air, though, and works normally again.

What causes a **bloody nose**?

The mucous membrane that lines your nose has many tiny blood vessels located close to the surface. It is easy to damage one or more of these vessels, resulting in some bleeding from your nose. Sometimes a hard bump on the nose will cause a nosebleed. A cold or infection—which can cause crusting that damages the nose lining—is another frequent cause. Sometimes the dry air produced by furnaces during winter can dry out the nasal passages and cause a nosebleed. Sometimes the reason for a nosebleed is unknown. Still, while it can be scary and look like a lot of blood is being lost, nosebleeds are generally harmless.

The best way to handle a nosebleed is to sit down and lean forward (leaning back leads to swallowing a lot of blood). Breathe through your mouth and press your thumb on the lower part of your nose on the side that is bleeding. Wait for about five minutes, until a blood clot can form on the damaged vessel and stop the nosebleed. An ice pack placed on the bridge of the nose can also help by constricting, or narrowing, blood vessels. Be very careful when handling your nose for about half a day afterward, so that you don't disturb the clot. A nosebleed that doesn't stop after 20 minutes should be treated by a doctor.

What starts a sneeze?

Anything that irritates the lining of your nose can start a sneeze. A cold or infection can irritate the inside of your nose, as can things that are breathed in—like dust and pollen. The fine hairs that line your nose are connected to nerve endings, and when they send a message to your brain that something is there that shouldn't be, your brain tells certain muscles to get rid of it. Your throat closes while air pressure builds up in your lungs; when the air is suddenly let go, it blows dust or germs or other things from your nose. During a powerful sneeze, air can exit your lungs at around 100 miles (161 kilometers) per hour!

Did you know that a few centuries ago people were so convinced about the health benefits of sneezing that they inhaled something called snuff into their nostrils to make themselves sneeze on purpose? Snuff, which is flavored and scented ground tobacco, was carried around in fancy little boxes and used throughout the day to cause sneezing. Sniffing snuff reached its greatest popularity during the eighteenth century, among wealthy men and women in Europe.

Why do people often say **"God bless you"** or **"gesundheit"** after someone sneezes?

Back before the development of modern medicines—especially antibiotics—a lot more people died from infectious diseases than they do today. Even things like colds could develop into serious and deadly infections. So a wish for God's blessings or "good health"—the meaning of the German phrase "gesundheit"—developed as an expression of care and concern for the health of the sneezer.

What starts a **cough**?

A cough starts with an irritation in the throat, windpipe, or lungs. Your body's automatic reaction to any such irritation is a very strong contraction of the muscles that control breathing, which causes a burst of air from the lungs to the mouth that is meant to clear your airways. The irritant may be dust, fumes from chemicals, or a particle of food. Colds and other respiratory infections often cause coughing because they inflame your airways and fill them with extra mucus. Coughs are important and, in most cases, should not be suppressed with medicines; you need to cough to keep your airways free of things that could damage your lungs or interfere with your ability to breathe. (If the cough is severe enough to interfere with sleep or to cause vomiting, your doctor may recommend medicine that will help suppress the cough.)

Why should I **cover my mouth and nose** when I **cough and sneeze**?

Coughing and sneezing spray germs into the air, where other people can breathe them in. It's very common for colds and other infections to be spread from one person to another by the germs expelled when a sick person coughs or sneezes. When you cover your mouth or nose when you cough or sneeze, you catch some germs in your tissue or hands, which keeps them from entering the air. But another common way of spreading germs is through physical contact, especially from the hand of one person to another. So it is important to wash your hands, too, after you cough or sneeze! Even better than covering your mouth with your hand is coughing or sneezing onto your shirtsleeve in the crook of your elbow. That way, the germs from your mouth end up on your sleeve, which is far less likely than your hand to have contact with other people. And the germs on your sleeve will soon die if they aren't passed along to another person.

What is a **booger**?

The mucous membrane that lines your nose is moist and sticky. That environment helps trap dust and other things in the air before they can pass into your lungs. When moisture evaporates from the thick film of mucus that covers the lining of your nose—which happens all the time as air passes over it—the mucus, combining with the particles you've breathed in, becomes dried and crusty, forming boogers.

Why shouldn't I **pick my nose**?

Your nose traps germs and dust and other impurities in the air before they can travel to your lungs, so it is a pretty dirty place. When you pick your nose those germs and more get on your fingers and can be passed to others through touch. A tissue—which can be quickly thrown away—should be used to wipe or clean your nose. Picking your nose could also damage the many blood vessels in your nose's thin lining, causing a nosebleed. (The insides of noses are not large enough for searching fingers!) Most people consider it bad manners (not to mention gross) to pick your nose in front of others: nose-picking is an unhealthy practice that shows a lack of concern for others as you spread your germs around.

Why do I have to **wash my hands** after I **blow my nose**?

Even when you use a tissue to blow your nose, you may get some of the impurities from inside your nose on your hands. You can keep from spreading germs to others—

or to surfaces that other people will touch—by washing your hands well. That doesn't mean running the tips of your fingers under cold water—a good hand-washing takes two minutes in warm, soapy water.

BATHROOM TALK

Why do I have to take a **bath or shower**?

Taking a bath or shower does a number of things. It removes some of the germs that your body comes in contact with throughout the day, germs that come from the air you pass through and from the objects, animals, and people you touch. A good washing of the skin also removes some of the dead cells that makes up its surface, allowing newer cells to take their place. Washing removes odors that may be caused by sweating; along with water and salt, perspiration contains waste products from body processes. Certain sweat glands called apocrines release a kind of sweat that can become particularly strong smelling.

Today we also wash to look good—washing with soap and water is the best way to avoid oily, dirty skin and hair, and it's generally agreed that those are things we want to avoid. But that wasn't always what people thought. Over the centuries, different people in various parts of the world have done crazy things in the name of personal cleanliness and beauty. A few thousand years ago, for instance, people in Europe washed themselves with mud, scraping it off with an iron tool. They then rubbed oil on themselves because oily skin was considered attractive. And long ago the Gauls of what is now southern France tried to make themselves more appealing by stiffening their hair with a mixture of fat and ash. Unexpectedly, they found that—when combined with water—their hair mixture made a good soap!

Why do I **pee**?

Food provides the energy that you need for your body systems to run smoothly. Once food is broken down during digestion into small bits of useful substances called nutrients, it passes into your bloodstream. While circulating through your body, nutrients are absorbed by your cells, where they are used for processes that release energy.

As nutrients and energy are used up, chemical waste products are left in your cells. These must be removed or the cells will eventually die. So the cells release waste into your bloodstream—the body's transportation system—which take the waste to your two kidneys. Containing more than one million microscopic filters each, your kidneys remove waste products like urea from your blood, along with any extra body

Taking a bath or shower removes dirt, oil, dead skin cells, and bad smells.

water. The waste and water mixture that the kidneys produce is called urine. It travels through tubes called ureters to your bladder, a flexible, balloon-like structure where urine is temporarily stored before you urinate, or pee. When your bladder has about one cup of urine in it, stretch sensors located in its wall send fullness signals to your brain, which then directs you to empty it.

Why don't **girls** have **penises**?

In both males and females, urine exits the body through a tube called the urethra. In males, the urethra is located in the penis. A male's urethra is also the pathway through which a fluid called semen passes. Made in the male reproductive organs in the lower abdomen and scrotum (the skin sack attached to the lower abdomen behind the penis), semen contains the sperm cells that fertilize female egg cells to create babies.

Females don't have penises because they don't need them. Their shorter urethra passes through the lower abdomen, expelling urine. Female reproductive organs are all located on the inside of the body, where a baby can safely develop. During sexual intercourse, a man inserts his penis into a woman's vagina, the passageway that leads to the uterus, the structure in which babies grow. Once semen is released, a sperm cell may fertilize the single egg cell that a woman releases each month from one of two ovaries, which are connected to the uterus. If that occurs, a baby eventually develops. **111**

Why do I **poop**?

The food that you eat—which provides the energy that your body needs to keep running and the materials needed for growth and repairs—goes through an amazing process once you put it into your mouth. First you chew it into smaller pieces with your teeth. These small pieces are softened by a watery liquid made by your mouth's salivary glands and molded by your tongue into a soggy ball for swallowing. The chewed-up food then begins a journey through a series of connecting tubes. Mushy food travels down your throat and esophagus into your stomach; powerful muscles in the stomach wall crush it even further and—along with strong digestive chemicals made there—turn it into a thick soup. Then it goes to your small intestines, where its nutrients pass through thin walls into your bloodstream and are delivered to cells throughout your body. Following that, the leftovers of your food—what your body can't use or digest—travel to your large intestines (along with other waste products of the digestive process). There moisture is removed and returned to your body, and what remains of your food becomes solid waste. This waste is stored in a large tube called the rectum. When the rectum gets full of solid waste, or feces, you get rid of it with a bowel movement through a small opening in your bottom called the anus. Your food makes the entire journey through your digestive system in about 24 hours (though it could pass through faster or slower than that, depending on the kind of food you've eaten).

While you may think that the indigestible part of your food—what becomes poop—is useless, it is actually very necessary. The unused portion of food, called fiber, makes the entire digestive system run smoothly. It gives the special muscles of the digestive tract—which move food along in traveling waves known as peristalsis—something to grip onto.

What causes **diarrhea**?

Diarrhea is simply food that moves through your digestive system too fast. It often occurs when the digestive tract is irritated and inflamed—by certain foods, or by an infection caused by germs (bacteria and viruses). In an effort to rid your body of these irritants or germs quickly, the special muscles of your intestines move food along faster than usual, cutting short the digestive process. Your small intestines may not be able to absorb all the nutrients in your food, then, and that part of food that can't be used—solid waste—isn't able to stay in your large intestines long enough to have its excess moisture removed and returned to your body. That is why diarrhea is so watery. Because that extra moisture stays in your waste instead of returning to your body, it is important to drink a lot of fluids when you have diarrhea. In addition, it is best to avoid eating solid food for a while, which will help quiet the hyperactivity of the digestive system.

Why do **babies and toddlers** have to wear **diapers**?

The bodies of babies and little children go through a lot of growing and changing. The ability of little ones to do things—like control the activity of their bladder and bowels—increases as their muscles and nervous systems develop and mature.

When a person's bladder is filled with urine, stretch sensors located in the bladder wall send a message to the brain, which sends back a message to empty it. Still, most people can delay this need to urinate by controlling the urethral sphincter, a muscle located at the opening of the bladder into the urethra, the tube through which urine exits the body. When a child is very young, however, he or she does not yet have this kind of muscle control. In addition, a small child's brain doesn't connect feelings of a full bladder with the urination that comes afterwards. In the bodies of babies and young children, urination happens automatically and often—like a reflex—and a diaper is needed to keep them and their surroundings clean. Between the ages of two and three, though, children become aware of their body signals and have greater muscle control, and they are able to be "potty-trained," or taught to use the toilet.

Likewise, when a person's rectum is filled with feces, nerve endings there transmit a similar message to the brain, which calls for it to be emptied. Whether the individual has a bowel movement, though, depends on whether he or she consciously relaxes the ring of muscles, called the anal sphincter, around the anus to allow the passage of feces. Before young children can do this--as with urination--they must learn to recognize the signals their bodies give them and have good muscle control.

Why do I have to **wipe myself** after I **go to the bathroom**?

It is important to wipe yourself after you go the bathroom for a couple of reasons. First, it keeps your clothes from becoming soiled. Second, it protects your skin from the irritation that can result if traces of urine and feces are left there. Feces contain a lot of bacteria that can multiply once they leave the body—especially in areas that are moist and airless, like around your bottom. A rash and sores can result when waste is left on the skin. So wiping helps you stay dry and clean.

Why should I **wash my hands** after I **go to the bathroom**?

Feces contain a lot of bacteria. Once solid waste exits the body it attracts more bacteria, which use it as nourishment to grow and multiply. While some types of bacteria are harmless, other kinds can cause infections and other problems. When you wipe yourself after going to the bathroom, you may get invisible traces of waste on your hands and transfer the bacteria in it to other parts of your body or to objects that others may touch. But this problem can be eliminated by a good hand-washing with warm water and soap, for about two minutes. Because we live closely with one anoth-

113

er, it is important to follow rules of cleanliness, or hygiene, to protect our own health and the health of others.

Why do some kids occasionally **wet the bed** in their sleep?

Usually, when you are asleep and your full bladder sends a message to your brain that it needs to be emptied, your brain wakes you up so that you can go to the bathroom. But once in a while you sleep through the message and wet the bed. Bed-wetting is a common occurrence in children up to about five years of age, because muscle control and nervous systems are still immature then. But older children can have the condition, too—called enuresis—and doctors really don't know why. A lot more boys than girls experience bed-wetting when they are older, and it seems to run in families. While challenging to deal with, the condition nearly always goes away by itself before adolescence. If a thorough check by a doctor reveals that no physical abnormality is the cause, a child can do a couple of things to limit bed-wetting: drink only small amounts of liquids in the evening, and set an alarm clock to wake up during the night and empty the bladder so that an accident will not occur.

FEED ME

Why do I **have to eat**?

Food and drink provide the energy that your body needs to function and the materials required for growth and repair. People can't live without food and drink for very long. A healthy diet requires a certain amount of six different substances: proteins, carbohydrates, fats, fiber, vitamins, and minerals. In addition, water is required to keep body processes running smoothly.

Proteins, found in meat, fish, eggs, dairy products, peas, beans, and grains, are required for the repair, replacement, and growth of body tissue. Carbohydrates, found in bread, pasta, potatoes, and cereals, are good sources of quick energy for the body. Fats, found in many animal and plant foods (like meat, eggs, and nuts), also provide the body with energy and are sometimes used for growth and repair. Vitamins are chemicals that the body needs to function well; minerals are metals and salts that the body also needs—in tiny amounts—to run. Different foods (like vegetables) contain different amounts of vitamins and minerals, so it is important to have variety in your diet so you can get a good balance. Fiber or roughage, parts of plant foods that the body can't digest, is important for the proper working of the digestive system. It provides the bulk that digestive muscles need to grip onto as they push food along and carry away body waste.

Water is also a very important part of a healthy diet. An adult's body loses about four pints (two liters) of water every day through urine, bowel movements, sweat, and the moisture in exhaled breath. Those fluids need to be replaced by drinking water (or other healthy beverages) and eating food (water makes up about 70 percent of the food we eat). An individual can survive weeks without food but only four or five days without vital water.

Why do I feel thirsty?

When your body is low on water, or dehydrated, the moist lining of your mouth and throat become dry. Thirst sensors there send a message to your brain, which tells you to drink at once. About three-fourths of the human body is made of fluids, and the average adult must take in about two and one-half quarts (about two and one-half liters) of water (and other healthy beverages, like fruit juice) every day to remain healthy (though some of the fluids we need also come from solid foods, which contain large amounts of water). Sometimes you may feel thirsty even when your body isn't dehydrated: things like dry, dusty air or salty food can draw moisture from your mouth and throat, alerting your thirst sensors. To demonstrate this, try swallowing dry crackers without taking a drink.

Why does my **stomach growl** when I'm hungry?

Your body changes food into substances it can use for energy. When your body is low on food, it cannot make the energy it needs. Your brain and nervous system go into action then, making the muscles of your stomach walls squeeze together in order to digest food—food that isn't there. The actions of your stomach make you feel hungry, insuring that you will seek out some food to eat that will soon be on its way to your stomach. In the meantime, though, gases and digestive juices in your empty stomach churn around, and you may hear growls. Scientists have a name for the rumblings in the digestive system that are caused by moving gas: borborygmi (pronounced BOR-boh-RIG-mee), a word that sounds a lot like the noises your stomach makes when it's empty.

Why should I **wash my hands before I eat**?

An important entranceway into your body, your mouth is connected to your digestive and respiratory systems. Germs from the outside world should be prevented as much as possible from getting inside these and other systems, where they can cause problems, keeping your body from running as it should. When you touch things or people that are carrying germs, it is easy to transfer them to your mouth while eating. The

115

problem can be easily solved, though, by washing your hands before you eat—about two minutes in warm, soapy water does the trick.

What happens if I **swallow** chewing gum or other **things that aren't food**?

When you accidentally swallow something that isn't food, you really shouldn't worry about it (unless the item is sharp, which could tear tissue as it makes its way through the digestive system, or unusually large, which could cause blockages). Once gum or other things enter your stomach, the powerful muscles in its walls crush and churn it, and the strong enzymes and acids produced there break down nearly everything into small particles that make a thick soup. The nutrients in this soup then pass into your bloodstream and travel to all the cells in your body. Those things that can't be broken down by the stomach (which includes parts of many plant foods)—or by more digestive juices in the small intestines—are moved along as solid waste and leave your body as part of a bowel movement. So things accidentally swallowed are either processed by your digestive system or find their way into the toilet!

So you shouldn't worry that the bug you swallowed will set up a new home inside you, or that the watermelon seed that slipped down your throat will grow into a big fat watermelon inside your stomach. Your stomach just isn't a good place for living things! One of the digestive juices made there, in fact—called hydrochloric acid—is so powerful that it can burn a hole though clothing and other things in its concentrated form. Why do people say that they feel like they have "butterflies" in their stomachs then? That's just a phrase that describes the fluttery feeling—like the beating of delicate butterfly wings— that some people get in their stomachs when they're nervous or excited.

What is **spit**?

Your mouth is kept moist and clean by a watery liquid called saliva, or spit, which is made by pairs of salivary glands located under your jaw, in front of your ears, and under your tongue. Saliva mixes with food as you chew, softening it so that it can be more easily swallowed. In addition, saliva starts the digestive process because it contains an enzyme, or chemical, that changes the starch in food into sugar. The production of saliva increases when food is in the mouth or even with the sight and smell of good food—hence the use of the word "mouthwatering" to describe delicious or fragrant meals.

How do the things that I eat and drink keep from **going down my windpipe**?

When you eat and drink, chewed food and liquids travel toward the back of your throat. Muscles there automatically close the passageway to your nose, so that your food and drink doesn't take a wrong turn (though some people can force liquid through these muscles, making it spout from their noses). More muscles make the epiglottis, a flap at the top of your windpipe, or trachea, automatically close so that food can't get into your lungs. Your food and drink then have a clear pathway down your esophagus, a muscular tube that runs from your throat to your stomach.

Sometimes, a trickle of liquid (from a drink, or from saliva in your mouth) passes into your windpipe before the epiglottis can close it. When that happens you feel like you're choking, and you cough and cough to expel the fluid from your lungs. It is said that what you swallowed "went down the wrong pipe," and that's exactly what happened: some liquid went down your windpipe instead of your foodpipe.

When food gets stuck in the trachea, though, more serious choking can occur. That food can partially or fully block the windpipe, leading to breathing problems. If the windpipe is partially blocked, a person may still be able to take in enough air to cough out, which will usually remove the piece of food. Remember, as scary and violent as coughing is, it is a good sign during choking, indicating the trachea is not completely blocked. When a person cannot cough, though, and holds his or her neck, that individual needs help. The Heimlich maneuver (named after the doctor who invented it) is a method of dislodging a piece of food from a choker's throat by reaching your arms around the person's body from behind and squeezing your fists up into his or her abdomen; the practice has saved many lives.

What is **throw-up**?

Throw-up, or vomit, is partly digested food that has come back up forcefully through your mouth. Vomiting usually happens when the stomach is irritated by certain foods or by an infection caused by germs (bacteria and viruses). The quickest way for your body to get rid of the irritants or germs in your stomach is to vomit them out. Your brain tells the muscles in your stomach walls to spasm (contract abnormally); it also tells your diaphragm—the large sheet of muscles that separates your chest from your abdomen and is most responsible for your breathing—to press downward on your stomach. These activities combine to force the contents of your stomach up and out.

Other conditions can cause nausea—that bad feeling in your stomach before you throw up—and bring on vomiting, too. Smelling a terrible odor, undergoing a frightening experience, or even, for some people, riding in a moving vehicle (called motion sickness) are some of the things that can send signals to the vomit center of the brain, which tells the stomach to empty itself to feel better.

What causes a **burp**?

When you get food and drink into your airway, problems occur. But when too much air enters your digestive system, it's not a big deal. It just comes back up in the form of a burp. Sometimes a person takes in gulps of air when he or she eats or drinks too fast. (Gum-chewing can also lead to swallowed air.) At other times, the food or drink— **117** like soda pop, for example—is responsible for the burp. Filled with carbon dioxide gas to make it bubbly, soda releases air once it's in your stomach.

What causes people to pass gas?

When there is too much air in your digestive system, there are two ways to get rid of it. It can exit from the top, through your mouth, in the form of a burp. Or it can exit from the bottom, through your anus, in the form of passed gas, better known as a fart.

Some of the gas in your digestive system comes from the air you swallow when you eat, while some of it is a natural by-product of food digestion in your large intestine. When your intestine encounters foods that are difficult to digest—including greasy or high-fat foods—it produces more gas than with foods that are digested easily. This gas travels through your intestine to your rectum and eventually passes out through your anus. While some may not like to admit it, everyone passes gas several times a day.

Why does some gas **smell worse** than others?

The gas expelled from our intestines actually contains many different kinds of gases, including nitrogen, hydrogen sulfide, and methane. When high concentrations of the sulfur-containing gas hydrogen sulfide are present, your gas has a particularly strong odor. Certain foods, like beans, cabbage, and eggs, contain a lot of sulfur and can result in this smelly gas.

What causes **hiccups**?

Hiccups are probably caused by eating or drinking too quickly or too much, which leads to irritation of the diaphragm, the large sheet of muscles attached to your lower ribs that separates your chest from your abdomen. The stomach rests just below the diaphragm, which is the main muscle used during breathing. When you have hiccups, the diaphragm contracts more strongly than usual, jerking and forcing you to take sudden noisy breaths. The sudden rush of air forces the flap at the top of your windpipe, called the epiglottis, to shut quickly, resulting in the "hic" sound. People have all sorts of crazy remedies for curing hiccups (like startling a person or eating certain foods, like peanut butter), but they usually go away by themselves after a few minutes. Some rare cases, however, do last for weeks, months, or even years!

If I eat **too much food** will I get **fat**?

Your body needs food to provide it with the energy it needs to run smoothly and to grow and repair itself. All of this requires calories, which is a measurement of energy.

Food provides the calories that make the body run. The amount of calories that a person needs depends a lot on how active he or she is and on whether that individual is still growing. Even though they are smaller than adults, children need comparatively more calories because they are so physically active and are always making new body tissue as they grow.

If you eat a lot more calories than your body needs for the energy you use each day, your body will store the extra calories as fat. Having a lot of body fat greatly increases your chances of getting a lot of different diseases. The easiest way to guard against being overweight is to lead a physically active life. Keeping fit through regular exercise like bicycling, swimming, or participating in team sports like basketball will burn up the calories you eat, keeping you trim. Regular exercise also keeps joints and muscles flexible and strong and the heart and lungs healthy. Exercise seems to make the brain work better, too.

In order to lose weight, you have to eat less and exercise more. If you burn more calories than the amount you take in through food each day, your body will use your stored fat for the energy it needs, and you will lose weight. Increasing your physical activities is one way to accomplish this; another way is to change your diet. By not eating "junk food"—food and drink that are high in fat and sugar but have few of the nutrients that your body needs—you will be able to reduce the calories that you take in, concentrating on foods that are good for you. But remember, the object of dieting is good health, not skinniness. People who make themselves too thin by not eating enough can have very serious health problems.

What are **eating disorders**?

Eating disorders are psychological, or mental, ailments that involve an obsession with food and with being thin. Eating disorders strike about one percent of teenagers in the United States, and girls are affected far more often than boys. People with eating disorders frequently feel depressed and anxious, and they often have a low opinion of themselves. They develop an obsession with food and sometimes devote many hours a day to an intense exercise routine. They frequently withdraw from friends and family, finding excuses to avoid social situations, particularly those that involve food.

The two most common eating disorders are anorexia and bulimia. People suffering from anorexia avoid eating whenever possible. What little food they do eat causes anxiety and fear that it will make them fat. Anorexic people usually lose weight rapidly, but even after they've become alarmingly skinny they still look in the mirror and see themselves as overweight. Anorexia can cause a severe drop in energy and ability to concentrate; it can also result in damage to internal organs, loss of hair, and weakening of bones. If it goes untreated, anorexia can become quite serious and even deadly. Bulimia is characterized by behavior known as binge and purge: people suffering from this disorder eat large quantities of food, but as soon as they've finished eating they make themselves throw up or take laxatives, which stimulates the colon to produce a bowel movement. Bulimia can cause damage to the kidneys and stomach, and the frequent vomiting sometimes causes the person's tooth enamel to decay. People with anorexia often appear dramatically thinner, but bulimia can be harder to recognize as a bulimic person does not actually lose much weight.

Doctors aren't exactly sure what causes eating disorders. Some believe they are a result of the tremendous pressure society places on young girls to be thin—models in magazines and celebrities on television reinforce the idea that being beautiful equals being thin. Some research has suggested that eating disorders may be the result of a chemical imbalance in the brain, and that the tendency to develop such a disorder can run in families. Regardless of the cause, it's vitally important that people with eating disorders seek treatment. Eating disorders can be very serious, and the longer they go on, the harder it becomes to treat them.

OPEN WIDE

What is my **tongue** for?

Without your tongue it would be nearly impossible to do three important functions: eat, taste, and talk. The tongue is a complex group of muscles that moves food around your mouth as you chew and finally molds it into a ball for swallowing. Just try eating anything without using your tongue! In addition, taste buds—clusters of special cells located on the surface of your tongue—are mostly responsible for your ability to taste food and drink. (Although other parts of your mouth have some taste buds, too.) Your 9,000 or so taste buds can recognize four types of flavors: sweet, salty, sour, and bitter. Besides helping you enjoy food, tasting is very important because it keeps you from eating food that has spoiled and is unsafe. Finally, your tongue—along with your mouth and lips—helps you to make the special sounds you use to speak.

How does my **voice work**?

Your vocal cords are stretched flaps of tissue located in your voice box, or larynx, which sits at the top of your windpipe or trachea. Your voice box is located in your throat (and if you put your fingers on it while you talk or sing, you can feel it humming). When air from your lungs passes over your vocal cords they vibrate; surrounding muscles open and close and stretch the vocal cords, changing their vibrations to produce a variety of sounds. (The more stretched your vocal cords, the more rapidly they vibrate and the higher the sounds they make.) Sounds made in your voice box are further changed when they are shaped by your throat, tongue, cheeks, and lips (and even teeth) into speech or song.

What happens when a person **"loses"** his or her **voice**?

When your vocal cords and the tissue that surrounds them are irritated or swollen you usually have a condition called laryngitis. Laryngitis makes your voice sound funny and hoarse and, in some cases, can even keep you from speaking altogether. Then it is said that you have "lost" your voice.

Usually the swelling in your larynx or voice box is caused by a cold or infection there. But sometimes smoking, or yelling, singing, and talking a lot can cause the problem. After a few days of resting the vocal cords and not speaking, or after the illness that has caused the swelling goes away, your voice will return to normal.

Eating, tasting, and talking would be almost impossible without your tongue. *Robert J. Huffman/Field Mark Publications © 2001*

What happens when people **stutter**?

People who stutter speak with many uncontrolled pauses and repetitions of sounds. It is caused when some of the muscles involved in speech spasm, or contract abnormally. Talking is a complicated process that involves muscles that work the lungs, vocal cords, throat, tongue, cheeks, and lips. When each part doesn't work precisely together, stuttering can occur.

Stuttering is not uncommon in young children. They are still learning about language and searching for new words and new ways of putting them together in speech.

By the time most people turn 18, they have 32 adult, or permanent, teeth.

But well before a child is ready to enter school, help for stuttering should be found. Children who cannot communicate well with others become frustrated and start to feel bad about themselves and their abilities.

Doctors don't really know why people stutter, though it seems to run in families and affects far more boys than girls. It is believed that a problem in the motor control center of the brain, along with nervous tension, causes the muscles of speech to spasm. Training to speak slowly and smoothly and to breathe deeply during talking often helps the problem.

Why do **boys' voices change** as they get older?

The shorter and thinner people's vocal cords are, the higher their voices. So children—with their small vocal cords—have high-pitched voices. As children grow, their vocal cords become longer and thicker, and their voices deepen. Especially during adolescence, boys may grow so fast that their vocal cords double in length and their voices change suddenly. Sometimes an adolescent boy's voice may "break," and he may talk in a combination of high and low pitches as he learns to control his growing voice box, or larynx, and the changing vocal cords inside.

You may have noticed that teenage boys and men have a pronounced bump in the front of their necks. Girls and women don't have this bump, which is called the Adam's apple. The Adam's apple is simply the result of men's larger vocal cords. The average man has vocal cords that measure 18 millimeters (about three-quarters of an inch) long, while the average woman's measure 10 millimeters (three-eighths of an inch). So men generally have deeper voices than women. And tall people, male or female, usually have longer vocal cords—and deeper voices—than short people.

How many **teeth** do I have?

You have two sets of teeth. The first set, your baby teeth, consists of 20 teeth. These teeth are small so they can fit in the small jaws of a young child. They usually break through—singly or in pairs—between the ages of six months and thirty months. At six years of age, a larger set of teeth begin to surface, slowly replacing your baby teeth. Thirty-two new teeth will eventually line your growing jaws, the last coming in around the age of 18. These permanent teeth will perform all your eating tasks for the rest of your life. Your four front teeth (top and bottom)—sharp incisors—cut and tear off food when you bite, along with your four pointed canine teeth. The flat-topped bicuspids (premolars) and molars near the back of your mouth crush and chew your food.

Why are **babies** born **without teeth**?

Babies don't have any teeth at first because they don't need them. They receive all their nourishment from liquid food—breast milk or formula—during their first few months. When babies are born their digestive systems are not yet fully mature, and they cannot process solid food well. While capable of sucking, their mouths and tongues are not yet ready for the complicated process of chewing and swallowing solid food.

Babies change quickly, though, and by about four months they need to eat some kind of solid food to get the calories they need to keep growing. But the food that they eat is soft or soupy because they still don't have any chewing teeth. Still, babies can use their gums and tongues pretty well to eat specially prepared solid foods. And gumming hard foods prepares babies for the time when they will have a full set of teeth in their mouths (at about two years old).

Why do teeth **fall out**?

Normally, only baby teeth fall out, and they do so when permanent teeth push up from below to take their place. As the permanent teeth push up, they destroy the roots, which are buried in the gums, of baby teeth. Without roots to anchor them to the jawbone, teeth become loose and fall out. Permanent teeth can fall out, too, when disease or injury destroys their roots.

Is there anything wrong with **thumb-sucking**?

During a child's early years, thumb-sucking is not a problem. In order to survive, all babies are born with sucking reflexes that help them feed right away on milk from the mother's breast or formula from a bottle. From the earliest moments, an infant associates sucking with milk filling his or her empty stomach and a feeling of comfort. When not feeding, a baby may frequently suck his or her thumb, fingers, or a pacifier to get that sense of comfort again. The habit often continues in young children when they are bored or frustrated or trying to get to sleep. Many children have a hard time breaking this habit: about 10 percent of school-age children in the United States—2.4 million—suck their thumbs.

While thumb-sucking doesn't cause problems in very young children who still have their baby teeth, it can have an affect on the bite of older kids who have their permanent teeth. Thumb-sucking can push upper teeth forward and lower teeth back so that the top teeth and bottom teeth don't line up the way they should. At this point, children should be strongly encouraged to give up their habit. An older child may want to stop thumb-sucking and be more grown up, especially if he or she feels some pressure from friends at school. But many kids go back to sucking their thumbs when under stress (or when they're sleeping). Keeping thumb-sucking children happy and busy, rewarding their efforts to stop, and even using reminders like a piece of tape wrapped around the thumb may help them quit the habit.

What are **wisdom teeth**?

Your four wisdom teeth are the last of your permanent teeth to appear. These molars, located at the back of the jaw, come in between the ages of 17 and 21. They emerge around adulthood—along with the "wisdom" that supposedly comes with maturity— which explains their name. In a lot of people, though, one or more of these teeth never come up, usually because there is not enough room on the jawbone. Long ago, primitive people had longer jaws that held these extra molars that were so important for chewing the tough meat that made up most of their diets. But as prehistoric men and women evolved and their brains became larger, the shape of their skulls changed, too, which included a shortening of the jawbone. So now we have an extra set of teeth not essential for our refined diets, and we have very little room in which to grow them. Wisdom teeth can cause problems whether above or below the gum surface. They can be difficult to keep clean and sometimes cause infections. Many people have their wisdom teeth removed before such problems occur.

Why do I have to **brush and floss** my teeth?

Brushing and flossing your teeth is critical to keeping them healthy and free from decay. With good dental habits, you can have your teeth for a lifetime. Because your mouth is dark, wet, and warm, it is a perfect place for germs like bacteria to grow, feeding on bits of old food. Removing food from your teeth after eating is a good way to limit the amount of tooth-damaging germs in your mouth. Because most food particles stick between your teeth and at the spot where your gums and teeth meet, keeping those places clean is especially important. Just scrubbing with a toothbrush usually can't do this, so dental floss should be used, too.

When bacteria break down certain foods in your mouth, they form an acid that dissolves the hard outer covering (enamel) of teeth. Over time a small hole, or cavity, may form on a tooth, allowing bacteria to travel farther inside. A dentist usually uses a filling made of metal or plastic to fill in the cavity and stop the decay. But if not caught and treated early, decay may spread, reaching tooth roots and nerves and causing pain and infection. When a tooth becomes too damaged, it may fall out or a dentist may have to remove it.

Why are sweets so bad for my teeth?

The sugar and starch in the foods you eat are what tooth-damaging germs, or bacteria, in your mouth like best. As bacteria feed on these food particles, they produce acid that dissolves the hard outer covering (enamel) of teeth. Sweet and starchy foods (like candy and potato chips) that stick to your teeth are the most damaging. Snacking on these foods between meals increases the damage they do, for each time you eat such foods your teeth undergo another acid attack. It is best to eat sticky sweet and starchy foods at mealtime, mixed with other foods. In fact, it really makes sense to eat your dessert first instead of last, so that other foods can clear some of the sugar from your teeth. Tell that one to your parents!

What causes **bad breath**?

Poor dental care is a major cause of bad breath. Old food particles between teeth and odor-producing mouth bacteria, as well as tooth decay and infected gums, can give breath a bad smell. Brushing your teeth for at least two minutes a couple times a day, flossing, and even brushing your tongue (the home to lots of bacteria) can make a big difference.

Sometimes bad breath can be caused by something you eat; certain foods, like onions or garlic, contain smelly substances that are absorbed into your bloodstream and then released into your lungs, causing bad breath. This smelliness will only last about a day, however, until the food leaves your body. Once in a while, bad breath can be caused by an illness in the body.

Why do I have to **go to the dentist**?

About every six months to a year, you should make a visit to your dentist's office. A dental hygienist there will give your teeth a good cleaning, removing built-up and hardened food and other substances that can't be taken care of through regular brushing and flossing (and that could lead to gum disease if not removed). Then your den-

Because few people have perfect teeth, braces are often put on to help make them work and look better. *Robert J. Huffman/Field Mark Publications © 2001*

tist will view your teeth with a tiny mirror, looking into hidden places, searching for cavities and decay. When cavities and tooth decay are not detected early, they can become serious, causing pain, infection, and even tooth loss. If your teeth have fillings, your dentist will make sure that they are in good shape. X rays of your teeth and jaws may be taken, too, to show cavities and other dental problems that cannot be seen during a regular examination. In addition, until you are about 13 years old, you will receive a fluoride treatment every year while the hard outer covering of your teeth (enamel) is still forming. Fluoride is a chemical that strengthens that enamel, helping it to resist decay.

Why do I have to **wear braces**?

Straight teeth that are spaced well in the mouth are easier to clean, they bite and chew better, and they last longer. They look nice, too. Few people have perfect teeth, but doctors called orthodontists can change the position of teeth to work and look better. These changes are usually done during childhood and early adolescence, when teeth and jaws are softer and still growing. Special appliances like braces, wires, bands, and more are used to slowly (over many months) push or pull teeth into their correct positions.

Why weren't you born with better teeth? One reason could be that you inherit different traits from each of your parents, and sometimes they don't work well together. If you inherited your mother's small jaw, for example, but your father's large teeth, you are going to have crowding problems in your mouth. Your teeth will slope back-wards or forwards, or turn, or overlap one another in order to try to fit into their small space. On the other hand, if your teeth are too small for your jaws, you will have big gaps between your teeth. These are just a few of the problems that an orthodontist tries to correct.

Try to remember that wearing braces for a few years when you are young will give you a lifetime of healthier, good-looking teeth. Also remember to brush and floss more often when you have braces, because they trap food particles against your teeth.

WHAT'S UP, DOC?

Why do I **get sick**?

When you get sick, part or all of your body isn't working as it should. The cause of sickness can come from the inside your body or from the outside world. Diseases that start on the inside are usually inherited in the genes that you receive from your par-ents, which make up the master plan that determines how your body will grow and run. Abnormal development or functioning of different body systems is the cause of many chronic (long-lasting) diseases.

Things in the outside world can cause sickness, too. Poisons in the environment can cause illnesses in people. Not eating the right foods, with their important nutri-ents, can also cause diseases. But the most common cause of sickness from the out-side world is infectious agents. These agents are usually microscopic organisms (living things so small that they can only be seen with the help of microscopes) like bacteria and viruses, which we commonly refer to as germs. Bacteria and viruses and other microscopic organisms live in the air, water, and soil that make up our world. They are on the things and people we touch and in the food we eat. Many of them are beneficial: bacteria are needed to make cheese; some bacteria help vegetables like peas and beans grow; and some bacteria clean the environment and enrich the soil by feeding on dead plants and animals. But there are other microscopic organisms that invade the bodies of plants and animals—and people—and cause diseases.

Your skin is a wonderful protective barrier that keeps a lot of the disease-causing germs that you run into each day from entering your body. Only when you have an opening in your skin—like a cut or a scrape—are germs likely to enter there. Most germs enter through your mouth and nose, making their way farther into your body through your respiratory or digestive tracts. But even then, certain chemicals in body tissues and fluids keep many harmful germs from causing problems. When an infec-

127

tion does begin, though—with the germs multiplying inside your body—your immune, or defense, system goes into action to get rid of the foreign organisms. Your white blood cells produce special substances called antibodies that attack and destroy the invaders, helping you to recover. Sometimes it takes several days for your immune system to stop the infection and for your body to repair the damage it caused. But after your illness you will have an immunity to the specific germs that were responsible for your sickness; this means that if the same kind of germs enter your body again, the antibodies already there will destroy them before any illness occurs. By the time you are an adult, you will get far fewer infections than you did as a child because you will have become immune to many of the common bacteria and viruses in the world. But when you are young and encountering different germs for the first time, you do get sick a lot.

What causes a **fever**?

The average temperature of the human body, when measured under the tongue, is around 98.6 degrees Fahrenheit (37 degrees Celsius). You have a fever when your body temperature goes higher than this. Scientists believe that fever is part of the body's defense system against infection: the higher temperature may kill the germs causing it or may speed up the body's defenses (like white blood cell and antibody production) against it. So a fever is a good thing, a sign that your body is working hard to get better. Medicines to reduce fever aren't really necessary unless a person's temperature gets dangerously high—above 102 degrees Fahrenheit (38.8 degrees Celsius) in children and 104 degrees Fahrenheit (40 degrees Celsius) in adults. At such high temperatures, the human body can no longer cool itself by flushing (releasing heat through surface blood vessels) and sweating. A cold bath or cold wet cloths on the skin can lower a very high fever before it does serious damage to the body.

When I take **medicine** for a headache, how does it **know where to go**?

When you have a headache or a toothache or any other kind of ache, you take a pain reliever like aspirin, and a few minutes later, the pain is gone. It's like that aspirin went directly to the spot that hurt and somehow took away the pain, but how would it know where to go? Actually, no pain reliever "knows" where to go. After you swallow the medicine, it goes through your digestive system and gets absorbed into your bloodstream, traveling throughout your body. So if you have a headache and at the same time happen to have a twisted ankle, the pain reliever you take will help both feel better.

When your body experiences pain—from a headache or a twisted ankle, say—your cells produce a chemical called prostaglandin. When your nerve endings pick up on the presence of this chemical, they send messages to your brain, telling it that the pain is located in your head (or ankle) and whether it hurts a lot or a little. As the medicine in pain relievers makes its way through your body, it prevents the injured cells from making prostaglandin. Therefore the pain messages don't get to your brain (or at least they don't get there as fast), and you no longer feel uncomfortable.

What are **tonsils**?

Tonsils are large bumps of special tissue located on either side of your throat at the back of your tongue. They are part of your lymphatic system, which helps your body defend itself against disease-causing germs and other foreign substances. Lymph glands, located in many parts of your body, make a special type of white blood cell (called lymphocytes); they also trap infectious invaders before they can enter your bloodstream.

Your tonsils are tiny when you are born, and they grow until you are about six or seven years old. (They begin to shrink in size after that.) So your tonsils are biggest when you are just starting out in school, a time when you are exposed to more new germs than usual. When you breathe in disease-causing germs, many of them are stopped in your tonsils and in other lymphatic tissue located around your mouth and throat in order to protect your lungs. But filtering out all those germs may cause your tonsils to become infected as a result—a condition known as tonsillitis. Tonsillitis usually results in a sore throat, fever, and difficulty swallowing, because your tonsils grow larger, or swell, when they are infected. As you grow older and your immunity to common germs increases, you should have less trouble with your tonsils. But some people have so many tonsil infections that their doctor recommends the tonsils be removed. A doctor cuts them away during a short operation in a hospital.

Why do I have to **get shots** even when I'm **not sick**?

The shots that you get when you're not sick are called vaccinations or immunizations. They prevent you from getting certain serious infectious diseases, like polio, tetanus, and diphtheria. Not too long ago, before vaccinations were used, people—especially young children—died in large numbers from such diseases. Most infectious diseases are communicable, which means they are easily passed from one person (or animal) to another, through infected air, contaminated food and drink, or an opening in the skin.

Ordinarily, when disease-causing germs (viruses or bacteria) invade your body, your immune or defense system springs into action to get rid of the foreign organisms. Your white blood cells produce substances called antibodies that attack and destroy the invaders, helping you to recover. The antibodies remain in your body, ready to attack the same germs—before any illness develops—should they ever invade again. After having one infection, you are said to have developed a natural immunity to those particular germs.

But you can also become immune to certain disease-causing germs through vaccinations. Developing immunity through vaccinations is a whole lot safer than devel-

129

oping it naturally from having a serious illness! Taken into the body by mouth (swallowed) or injected in a shot, vaccinations are dead or harmless versions of specific disease-causing germs; these inactive germs are unable to cause sickness but can still make the body's immune system produce antibodies against them. So if a vaccinated person is exposed to the live germs in the future, antibodies will already be present in his or her body, waiting to attack before any illness can start. Sometimes it takes several doses of a vaccine—spread out over time—to produce full immunity in an individual. The immunity given by other vaccines may weaken after a number of years and have be strengthened with a "booster shot."

Where do **medicines** come from?

Medicines or drugs are chemical substances used to prevent, treat, or stop diseases, to heal wounds, and to stop pain. Since ancient times, people have used natural products—from plants, animals, and minerals in the earth—to help themselves and others. For example, a substance called digitalin, found in the leaves of the flowering foxglove plant, has long been used to help people with heart problems. Likewise, the dried sap of the seed pod of a certain poppy plant (opium) has a long history of use as a powerful painkiller. Even today, about 25 percent of all the drugs that doctors prescribe—and many more medicines that can be bought "over the counter," meaning without a prescription—are made from plant products. (Scientists have yet to explore the full potential of plant-based medicines; many useful plants come from the world's rain forests, which are unfortunately being destroyed at a rapid rate.)

Companies that make drugs study the healing effects of natural substances and try to recreate similar substances in laboratories. They test these and other man-made chemicals on samples of diseased and ailing cells, on animals, and sometimes on people over long periods of time. If these substances are shown to be useful (without causing harmful side effects), they are then sold as new drugs. In the United States, a government agency called the Food and Drug Administration (FDA) controls the testing and marketing of new medicines, making sure that they are safe and effective.

SLEEPY TIME

Why do I **need to sleep**?

During sleep, your body systems don't work as hard as when you're awake. Your skeletal muscles relax and need less oxygen, so your breathing and heartbeat can slow down. Other functions like digestion slow down, too. (During one stage of sleep—

when you dream—your muscles are even temporarily paralyzed!) As your body uses less energy to run itself, it can use more energy for other important things, like growth and repair. In fact, a body chemical known as growth hormone, which is responsible for how big you will become, is produced mostly during sleep. Scientists have found that children who do not get proper sleep over long periods of time do not grow nearly as much as they should. So even though you don't feel like going to bed sometimes, do it for your body's sake. It will thank you in the morning, when you awake rested, repaired—and even a little bit bigger.

How does my body know to **wake up** when morning comes?

Parts in the center of your brain (the thalamus and hypothalamus) control your body's sleep-wake cycle. These parts act like an internal alarm clock. Sunlight is what sets the alarm off and keeps your body on a 24-hour schedule (like Earth), resetting your internal clock every day. If you didn't have to follow a busy schedule that sometimes required you to get up before sunrise, and if there were no artificial lights at night to extend your day past sunset, your body clock would follow the cycle of the Sun even more closely than it does now.

Why do some people need to take naps?

Young kids need naps to keep them healthy and safe. Their bodies are growing and changing at a rapid rate, which requires a lot of energy. In addition, the world is filled with so many interesting things to discover and so many new skills to learn, and all that stimulation can make a child pretty tired. Whether big or little, people don't perform at their best—mentally or physically—when they are too tired. Often when you're tired it takes twice as much energy to perform a task that you could easily do if you were rested. Sometimes being too tired makes you less coordinated and clumsy, and you might think less clearly, which could lead you to hurt yourself. Taking a short rest allows your body to slow down for a while so that it can regain the energy it needs to continue performing at its best.

What causes **snoring**?

When people breathe through their mouths rather than their noses when they sleep—because the nasal passageways are swollen or stuffed for some reason—snoring may occur. The rough, hoarse snoring noise results when the soft tissue at the back of the roof of the mouth (called the soft palate) vibrates during breathing. Males snore far more often than females; scientists think that may be because men are generally bigger and have more tissue in their soft palates. Some people snore so loudly that they wake themselves up.

131

Why do I **dream**?

When you sleep your brain does different things. Most of the time it is quiet, resting with the rest of your body and producing little of the electrical activity seen during waking hours. But every one and one-half to two hours, you dream. During dreams, your brain shows the same electrical activity as if you were awake, and your eyes move about very rapidly (that is why this is known as REM sleep, referring to the *R*apid *E*ye *M*ovements). Oddly, during all this brain and eye activity, your body is very still, its muscles limp. Scientists think that this inability to move the body is protective, keeping people from hurting themselves as they respond to what happens in their dreams. In scientific experiments, cats were operated on so that their muscles were able to move when they dreamed. Some began to run and even attack imaginary mice while they slept.

If you sleep for about eight hours, you have four or five dreams during that time. Dreams usually last anywhere from five minutes to thirty minutes, so in one night you can spend between half an hour and more than two hours dreaming. What is the purpose of dreaming? While scientists aren't sure, they know that people who are prevented from dreaming—people whose sleep is interrupted—become crabby, slow-thinking, and clumsy. So it is clear that dreams are needed to keep the brain healthy for some of its complex functions, like memory and concentration. Many psychologists and psychiatrists, professionals who study mental and emotional behavior, believe that dreams provide us with ways of working through fears and anxieties. These professionals often analyze their patients' dreams to figure out what might be troubling them. Our dreams often feature people we know and events that recently happened in our lives, though dreams are frequently so strange and unreal that it's hard to recognize the familiar in them.

OUR ANIMAL NEIGHBORS

ODDS AND ENDS

What are **animals**?

Animals are all the creatures belonging to the kingdom Animalia, ranging in complexity from simple organisms like sponges to highly developed human beings. (Some of the other kingdoms are Plantae, which encompasses things like grass, trees, and flowers, and Fungi, which are things like mold and mushrooms.) Animals make up at least three-quarters of all the species on Earth, and they are distinguished from plants and other organisms by their ability to move. Even tiny animals have muscles and therefore can get around—to find food or a mate, or to get away from enemies.

While humans are animals, often when people use the word "animal" they are referring to all animals *except* humans. Sometimes people are referring specifically to mammals—warm-blooded creatures like dogs, cows, or lions—as opposed to birds, reptiles, or fish.

How many **different kinds** of animals are there?

Experts estimate that over one million different kinds of animals have been identified in the world. There may be millions more, particularly insect species, that have not yet been identified or discovered by scientists. Hundreds of years ago scientists began dividing the animal kingdom into categories based on certain characteristics like body type, ways of reproducing, and what the animals can do (fly, swim, walk on two legs, and so on). The animal kingdom (and every other kingdom as well) is divided and subdivided into numerous other categories. If animal classification categories were viewed as an upside-down pyramid, kingdom—the largest and broadest classifica-

133

Animals (like this family of lions) make up at least three-quarters of all the species on Earth.

tion—would be at the top. The animal kingdom is divided into several different parts, called phyla (the singular form of that word is "phylum"); each phylum is further divided into classes. The other levels of division are order, family, genus, and species, with species being the tip of that upside-down pyramid, or the most specific way to categorize. When scientists give the official name for a type of animal, they use the genus and species names. Human beings are part of the genus *Homo* and the species *sapiens*; therefore, our scientific name is *Homo sapiens*.

What are **vertebrates**?

Vertebrata, or vertebrates, are a subphylum of the phylum called Chordata. Human beings, as well as most of the animals we experience in our everyday lives—mammals, birds, reptiles, amphibians, fish—are classified as vertebrates. The most obvious characteristic of vertebrates is a backbone (which can be made of bone or cartilage). Vertebrates have a complex spinal cord that runs along the length of the animal's body and contains a nervous system. At the top of the spinal cord is a brain and sense organs that allow animals to see, hear, and smell. Vertebrates also have bodies that are bilaterally symmetrical, which means that the left side is basically a mirror image of the right. There are 45,000 living vertebrate species. Vertebrates live in nearly every region of the world, adapting to life on land, in the air, and in the sea.

What are **invertebrates**?

It may seem that most of the world's animals are vertebrates—what's left after mammals, birds, reptiles, amphibians, and fish? In fact, invertebrates make up more than 90 percent of the world's living animals. Any animal that lacks a backbone is an invertebrate. They do not have a bony skeleton, but many do possess a hard, shell-like exterior. Invertebrates include insects, worms, crustaceans (like crabs and lobsters), mollusks (clams and oysters), and arachnids (spiders, scorpions, and ticks).

What are **cold-blooded** and **warm-blooded** animals?

Cold-blooded, or heterothermic, animals have a body temperature that is regulated by the temperature of their environment. Such animals—including fish, amphibians, and reptiles—generally cannot survive in climates of extreme temperatures. When it's very cold (or very hot) outside, cold-blooded animals cannot function. Warm-blooded, or homeothermic, animals have the ability to maintain the temperature inside their bodies without being affected by changes in outside temperatures. While extremely cold or extremely hot temperatures can cause even warm-blooded animals—like mammals and birds—to suffer, their bodies have mechanisms to regulate internal temperature under most conditions. Shivering when you're cold, for example, is your body's way of increasing its temperature. Dogs can release excess heat by panting, and animals that hibernate have ways of slowing down their bodily functions so they can preserve heat.

What is **hibernation**?

During the coldest winter months, some animals migrate, traveling hundreds or even thousands of miles to a warmer climate. Others stay in their wintry homes, preparing for the cold by putting on extra fat, stockpiling food, and creating cozy dens where they will be protected from wind and snow. A few animals survive freezing temperatures by slowing everything down—their breathing, heart rate, body movements—and entering into a dormant, or inactive, state called hibernation.

Animals that are true hibernators lower their body temperatures close to the freezing point (32 degrees Fahrenheit, 0 degrees Celsius) and spend the winter in a state close to death. They cannot be easily wakened, and they don't appear to be breathing at all (in fact, they breathe a few times a minute). Among mammals, true hibernators include some types of bats, some rodents (like squirrels), and hedgehogs. These animals will wake up from their dormant state every few weeks to eat something, and then they return to hibernation. Bears and many other large animals are not true hibernators; they do spend much of the winter sleeping, but their body temperatures don't lower much, and they can be awakened easily.

The summer version of hibernation—experienced by some animals that live in extremely hot, dry desert regions—is called estivation.

What are **predators** and **prey**?

A seal swims through cold ocean waters in search of a meal. He spots a nearby fish, swims to it, and eats it. In that situation, the seal is the predator, an animal that hunts down and eats another animal for food. The fish, on the other hand, is the prey, an animal that is hunted as a food source by another animal. In the ever-shifting world of the animal kingdom, however, an animal that is a predator in one situation could be the prey in another. The fish-eating seal, for example, might later find itself the intended prey of a hunting polar bear.

While it may seem harsh and cruel (and it's always difficult to watch on television nature shows), animals hunting one another is a natural and necessary process. Animals don't hunt other animals for sport—they do so because they need to eat in order to survive. All living things depend on each other for survival—many animals (herbivores) need to eat plants; other animals (carnivores) need to eat those plant-eating animals; and some animals, called omnivores, eat both plants and meat. The waste produced by animals (as well as the nutrients that result when an animal's body decomposes, or breaks down, after death) enriches the soil, providing necessary ingredients for plants to thrive. An animal that primarily eats the leaves of a certain tree (or that requires that tree to make its home) would have trouble surviving if all of those trees were destroyed. And if that animal cannot survive, its predators cannot survive—and such struggles for survival echo all the way up the food chain.

What is a **food chain**?

Each animal in a predator-prey situation is a link in a food chain, which is a way of looking at the relationships among plants and animals that guarantee the survival of all. Every food chain begins with the Sun, which provides the energy that makes plant life possible. The next link in the chain is a plant, which passes on the energy of the Sun when it is eaten by the next link in the chain (a mouse, let's say), which passes energy on once again when it is eaten by the next link (a fox, perhaps), and so on. Because most plant-eating animals and most meat-eating animals have more than one food source, many scientists look at the relationships among them as a food web, rather than a food chain. A diagram showing a food web indicates the variety of foods eaten by a rabbit as well as the many different predators for whom a rabbit is prey.

Why are some animals active **only at night**?

Many animals, including lots of large predators, are diurnal, meaning they are active during the day and sleep at night. Others are nocturnal—sleeping throughout the day in burrows, dens, caves, or trees—emerging at night to find food. Nocturnal animals that are predators use the cover of darkness to hunt their prey without being seen; those that are prey can also use the darkness to hide. In general, there is less competition for food at night. In desert climates, nights have the added advantage of being cooler; many animals spend the hottest part of the day sleeping and conserving energy, coming out in the cool night air to hunt for a meal.

Nocturnal animals have special adaptations that allow them to function in darkness. Several nighttime creatures, including owls and cats, have eyes that are a certain shape and have a particular kind of cell that helps them see with very little light. Bats, the only flying mammals, are usually nocturnal, and some species get around in the dark by using a kind of sonar called echolocation: the bats make sounds that bounce off nearby objects, and when the sound waves return they carry information about the location and size of those objects. Good hearing and senses of smell also come in handy for nocturnal animals. Some animals leave a scented trail, excreting fluid produced in glands in their bodies, to make it easier for them to find their way back in the dark.

What is the largest animal in the world?

The largest animal in the world is the blue whale. It can reach a length of 110 feet (33.5 meters) and weigh more than 150 tons (300,000 pounds). Its head makes up nearly one-quarter of its body, and its heart is the size of a small car. It is thought to be the largest animal that has ever lived, bigger than the largest dinosaur. Even a baby blue whale is bigger than an elephant, which is the largest land animal.

The are two types of whales: toothed whales, which use their teeth to catch fish and squid (that they usually swallow whole), and baleen whales, which are toothless, but have sheets of a horny substance called baleen attached to their upper jaws. The baleen works like a giant strainer, letting water—including tiny plant and animal life called plankton—move back and forth through it. Loads of plankton are trapped behind the baleen and then swallowed. The blue whale is an example of a baleen whale, which means that the largest creature in the world feeds on some of the smallest plants and animals that exist.

What are some of the **smallest animals** in the world?

Some people consider protozoa, which are a type of single-celled organisms including amoebas, part of the animal kingdom. According to that classification, the microscopic protozoa would be the smallest animals. But many classification systems place protozoa in their own kingdom called Protista, a group separate from the animal kingdom.

Several types of insects are nearly microscopic, measuring only a fraction of a millimeter in length. The smallest mammals are considerably larger than that: Commerson's dolphin, weighing around 50 to 70 pounds (23–32 kilograms), is the smallest sea mammal. A bat that is about the same size as a bumblebee, called Kitti's hog-nosed bat, may be the smallest land mammal. It is only about an inch long (29–33 millimeters) and weighs around .07 ounces (2 grams).

Which animal is the **fastest**?

The cheetah—clocked at speeds of 70 miles (112 kilometers) per hour—is the fastest animal on land. Cheetahs' bodies, with their small heads, long legs, and ridged foot pads that give them extra traction, are designed especially for speed. (Humans, by the way, have been known to travel short distances as fast as 28 miles [45 kilometers] per hour.) Measuring speed in sea animals is very difficult, but studies have shown that the sailfish is the fastest creature in the sea, swimming at speeds up to 68 miles (109 kilometers) per hour. The fastest animal in the air is the peregrine falcon. When flying horizontally, the peregrine falcon can go around 60 miles (97 kilometers) per hour. It is during its high-speed dives for prey that this bird breaks speed records, however. Flying at a speed of more than 200 miles (322 kilometers) per hour, the peregrine falcon frequently kills its prey just by the force of impact.

Which animal is the most **intelligent**?

Ask five scientists to list the most intelligent animals, and you'll get five different lists. Most experts believe that humans are the most evolved, complex, intelligent animals, but there are some people who question this. Part of the problem in determining the most intelligent animals is that there are several different kinds of intelligence: the ability to communicate, to adapt to the environment, and to solve problems. And scientists have always struggled to learn how an animal's mind works when communication between animals and humans is so limited.

Many studies have shown that primates are the most intelligent animals. The primate family includes human beings as well as chimpanzees, gorillas, orangutans, baboons, gibbons, and monkeys (those animals, with chimps at the top of the list, hold the top six spots on biologist Edward O. Wilson's list of the ten most intelligent animals—aside from humans). Primates have large, complex brains, and they can build complicated cultures and, to some degree, control their environment. They can communicate with others of their species and develop language skills. Several marine animals, including the killer whale and many dolphin species, have been listed as some of the most intelligent animals on the planet. Elephants and pigs are also believed to be highly intelligent.

Can any animals **talk**?

Most animals have the ability to "talk" to other animals of the same species—they make one kind of noise to attract a mate, another to sound the alarm that a predator

Primates, like this orangutan, are thought by many scientists to be among the most intelligent animals. *Robert J. Huffman/Field Mark Publications © 2001*

approaches, and so on. Animals can also communicate with each other through gestures, touch, and even by releasing certain odors. The more evolved the animal, the more complex their communication becomes. Animals that live in complicated social structures, with a leader and followers, communicate the details about that social order to each other.

As for whether animals can talk to humans, this simple question has sparked heated debate among scientists for many years. Experiments teaching chimpanzees sign language so they could communicate with their human observers resulted initially in exciting discoveries: it appeared that the chimps had learned to put together simple sentences from the signs they had learned. A closer look, however, revealed that the animals had simply learned to move their hands in ways that pleased the humans. The scientists, eager to believe communication with the chimps was possible, misinterpreted the animals' gestures. A few years later, in the mid-1990s, scientists in Atlanta, Georgia, worked with Bonobo, or pygmy, chimps to teach them to associate words with dozens of different symbols on a keyboard. The scientists believe that these chimps learned to communicate—following instructions and offering information—at the level of a human toddler.

While many experts agree that such basic communication between the smartest primates and human beings is possible, some linguists, or human-language specialists, don't think that animals can learn our languages. They feel that studies like the ones done with the Bonobo chimps simply show that the animals are very good at

139

being trained. They can figure out which buttons to push to get food and other rewards from the scientists.

Many pet owners and scientists have had great success teaching parrots, particularly the African gray parrot, to talk. Parrots have outstanding mimicking abilities: they can imitate a human voice with surprising accuracy, and they can learn a great number of words. What is unclear, however, is whether parrots can really understand the words they say, or if they are merely imitating what they hear.

Which animal has the **longest** life?

The animal believed to have had the longest life span ever recorded was a Marion's tortoise that lived over 152 years. Several other types of tortoises have been known to live longer than 115 years. Clams also tend to live a very long time, with a quahog (pronounced KO-hog) living around 150 years and a deep-sea clam living around 100 years. The oldest person on record lived 122 years.

Which animal has the **shortest** life?

Many insects have very short lives, existing for only a few days. The mayfly has the shortest life span. In the adult stage, the mayfly often lives just a few hours—long enough to mate and, for the females, to deposit their fertilized eggs. Male mayflies perform an acrobatic mating dance over water as the Sun goes down. They are then joined in the dance by the females. Mayflies, also called fishflies, arrive in swarms in areas near bodies of freshwater (the pre-adult stages are aquatic, meaning they live in water). They coat streets and driveways and cling to screen doors and cars. While their fishy odor is unpleasant, the presence of mayflies indicates that the body of water is healthy.

Which animal is the **deadliest**?

The poison dart frog, found in the rain forests of the South American country Colombia, produces one of the most toxic poisons in the animal kingdom. Many amphibians (the animal group to which frogs belong) produce toxins that make their skin taste bad so predators won't want to eat them. Some frogs, usually the brightly colored ones, produce poisonous secretions that can harm or even kill their enemies. The toxin made by the poison dart frog, if it enters an animal's bloodstream, can paralyze and even kill. There are many different types of these frogs, the most poisonous being a bright yellow frog whose toxin can kill a human if it gets into the person's mouth or into an open wound. The toxin can even work its way through unbroken skin. As little as one drop of this frog's poison can cause the heart to stop beating. Certain tribes in Colombia use the poison dart frog's secretions (obtained without killing the frogs) to coat their darts and arrows (hence the name given to the frog).

What does it mean when an animal is **extinct**?

Extinction happens when a species of plant or animal dies out completely. Extinction is a permanent state: once a species is extinct, it cannot be revived. Scientists believe that extinction usually occurs when a species cannot adapt to major changes to its environment. (Some species adapt dramatically to such changes, and in doing so they become an entirely new species, meaning the species they evolved *from* becomes extinct.) The actions of human beings have caused numerous extinctions: at one time many people believed that Earth's resources—fresh water, trees, fuel sources, animals

The toxin made by the poison dart frog can paralyze and even kill.

used for food—were unlimited. People have hunted or fished for an animal in such great numbers that the deaths outnumbered births, and the species could not survive. Tearing down forests or filling in swamps to build homes, golf courses, or shopping malls has had a great impact on animal life: many animals can no longer survive if their habitat is destroyed. Pollution of the air, soil, and water has also been a factor in the destruction of many species.

It's important to remember that while human beings have caused the extinction of many species, we also have the ability to protect and save endangered plants and animals. Wildlife preservation laws and organizations like the Sierra Club first arose in the late 1800s after people began to realize the devastating impact their actions could have on animal species. Widespread hunting of the American bison, for example, reduced the animal's population from 60 million in 1860 to only about 550 just 30 years later. Such a huge and fast reduction in the bison's numbers alarmed many people.

In 1966 the U.S. Congress passed the important Endangered Species Protection Act, which meant that animals whose populations were shrinking could be protected from hunters and land developers. That law, and many others passed since then, has generated controversy in situations where the building of a bridge or dam or airport could threaten an endangered species but would help the people living nearby. As the world's population continues to grow, with more and more people living in what used to be animal habitats, such conflicts are likely to increase.

Of all the animal and plant species that have ever lived, far more than half are now extinct. On the other hand, new species develop and are discovered all the time, so a balance between death and new life is maintained.

141

What does it mean if an animal is an **endangered species**?

There are many organizations in the United States and all over the world that study and research plant and animal species, determining which ones may be headed for extinction. Any species in such danger is described as endangered. Once a species is endangered, it becomes illegal to hunt that animal or destroy its habitat. In 2001 the U.S. Fish and Wildlife Service, the organization that maintains the nation's list of endangered and threatened plants and animals, listed over 1,000 animals and nearly 750 plants worldwide ("threatened" species are those that might soon become endangered). The goal of such organizations is to help a species recover to the point that it no longer needs to be listed as endangered.

AMAZING ANIMAL BEHAVIOR

What is **bioluminescence**?

Bioluminescence is the ability of some organisms, like fireflies, to light up. This phenomenon occurs in some protozoa, fungi, ocean-dwelling invertebrates (such as some species of shrimp and squid), and even some fish (anglerfish and hatchetfish). It does not occur in more highly developed animals like birds, reptiles, amphibians, and mammals. The light results from a chemical reaction, and scientists believe it serves a variety of functions in animals. Sometimes animals use their light to confuse or scare their enemies, and sometimes it is used to attract a mate. For some deep-sea creatures, their body light may help them see in an otherwise completely dark environment.

Why (and how) do animals **change color**?

Many animals can change their color, some over a period of seconds and others over several months. Cephalopods, a group including octopuses and squids, are especially skillful at changing color rapidly; they can turn different colors in less than a second. Their color changes are usually triggered by a heightened state—excitement or fear—which brings on an amazing display of different colors spreading over their bodies. Several kinds of fish and some amphibians and lizards are also able to change colors, though their transformations take a bit more time than those of the cephalopods. Color changes take place in special pigment cells called chromatophores. Changing the size of these cells moves the pigment around, altering the animal's coloration.

Such animals change their colors for a number of reasons. Those that can rapidly change colors do so to startle or confuse predators or to better blend in with their environments, a technique known as camouflaging. Camouflaging can either be used by an animal that wants to hide from an attacker, or by an animal that doesn't want to be seen by its prey. Color changes can also be used to attract a mate.

Some animals undergo color changes with a change in seasons. Certain mammals and birds that live in cold climates, for example, have white fur and feathers in the winter so they can blend in with the snow and be less noticeable to their predators. Some songbirds will grow brightly colored, attractive feathers for the mating season. Those feathers are replaced by duller colors after mating is over. These color changes are also caused by pigment cells, located beneath the fur or feathers.

What is **mimicry**?

Mimicry is the ability some animals have to resemble another animal so closely that they can fool either their prey or their predators. For example, the beautiful and brightly colored monarch butterfly has a foul taste, and most birds will avoid eating it. The viceroy butterfly, with its similarly colored orange-and-black wings, looks so much like the monarch that most birds are fooled and will also avoid the viceroy. The American zone-tailed hawk has similar color and body shape to that of a certain kind of vulture. Vultures do not attack live animals; they eat only carrion, which is the flesh of animals that are already dead, so small animals on the ground are not afraid of them. The zone-tailed hawk flies in groups with these vultures, disguising itself among them, and then swoops down on unsuspecting rodents that didn't recognize the hawk in time to scurry away. The red milk snake, which is harmless, has color patterns similar to the deadly coral snake. A potential enemy could easily mistake the milk snake for the coral snake and, thinking it is venomous, leave it alone.

Can some animals **grow a new limb** after one has been cut off?

There are many creatures that have the ability to replace body parts that have been lost. In fact, this process, called regeneration, happens in all living things at some level; life is not possible without regeneration. Generally, the more complex the organism, the less dramatic the regeneration. Human beings can replace old skin cells with new ones, for example, while a certain species of flatworm can regenerate a new head and tail—basically a whole new worm—from any one of its segments. A hydra, a freshwater invertebrate with a tube-like body that has several tentacles at one end, has such amazing regenerative ability that an entirely new hydra can be regrown from just a tiny fragment of the animal. Several insects, if they lose a limb before they reach their adult stage, can grow a new one. Crustaceans like crabs and lobsters can replace lost claws or legs with new ones.

Even some vertebrates, which are more highly developed than invertebrates, are capable of some amazing regeneration. Bony fish, a group that includes salmon, tuna, and most other creatures we think of as fish, can regrow a fin (though the group of

143

fish that includes sharks cannot). Some amphibians can replace lost limbs with new ones, while some lizards can grow a new tail if the old one gets cut off. Birds cannot grow new limbs, though their ability to replace old feathers and sometimes beaks with new ones is a type of regeneration. The regeneration that mammals are capable of is more modest—deer produce new antlers every year, for example, but no mammal can regrow a new limb or tail.

INSECTS, SPIDERS, AND WORMS

What are **"bugs"**?

Most people use the word "bug" when talking about insects like beetles, bees, and butterflies, and other small, many-legged creatures that crawl, jump, or fly, such as spiders and centipedes. All of these critters belong to the same phylum, called Arthropoda, which also includes crustaceans (like lobsters and crabs). Arthropods have hard skeletons on the outside of their bodies, called exoskeletons, and they also have jointed limbs (arthropod means "jointed feet"). Arthropods make up more than 80 percent of the world's animal species.

The word "bug" does correspond with an official category, though: in the scientific world, a "true bug" is classified as an insect that belongs to the order Hemiptera. The insects in this order can be recognized by the X-shaped pattern on their backs, a design formed by their wings at rest. They also have sucking mouth parts and a hardened gula, which is the underside of the head. The 30,000 species of the Hemipteran order include bedbugs, fire bugs, and some water bugs.

How many **different kinds** of insects are there?

More than 980,000 species of arthropods exist, and most of those are insects. Estimates vary, but some scientists believe there are around 900,000 known species of insects, and many more species are yet to be discovered. Some experts believe there may be as many as 10 million different kinds of insects.

Why are there **so many** insects?

There are so many insects because they are essential to life on Earth and play many important roles in keeping our planet healthy. Most of the world's flowering plants (about 80 percent) are pollinated by insects; insects carry pollen from the male parts of a blossom to the female parts of another plant's flower, allowing reproduction. Most of our fruits and vegetables are the result of this kind of plant reproduction. Insects also feed on the remains of dead plants and animals, keeping our environment clean and returning nitrogen, carbon, and other valuable elements to the soil in their waste. In addition, insects are a vital part of Earth's food chain, providing nourishment for one another (there are many thousands of insect-eating insects) as well as for reptiles and amphibians, for birds and fish, and for mammals, such as mice and bats. In many parts of the world, insects even make up an important part of the human diet!

If there are so many insects, why don't I see more of them?

A great many insects are so tiny that they can't be seen without magnification. Others are small enough to fit into the cracks and hidden spots of our environment, so we simply don't see them unless we really look for them. Many other insects blend in with their surroundings so that they are practically invisible, a technique called camouflaging. An insect known as the walkingstick, for instance, has a slender body that looks just like a twig.

Why do **mosquitoes bite**?

Just female mosquitoes bite; male mosquitoes feed only on fruit and plant juices. The female mosquito bites people (and other animals) to feed on their blood. She needs blood so that her eggs can develop properly before they are laid. One way a female mosquito locates a victim is by feeling the body heat of an animal as she flies by it.

Why do mosquito bites **itch**?

With her long, slender mouthparts, a female mosquito pierces the skin of her victim in order to suck its blood. She injects a substance that keeps the blood from clotting (an anticoagulant) before she drinks her fill. This foreign substance in the blood activates the victim's immune system, causing an allergic reaction around the bite. This reaction causes the swelling and itching that drive us crazy!

How do bees make **honey**?

Honeybees collect sweet nectar from flowers and bring it back to their nests or hives. There it is stored for future use, for its sugar provides honeybees with the energy they need. The nectar is stored as honey, which is a thick, concentrated form of nectar that has been converted in the bees' digestive tracts. Honey is stored in many little compartments or cells in the nest (called a hive), which the bees seal over with wax—something they also produce. We call this honey-filled wax honeycomb. Beekeepers take honeycomb from the hive (leaving enough behind for the bees), using the wax for candlemaking and the honey to sweeten all kinds of foods.

Bees make honey from the nectar they gather from flowers. *Robert J. Huffman/Field Mark Publications © 2001*

Why do bees, wasps, and other insects **sting**?

An insect's sting is a defensive weapon used when it senses danger. It was developed to keep predators away from it or from its colony in a hive or nest. It is designed to pierce the skin and inject a poison or venom into the predator.

If you have the bad luck to be stung by an insect, there are a few things you should do. First, move away from the hive or nest if one is nearby (a stinging bee sends out a chemical signal that excites other bees). Second, try to remove the stinger from your skin by scraping it with something hard instead of pulling it, which could squeeze the attached venom sack, releasing more of the irritating substance into the wound. Put some ice on the sting to ease the swelling and pain. If you develop a lot of swelling, a rash, or, most important, have trouble breathing, see a doctor, because you are having a serious allergic reaction.

What are **killer bees**?

Killer bees are the result of a scientific experiment begun in the mid-1950s, when European honeybees and African bees (which are accustomed to hot temperatures) were brought to Brazil and bred with each other in an effort to create a honeybee that would produce honey in hot, tropical climates. The experiment was a big failure because—unlike the mild-mannered European honeybee—the new Africanized honeybee had an aggressive nature. Quick to attack intruders, the new bees have been responsible for a number of human deaths. The danger of these bees comes from their tendency to attack in swarms; if a person is stung by enough bees at one time, it could trigger a severe allergic reaction. These "killer bees" have made their way into the southern United States, but the American beekeeping industry is working on ways to correct this experiment gone wrong.

Why do yellowjacket wasps **bother picnickers**?

Yellowjacket wasps only appear at picnics in the late summer and fall, when there is less work for them to do in their colonies. The nectar-producing flowers that they usually feed on are almost gone at that time of year—so they settle for sweet things like soda and other picnic food.

Why do bees and other insects **buzz**?

The buzzing sounds that insects make are the beating of their wings. Some insects flap their wings slowly, like the butterfly (8 to 12 beats per second), and make no sound. Others, like the mosquito, beat their wings very fast. At 600 beats per second, the mosquito's buzz sounds more like a high-pitched whine.

How do insects make **other sounds**?

Most of the time, insects make noise for mating purposes; male insects produce sound to attract females, sometimes over long distances. A male insect can make such sounds by rubbing parts of his body together. The grasshopper, for instance, rubs the rough edge of his hind leg against the edge of a forewing. Similarly, the cricket scrapes his forewings together. Other insects have membranes that vibrate, which also produces sound.

Can you figure out the temperature by listening to a **cricket chirp**?

Yes—the warmer the night, the faster a cricket "sings." This phenomenon is so reliable that a mathematical equation can be used to calculate air temperature: count the number of cricket chirps made in 13 seconds and add 40, and you will get the temperature outside (in degrees Fahrenheit).

Why do fireflies **light up** at night?

It is believed that fireflies (beetles also known as lightning bugs) flash signals to one another to show their locations in the dark and to indicate their willingness to mate.

Butterflies like this monarch fly from flower to flower to eat the nectar, spreading pollen as they go. *Robert J. Huffman/Field Mark Publications © 2001*

Fireflies have organs near the ends of their bodies that convert a special biochemical into flashes of heatless light. This ability of living things to produce their own light is called bioluminescence.

Why do butterflies and other insects fly from **flower to flower**?

Butterflies and other insects fly from one plant to the next to feed on the sweet nectar—and sometimes the pollen—located in the interior of flowers. The sugar in nectar supplies insects with the energy they need, and pollen contains protein, fat, vitamins, and minerals. In the process of feeding, many insects transfer pollen—which sticks to their bodies—from one plant's flower to another. Pollen, which is a fine powdery grain from a flower's male reproductive organ, must be transferred to the female reproductive organ of a flower for fertilization to take place and seeds to form.

How are **moths** different from **butterflies**?

While moths and butterflies are very similar and belong to the same order of insects, Lepidoptera, there are noticeable differences between them. Butterflies are generally active during the day, and moths are usually nocturnal, or active at night. Butterflies have knobs on the ends of their antennae, while moths do not. Butterflies tend to be more colorful than moths. And moths and butterflies hold their wings differently when at rest: moths lay theirs out flat, like an airplane, while butterflies hold theirs vertically above their bodies.

What is a **cocoon**?

A cocoon is an envelope-like structure made of silk that is spun by an immature insect or larva. It is a protective covering in which the larva passes through its inactive pupa stage before it becomes an adult insect. These cocoons are often attached to branches or twigs. Caterpillars are the larva that eventually change, or metamorphose, into butterflies and moths. Only a few types of butterfly caterpillars spin cocoons (a butterfly's cocoon is called a chrysalis), while the caterpillars of many moths do. The cocoon of the silkworm, caterpillar of the silk moth, is collected and processed and woven into the beautiful cloth we know as silk.

Why are some flying insects **drawn to lights** at night?

Scientists aren't exactly sure why this happens. They have noticed that on clear nights, when the Moon is visible, fewer insects gravitate to artificial lights. This observation has given rise to a theory: for millions of years, insects have used the light of the moon, coming from one direction—above—to guide them during night flight. But artificial lights, which put out rays of illumination in all directions, confuse this ancient navigational system. Flying in a straight line is impossible when an insect is around an artificial light, which causes it to fly in circles.

Where do insects go in the **winter**?

Most insects survive the winter in an inactive state known as diapause. It is a type of hibernation, in which all body processes slow down and little energy is required for survival. A few types of insects, like the monarch butterfly of North America, migrate to a warmer place—just like many birds—to spend the winter, returning in the spring.

Are **spiders** insects?

Many people think of spiders as insects, but actually they are classified in a separate category. Spiders are part of a group called arachnids, which also includes mites, ticks, and scorpions. Arachnids share many features with their arthropod cousins, but they differ in that they do not have antennae. Also, spiders have eight legs (insects have six), and their bodies are segmented into two parts (insects' bodies have three parts).

Can spiders **fly**?

Spiders do not have wings and cannot, technically, fly. Several types of spiders, however, can travel long distances through the air by a process called ballooning. The spiders spin long strands of silk that are caught by the wind, carrying the spiders along the currents. Spiders can travel far by this method (as far as hundreds of miles), and in

Spider webs look delicate, but they are incredibly strong. *Robert J. Huffman/Field Mark Publications © 2001*

some cases they can "fly" as high as 2,600 feet (800 meters). One spider was even recorded at an altitude of 15,000 feet (4,572 meters).

How do spiders **spin webs**?

Not all spiders spin webs, but most do. The webs can be spun into many different shapes, and they are used to protect eggs, catch insects for food, or move a spider through the air. Most spiders possess three pairs of tube-like spinnerets near the ends of their bodies that produce a fluid that hardens as it is drawn out into silky threads. Spider webs look delicate, but they are actually very strong: when compared with an equal amount of steel, spider silk is five times stronger.

Spider webs do not last long—they are damaged by the capture of prey or by weather conditions, and some webs simply dry out after a day or two. Some spiders need to spin a new web every day, a task that can take about an hour. Rather than spin a web, certain spiders spin a silk tube with a trap door at one end. They hide in the tube until they feel the vibrations of a passing insect; then they dart out and capture their meal.

Do spiders really **eat the bugs** they catch in their webs?

Yes, most spiders live on insects and other related arthropods. Very large spiders can capture small birds and snakes in their silk traps. Spiders know they've made a catch because they can feel the vibrations caused by struggling bugs caught in their strong, sticky webs. Sometimes spiders tightly wrap their prey in silk to subdue them. They usually kill their prey by injecting them with a paralyzing poison or venom that they produce.

Why don't **spiders get stuck** in their own webs?

Some of the strands of a web are made of a different kind of silk that is not sticky, and spiders walk across these. But if a spider should happen to fall into the sticky strands, an oily covering on its body keeps it from getting caught.

How large is the world's **biggest spider**?

The largest known spiders in the world are the Goliath bird-eating spiders, which live in the coastal rain forests of northeastern South America. They can become as big as dinner plates! The largest recorded specimen had a leg span of 11 inches (28 centimeters). This spider, a type of tarantula, has a somewhat misleading name. So-called bird-eating spiders don't usually eat birds but instead dine on snakes, frogs, and insects.

Which spiders are **poisonous** to people?

Most spiders are capable of injecting venom into the animals they bite, but only a few can cause harm to humans. Two spiders most often associated with harmful bites are the black widow and the brown recluse. The black widow can be found all over the world, including throughout the United States (except Alaska). Females are far more common than males; the male usually gets eaten by the female after mating. Their shiny black bodies have red markings on the underside that are frequently in the shape of an hourglass. Black widows feed on insects, but they will occasionally—if they feel threatened—bite a human. A bite from a black widow, while it can cause a person severe pain and nausea, is not generally life-threatening.

The brown recluse spider can most commonly be found in the southern and western United States, but it can also be seen in the northern states. A bite from this small spider may not be immediately detected, but after a few hours a painful blister may form. The wound can take several weeks to heal. In very rare cases, the bites of brown recluse spiders have been known to cause death in humans. These shy spiders are not aggressive and generally only bite when they are disturbed or handled.

The funnel weaver spider, found in southeastern Australia, and certain kinds of tarantulas that live in Africa and South America have also been known to cause harm to humans. The Brazilian huntsman is believed to be the spider with the most toxic poison—it would take only .00000021 ounces (.006 milligrams) of this spider's venom to kill a mouse.

151

If a spider bite occurs, the best thing to do is to try to collect the spider so it can be identified and to see a doctor as soon as possible. Most spider bites are harmless, though mildly annoying.

Are **worms** insects?

While some insects are worm-like in their immature, or larval, stage, the invertebrate creatures classified as worms are not insects. There are many different types of worms; in the earthworm category alone, there are thousands of species. Earthworms are very beneficial little animals. They are part of the diets of a huge variety of birds and other animals, and they also help keep the soil they live in healthy and nutritious for plants. The tiny tunnels created when worms burrow into dirt (they're actually eating the dirt as they go!) help the roots of plants get more nutrients, air, and water. Even the worms' manure, called worm castings, is beneficial: it's a great fertilizer.

Earthworms are hermaphroditic, meaning that each worm has both male and female sex organs. A single worm is not capable of reproduction, however—each worm still needs a partner in order to get its eggs fertilized. While earthworms cannot actually hear or see, they can pick up vibrations and can sense light. The species of earthworm most common in the United States is rather small; these usually grow to be about 10 inches (25 centimeters) long. There is a species found in Australia, however, that can be as long as 11 feet (3.3 meters).

Why do worms come out after it **rains**?

Go outside near any patch of dirt on a warm summer afternoon after a rainfall, and you are sure to find plenty of earthworms on driveways and sidewalks. Scientists are not certain why this happens, but the worms may emerge from the soil to escape from the rainwater that has filled their tunnel homes. While earthworms require a certain amount of moisture, they can drown if they're submerged in water. Unfortunately, their escape from the rain-soaked soil onto a warm driveway can also prove deadly: if the Sun comes out before a worm can make it back to some dirt, it can get dried out.

FISH AND OTHER SEA CREATURES

How many kinds of **fish** are there?

There are around 25,000 different species of fish, with hundreds of new species being discovered every year. Of all the vertebrate groups—including fish, mammals, reptiles,

Fish are the most diverse vertebrates on Earth, with hundreds of new species being discovered every year.

amphibians, and birds—fish are the most diverse. Most fish have scales, but some do not. Some are brilliantly colored, others blend in with the muddy sea bottom or the plants they live amongst, and certain fish can even change their colors to match their changing environment. There are even fish that can glow, a function called bioluminescence, in the pitch-black world of the deep sea. Some fish have sleek, torpedo-shaped bodies with fins, some have spiny or puffed-up bodies, others are flat, and still others have long, snake-like bodies.

The largest class of fish by far are the bony fish, or Osteichthyes. This class includes most of the fish that people catch for fun and for food, like salmon, trout, tuna, sole, and perch. All bony fish have a skeleton that is at least partly made up of bone, and most have platelike scales, a cover over their gills, and a swim bladder, which is a sac filled with gas that the fish can empty or release to control how closely they swim to the surface. The bony fish range in size from the goby, which is one of the world's smallest vertebrates at about one-half inch (one centimeter) in length, to the enormous whale sharks, which can get as long as 50 feet (15 meters).

Among the most fascinating classes of fish are the cartilaginous fish, or Chondrichthyes, including sharks and rays. Chondrichthyes have skeletons made of cartilage instead of bone. (Cartilage is an elastic tissue that is more flexible than bone but can still provide support. Pinch the tip of your nose, and you'll see what cartilage feels like.) Sharks have scales, but not like the ones found on bony fish. Sharks' scales feel rough, like sandpaper, and they are made of a material similar to teeth. In fact, the

153

teeth of sharks are actually modified scales. Sharks usually have powerful tails, a blunt snout, and powerful jaws with multiple rows of teeth. If a shark loses teeth while feeding or fighting, new teeth from the back rows will move to the front. Many people think of sharks as savage and dangerous, but in fact only a small number pose a threat to people. While some sharks can get extremely large, most species are smaller than three feet (one meter) in length, with the smallest shark, the dwarf dogfish, measuring only about eight inches (twenty centimeters) long.

Another type of Chondrichthyes, the rays, have wide, flat bodies with the eyes on top and the mouth and gills underneath. They live at the bottom of the ocean, moving slowly through the water by gracefully flapping their winglike fins. While many rays are harmless to humans, some, such as stingrays, have narrow tails with sharp, poisonous spines. If the stingray feels threatened, it can whip its spiny tail at its enemies, causing extremely painful and sometimes severe wounds. Rays range in size from a few inches to more than 20 feet (6 meters) in width.

Another class of fish, known as the jawless fish, or Agnatha, includes lamprey eels and hagfish. Many of these primitive species are parasites, meaning they live off other organisms. Lampreys in particular have caused major problems for commercial fisheries, destroying large numbers of trout and other fish in the Great Lakes and other regions of the United States. They have long, eel-like bodies and round, jawless mouths. They attach onto their prey by suction, biting into a fish's flesh with their small, sharp teeth. Their skeletal structure consists only of a chord made of cartilage, called a notochord, running the length of their bodies.

How can fish **breathe** underwater?

Just like people and, indeed, all animals, fish need to take in oxygen and release carbon dioxide to survive. And while oxygen isn't as plentiful in water as it is in the air, there is enough dissolved oxygen in water to allow fish (and all other water creatures) to live. Fish conduct the exchange of oxygen and carbon dioxide with the help of gills, breathing organs consisting of flaps of tissue located on the outside of the fish's body. Gills are loaded with tiny blood vessels called capillaries; it is these vessels that take in oxygen from the water and transport it to other blood vessels that distribute it where it's needed in the fish's body. The gill capillaries also bring carbon dioxide from other vessels to the gills, where it is then returned to the water.

If fish breathe **oxygen,** why can't they survive on land?

Some fish can breathe on land. Of these, a few actually must breathe air—these are called obligate air breathers. Others, like the eel-like lungfish, the bowfin, and the gar, are adapted to breathe either air or water. These fish probably evolved to breathe air because they live in warmer water where oxygen is present in smaller amounts.

For the most part, however, fish must get their oxygen from water and not from air. If such fish are taken out of water, they suffocate. Fish are able to get oxygen from water through the many tiny blood vessels spread over the surface area of their gills. When fish are out of water, their gill arches collapse, and the blood vessels are no longer exposed to the oxygen in the air.

Even fish that can breathe air must still live primarily in the water because it is in water that they are capable of movement. If they can't move, they can't get food or escape from enemies.

Do fish **sleep**?

While fish don't sleep in quite the same way as people, scientists believe they do enter a resting state. People are generally still, with eyes closed, during sleep. Most fish don't have eyelids, so they obviously can't close their eyes to go to sleep. And some fish do seem to stop moving when they sleep, but others cannot afford to stop moving. Tuna, for example, must stay in motion because they need to have water moving constantly over their gills to get oxygen. Some fish find a nook between rocks or in a coral reef to rest in, and others actually build a nest for sleeping. When it's ready for a rest, the parrotfish releases a jellylike substance that surrounds its body, offering some protection while it dozes.

Can flying fish really fly?

There are about 40 species known as flying fish. These small fish (around 18 inches, or 45 centimeters, long) are found in warm waters all over the world. They don't technically fly, but they can glide through the air, using winglike fins and a powerful tail. When chased by a predator, a flying fish heads straight for the water's surface at a rapid speed, with its fins tucked in close to its body. As it breaks the surface of the water, it spreads its "wings" and uses its flapping tail, still underwater, to give it an extra boost.

Flying fish don't go very high—usually just a few feet above the water—but they can glide for fairly long distances. As it reaches the water after a glide, a flying fish can use its tail to propel it up again for another run, like a skipping rock that makes several bounces. A single glide can take a flying fish as far as 600 feet (180 meters), and the total distance traveled over a series of consecutive glides can be as far as 1,300 feet (400 meters).

What do fish do in the winter when **water freezes**?

If a body of water freezes completely, from the surface to the bottom, fish cannot survive for long—unless they are like the Antarctic icefish, which has chemicals resembling antifreeze in its blood to help it survive in water below freezing temperatures. For other kinds of fish, as long as there is some unfrozen water beneath the ice, they can generally survive the winter. The danger in such wintry conditions is not freezing to death but suffocating: ice on the water's surface makes it hard for oxygen in the air to dissolve in the water. Fish can survive in very cold water in the same way land animals like bears can live out the winter: by becoming dormant, meaning slowing down bodily processes, eating very little, and consuming less oxygen.

What is the **largest** fish?

The largest living fish is the whale shark. It usually grows to about 30 feet (9 meters) in length, but some have been measured at more than 50 feet (15 meters) long, weighing several tons (a ton is 2,000 pounds, or 908 kilograms). These gentle giants pose little threat to humans, however. They have very small teeth and eat mainly fish and plankton, which are tiny organisms that drift in both saltwater and freshwater, providing food for numerous animals. Whale sharks, recognizable by their distinctive skin pattern of small dots and stripes, swim very slowly, just beneath the surface of the water.

Do **piranhas** ever attack people?

Piranhas have a reputation for being vicious hunters with a strong attraction to the scent of blood. While they do have very sharp, pointy teeth and powerful jaws, and they sometimes hunt in large groups, piranhas rarely attack humans or any other large animals. Found mostly in the rivers and lakes of South America, piranhas can grow to be 2 feet (60 centimeters) long. Their preferred prey are fish that are smaller or only slightly larger than themselves. Groups of piranhas have been known to attack larger animals that have wandered into their territory, engaging in a feeding frenzy and rapidly removing hunks of the animal's flesh. But such incidents are quite rare, and many species of piranhas get most of their food from scavenging, meaning they feed on the remains of fish that are already dead.

Which sharks pose a **danger** to people?

There are more than 350 shark species, and only a few of them have been known to attack people. Contrary to the habits of the bloodthirsty shark featured in the *Jaws* movies, scientists don't believe that sharks purposefully hunt people. In most cases where sharks have attacked humans, they were probably protecting their territory or mistaking the person for a seal or another type of shark prey. (Unprovoked shark attacks do happen, but they are pretty rare: the International Shark Attack File at the University of Florida recorded fewer than 80 such attacks throughout the world in 2000; 10 of those resulted in death.) Around 30 different kinds of sharks have been known to attack people, with the white shark, the bull shark, and the tiger shark being the most common aggressors.

Most sharks, like this blue shark, are basically harmless unless provoked.

How does an eel make **electricity**?

The electric eel is a South American fish with a long, wormlike body. It can grow to a length of 9 feet (2.75 meters) and weigh nearly 50 pounds (22.7 kilometers). The electric eel floats through slow-moving water searching for fish to eat. It breathes air, which means it must come to the surface every few minutes.

The electric eel has organs made up of electric plates that run the length of its tail, which makes up most of its body length. This eel—which has no teeth—uses electric shocks to stun its prey, probably to protect its mouth from the struggling, spiny fish it is trying to eat. The eel shocks the fish with several brief electrical charges, temporarily paralyzing it so the eel can suck it into its stomach. The electrical charge can be anywhere from 300 to 600 volts, enough of a shock to jolt a human being. Electric eels are not aggressive, though, and primarily use their electricity to ward off enemies and stun their prey.

What kind of animal is a **sea horse**?

These unusual and fascinating creatures offer many surprises. They are fish, though with their bony rings, horselike heads, and curly, gripping tails, they don't look anything like other fish. Most sea horses are quite small, around 1.5 inches (4 centimeters) in length, though the largest of them can be nearly 12 inches long (30 centimeters). Scientists believe that sea horses mate with a single partner, a behavior called

157

monogamy that is rare in the animal world. And, even more unusual, it is the male sea horse that gets "pregnant," carrying and nurturing the fertilized eggs in a pouch in his body. The female deposits the eggs in the male's body, and he provides oxygen and nutrients until the young are ready to hatch.

The sea horse population has been threatened in recent years by destruction of its habitat and by overfishing. Hundreds of thousands of sea horses are caught and sold each year to large aquariums and to people who simply like to collect unusual animals. Many more are sold to several countries in the Far East, where sea horses are believed to have medicinal value.

Is a **starfish** really a fish?

In spite of their name, starfish are not true fish. They are invertebrates known as echinoderms (all fish are vertebrates). There are actually close to 2,000 species of starfish, and they can grow to as large as 25 inches (65 centimeters) across. They usually have five arms attached to a disclike body, and they can grow a new limb if one is lost. Starfish have tube feet on the underside of their arms that allow them to move and to cling to rocks or coral. The starfish's mouth is located on the underside of the disc, and some species actually turn their stomachs out of their bodies to surround and digest their prey (including oysters, mussels, and clams).

Where do **seashells** come from?

Seashells are more than just pretty souvenirs to take home from a trip to the beach. Shells are the hard outer coverings, or exoskeletons, of small, soft-bodied, invertebrate animals. Most animals that live in seashells are called mollusks. Some live in the water and others live on the shore. Some mollusks—usually the ones called bivalves, named because their shells are divided into a left and right valve—are delicacies for humans, like mussels, clams, oysters, and scallops. Snails are also mollusks.

Seashells are made mostly of calcium carbonate and other minerals found in the sea. The shell is formed in layers when the mantle, a tissue that is part of the mollusk's body, secretes a substance that hardens. Some shells have a glistening, pinkish-orange interior that is called nacre, or mother-of-pearl. Seashells come in a wide variety of shapes and sizes—some are curvy spirals, others are spiny, others are fan-shaped with grooves spreading across the surface—and a glorious range of colors. Scientists aren't exactly sure why some shells are shaped or colored the way they are, though they believe certain shapes help the mollusk burrow into the sand or intimidate its enemies, and certain colors help to camouflage the shell from predators.

Why do we hear **ocean sounds** when we hold shells up to our ears?

Many of us have held a large shell, usually a conch (pronounced "konk"), up to our
ears and heard what sounds like waves crashing against the shore. The magical part is

that you can be miles from the ocean and still hear that sound. How does it work? It seems very mysterious, but the answer is actually pretty simple. The curved inner chambers of the shell are just bouncing back into your ear the noises that are around you all the time but that you don't usually notice. The louder it is around you—if you're near a construction site or at a party, for example—the louder the "ocean" sound in the shell will be.

If you don't have a conch shell handy to test this out, don't worry: you can use a cup or even your curved hand to demonstrate. Shells of different sizes and shapes will reflect noises in varying ways, and so will different kinds of cups. Try holding a large plastic cup over your ear; pull it back a bit and see how the noise changes. Then try it with a coffee cup to see if it's different.

How do oysters make pearls?

Pearls are round, iridescent jewels strung together to make necklaces or bracelets, or mounted onto earrings or rings. Unlike most kinds of jewelry that are made from stones or metals, pearls come from living creatures. They are produced by oysters (and, in rare cases, by some other mollusks). The mantle, the part of a mollusk that secretes the substance that becomes the shell, also produces the smooth, shiny nacre (referred to as mother-of-pearl) found on the shell's inner layers. If an irritating substance— like a grain of sand—finds its way into the mantle, the mantle will start secreting nacre to cover up that irritant. Layer upon layer of nacre builds up until eventually a pearl is formed. The pearls with the roundest, smoothest shape are the most expensive. Most pearls that we see are a creamy, off-white color, but they can be several different colors. Some oysters in the South Pacific produce black pearls.

People can create conditions that encourage oysters to produce pearls. Pearl harvesters make a small cut in the oyster's mantle and insert an irritating substance. Then they sit back and wait for a pearl to form. The pearls that result from this process are called cultivated pearls, while those that occur without human involvement are called natural pearls. It can take three years or more for a pearl, whether natural or cultivated, to form.

Can an octopus really make **ink**?

An octopus (so named because it has eight arms) is generally a shy, gentle creature. But if it is attacked, it will fight back. One method it has of escaping from a predator is to eject an inklike substance into the water that makes it hard for the attacker to see what's in front of it. Before the ink clears, the octopus has scurried away. Some octopuses (or octopi) can even produce an ink that temporarily paralyzes the predator's senses. Another way for the octopus to escape is to shoot out a powerful stream of

159

water, using jet propulsion to rapidly push itself away from danger. Octopuses can also quickly change the color of their skin, camouflaging themselves from predators.

There are many different kinds of octopuses, and they vary widely in size. The smallest ones are only about 2 inches (5 centimeters) long, and the largest can be 18 feet long (5.4 meters). The armspan of the largest octopuses can reach 30 feet (9 meters). The best-known species is a medium-sized one (about 3 feet, or 90 centimeters) known as the common octopus. In terms of intelligence, this animal is not so common: scientists believe that the common octopus is the smartest of all the invertebrate animals. Unlike most invertebrates, octopuses and such relatives as squid have complex, highly developed eyes, giving them the ability to see images.

How many **suckers** does an octopus have on its arms?

The common octopus has 240 suckers lined up in two rows on each arm. Multiply 240 by 8 arms, and you can calculate that this octopus has 1,920 suckers! Its suckers are extremely powerful, and the octopus uses them to move along the sea bottom and to capture and hold its prey. The suckers don't just stick like suction cups to whatever they touch, however—the octopus can control what it wants to hold in its grip, and if it needs to swim away quickly, it can instantly release the suction.

Octopuses eat mainly crustaceans like crabs and lobsters. The octopus's mouth is located in the center of the skirt, which is the tissue at the base of the arms. It uses sharp beaklike structures and a built-in file, called a radula, in its mouth to tear away the shells of its prey. Octopuses are, in turn, eaten by a number of large fish as well as by humans.

What is the difference between a **squid** and an **octopus**?

Both are marine creatures, and both are cephalopods, a type of mollusk. An octopus has eight limbs, while a squid has ten—eight arms and two long tentacles with flattened ends. Suckers line the undersides of their arms in rows, appearing also on the flattened parts of the tentacles. The tentacles are much longer than the arms and are used to capture prey and bring it to the squid's mouth. Squids can swim very fast (up to 23 miles per hour), usually backwards, and they travel in schools, unlike the slow and solitary octopus. A squid's body is also quite different from an octopus's; while the octopus has a bell-shaped body, the squid has a long, cigar-shaped body. Its eyes, complex like those of the octopus, are located on the sides of its head.

How big can a **giant squid** get?

Squids range in size from tiny (less than three-quarters of an inch, or 1.5 centimeters) to gigantic. The giant squid, scientifically known as the *Architeuthis*, can reach 65 feet (20 meters) in length, with tentacles that are close to 20 feet (6 meters) long. The eye of a giant squid can be as big as a foot (30 centimeters) across! They can weigh nearly

There are many similarities—and many differences—between octopuses (like this one) and squids.

a ton (2,000 pounds, or 908 kilograms). Giant squids are the largest invertebrates ever to have lived.

Scientists don't know much about the giant squid, and what they do know comes entirely from observations of dead specimens that have been washed up on shore or found in the stomachs of sperm whales, giant squids' number-one (and possibly only) predator. Although numerous scientific teams have searched for giant squids using some of the most sophisticated tracking equipment available, none has been able to catch sight of this mysterious animal. Part of the problem in finding a giant squid in its natural habitat is that these creatures may live in the deepest part of the ocean, a very difficult area for humans to explore. Because so little is known for sure about giant squids, many myths and stories have been told over the years about this supposedly ferocious sea monster attacking ships and eating people. No such stories have ever been proven, however, and many scientists believe they are completely inaccurate.

REPTILES

What is a **reptile**?

Reptiles are cold-blooded vertebrate animals with scales, shields, or plates covering their bodies. They include snakes, lizards, alligators, crocodiles, and turtles. There are

161

around 6,000 living reptile species (dinosaurs are among the many extinct types of reptiles), and while they prefer warmer climates, reptiles can be found all over the world. Most reptile babies develop in eggs with a hard outer shell that have been laid by the female; a few develop in eggs within the mother's body.

Do snakes have **slimy** skin?

Looking at a snake, many people might assume that its skin feels wet and slimy. But snakes, like all reptiles, actually have dry, scaly skin. This tough outer covering helps reptiles keep necessary amounts of moisture in their bodies. Some snakes have a ridge in the middle of their scales, but many are smooth to the touch. Depending on its external conditions—if it's lying in a cold, shady spot or basking on a hot, sunny rock—its skin will either feel cool or warm to the touch.

How do **snakes move** without legs?

Snakes have no arms or legs, yet they can move fairly swiftly through grass, sand, and, in some cases, water, and they can easily climb trees. Snakes can achieve such amazing mobility thanks to well-developed muscles and a row of scales, called ventral scales, on the undersides of their bodies. They usually rely on the ground's rough surface to provide resistance, something for them to push against that isn't slippery. Most snakes move by coiling their bodies into a series of S-shaped loops, with each loop pushing against the ground. Some large snakes, like boas, move in a way similar to a caterpillar, inching along the ground. Snakes that live in the desert have a harder time getting the traction necessary for movement. These snakes, called sidewinders, move in a sideways motion that allows them to slither along on the ever-shifting sandy surface.

While the absence of limbs might seem like a handicap, snakes have certain advantages thanks to their unique bodies. Not only can they move quickly and easily over and through a variety of landscapes, they can also move in near silence, making it easy for them to sneak up on their prey. And their narrow, flexible bodies allow them to fit into small crevices and holes where they can wait for unsuspecting animals to come along (or where they can hide from predators).

Are all snakes **poisonous**?

Snakes are among the most frightening animals to humans, and because of this fear many people would sooner try to destroy these animals than understand their benefits to the environment. Snakes are beneficial in that they eat pest insects and rodents, helping to control the populations of animals that can be nuisances to humans. Only about one-tenth of all snakes are venomous, and not all of the venomous snakes are dangerous, or even deadly, to humans. Most snakes are completely harmless. And poisonous snakes do not hunt people; they bite when they are handled, stepped on, or otherwise disturbed. Their venom is most often used on their prey, not on people.

There are about 20 species of poisonous snakes in the United States, mostly rattlesnakes, cottonmouths (also called water moccasins), coral snakes, and copperheads. Many venomous snakes (with coral snakes as one exception) are categorized as pit vipers because they have pits on their heads between their eyes and nostrils. These pits help the snakes detect heat, making it easier for them to locate prey. Most venomous snake bites are treatable and don't result in any lasting problems. The deaths that do occur from snake venom frequently happen because the person was unable to get to a hospital soon enough. If a snake bite occurs, try to get to a hospital as soon as possible. In the meantime, a bandage can be wrapped lightly around the area just above the bite, and the limb where the bite occurred should be moved as little as possible.

How do snakes make venom?

Snakes make venom in glands like those used for making saliva. These glands are located at the back of the snake's head, and the venom travels through ducts, or tubes, to the fangs. Different kinds of venom damage different parts of the snake's prey: some venoms affect the heart, some attack the nervous system, and some work to digest the prey, making it easier for the snake to swallow it.

Why don't **predators of poisonous snakes** die from eating venom?

When animals that feed on poisonous snakes eat their prey, they also eat the venom that snake has stored up. But this venom that would kill other animals does not kill the snake's predator. Why? Because these predators have a built-in resistance to the venom of the snakes they eat. An opossum can eat a rattlesnake, venom and all, and only suffer a mild reaction. The same amount of venom that goes into the opossum's stomach would be enough to kill a horse.

Why do some snakes **"rattle"**?

Scientists believe that rattlesnakes shake the rattles at the end of their tales as a warning of their presence. Snakes would rather warn potential enemies away than get involved in a fight, and most creatures familiar with rattlesnakes would probably rather flee than tangle with a rattler. Rattlesnakes might also shake their rattles to attract small birds that could mistake the rattling for a buzzing insect and swoop down for a bug snack, only to be caught themselves by the snake.

The rattle is a series of small, hard segments made of dried skin. Each time the rattlesnake sheds its skin, or molts, another segment is added. In its first few years of life, a rattlesnake may molt three or four times a year; in adulthood, rattlesnakes molt

163

less often. Counting the rattles is not an accurate measure of a snake's age because it's common for some of the rattle segments to break off. Most adult rattlesnakes have between six and ten rattle segments.

Why do snakes always **stick out their tongues**?

Although a snake's forked tongue darting constantly in and out of its mouth can look scary, it is actually quite harmless. Snakes repeatedly stick out their tongues not because they're rude, but because they are using their tongues to gather information. Snakes have an organ located on the roof of their mouths called Jacobson's organ. This organ processes tiny amounts of chemical substances that are picked up by the snake's flicking tongue. Each time the tongue goes out of the snake's mouth, it picks up chemicals from the air. The snake then inserts the tips of its delicate forked tongue into the two openings of Jacobson's organ, which can analyze the chemicals to tell if a nearby animal is potential food, or perhaps an enemy.

Male snakes also use their tongues as part of a courting ritual, that is, the process by which they figure out if a certain female snake is interested in mating with them. The male snake jerks his body around, snapping his tongue in and out, and if the female ignores him, he knows to keep looking for a suitable partner. If she responds favorably, he's found his mate.

Do snakes have **bones** in their bodies?

Snakes have such flexible and winding bodies, it seems strange to think that they have bones under those scales. Snakes do not have any arms or legs, but they do have bones in their skull, and they have a long backbone. The backbone is made up of vertebrae (plural of vertebra), the segments that make up the spinal column in all vertebrates, and a pair of ribs is attached to each vertebra above the tail section. Therefore, very long snakes have more vertebrae, and more ribs, than any other kind of animal; some snakes have more than 400 vertebrae (people have 12). The way the vertebrae fit together allows for swiveling flexibility in both side-to-side and up-and-down motions, allowing the snake to move the way it does without straining its skeleton.

How can snakes **swallow** animals larger than their own bodies?

Snakes do not always eat animals whose bodies are wider than their own, but they are certainly capable of it. And because they swallow their prey whole without bothering to chew it up first, they need to be equipped with special characteristics for getting food to their stomachs. First of all, snakes have unique jaws. The lower jawbone is only loosely connected to the upper jaw, and the lower jaw is made up of two bones that are connected by an elastic, or stretchy, tissue. So the snake can open its mouth very wide (several times as big as its own head), accommodating a relatively large ani-

Snakes use their tongues to pick up chemicals from the air that provide lots of information about the world around them.
Robert J. Huffman/Field Mark Publications © 2001

mal. Also, the two sides of a snake's jaw move separately from one another. The snake sinks its fangs, which are curved backward, into its prey; it moves first one side of the jaw backward and then the next, gradually pulling the prey into its mouth.

It can take a snake 30 minutes to an hour to swallow an animal. During that time, its trachea, or windpipe, gets pushed forward, out of its mouth, so the snake can continue to breathe during the long swallowing process. The snake's flexible ribs then expand to allow the body to widen as the food makes its way to the stomach and intestines. Given that eating is such a time-consuming and body-expanding process, it is perhaps fortunate that a snake doesn't need to eat very often. Snakes may eat once a week or once a month, and some large snakes in captivity have been known to go several months between meals. During colder seasons, snakes are dormant, or inactive, and can go much longer than usual without eating.

How do **boa constrictors** kill their prey?

Injecting animals with venom is not the only method used by snakes to control their prey. One group of snakes, called the constrictors, do not produce venom but are every bit as deadly to the animals they hunt. The constrictors, including boa constrictors and pythons, use the powerful muscles in their bodies to squeeze the life out of their prey. They coil themselves around the animal they've caught, squeezing until its blood can no longer circulate. Boa constrictors eat mostly birds and mice, and

165

they can grow to be around 14 feet (4.3 meters) long. The female boa is among the few snakes whose young develop within her body; she gives birth to live snakes, perhaps as many as 50 at one time. Pythons, which live in parts of Asia, Africa, and Australia, are among the biggest snakes in the world, with the larger species getting as long as 30 feet (9 meters).

Why do snakes **shed their skins**?

Snakes grow rapidly when they are young, and they continue to grow throughout their lives. Their skin does not grow along with them, however, so they must shed their outer covering regularly, replacing it with a new, larger skin. Additionally, the scales covering a snake's body occasionally get damaged or wear out. All animals produce new cells to replace old, worn-out parts of their outer covering. For snakes, the replacement process does not happen bit by bit, but all at once, in a process called molting, or shedding.

When the new skin is ready, the outer layer begins to loosen. The snake's eyes turn a milky blue color because the skin covering the eye cap has loosened. To help get the molting started, the snake may rub its head against a rock, pulling the skin loose from its head. It then crawls completely out of its old skin, turning it inside-out in the process and revealing its brand-new skin. The new skin has the exact same pattern of scales as the old. Snakes shed more when they are young and growing quickly than when they get older, but on average a snake will molt between two and four times a year.

Which snake is the **biggest**?

It depends on how the snake is measured. Many people believe that the giant, or green, anaconda is the largest overall—thickest and heaviest—while the reticulated python is the longest. Either way, these are both extremely large snakes. The anaconda, which lives near water in tropical regions of South America, commonly grows to be about 16 feet (5 meters) long. But these snakes have been known to get as long as 30 feet (9 meters), and they can weigh several hundred pounds. They capture prey by lying in the water at night, waiting for animals to come to the water's edge for a drink. Anacondas belong to the group of snakes known as constrictors, meaning they squeeze their prey to death rather than using venom. While they will sometimes capture animals as large as deer when in search of a meal, anacondas are typically not very aggressive in the wild.

Pythons are also nonvenomous constrictors. The reticulated python, one of about 25 species of pythons, is thought to be the longest snake in the world. It often grows to be about 26 feet (8 meters) long, though longer specimens have been recorded. The *Guinness Book of World Records* notes that the longest snake ever measured was a reticulated python that was around 33 feet (10 meters) long. Pythons frequently live near cities and can often be found by riverbanks. They live in many regions of the world, including Africa, India, southeastern Asia, and Australia. Unlike anacondas, pythons have a reputation for being vicious, though they don't usually bother humans unless the humans are bothering them.

Which lizard is the biggest?

The Komodo dragon, part of the monitor family of lizards, is the largest living lizard. It can grow to be 10 feet (3 meters) long, and it can weigh up to 300 pounds (136 kilograms). The Komodo dragon has been known to attack and kill humans, and sometimes it will even eat members of its own species. But generally its diet consists of carrion, which is the flesh of animals that are already dead. Found on Komodo Island in Indonesia, this lizard has been popular with collectors of rare and exotic animals, and because of that the Komodo dragon is nearly extinct. The Komodo dragon is now protected by laws that prohibit people from hunting or capturing it.

What is the **smallest** lizard?

Geckos (sometimes spelled gekkos) are the smallest types of lizards. They are only about one inch (three centimeters) long. Geckos got their name from the frequent chirping and clicking noises they make (most reptiles don't make any noise at all). They like warm climates, and, unlike many other reptiles, they frequently live peacefully among humans—probably because they are harmless, they are less threatening because of their small size, and their insect diet is helpful to humans. The tiny, hairlike coverings on their flattened feet make geckos extraordinary climbers. They are able to grip even very smooth surfaces, and they can climb straight up walls and even walk across ceilings.

Are there any **poisonous** lizards?

Two lizards are known to inject venom into their prey: the Gila (pronounced HEE-luh) monster and the Mexican beaded lizard. The Gila, found in northern Mexico and the southwestern United States, produces venom that is secreted into grooves in their teeth; when they bite into their prey, the venom gets into the other animal's blood. Around 20 inches (50 centimeters) long, Gila monsters eat small mammals and birds as well as eggs. They have been known to bite people, but while their bites may be painful, they rarely cause serious harm to humans. The Mexican beaded lizard, a close relative to the Gila, can be a bit larger (around 31 inches, or 80 centimeters). It lives throughout much of Mexico and parts of Central America. Both of these lizards, during seasons when food is hard to find, can live for months off fat stored in their tails.

167

Do any lizards live in **water**?

Lizards need to breathe air, so there are no living species that live in water all of the time. Several species of lizards can and do swim, spending part of their lives in the water looking for various freshwater organisms to eat. Only one species, the marine iguana of the Galápagos Islands, is known to get its food from salty seawater. It eats seaweed and algae, and some marine iguanas have been known to dive underwater in search of food for periods of up to half an hour. As they eat, marine iguanas naturally swallow lots of saltwater, but they are able to remove the salt from their bodies because they, like all iguanas, have salt glands between their eyes and nostrils. These glands concentrate and remove the salt, depositing it in the iguana's nostril. The lizard then gets rid of the salt by "sneezing." The resulting bit of salt that shoots out of the iguana's nostril is used to scare off potential enemies.

How is an **alligator** different from a **crocodile**?

Alligators and crocodiles share many similarities and are close relatives, both belonging to the order Crocodilia. Some distinguishing features can help in telling them apart, however. Alligators usually have broader, flatter, rounder snouts than crocodiles; crocodile snouts are narrow and V-shaped. Both have extremely powerful jaws, but the wider jaw of the alligator has the edge. Another difference can be seen in the way their jaws fit together. In alligators, the upper jaw is wider than the lower jaw, so when their mouths are closed, the upper teeth can be seen outside the mouth, while the lower teeth are almost completely hidden. Crocodiles' upper and lower jaws are about the same width, so when their mouths are closed, their teeth (also visible outside the mouth) interlock. The crocodile's large fourth tooth on the bottom is especially noticeable.

Both animals tend to prefer freshwater environments, but crocodiles have a higher tolerance for saltwater than alligators because they have salt glands on their tongues that help them get rid of excess salt. Crocodile skin also looks different from alligator skin because crocodiles have small black specks all over their bodies, while alligators have them only around their jaws. These dots are special sensory pits that help the animals detect the presence of prey and sense changes in water pressure. Crocodiles are thought to be more aggressive than alligators, and while that is true for some species, there are several different kinds of both animals, and there are many behavioral differences among them.

Why are crocodiles and alligators such **good hunters**?

One advantage crocodiles and alligators have over their enemies and prey is that they can grow to be fairly large. Alligators can be as big as 19 feet (almost 6 meters), and crocodiles, considered the largest and heaviest living reptiles, can be slightly bigger.

Crocodiles, like the one pictured above, share many similarities with their relatives the alligators.

They have huge, crushing jaws and massive, powerful tails that help them swim and can be used to thrash their opponents. Perhaps their most useful feature as hunters is the positioning of their eyes and nostrils on the top of their heads. This trait allows alligators and crocodiles to keep most of their bodies submerged in the water, hidden from view, while they wait for an animal to come to the water's edge for a drink. The water-loving reptiles can then snatch their prey, pulling the animal into the water to drown it before eating it.

What is a **caiman**?

A caiman (also spelled cayman) is a close relative of the alligator that can be found in Central and South America. Like their crocodilian cousins, caimans live near rivers and other bodies of water. Most caimans are around six or seven feet (two meters) long, but the largest species, the black caiman, can grow to a length of 15 feet (4.5 meters).

How is a **tortoise** different from a **turtle**?

Depending on where you live in the world, the words "turtle" and "tortoise" can be used to mean different things. Generally, in the United States, the word "turtle" is used to describe all members of the order Chelonia, the reptiles characterized by the shell that covers their bodies—those that live on land, in the sea, and in freshwater.

"Tortoise" refers specifically to the group of turtles that live on land. In other words, all tortoises are turtles, but not all turtles are tortoises.

Turtles look like ancient and primitive animals because that's what they are: they have survived relatively unchanged for hundreds of millions of years, thanks in large part to their hard, protective shells. Turtles can pull their arms, legs, tail, and head completely inside their shells, which in some species are strong enough to support a weight 200 times greater than their own. Not only have turtle species survived an incredibly long time, but individual turtles also have a longer life span than any other vertebrate, with some being known to live longer than 150 years.

Turtles are legendary for their slow movement, particularly the lumbering tortoises that have been clocked at a pace of less than one-third of a mile (about half a kilometer) per hour. Turtles don't have teeth, but many types do have sharp, horny beaks that they can use to chew food. Most tortoises eat small, soft invertebrates like worms, slugs, and insects, while water-living turtles eat fish and even some small birds and mammals. Turtles come in a huge range of sizes. Smaller species weigh less than a pound (454 grams) and reach only about 5 inches (12.5 centimeters) in length. The largest tortoises have shells just under 3 feet (1 meter) long, weighing more than 500 pounds (225 kilograms). The Atlantic leatherback, the largest of the sea turtles, can reach 7 feet (2.1 meters) in length and weigh around 1,200 pounds (540 kilograms).

Can a turtle **climb out** of its shell?

A turtle can no more climb out of its shell than a person can remove his or her backbone. The turtle's shell is fused, or attached, to its backbone, ribs, and parts of its shoulder and hip bones. If an empty turtle shell is found, it means that turtle has died, and its shell is all that remains.

AMPHIBIANS

What is an **amphibian**?

Amphibians are cold-blooded vertebrates that spend part of their lives in bodies of water (or watery places) and part on land. The name comes from the Greek word *amphibios,* which means "living a double life." This class includes frogs and toads, salamanders, and caecilians, which look like large earthworms. Amphibians start out as eggs that are usually laid and hatched in water or moist ground, and the early stage of most amphibians' lives are spent in the water. Baby amphibians, called larvae, don't resemble the adults at all. As they mature, they go through major changes, called a metamorphosis. Adult amphibians usually live on land, never straying far from the water and returning to it when it's time to breed. Frogs and toads, for example, emerge from their eggs as tadpoles (sometimes called polliwogs), little creatures with a rounded head and a tail. They have gills for breathing in water and cannot survive on land. Over time, the gills become air-breathing lungs, the tail disappears, and limbs develop. Adult frogs and toads may spend a good amount of time in and around water, but they need air in order to breathe.

Not every amphibian follows the usual pattern of spending the larval stage in water and the adult stage on land. As with every part of the animal kingdom, there are some creatures that don't fit the mold. For instance, some tree frogs living in tropical regions never leave their leafy homes. Their eggs must be kept moist, however, so the female frogs lay them in the drops of water that gather on the tree's leaves after a rain.

For the most part amphibians are fairly small creatures, with most being only a few inches long. The smallest frog in the world is no bigger than a person's thumbnail. The largest amphibian is the Chinese giant salamander, which can be around 5 feet (1.5 meters) long. Amphibians do not have scales, plates, or fur—their skin is usually smooth (with some toads being notable exceptions) and moist. In addition to breathing through their lungs, amphibians breathe through their skin, and that moistness is necessary for them to do so. To make sure their skin stays moist, amphibians secrete a fluid that spreads over their skin and locks in moisture.

How is a **frog** different from a **toad**?

Frogs and toads have many features in common, but there are a couple ways to tell them apart. In general, frogs spend more time in the water, while toads spend more time exploring land. Frogs have smooth, moist skin, while toads' skin is generally bumpy. Toads get around by walking and hopping, while frogs, which generally have longer legs, do more leaping. Frogs' feet are more fully webbed than toads', and their legs are usually longer.

Frogs and toads make up the order Anura, and within that order there are almost 25 families of frogs. The toads in the family Bufonidae are called "true toads," while the frogs in the family Ranidae are called "true frogs." The hundreds of other types of anurans in the remaining families are commonly described as frogs if they resemble the Ranidae and toads if they resemble Bufonidae. This rather unscientific method of describing these animals sometimes means that one animal from a particular family is called a toad while a close relative from the same family is called a frog. Sometimes, since there is no commonly used word that refers to frogs and toads together, scientists will simply use the word "frog" to cover both types of animals.

There are about 3,800 species of frogs and toads, and they come in many different shapes, sizes, and colors. The smallest, a Brazilian frog, measures no more than .39

inches (around 10 millimeters) in length, while the goliath frog from West Africa is almost 12 inches (30 centimeters) long.

Is the **horned toad** really a toad?

In spite of its name, the horned toad (also called horny toad) is not a toad, or even an amphibian. The horned toad is actually a lizard (and therefore a reptile), also known, more accurately, as the horned lizard. It lives in dry, sandy regions in western North America, where it burrows itself up to its head in sand. This animal has a very specialized diet, eating mostly ants, and unusual ways of defending itself from predators: the horned toad can puff itself up to a larger size by sucking in air, and in rare cases, the horned toad has been known to shoot blood out of its eyes to frighten attackers.

How do frogs **croak**?

Frogs croak for the same reason that many animals make noises: to track down and then select a mate. Scientists have discovered that females can recognize the sounds made by their own species, so they don't waste their time seeking out a male that they wouldn't be able to breed with. Frogs can make their croaking noises because they have simple vocal cords consisting of two slits in the bottom of the mouth. These slits open into what is called a vocal pouch. When air passes from the lungs through the vocal cords, a sound is produced. The inflating and deflating vocal pouch makes the sound louder or quieter. That sound changes depending on the kind of frog—there are as many different kinds of croaks as there are frogs.

Can you get warts from touching a toad?

Warts are caused by a virus and have nothing to do with touching a toad. This myth may have come from the fact that most toads have wartlike growths on their skin, and people may have thought that those "warts" were contagious. In fact they are not warts but glands, some of which are responsible for producing the fluid that toads use to help keep their skin moist. Some of those other bumpy glands produce a toxic liquid that tastes horrible and deters other animals from eating the toad. This liquid can be irritating to human skin, so it is best to wash your hands with soap after holding a toad (or any wild animal, for that matter).

What is a **salamander**?

A salamander is an amphibian that usually has four legs and a tail that is almost as long as its body. There are hundreds of different types of salamanders, including newts, mud puppies, and hellbenders. Like other amphibians, salamanders hatch from eggs laid in water or moist areas. They then go through a larval (youth) stage as aquatic creatures with gills, eventually metamorphosing, or changing, into air-breathing adults that live on land. Some salamander species, like the mud puppy, keep their gills in adulthood.

Some types of newts, after graduating from aquatic larvae to land-dwelling adults (at which point they are called "efts"), will spend a couple years on land only to return to water permanently. They continue to breathe through lungs (and through their skin), but they spend the rest of their days living in the water.

BIRDS

How do birds **fly**?

Birds have one major feature that distinguishes them from all other animals: feathers. These strong but lightweight feathers, in combination with the structure of their bodies, allow birds to fly with amazing skill and speed. Many birds have hollow bones, making their bodies very lightweight, and the muscles that move their wings are extremely powerful. Birds fly, basically, by flapping their wings and using their tails to steer. A bird's wing is a very complicated instrument that can be adjusted in many different ways to control the flight's speed, angle, height, and direction. The wider base of the wing, the part closer to the bird's body, gives it support, while the tip of the wing propels the bird forward. The way the bird's body is built, particularly the shape and structure of the wing, determines the way the bird flies. Some fly at high altitudes, while others stay low to the ground. Some fly quickly with small, rapid wing movements, others flap their wings slowly but powerfully.

Can **all birds** fly?

All birds have wings, but not all of them can fly. Scientists believe that all birds could, at some point in their evolution, fly, but that some have lost the ability over millions of years. Some of the best-known examples of flightless birds are penguins and ostriches (and ostrich relatives like emus and kiwis). One of the primary benefits of flight is being able to escape enemies quickly; flightless birds must rely on other techniques to save themselves. Penguins have made up for their flightlessness by being outstanding swimmers (they use their wings as flippers). Ostriches can use their great size to scare away many predators, and if that doesn't work, they always have their legs. Ostriches can run at speeds of 40 miles (65 kilometers) per hour, and if the attacker does manage to get close, the ostrich might just give a powerful kick.

Scientists think that some birds lose the ability to fly (over the course of many generations) when they live in isolated regions where they don't have predators. The

A bird's wings control the speed, angle, height, and direction of flight. *Robert J. Huffman/Field Mark Publications © 2001*

great auk, which is now extinct, inhabited an island where flight was unnecessary because there were no mammal predators present. Therefore, from lack of use, the great auk's wings became useless over time. Other birds in the same family as the great auk that live in regions populated by predators have never lost the ability to fly.

How **high** can birds fly?

In their regular, everyday lives, most birds fly below 500 feet (150 meters), while during migration many birds fly at an altitude of around 10,000 feet (3,000 meters). Some extraordinary birds have been spotted flying as high as 29,000 feet (8,700 meters). That's more than five miles (and nearly nine kilometers) off the ground. Bar-headed geese were seen at that altitude flying over the Himalayas, and an airline pilot spotted whooper swans at that height over Northern Ireland. Migrating birds know not only what direction to fly in, but how best to get there. They seek the altitude that allows them to fly most efficiently, rising high where the wind is fastest when it's behind them, and staying low to use trees and buildings to block the wind when it's coming at them.

How **fast** can birds fly?

There is great variation in flight speeds among the nearly 8,000 species of birds. Small songbirds like wrens and sparrows fly 10 to 20 miles (16 to 32 kilometers) per hour, while ducks, geese, and pigeons can fly at speeds up to 60 miles (97 kilometers) per hour. Some birds, like the peregrine falcon and golden eagle, have been timed diving at speeds exceeding 170 miles (274 kilometers) per hour.

Scientists have had a hard time measuring how fast a bird can fly, due in part to the variable effects of wind. A strong wind at a bird's back can help it fly much faster, while flying directly into a wind can slow the bird down considerably.

How **far** can birds fly?

Some birds go very short distances in their migrations. The blue grouse, for example, lives in the mountains in North America and flies less than a mile down to lower, warmer altitudes for the winter months. That's one extreme. Another extreme are the long-distance fliers like the Arctic terns. These birds hold the distance record for flight; they've been known to fly from their summer home in the Arctic to a winter spot in the Antarctic, covering distances of around 10,000 miles (16,100 kilometers). And in the spring they go back the other way. The long-tailed jaeger flies more than 5,000 miles (8,050 kilometers) in each direction of its migratory flight. And even the tiny barn swallow has been known to cover 6,000 miles (9,660 kilometers) round-trip.

Why do birds **migrate**?

Many species of birds spend part of the year the warmer months—in northern regions, and then migrate south when the weather starts to get cold. Birds follow this southward path primarily in search of an abundant, accessible food supply. Birds use up the energy they get from food very quickly, and they need to eat often. So when the ground begins to freeze and food supplies (particularly insects) are harder to find, many birds head south. (Birds that spend a lot of time in water—ducks and geese, for example—have an additional reason to migrate: the northern lakes and ponds where they live freeze over in the winter.) Migrating birds spend the winter months in the warmer, southern climate, and as spring returns to the north, so do migrating birds.

How do birds know when it's **time to migrate**?

Scientists believe that in some species, young migrating birds learn when and how to migrate from the older birds in the flock. Experts have also noted that changes in the temperature and amount of daylight seem to trigger a migrating impulse in birds. As the days get shorter and the amount of sunlight decreases in the autumn, migrating birds begin to produce hormones. These hormones cause the birds to store up more fat in their bodies, fat that can be converted into energy to help sustain them on their long flights. As the time for migrating approaches, birds display signs of restlessness. Some people have even observed such restlessness among captive birds, which have a steady food supply and little contact with outside temperatures and sunlight.

175

How do migrating birds know how to **navigate**?

Twice a year, migrating birds vacate their homes to travel hundreds and sometimes thousands of miles—over land and over sea—to a new residence. Some migratory birds travel to the same exact place year after year, and some are even so punctual as to arrive at the same time year after year. How do they know how to do that? Scientists have studied migratory patterns of many different species, and they have developed theories as to how birds can find their way, but ultimately, they don't know for sure what techniques birds use. Birds might use the stars and the Moon to guide their way, or they may have a sort of internal compass that helps them detect Earth's magnetic field (thereby showing them which way is north). Some birds may also be able to detect low-level sounds made by ocean waves, sounds that can provide clues about direction. Perhaps many birds are capable of using more than one navigational technique; if not, the birds that use the stars to find their way would be lost on cloudy nights.

What are **feathers** made of?

Birds have many different kinds of feathers, each of which performs a different function. Some feathers (the small, soft down used in pillows and winter jackets) are designed to keep the bird warm, others are specifically used for flight, while some feathers are pure decoration, intended to help the bird find a mate. Feathers consist of a shaft in the middle with pairs of branches, called barbs, attached. The surface formed by the barbs is called the vane. On the feathers of some birds, the barbs in turn have smaller branches called barbules. The barbules from one barb connect to those of the barb next to it by little hooks, making the feather stiffer and stronger.

Before the invention of the modern ink pen, people filled the hollow shafts of feathers, called quills, with ink and used them as writing instruments. In societies all over the world, people have also used feathers to decorate clothing or hats, or to make garments worn during important ceremonies.

Why are male birds **more colorful** than female birds?

In some species, like the North American cardinal, the male bird has brilliantly colored feathers while the female's feathers are drab and dark. One reason the males have a more colorful appearance is so they can capture the attention of the female bird they wish to mate with. The male's bright colors also come in handy after mating, when he's protecting the nest and sending a clear signal to other males to keep away from his territory. The female's dull colors, on the other hand, help her blend in with the branches surrounding her nest and avoid being seen by enemies. If her feathers were bright like the male's, she would be easily spotted by predators, and she would have to leave her nest unprotected if attacked.

The male ostrich can grow to be nearly 8 feet (2.5 meters) tall. *Robert J. Huffman/Field Mark Publications © 2001*

Will wild birds **reject their babies** if people touch them?

Many people believe that if a person touches a wild baby bird to put it back in the nest, the bird's parents will be able to detect the human scent and will then reject the baby, pushing it right back out of the nest. This widely held belief is simply not true. If a baby bird is found on the ground and appears to be able to fly, leave it alone and trust that it will find its way back to the family nest. If it clearly cannot fly, and you know where its nest is, pick it up gently and place it back in the nest. If the nest can't be found, some experts suggest putting the baby bird in a small basket and hanging it on a nearby bush or tree. The bird's parents will care for it in the basket until it is able to fly.

What is the **largest** bird?

The ostrich is the largest living bird (some extinct species were larger). Found primarily in Africa, the male ostrich can grow to be nearly 8 feet (2.5 meters) tall, with its neck making up almost half of its height (females are a bit smaller). Ostriches can weigh almost 350 pounds (159 kilograms). These flightless birds travel in groups and can frequently be found in the company of other grazing animals. People have harvested ostrich feathers for hundreds of years to decorate hats and other items, and in recent years ostrich meat has become more popular.

Which bird lays the **largest eggs**?

The largest eggs, not surprisingly, are laid by the largest bird, which is the ostrich. An ostrich egg averages around 6 inches (150 millimeters) in length and around 5 inches (125 millimeters) in diameter. It weighs about 3 pounds (1.35 kilograms). A male ostrich mates with several females during one mating season, and all of those females lay their eggs in one large nest, which can contain several dozen eggs at one time. Over the course of the 40 days it takes the eggs to hatch, the male sits on the nest at night, and the females take turns during the day.

Do ostriches really **bury their heads** in sand?

This supposed ostrich behavior has been referred to countless times in warning people not to "bury their heads in the sand" and ignore their problems, but the fact is that ostriches do not bury their heads in sand when danger approaches. They kick up their heels and run. Sometimes, to avoid being seen by nearby predators, the very tall ostrich will lie down and stretch its neck out on the ground. This behavior may have been spotted—and misunderstood—by people who began the tale of an ostrich burying its head in the sand. Ostriches also occasionally nibble on small pebbles or sand, a behavior that may give an observer the impression that they are trying to burrow into the sand.

Which bird has the **largest wings**?

The largest measured wingspan belongs to the wandering albatross, a large seabird that can be seen gliding over southern oceans. When spread, its wings can measure nearly 12 feet (3.6 meters). Their long, narrow wings allow them to fly great distances with minimal effort: albatrosses can glide for several hours without flapping their wings once. Their gliding ability helps them save energy, which comes in handy when they have to fly hundreds of miles in one trip to find food for a just-hatched baby. Albatrosses only come to shore for breeding, and they are unusual among birds in that the female only lays one egg each year. (Most birds lay several eggs a year—ducks can lay around 10 eggs at a time, for example.) Baby albatrosses require a lot of care from their parents: it can take them almost a year to grow the feathers they need for flying, and during that time the parents must search far and wide to get food for the whole family.

Albatrosses eat fish and squid, and sometimes they follow boats, looking for food scraps. At one time sailors believed that killing an albatross brought bad luck, an idea explored in the famous poem by Samuel Taylor Coleridge, "The Rime of the Ancient Mariner." Others ignored that superstition, catching the birds on baited fish hooks for their meat and feathers.

What is the **smallest bird**?

The smallest living bird is the bee hummingbird. Including its beak and tail, this bird measures only about 2 inches (5.5 centimeters) and weighs about two-thirds of an ounce (20 grams). The more than 300 species of beautiful, brightly colored hummingbirds live throughout North and South America. They can flap their wings at amazing speeds—the smaller species beat their wings from 60 to 80 times *per second*—and they are the only birds who can fly upside-down. The special structure of their wings also enables them to fly backwards, sideways, and straight up and down. Hummingbirds get their food by hovering over plants and inserting their long, thin beaks into flowers to get the nectar (and insects) inside. Some can hover for close to an hour at a time. Like bees and other nectar-eating creatures, hummingbirds help to spread pollen, the dusty grains that allow fertilization in plants. The pollen clings to their feathers when they come in contact with the male parts of a flower and gets deposited in another plant's female parts, thus helping to produce new plants. Because of their unusually small size, often brilliantly colored feathers, and extraordinary methods of flying, hummingbirds are favorites with birdwatchers.

The hummingbird's hum is created by its rapidly flapping wings. *Robert J. Huffman/Field Mark Publications © 2001*

Why do hummingbirds **hum**?

The joke answer: Because they don't know the words. The real answer: Hummingbirds' wings flap so quickly that they create a high-pitched humming sound, just as mosquitoes and other insects generate a buzzing sound from their high-speed wing-flapping.

Why do birds **sing**?

Just as people talk to each other to accomplish a number of different things, so do birds sing for a variety of reasons. Perhaps the primary reason birds sing (and squawk, call, or chirp) is to attract or communicate with a possible mate. Once a mate has been chosen, the male bird sings to announce his choice and warn other males away from his mate. If approached by a hostile male, a bird might make threatening noises

179

Birds chirp and sing mainly to attract mates and warn of predators, but sometimes they sing just because they can. *Robert J. Huffman/Field Mark Publications © 2001*

to scare his opponent away without having to fight. Birds also call to other birds to alert them to a good food source, or warn them that a predator is coming. Baby birds sing to let their parents know they are hungry. And sometimes birds sing for no apparent reason, just because they can.

There is an actual scientific category of birds called songbirds. It includes several thousand species—nearly half of all bird types—and covers larks, swallows, and most birds that people keep as pets. Not all songbirds have pretty voices (like the harsh-voiced crow, for example), and some sing very rarely. On the other hand, some birds that are not classified as songbirds have beautiful songs. A bird is classified as a songbird because it has special voice-producing organs, not necessarily because it produces the most lovely song.

Why do **woodpeckers** make such a racket?

Most woodpeckers spend most of their lives in trees. But instead of perching on a branch, woodpeckers spend their days climbing up the tree in a spiral pattern, searching for insects to eat (some also eat berries and fruit, and others, called the sapsuckers, eat tree sap). They find insects by repeatedly and rapidly pecking at tree bark with their sharp bills, an action that produces the telltale hammering noise. Woodpeckers have long, thin tongues that they use to reach into the holes they've created and pull out insects. Woodpeckers also peck at trees to carve out holes they can use for nests. Male woodpeckers make such tapping noises to attract a mate and to tell other males where their territory is (and to keep away from it). Woodpeckers have thick, strong skulls that protect their brains and other organs from the stress of their repeated pecking.

How do **penguins** keep their eggs warm?

Some penguins lay their eggs in nests like other birds. The emperor and king penguins, however, have an unusual method of keeping their eggs warm. While the female makes a long trek from the penguin colony to the water in search of food, the male places the egg on top of his feet, where it can nestle up against his warm body. For this entire incubation period, the male penguin carefully balances the egg on his feet, living off stored fat while he is unable go find food. When a storm hits, all of the male penguins huddle together into a circle to provide some protection from high winds. After the egg hatches, the parent must continue holding it

Countershading helps animals like this penguin blend in with their surroundings. *Robert J. Huffman/Field Mark Publications © 2001*

on its feet because the baby doesn't have enough insulating feathers, or down, to keep it warm on its own. When it's old enough, the baby penguin joins a large group of other babies. A few adults stand guard over the little ones while their parents seek food; when the parents return to the colony, they call to their chick. The parents can recognize their baby among the dozens of others by its appearance and its distinctive voice.

Why are penguins **black and white**?

The trademark tuxedolike coloring of penguins, with their black backs and white fronts, is called countershading. This kind of coloration is found in many fish and

181

other aquatic animals that swim close to the surface because it helps hide them from sight in the water. When viewed from below, the white-bellied penguin blends in with the lighter appearance of water near the surface; when seen from above, the penguin's black back can't be distinguished from the dark depths of the sea.

Why does a flamingo **stand on one leg**?

Scientists don't know for sure why flamingos stand on one leg at a time, sometimes for several hours, but they have several theories. Some people believe that flamingos lift up one leg so they are less visible to their prey; standing on one leg, they may resemble a tree to the aquatic creatures they are hunting. During cooler weather, bringing one leg up close to the body can help conserve heat. Some have suggested that standing first on one leg and then the other helps promote the circulation of blood down flamingos' long, skinny legs. Flamingos can even sleep while standing on one leg, and some scientists think there is a connection between their one-legged position and the way their brains function during sleep: one-half of their bodies (and brains) can sleep while the other half, including the leg they stand on, remains somewhat alert.

Why do flamingos' knees **bend the other way**?

If you've seen flamingos (and some other long-legged birds, like cranes), you've probably noticed that, when they walk, their legs bend in the opposite direction of human legs. How can their knees bend that way? The answer is, they don't. What appear to be flamingos' knees are actually their ankles. Their knees are up closer to their bodies, hidden by feathers, and they are actually standing on their toes.

How does a vulture **find its food**?

Most vultures dine on such appealing items as garbage and carrion, or the flesh of dead animals. They soar high above the ground on their large, wide wings for hours at a time, searching for a food source. Scientists aren't sure how they know where the carrion is, but they suspect it may be a combination of sight and smell. Turkey vultures, common in North America, have a well-developed sense of smell, though scientists aren't sure how they could smell their food from such lofty heights. It's more likely that they rely on their vision to spot animal carcasses, or to find other scavengers that have already located a feeding site. While the idea of an animal eating garbage and carrion may be disgusting, it is actually a very beneficial practice. Vultures and other scavengers perform a valuable service, cleaning up carcasses that would otherwise take a long time to decompose.

Owls have special eyes that help them see with very little light. *Robert J. Huffman/Field Mark Publications © 2001*

How can an owl **see at night**?

Most owls are nocturnal hunters, meaning they are active at night rather than during the day. Their large eyes have special features that allow them to see well even on very dark nights. An owl's retina, the part of the eye that controls sensitivity to light, is equipped with a certain kind of cell that gives the owl excellent vision even when there is very little light. While many animals can move their eyes without moving their heads, owls' eyes are practically immovable. They make up for this limitation by having extremely flexible necks: owls can turn their necks more than 180 degrees, meaning they can look directly behind them. There is a popular misconception that owls are blinded by bright light. In fact, their pupils can act just like people's pupils do, reducing to a very small size in bright light in order to protect the retina. Not only can owls see in bright daylight, but they actually have better vision in that kind of light than do people.

MAMMALS

What is a **mammal**?

A mammal is an animal that belongs to the highest class of vertebrates. A vertebrate is an animal that has a backbone and a spinal cord; the other types of vertebrates are birds, reptiles, amphibians, and fish. Human beings are mammals.

All female mammals give birth to live young, with the exception of the platypus duck and the spiny anteater, which reproduce by laying eggs. But regardless of how their babies are born, all female mammals nurse their young with milk, which they produce from mammary glands. A mammal is warm-blooded, which means that its body temperature is internally regulated and constant, and does not change with different surroundings. Most mammals are covered—either partially or completely—with hair or fur, as opposed to the scales of reptiles and fish and the feathers of birds. Mammals also share certain features in their bone structure, muscles, and even cells that separate them from other vertebrates.

When we think of wild animals, farm animals, or pets, we usually think of creatures that belong to the mammal class. Chimpanzees, elephants, bears, horses, pigs, dogs and cats, and countless other land animals are all mammals. Some mammals also live in unexpected places: whales and dolphins, for example, are uniquely adapted to spend their lives in the water. They have fishlike, hairless bodies, and their limbs have been modified into flippers. But unlike their fish neighbors, these mammals have air-breathing lungs instead of water-breathing gills. Bats, the only true flying mammals, spend much of their time in the sky. Their wings are made of skin stretched from their very long fingers along the sides of their bodies to their hind legs and tails.

What is the difference between **fur** and **hair**?

While there is some debate about this, most scientists agree that there is no real difference between fur and hair. There are many different kinds of hair—the hair on a dog is different from the hair on a polar bear, which is different from the hair on a person's head. And the hair on a person's head is different from the whiskers on a man's face. But it's all hair. Many fur-covered animals actually have two different kinds of fur: the ground hair, sometimes called secondary hair, which is the dense, soft undercoat of hair, and guard hair, also known as primary hair, which is the longer, coarser outer layer of fur. Ground hair helps the animal maintain its body temperature, while guard hair protects the ground hair from water, snow, or insects. Some animals, like certain kinds of lambs, only have ground hair. And some animals—such as horses, primates (a group that includes people), and some dogs—have only guard hair.

Animal fur has long been used to create clothing for people. At one time, fur outerwear was necessary to protect people from harsh winter weather. In modern times, however, fur coats are a luxury item. Many of the animals whose fur is prized for its beauty and warmth—like minks and foxes—are raised on fur ranches that were set up expressly to produce fur coats to sell.

Do any mammals have **scales**?

Mammals are usually identified by their furry outer layer, but there are some mammals with a hard, scaly covering that makes them look more like reptiles than mammals. The pangolin, which lives in parts of Asia and Africa, is covered with scalelike plates that are actually modified hairs. Pangolins eat mostly ants and termites, foraging with their pointy snouts and their long, wormlike tongues. They protect themselves from predators by rolling themselves into a tight ball and sticking their sharp scales out.

The armadillo is another mammal with an unusual outer layer. Covered in protective, solid plates of armor over most of its body, the armadillo looks like an animal from prehistoric times. These shy, nocturnal animals are more likely to run away from potential enemies than to fight. When threatened, some species can pull their legs underneath their armor like a turtle retreating into its shell, and some armadillos will curl into a protective ball like the pangolin.

Why do some animals carry their young around in **pouches**?

Some mammals, like kangaroos, koalas, and opossums, are called marsupials. When marsupial babies are born, they are incompletely developed. They continue developing outside the womb, in many cases living for a time in a pouch (a large fold of skin called a marsupium) on the mother's body. The marsupium keeps the developing baby warm and close to the mother's nipples, where it can feed around the clock on the milk the mother produces. Most marsupial species are found in and around Australia, but several species, including the opossum, can be found in North and South America.

What does it mean to **"play possum"**?

The opossum (whose name is frequently shortened to "possum") is a small animal that spends a lot of its time in trees looking for food: insects, fruit, small birds or mammals, and eggs. Its teeth and sharp claws help it get the food it needs, but in a contest with a larger predator, the opossum doesn't have many defenses. It does have one fairly effective trick, however: if an opossum is caught off-guard on the ground by a potential enemy, it might pretend to be dead so the predator will leave it alone. (Sometimes this works for the possum, and sometimes it doesn't.) This behavior gave rise to the expression "play possum," which means to pretend to be sleeping or dead to avoid trouble. It can also generally refer to deceptive or dishonest behavior.

Why do porcupines have **quills**?

The porcupine's quills are its best method of defending itself from predators. The sharp quills, which are modified hairs, are all over the porcupine's body, including its tail. When the North American porcupine, the most common species in the Americas, is threatened, it turns its tail toward the approaching animal. If attacked, this porcupine will thrash its predator with its tail, thrusting its quills into the other animal's hide. Often some of the quills will come off the porcupine's tail, and their barbed ends

185

Opossums spend much of their time in trees looking for food. When approached on the ground by a predator, their best defense is playing dead.

(like a fishhook) will stay embedded in the attacker's skin. The average porcupine has around 30,000 quills.

Porcupines are rodents, a group that makes up around half of all mammal species and includes mice, squirrels, and beavers. They are nocturnal, meaning active at night, and they eat tree bark, roots, and other vegetation. Their diet doesn't do much to satisfy their intense salt cravings, so porcupines have been known to chew on things like canoe paddles, animal bones, and even the discarded clothing of humans to get to the salt and oils in these items.

Why do beavers **build dams**?

Beavers have amazing construction and engineering skills; they are among few animals that make dramatic changes to their environment to provide shelter for themselves and their young. Beavers are semiaquatic, which means they spend much of their time in water, usually streams, rivers, and lakes. These hardworking creatures build dams—using sticks, branches, mud, and anything else they can find—to change the course of a stream, sending some of the stream's water to flood another area in order to create a small pond. In that pond they can then build a lodge, a large, domed structure where the beaver family can spend the winter. The lodge is built of the same materials used for the dam.

Beavers use their long, powerful teeth to cut down branches and even whole trees. They then drag or float the wood over to the site of the lodge, sometimes using canals, or narrow passages filled with water, that they built themselves. They pack the sticks together using mud, which freezes in the winter, turning the beaver lodge into a strong fort that predators can't get into. While the lodge itself sticks out above the surface of the water (sometimes nearly six feet, or almost two meters), the entrance to the lodge is underwater, giving the beavers further protection. In the months before winter approaches, beavers begin stockpiling food, including water plants, branches, and leaves. They anchor their food stash in the water just outside the lodge's entrance, so throughout the winter their food supply is nearby.

Beavers have thick, shiny coats that have long been attractive to people in the fur trade. The North American beaver nearly became extinct in the 1930s due to extensive trapping for its fur. Another notable feature of these animals is their broad, flat tails that can be up to a foot long in some larger beavers. Beavers use their tails to steer when they are swimming and to help prop them up when they are standing. They also use them to communicate with other beavers, slapping their tails on the water to produce a loud warning sound when a predator approaches.

Why does a skunk **stink**?

These furry black-and-white animals have a powerful secret weapon. If they feel frightened or threatened by the approach of another animal, they will first give off warning signals, like stamping their feet and, in some types, doing handstands on their front feet. If these warnings don't work, the skunk will spray the attacker with a horrible-smelling, oily liquid produced in glands near its anus. A skunk can shoot this liquid up to 12 feet (3.6 meters), and its powerful odor can be detected more than a mile away.

The foul smell of this liquid can be very difficult to remove from the fur of a cat or dog that has been sprayed. Pet stores sell cleaners especially designed for this problem; bathing the pet in such products as tomato juice or diluted vinegar can also be effective.

Why do raccoons **wash their food** before they eat?

Raccoons have small, slender feet that they use to catch and hold on to their food. Their front feet resemble little hands, and their slender fingers can be used to remove garbage can lids and open containers and even door latches. Raccoons in the wild have often been observed swishing their food through the water of a lake or stream before eating, giving the appearance of washing their food and their hands. Raccoons kept in cages will also wet their food, dipping it into their water bowls.

Scientists are not sure why raccoons exhibit this behavior. At one time they believed raccoons did not have enough saliva and needed to moisten their food before swallowing it. They now know that isn't true. Some believe raccoons might wet their food so they can mush it up a bit to make sure they've removed any sharp sticks or bones. Some have speculated that raccoons have a highly developed sense of touch, and they just like to handle their food in many different ways—putting it in water, rubbing dirt on it—to figure out what it is they are eating. Sometimes raccoons have been seen "washing" food in dirt instead of water, which indicates that this is an instinctive behavior that may not have any purpose at all.

Are bats blind?

The expression "blind as a bat" would indicate that bats are blind, but in fact scientists believe they have fairly good eyesight. Bats are nocturnal creatures, coming out after dark to find insects and other food. Some bats, just like humans, can't see very well in the dark, but they make up for this with a unique navigating system called echolocation. These bats make a series of high-pitched sounds (frequently above the hearing range of humans) that bounce off nearby objects, like rocks, trees, or insects. The echoes of these sounds, when they reach the bat's highly sensitive ears, tell the bat where the object is and even, in the case of insects and other animals, what direction it is moving in.

Do bats really **suck blood**?

There are more than one thousand different kinds of bats. They live all over the world, except in the coldest regions. Most bats eat insects—lots of them—helping to protect food crops and other plant life. Some bats also eat fruit, as well as the nectar of flowers.

There is only one kind of bat that drinks blood; called the vampire bat, it lives in South America, Central America, and Mexico. Vampire bats are pretty small, their bodies only about three inches (eight centimeters) long. They have big pointed ears and sharp teeth, which they use to quietly bite their victims while they are sleeping. In the saliva of the vampire bat is a substance known as an anticoagulant, which keeps the blood from clotting. They often bite livestock—farm animals like horses and cows—and they, like many types of bats, can spread rabies through their bites.

How do whales and other mammals **stay underwater** so long?

All aquatic mammals (meaning those that live in water) have lungs and require air to breathe. Some, like dolphins, live close to the water's surface and come up for air around once or twice a minute. Other sea mammals find their food by diving deep into the ocean, so they must be able to hold their breath for longer periods of time. They can do this because they take in a great deal of air with each breath—their lungs take up a larger percentage of their body than do human lungs. Their bodies can also hold on to the oxygen they've breathed better than human bodies can. Oxygen is required in every part of the body, for every bodily function. But when marine mammals go down for a deep dive, their oxygen is only sent to the most important parts: the heart, brain, and muscles used for swimming. The rest of the body—the stomach, for example—must wait until the dive is finished to get its oxygen.

Human beings can hold their breath under water for an average of one minute. A hippopotamus can stay underwater for 15 minutes. The sperm whale and bottlenose whale can stay underwater the longest: some have been recorded on dives that lasted nearly two hours.

How can mammals that live in the water **sleep**?

Some marine mammals, like seals, climb out of the water to sleep. Others, like whales, cannot leave the water: for one thing, they cannot move on land, and for another, a large whale's body weight would crush its lungs if it were stuck on land. Therefore, many of these animals must sleep while in the water, but they also need to be alert enough to rise to the surface every so often to get a breath of air. Human beings (and many other animals) have an involuntary breathing system, which means that we continue to breathe even when we are sleeping and not conscious of doing so. Scientists suspect that whales and dolphins have voluntary breathing, which means they have to be somewhat alert to bring their blowholes to the surface and open and close them.

In order to rest and yet still be conscious enough to breathe, marine mammals must sleep lightly, many doing so while swimming slowly near the water's surface. When bottlenose dolphins sleep, half of their brain rests while the other half remains alert (and one eye stays open) to detect food or danger signs in the water. After a couple hours, it switches, with the other half resting and the first half staying awake. Sea cows and manatees, which usually live in warm, shallow water, float at the surface when they are resting. If the water is shallow enough, they can rest their bodies on the ocean bottom and keep their heads above water.

Why do whales **blow water up into the air**?

A whale has one or two nostrils or blowholes located far back on the top of its head. (A toothed whale has one, a baleen whale has two.) Whales can only breathe through their blowholes, which are directly connected to their lungs. Their mouths lead only to the stomach. Blowholes have valves that close when a whale dives. A whale may dive as deep as one mile below the ocean surface and stay under water for well over an hour. When a whale returns to the surface it spouts, blowing the warm, moist air that has formed in its lungs out through its blowholes before it takes a fresh breath. The water that has collected on top of the blowholes gets blown into the air along with the whale's breath. Sometimes, the spouting of a large whale can be seen for miles. The type of whale can often be identified by the shape of its spout.

Why do some whales **make sounds** underwater?

With special instruments, people have been able to record the deep sounds that some whales make as they swim underwater. The mellow sounds are so lovely to listen to that they have been recorded on compact discs and tapes and sold in stores! Some whale sounds resemble barking and can be heard by humans. Whales also make clicking sounds that people can only hear with the help of special equipment. Scientists think that whales use these sounds to help them find their way and keep track of one another (whales travel in groups, called pods) as they swim in the deep and often dark ocean. This technique is called echolocation: the vocalizations bounce off objects, creating echoes that return to the whale. (Whales can see fairly well with their small eyes, but their hearing is extraordinary.) Echolocation can tell the whale how big an object is, how far away it is, and in what direction it is traveling.

How is a **porpoise** different from a **dolphin**?

Both porpoises and dolphins are types of whales; they are closely related to one another. Porpoises are usually smaller, 4 to 6 feet (about 1 to 2 meters) long, while dolphins average about 8 feet (2.4 meters) in length. The snout of a porpoise is more rounded, and its teeth are flatter; a dolphin has a long snout and cone-shaped teeth.

Dolphins have long been studied for their intelligence (they are very fast learners), for the enormous variety of sounds that they make to communicate (whistles, clicks, and squeaks), and for the tender way that they care for one another and—sometimes—for human beings. There have been many reports of dolphins saving the lives of people who were drowning or divers who were lost.

The most familiar dolphin species is the bottle-nosed dolphin (most dolphins in aquariums are this type). Like many dolphins, this animal is graceful and very playful. Its snout gives the impression that the dolphin is smiling when its mouth is open. They can often be spotted on the open sea, following ships and playfully leaping out of the water.

Are all dolphins **mammals**?

When we refer to dolphins, we usually mean the mammals that are in the same family with whales and porpoises. But there are some types of fish that are also referred to as dolphins—one that is known as mahimahi or dorado and another called pompano dolphin. These fish—popular in sport fishing and as food—do not resemble the mammalian dolphins.

Do **killer whales** attack humans?

The killer whale, also known as orca, is a type of dolphin that can grow to be 31 feet (9.5 meters) long and weigh 11,000 pounds (5,000 kilograms). It eats fish, squid, and

Bottle-nosed dolphins are known for their intelligence, curiosity, and gentleness with people.

occasionally such sea mammals as seals and other dolphins. Despite its frightening name, the killer whale has never been known to attack a person. Killer whales are intelligent and, with their stark black-and-white coloring, dramatic-looking animals. They learn quickly and can perform complex tasks, abilities that have made them a favorite at aquariums and marine parks.

How is a **seal** different from a **sea lion**?

Sea lions are just one of many different types of seals. Seals (along with walruses) are classified as pinnipeds, a Latin word meaning "fin-footed." As the name suggests, seals' limbs are flippers; they have one pair in front, and one pair in back. Seals are divided into two categories: earless (or "true") seals, which have tiny ear holes but no external flaps, and eared seals, so named because they have small ear flaps on their heads. Earless seals include the gray seal, harp seal, and the huge elephant seal, which can reach a length of 21 feet (6.5 meters) and weigh 7,780 pounds (3530 kilograms). Sea lions and fur seals are eared seals.

There are several differences, in addition to the ears, between sea lions and their earless seal relatives. The sea lion's flippers are longer than those of earless seals. They look like wings and usually don't have hair on them, while seal's flippers are covered with hair. Sea lions can turn their hind flippers forward, allowing them to use all of their limbs when moving on land. Seals cannot turn their hind flippers forward, and

191

in order to move on land they slide on their bellies and pull with their front flippers, moving in much the same way as a caterpillar.

How can animals live in a **desert**?

The harsh conditions of desert life present many problems for the animals living there: temperatures get extremely high, water is scarce, and food supplies, whether in the form of plants or other animals, dwindle. Desert animals have developed numerous techniques, however, to adapt to their unique climate. Just as animals living in cold climates hibernate in winter, so do some desert animals live through dry periods by becoming dormant, or inactive. Desert toads bury themselves deep in the ground, emerging only after a rainfall to get water and food and to breed. Many desert animals live in underground burrows or in caves; such animals spend hot, dry days in their dens, away from the sun, coming out in the early morning or at night when it's cooler.

Several desert animals are especially equipped to handle hotter temperatures. The large ears of jackrabbits can release heat while they rest in the shade. Owls and some other birds release body heat through their open mouths, letting their saliva evaporate to cool down their bodies. Many desert residents have pale fur, feathers, scales, or skin, an adaptation that means they absorb less of the sun's heat (they also blend in better with their sandy surroundings, which means they are less visible to predators). The meat-eaters in the desert can sometimes get all of the moisture they need from eating their prey (or, in the case of vultures, from eating carrion, or the flesh of already dead animals). Other desert animals are able to conserve the moisture they do get in amazing ways. The kangaroo rat, for example, can actually create water from the dry seeds it eats, and its kidneys can remove most of the water from its urine, sending the water back through the rat's bloodstream.

Thanks to their ability to fly, birds probably have the easiest time escaping the desert's difficult conditions. They can fly great distances if necessary to find areas where rain has fallen and vegetation is growing. Large-winged birds can spend the hottest part of the day soaring way up high where the winds are cooler.

Do camels really **store water** in their humps?

Camels store fat, not water, in the humps on their backs. Living in desert environments, camels use this stored fat for energy if food is not available; the animals can go days without eating. A camel can also go days without drinking because there are pockets in the walls of its stomach that hold water, released bit by bit as the animal needs it. A camel can drink up to 50 gallons (189 liters) of water at one time and store it. There are two types of camels: the Arabian camel or dromedary—native to northern Africa—which has one hump, and the Bactrian camel—native to central Asia—which has two. For centuries, camels have been used by people to cross the desert, either rid-

Given the polar bear's Arctic surroundings, its white fur provides excellent camouflage. *Robert J. Huffman/Field Mark Publications © 2001*

den or used as pack animals carrying supplies. That is why the large, strong beast has often been called the "ship of the desert." Able to endure intense heat, camels have many other features that make them well-suited to desert surroundings: their broad, padded hooves do not sink in the sand and their long eyelashes and hair-filled nostrils protect their eyes and airways from blowing grit. But their most unique features are their stomachs and humps of fat. At the beginning of a desert journey, when a camel is well fed, its hump can weigh nearly 100 pounds (45 kilograms). At the end of a long, hard trip, the hump nearly disappears, and all that is left is the loose skin that once covered it—kind of like a furry balloon that has lost its air.

Why are polar bears **white**?

The polar bear lives in the Arctic, the region of the North Pole. Most of its environment is barren, covered year-round with ice and snow and not much else. A polar bear might eat what few plants it can find, but it feeds mostly on water animals like seals and small walruses, which share its frozen home. The polar bear's yellowish-white coat helps it blend into its snowy surroundings as it hunts its prey. After all, there is not much in the Arctic to hide behind! The fur of a polar bear is also extremely thick, allowing it to withstand polar temperatures and swim in Arctic waters, where its prey is often found. Polar bears are excellent swimmers, and their unique paws—with hairy soles—allow them to run very quickly over ice and snow without slipping.

193

Why are zebras **striped**?

Zebras are black-and-white (or brown-and-white) striped members of the horse family that live and graze in the grassy open plains and brush country of Africa. They usually live in large herds of several hundred. Although they are fast runners (up to 40 miles, or 60 kilometers, per hour), they are often overtaken by lions and leopards, their main predators. It would seem that such bold stripes and stark colors would make the zebra an easy target for its predators. But scientists believe that their stripes help zebras blend in with each other, making it difficult for a predator to single out one zebra to attack. Some have suggested that zebra stripes resemble patterns of light and shadow in brush and grass, fooling the animals' predators from a distance.

Why are leopards **spotted**?

Like the fur of many animals, the leopard's coat is a form of camouflage. Camouflage helps animals blend in with their environments, making them less visible to predators (the animals that hunt them) and prey (the creatures they hunt). Mostly found in the forests of Africa and Asia, leopards, which hunt in trees and on the ground, blend in with the dappled sunlight shining through leafy tree branches and other plant life. Melanin is the organic chemical responsible for the pigmentation or color of animal (and human) skin; the more pigmentation, the darker the color. Black panthers are really leopards that have melanism, a condition of excess pigmentation. If you look closely at a black panther (careful!) you may be able to see the same spots that a normal leopard has against a very dark background. Because leopards are mostly nocturnal—resting during the day and active at night—this dark coloration causes little problem for black panthers.

Why is the lion known as the **"king of beasts"**?

The lion is one of the largest members of the cat family, found mostly in the open country of central Africa. A male lion can reach up to 9 feet (2.7 meters) long, including his tail, and weigh almost 400 pounds (182 kilograms); the female is somewhat smaller. Powerfully built, lions can take down large, swift-running animals like zebra and antelope, on which they feed. Unique to the cat family, the male lion possesses a black or brown mane of long hair that grows on its neck, head, and shoulders. The mane can become quite enormous. The size and power of the male lion, his hunting habits, and his impressive mane have all likely contributed to his label as "king of beasts." Lions also have commanding, thunderous roars (which can sometimes be heard more than a mile away) that, undoubtedly, have also contributed to their kingly reputation.

A giraffe may have a neck that measures up to seven feet (two meters) long. *Robert J. Huffman/Field Mark Publications © 2001*

Which of the "big cats" is the **largest**?

The colorful, striped tiger is the largest of the cat family. One type of tiger—the Siberian—is bigger than any lion. A male Siberian tiger can reach 13 feet (4 meters) in length, including his tail, and weigh up to 650 pounds (295 kilograms).

Which of the big cats is the **most dangerous**?

Probably, for people, the most dangerous of the big cats is the leopard. Although not as large as the lion or tiger, the leopard—a good climber that lurks in trees and on the ground—will attack a human when hunting or when startled. Lions and tigers usually try to avoid fights with people.

Why do giraffes have such **long necks**?

Giraffes, the tallest of all animals, have such long necks because they eat leaves from the tops of some very high trees, beyond the reach of other animals. Living in the grasslands of Africa, they feed chiefly on acacia and mimosa trees, using their long tongues and strong lips to pull off the highest leaves. A baby giraffe is about 6 feet (1.8 meters) tall at birth, and a full-grown male giraffe can reach a height of 18 feet (5.4 meters) from his hooves to the top of his head (about as high as a two-story house). A giraffe may have a neck that measures up to 7 feet (2 meters) long! Still, giraffes have

195

the same number of bones or vertebrae in their necks as we do—the giraffe's bones are just much longer. Giraffes also have very long legs, which contribute to their great height. While their long legs allow them to outrun most of their enemies, they also cause a problem: giraffes must spread their legs wide apart in order to reach anything on the ground, like water or grass. The position is an awkward one and leaves them vulnerable to attacks from predators. But they can protect themselves with their large hooves, kicking a beast even as powerful as a lion to death.

Why do hyenas **laugh**?

Hyenas aren't really laughing, but some of the noises they make to communicate sound like loud, crazy laughter. Hyenas are usually scavengers, living on carrion, which is the rotting remains of dead animals. (They have even been known to rob human graves for food.) Sometimes hyenas do hunt live animals, however, attacking in packs. Mostly nocturnal, which means that they rest during the day and are active at night, hyenas have—on occasion—entered villages and attacked livestock and sleeping people. The unsavory diet of the hyena gives it a bad smell. It is also not an attractive animal, with scruffy fur and hind legs that are much shorter than its forelegs, giving it a skulking appearance. Still, hyenas perform a valuable service in Earth's food chain as scavengers, ridding the environment of dead animal remains.

Why do rhinoceroses often have **birds riding on their backs**?

The small birds seen on the huge backs of rhinos—giant horned animals that come from Africa and southern Asia—are called tickbirds. These birds feed on the parasites or bugs hidden in the thick, deeply-folded skin of the large animals, keeping them clean and healthy. The cries of tickbirds also warn rhinos when danger is approaching. Such warnings are helpful because rhinos have very bad eyesight.

Is an **elephant's trunk** really its **nose**?

Yes, an elephant breathes through its trunk, or proboscis, which has two nostrils through which air can pass. But an elephant's muscular trunk—which nearly reaches the ground—can do several other remarkable things. On the end of the trunk is a sensitive, fingerlike lip or protuberance (an African elephant has two) that can feel and pick up food and other objects. (The end of an elephant's trunk is so sensitive that it can pick up a piece of thread from the floor.) An elephant can also pick up and carry large things like logs by wrapping its strong trunk—which contains hundreds of individual muscles—around them. Because elephants are intelligent and easily trained, people have used them for centuries to do heavy work in certain parts of the world.

An elephant can draw water up into its trunk and either release it into its mouth for a drink or shower it onto its back. It can do the same with dust and dirt, giving itself a soothing spray. An elephant also uses its trunk to make noise. The trumpeting sound we associate with elephants comes from its trunk.

How many different kinds of elephants are there?

There are two species of the elephant, the largest of the land animals. Both have descended from the ancient, extinct mammoth and mastodon. The African elephant is a good deal bigger than the Asian elephant; an African male can reach a height of 13 feet (4 meters) at the shoulder and weigh more than 8 tons (16,000 pounds, or 7,264 kilograms). In comparison, an Asian male can reach 10 feet (3 meters) at the shoulder and weigh about six tons (12,000 pounds, or 5,448 kilograms). Another difference between the two species is the size of their tusks, the elongated pair of upper teeth that the animals use for digging up roots and other food and for fighting. In African males they can measure more than 10 feet (3 meters) and weigh up to 200 pounds (91 kilograms) each, while in Asian males they can reach a length of 6 feet (1.8 meters). African females have tusks, but Asian females do not.

The ears of the two species differ also. African elephants have very large ears, which they flap to cool themselves. One ear can measure 42 inches (107 centimeters) across! Asian elephants, on the other hand, have much smaller ears. Other differences between the species include trunk size and shape: African elephants have two long fingerlike lips on the ends of their trunks while Asian elephants only have one. In addition, the trunks of Asian elephants are usually shorter and covered with smoother skin. The back of an Asian elephant is a bit humped, unlike the smooth back of its African cousin. Asian elephants are thought to have the better nature of the two species, being more trainable and even-tempered.

How much food does an elephant **eat each day**?

As the largest land animal, the elephant needs a lot of food to keep it going. An elephant eats all day long, browsing or grazing on vegetation like grasses, leaves, and fruit. It can consume hundreds of pounds of food each day, when available, and drink up to 50 gallons (190 liters) of water. Elephants usually live in large herds, making it necessary to continuously travel over a large region; they are such big animals and big eaters, if they didn't keep moving they could easily strip an area of vegetation.

Why are elephants **hunted for their tusks**?

Elephants' tusks—the huge, elongated pair of upper teeth that they use for digging and fighting—are the source of ivory, a hard, creamy-white material that has long been carved and polished to create beautiful objects. There are two types of ivory: live ivory, which is taken from a recently killed animal, and dead ivory, from an animal long dead, which is usually found on or buried in the ground. Dead ivory is harder and more brittle, cracking easily. Live ivory is more moist and easier to work with. The quest for live ivory has led to hundreds of thousands of elephants being killed for their tusks. Once very widespread, the world's elephant population has dwindled alarmingly because of this slaughter, but these great animals are now protected in many areas by strict laws that punish elephant hunters.

Unfortunately, even the threat of punishment is not enough to stop some poachers, or hunters who illegally kill protected animals. In spite of an international ban on the sale of elephant ivory, hundreds of elephants are killed each year by people wanting to sell the ivory.

A DAY AT THE ZOO

Why are there **zoos**?

Zoological gardens—commonly known as zoos—were created for a number of reasons. Since ancient times people have captured wild animals for collections, for the pleasure of owning and observing them, and in order to learn more about them and their habits. Very few people can travel to the wilds of Africa and other exotic places, but by visiting a zoo they can see firsthand some of the world's huge variety of creatures. Today, most large cities have zoos. People can learn more about animals there and about how to protect the native habitats from which these creatures come. Many zoos are havens where endangered animals can live protected and where there are breeding programs that try to increase the population of such creatures to keep them from extinction. Zoos also provide homes for animals that have been injured and could no longer survive in the wild. Zoos both entertain and educate those who visit them.

Why are animals sometimes **kept in cages** at zoos?

For many decades, most zoo animals were exhibited in cages with bars. It was a way to allow zoo visitors a good view of the animals while keeping people safe from unexpected attacks. Cages also kept animals in small areas, which was economical—saving the zoo money—and they were made of hard materials that could be hosed down, making them easy to keep clean.

While cages are still used at zoos today, it is not often that an animal is kept in one all the time. Zoologists now realize that it is unhealthy—and even cruel—for an animal to always be confined to a cage where it cannot get the exercise it would ordinarily get in the wild. In recent years, many zoos have built large enclosures for zoo animals that resemble the creatures' own natural habitats. While zoo visitors may not be

By visiting a zoo, people can see firsthand some of the world's huge variety of amazing creatures.

able to look as closely at an animal in such enclosures—where a creature can hide in caves or trees—the accommodations are much better for the animal, which can now exhibit more natural behavior.

Do zoo animals **hibernate**?

Animals that hibernate in the wild do so because temperatures drop and food supplies become scarce. In the zoo, however, animals live in a controlled environment. They are given a constant supply of food and warm pens or buildings to retreat to when it gets chilly outside. Some animals, including bears, may get sluggish during the coldest months at the zoo, but they will not spend months at a time sleeping as they might do in the wild.

Why can't people **pet the animals** at the zoo?

Most animals at a zoo have been captured from their natural habit. They are wild creatures unused to human contact, and their behavior is unpredictable. It isn't safe to pet most of the animals at the zoo, because some might scratch or bite or attack. But many zoos have some animals that zoo officials know are safe to pet. They may be baby animals that have been raised in captivity by humans or types of animals known to be gentle. These animals are often put in "petting zoos" where visitors are allowed to touch and sometimes feed them.

TREES, FLOWERS, AND OTHER GREEN STUFF

PLANT BASICS

What are **plants**?

Plants and animals make up almost all of the living things in the world. They are alike in a lot of ways. Both are made up of cells, tiny building blocks of life that produce chemicals that control growth and activity. Often these cells become specialized in a plant or animal, with different types doing particular jobs. In addition, both plants and animals use gases, water, and minerals to carry on life processes. Both experience life cycles in which they are created, grow, reproduce, and die.

But plants are very different from animals in one big way: most don't move around. Because they are rooted to one spot, plants are able to perform a special process called photosynthesis. For this remarkable process, plants use energy from sunlight, a gas in the air called carbon dioxide, and water and minerals from soil to produce their own food. Animals can't do this; they must look for food, eating plants or other animals in order to get the energy they need to live.

The waste product produced by photosynthesis is oxygen, the gas that all animals need to breathe. So without plant life, there would be no animal life on Earth. And without plants around to absorb carbon dioxide, an excess amount of this gas would linger in our atmosphere, trapping the Sun's heat and causing an unwanted increase in the planet's average temperatures. Plants, then, are essential not only because they provide so much of the food we eat (and provide nourishment for many of the animals we eat), but because they make our air healthier, using up carbon dioxide and releasing oxygen. In addition, we depend on plants to provide us with other things we need, like wood for building, fibers for making clothes, and medicines to improve our health.

201

How many **different** plants are there?

Scientists have found and described more than 275,000 kinds of plants, but they believe that many more are yet to be discovered. Plants vary greatly in size and appearance. Some, like single-celled algae, are so small that you can only see them with the help of a microscope. Others, like giant sequoia trees, are so big that you can't even see the tops of them. Plants are very different from one another because they have developed features—over millions of years—to help them live in the world's many different environments.

What did the **first plants** look like?

When you look at the green slime covering a still pond, you are looking at types of plants—single-celled green algae—that are thought to be among the first that appeared on Earth. (Though they share many characteristics, some scientists do not actually classify algae as plants, but as part of the kingdom Protista.) About 630 million years ago plants like these first grew in the oceans and spread to other watery environments. While they have no roots, stems, or leaves, algae do contain chlorophyll and make their own food through photosynthesis—using the energy of the Sun, carbon dioxide, and water—and give off the waste gas oxygen. (Because so much of Earth's surface is covered with water, algae—including seaweeds—are a major source of the oxygen we breathe.) Over time, plants with more complex parts evolved and eventually adapted to life on land, beginning about 400 million years ago.

What do plants **eat**?

Plants really don't eat in the way that animals eat. A better question would be, "How do plants make their own food?" Green plants get nourishment through a chemical process called photosynthesis, which uses sunlight, carbon dioxide, and water to make simple sugars. Those simple sugars are then changed into starches, proteins, or fats, which provide a plant with all the energy it needs to perform life processes and to grow.

Generally, sunlight (along with carbon dioxide) enters through the surface of a plant's leaves. The sunlight and carbon dioxide travel to special food-making cells (palisade) deeper in the leaves. Each of these cells contain a green substance called chlorophyll—which gives plants their green color—that traps light energy, allowing food-making to take place. Also located in the middle layer of leaves are special cells that make up a plant's "transportation" systems. Tubelike bundles of cells called xylem tissue carry water and minerals throughout a plant, from its roots to its outermost leaves. Phloem cells, on the other hand, transport the plant's food supply—sugar dissolved in water—from its manufacturing site in leaves to all other cells.

The plant food that we buy in stores is simply a mixture of minerals that plants need to grow well. These include nitrogen, phosphorus, and potassium. Usually a

Algae, a group of simple plants including seaweeds like these, were probably among the first plants on Earth.

plant is able to get these things from the soil in which it grows, drawing them up with water through its roots. But gardeners, farmers, and other plant growers add to this natural mineral supply so plants can thrive.

If a plant **isn't green,** can it still perform **photosynthesis**?

Many plants contain other pigments in addition to the green pigment chlorophyll, which traps light energy for photosynthesis. These other pigments can mask chlorophyll's green color, so the leaves and stems of such plants may appear red, purple, or even brown. But these plants still contain chlorophyll and can still use photosynthesis to produce food.

How do plants **grow**?

Special cells in plants produce hormones, chemical messengers that tell different plant cells to perform certain activities. Plant hormones are responsible for things like fruit development, the death of flower petals and leaves, and, most importantly, for growth. Cells in stem tips, new leaves, and buds, for instance, produce various growth hormones that tell plant cells to multiply by division or to become larger.

The pattern of growth in plants offers an important example of how they differ from animals. While animals eventually become fully grown (and live for a long time after that point), plants never stop growing throughout their life cycles. In other words, there is no such thing as an adult plant that no longer grows but continues to live.

Why do plants grow **toward light**?

A plant's ability to make food depends on its ability to absorb enough light energy. So, many plants move—in the small ways that they can—toward the Sun or other light sources (a characteristic known as phototropism). Some plants hold their leaves flat and open during the day—to catch as many of the Sun's rays as possible—and close them at night. Other plants change the direction their leaves face throughout the day, following the path of the Sun as it moves across the sky. When a plant grows in uneven sunlight—with the light hitting just one side of the plant, let's say—chemical messengers called hormones will cause more stems and leaves to grow on the lighted side so that the plant can gather enough of the sunlight it needs to make food. Phototropism explains why houseplants turn their leaves toward windows, growing into lopsided shapes unless they are rotated once in a while.

Why do plants sometimes **wilt** in the Sun?

In order to take in and get rid of the gases—carbon dioxide and oxygen—involved in food production, plants have thousands of microscopic openings called stomata on their leaves and stems. Most of the stomata are located on the underside of leaves. A leaf on a cucumber plant has 60,000 stomata in just over one-tenth of a square inch (one square centimeter).

Water that circulates throughout a plant escapes through these many openings in a process called transpiration. Usually a plant takes up more water through its roots than it loses through its leaves, and it is able to keep its firm shape. But on a hot, dry, or windy day, a plant can lose a lot of water through its leaves, at a much faster rate than it can take it in. On such days, wilting can occur. Water pressure in plant cells helps give plants their form; without that pressure, the cells shrink, causing a plant to wilt.

At night, when there is no sunlight for photosynthesis, the stomata on plants are closed by special guard cells that surround their openings. Little transpiration occurs then, and a plant can refill its supply of water through its roots. Water pressure will return to normal in plant cells, then, along with the normal shape and appearance of the plant.

Do all plants have **roots**?

The simplest types of plants don't have roots. Single-celled green algae, for instance, float on water surfaces, as do many types of seaweed, which are larger types of algae. Those seaweeds that do cling to the seabed do so through growths called "steadfasts," which are not true roots. Seaweed absorbs water and minerals from the sea through

Attaching themselves to trees and the forest floor, mosses survive without the help of roots. The Spanish Moss shown here, while not a "true" moss, also exists without roots.

all its parts. Similarly, simple plants like mosses form low-growing mats in damp places, soaking up the moisture they need directly from their environment. Instead of roots they have thread-like growths called rhizoids that anchor them to rocks or trees. More complex forms of plants, though, like ferns, conifers (cone-bearing plants), and flowering plants, all have true roots and stems—an internal transportation system that can move water and minerals from their source to wherever they are needed.

Land plants have two types of roots: tap roots and fibrous roots. A plant's root type is often determined by its water source. A tap root is a large, single root that grows straight down to reach water deep in the soil (with smaller roots branching off of it). Fibrous roots have no main root but spread out in a wide web to gather water located in the top layers of soil. In places like rain forests—where there is abundant plant growth with little ground space for roots and plenty of moisture—some plants grow high up in trees. These epiphytes, or air plants, have fibrous, spongy, aerial roots that get moisture from the frequent rains and take minerals from the surface of the tree on which they grow (or from the plant debris that gathers around their roots). Many orchids are epiphytic plants.

Do all plants have **leaves**?

The simplest types of plants, like algae, don't have leaves. But they do have chlorophyll in their cells and make their own food through photosynthesis, using sunlight, water,

205

and minerals. Mosses have leaf-like structures that carry out photosynthesis, but they are not true leaves because they don't have the special tissues—xylem and phloem—that distribute food, water, and minerals throughout most plants. The lack of a transportation system is the reason that mosses are so tiny and low to the ground.

More complex types of plants have leaves. Leaf shape is often determined by conditions in the environment. Usually, where sunlight and water are plentiful, leaves are flat and broad, providing a large surface area where photosynthesis can take place. Where weather is cold and dry, however, water loss can be a problem. The long, needle-shaped leaves of conifer trees (including pines), for example, help retain water, allowing the plants to grow in very dry, cold places, far north or high in the mountains. The extreme environment of the desert—intensely hot and dry—has brought about other special leaf adaptations. Many desert plants have fleshy leaves (and stems) in which they are able to store large amounts of water. Over millions of years the leaves of desert cactus plants became so small—to restrict water loss through transpiration—that on many only sharp spines remain. The thick-skinned stems or branches of cactus plants now do the job that leaves do for other plants, making food through photosynthesis.

What plant has the **biggest leaves**?

Two species of palm trees have the largest leaves in the world. The raffia palm that grows in the Mascarene Islands in the Indian Ocean and the Amazonian bamboo palm of South America both have leaf blades (leaves with supporting stems) that measure up to 65 feet, 6 inches (about 20 meters) long.

How do vines **climb**?

Some plants, referred to as vines, need support to grow to their full height. Vines climb in different ways. Some have soft, twisting stems, or tendrils, that they use to climb up other, stronger plants or supports. (In such vines, once they touch supports, hormones make their stems grow more quickly on one side than the other, producing clinging spirals.) Other climbing plants have special growths, like tiny aerial roots or padlike suckers on their stems, that help them cling to walls and trees. Still others use hook-tipped leaves or sharp thorny spines—like climbing roses—to hold onto upright surfaces. Vines occur in many different groups of plants—they can be deciduous (losing their leaves in winter) or evergreen (keeping their leaves year-round) and they can live one season (annuals) or many (perennials). Some vines commonly found in gardens include grapes, zucchinis, and bougainvillea.

Do plants **feel** when they are **cut**?

Plants don't have nervous systems like animals do. The nervous system of an animal controls its actions and reactions to its environment. In complex animals, special senses send information (electrochemical impulses) along nerve pathways to their brains about things occurring inside and outside their bodies. Without such a message system, plants can't feel or react like animals do. So plants don't feel when they are cut.

But plants do respond to things in their environment, like gravity, light, and even touch. Chemical messengers called hormones tell special cells and tissues how to respond to different conditions inside and outside a plant. Hormones tell seedlings to grow up from the ground, away from the pull of gravity. They tell houseplants to turn their leaves toward windows, where light comes in. They tell certain insect-eating plants to snap their leaves shut when prey lands there. They tell other plants to develop fruit following pollination. Although the many hormones that affect the lives of plants are not fully understood by scientists, it is clear that plants function remarkably well, though in very different ways from animals.

Will a plant **grow better** if you **talk to it**?

Studies have shown that plants seem to grow better if they are talked to. But plants don't have sound receptors or nervous systems, so scientists know that plants aren't responding to the specific words people say. What could it be, then?

When you talk, you breathe out carbon dioxide and water vapor, two things that plants need to grow. And sound waves from your voice cause plant cells to vibrate. Experiments have shown that certain types and strengths of sound can cause plants to grow better—or worse—than usual. Plants exposed to classical music, for instance, grew thick, healthy leaves and developed good roots. Jazz had the same beneficial effect. Plants exposed to country music had normal growth. But those that were exposed to rock music did very poorly. Their root development was so terrible that the plants began to die.

SEED FACTS

Do all **new plants** grow from **seeds**?

Plants can reproduce in a number of ways, and many of those ways don't involve seeds. Simple, single-celled plants like algae (the living green covering that you see on some ponds, for instance) produce asexually, which means that male and female cells are not needed to create new life: the parent cell simply divides to create a new plant cell identical to itself.

This method of reproduction—where an identical plant, or clone, is created—also occurs in more complex plant life. Often growing from a parent plant's stems or roots, 207 new plants receive water and food through connecting runners until they develop roots and leaves of their own. A strawberry plant, for example, often uses this method of reproduction. Bulb plants like tulips frequently reproduce in a similar way, growing new bulbs on the sides of parent bulbs. And cuttings—parts of roots, stems, or leaves—can be taken from many, many kinds of plants and grown into identical versions of the plants from which they came.

But sexual reproduction, where male and female cells unite to create a new plant, is the most common method of plant reproduction. Plants like ferns do this through spores, and conifers (cone-bearing plants) and flowering plants achieve it through seeds. A plant created through sexual reproduction inherits genes from both parents (unless it is self-pollinated) and will not be identical to either. The changes that come about in offspring from the combination of genes works well because the plant's new genetic traits may allow it to survive better in an environment that is always changing.

How are **seeds made**?

Conifers—plants that bear cones—and flowering plants all make seeds. Plants that produce flowers, called angiosperms, cover 90 percent of Earth's land surface. Most of the plants we know, like broad-leafed trees, vines, grass, and more, are flowering plants, although sometimes their flowers are so small and colorless that we barely notice them. While flowering plants now dominate the world, that was not always the case. They are relatively new to Earth, appearing just 135 million years ago. In ages before then, simpler plants dominated. The great age of conifers, which bear seeds in cones, began 300 million years ago.

Coniferous trees (which are part of the plant group gymnosperms), like pines, spruces, firs, and cypresses, bear male and female cones. Male cones contain sacs that release millions of tiny grains of pollen—male reproductive cells—into the air. They are carried by the wind to female cones that have reproductive cells located in ovules, which are sticky and attract pollen grains. When male and female cells meet, fertilization occurs, and seeds form in the scales of a female cone, which increases in size as the seeds grow. Once the seeds are mature (which takes a couple of years), the cone opens to release them. Equipped with a wing to help it to travel in the wind, each seed has a tough outer coating and some food inside to use if it finds a good spot to start growing.

Seed-making in flowering plants is a little more complicated. Most flowers contain both male and female sex cells. The typical flower has four main parts: an outer cup of leaflike sepals, a ring of petals within the sepals, and inside, male reproductive organs surrounding female parts. Male cells develop in structures called stamens and travel enclosed in the hard shell of pollen grains. Female cells, or ovules, develop deep in a flower's ovary, enclosed in a structure called a pistil. The top of the pistil—known as the stigma—is long and sticky and a good target for pollen. After it reaches the stigma,

Dandelion seeds have parachutes made of tiny hairs that allow them to be carried great distances.

a small tube grows out of the pollen grain. The male cells travel down the pollen tube, eventually reaching female ovules. Then fertilization occurs and seeds start to grow.

Since flowers possess both male and female parts, some flowers can fertilize themselves (or fertilize another flower on the same plant), which is called self-pollination. Or the ovules of one flower may be fertilized by the pollen of a different flowering plant of the same species, a method called cross-pollination. The wind, water, insects, and other animals help to carry pollen from one flower to another. Cross-pollination usually produces a better plant: the offspring of cross-pollination possesses the genetic traits of two parents, which may give it new characteristics that will help it survive in an always-changing environment. Cross-pollination is so desirable, in fact, that many flowering plants have developed different ways to keep self-pollination from happening. In the flowers of a spiderwort plant, for example, the stamens are ready to release pollen grains before the pistils are ready to accept them, so the pollen has to travel to other spiderwort plants in search of a ripe pistil.

How do **seeds become plants**?

Once seeds are fully developed, they need a good place to grow. If they just fell to the ground beneath their parent plant, they would struggle, competing against each other for sunlight, water, and minerals. Most seeds need to travel, then—by wind, water, or with the help of insects and other animals—to better places to germinate, or start to grow into new plants.

Some seeds, like those from conifer and maple trees, have wings attached. Others, like those of dandelions, have parachutes made of tiny hairs. Both features allow the seeds to be carried great distances by the wind, and they sometimes land in spots that are good for germination. Water carries other seeds to good growing places; the hard, watertight shell of a coconut, for instance, allows it to travel many miles at sea before finding a beach where conditions are suitable for growth.

Animals are great seed carriers. They take them from one place to another in their mouths (as does a squirrel preparing for winter), or sometimes seeds stick on their fur or feathers. But most often seeds travel in animals' digestive systems. Some plants grow colorful and tasty fruits, which are really just fleshy seed coverings meant to attract hungry animals. When creatures like birds, bats, raccoons, or bears eat berries and other fruits they usually swallow the seeds whole. Safe inside a hard coating, the seeds pass through unaffected by digestive juices, appearing many hours later in animal waste. The seeds sometimes emerge in places far from their parent plants, in locations better for germination.

Seeds, then, sometimes have to wait a long time before they find good places to grow, places where the sun, moisture, and temperature are right. Most seeds are designed for the wait, protected by a hard outer pod (except those of conifers). Some seeds wait years to germinate, and some just never do. But inside each seed pod is a baby plant, or embryo, and endosperm, a supply of starchy food that will be used for early growth if germination takes place. Then a tiny root will reach down into the soil, and a tiny green shoot will reach up, toward the light.

How does a **sprouting seed** know **which way is up**?

Earth's gravity is the force that guides the direction of a sprouting seed's roots and shoots. (In scientific experiments where plants are put in zero-gravity environments, they grow in all directions.) Roots respond to the pull of gravity (which generates from the center of Earth) by growing toward it, and shoots, or stems, respond to gravity by growing away from it. Scientists do not completely understand how a plant's cells receive the signals that point different parts in different directions, but simple experiments show that no matter which way a seed is planted (with the root-producing part facing down or up), the roots will grow down and the shoots will grow up. Heavy starch grains found in certain cells help the growing plant keep its balance by shifting their place if the plant loses its upright position. This shifting directs growth hormones to affected areas in the plant. These hormones will cause new growth in stems and roots to correct their position in relation to gravity. In the shoot, for example, growth hormones will make cells toward the bottom grow faster than cells toward the top, pushing the shoot upward.

What plant makes the **largest seeds**?

Coco palm trees produce coconuts, which are among the largest seeds in the world. Giant fan palms that grow wild in the islands of the Seychelles Republic, located in the Indian Ocean, produce what are known as double coconuts, which can weigh up to 50 pounds (23 kilograms).

What plants produce some of the **smallest seeds**?

Orchids produce the smallest seeds. They measure no more than .04 inches (one millimeter) in length, and one million orchid seeds might weigh less than an ounce (less than 28 grams). Seed size has no bearing on the size of the plant that grows from it; orchids grow to a larger size than many plants that have much larger seeds. And a huge redwood tree begins as a tiny seed no more than one-sixteenth of an inch (1.6 millimeters) long.

FLOWERS

Why are flowers **brightly colored**?

To accomplish reproduction through cross-pollination, flowering plants must rely on other forces (as they can't move themselves). Many flowering plants depend on insects

Insects, like this butterfly, help create variety in flowers through cross-pollination.

and birds to carry their pollen from one plant to the next, and these plants can attract particular animals with brightly colored or fragrant flowers. The nutritious pollen and nectar in flowers is an important part of many creatures' diets. When insects and birds visit a flower to feed, sticky pollen grains cling to their bodies. As the creatures continue to feed from flowers of other plants of the same species, they leave some of the pollen behind, and cross-pollination occurs.

Many flowering plants—like grasses and several kinds of trees—rely on wind for pollination. This method is less reliable than the animal carrier method of cross-pollination, so wind-pollinated plants produce huge amounts of pollen grains to improve their chances of success. (The large amounts of fine, dry pollen in the air are the cause of the allergies that we call hay fever.) The flowers of wind-pollinated plants are usually small, plain, and not brightly colored (and many don't produce nectar) because they don't need to attract the attention of insects or other animals to help spread their pollen.

Why do flowers **look different** from one another?

The way a flower looks depends a lot on the way it is pollinated. Flowers that depend on the wind for pollination are usually small and plain-looking because they don't need to attract the attention of insects and birds to carry their pollen. But flowers that do depend on the carrier method need ways to attract the animals that will help them cross-pollinate. And flowers are often structured—in terms of color, scent, and shape—to suit a particular insect or animal visitor.

Many flowers attractive to bees have parts that act as "landing platforms," so the bees that visit them can rest their heavy bodies while feeding. Bees can see most colors (except red), and they are attracted to colorful flowers. And because bees use long sucking tubes to collect pollen and nectar, the flowers that they visit often have long, narrow shapes.

Butterflies like many of the same flowers that bees do. They, too, have long, sucking mouth parts and like to land when feeding. Their large wings keep them from traveling deep into flowers, though; for this reason they prefer flowers that are flat, broad, and clustered. Butterflies are attracted to all bright colors. Moths, which are similar to butterflies, are nocturnal, which means they are active at night. So the flowers they are attracted to tend to be light-colored or white—the kinds of flowers that show up well in the dark. And because moths tend to hover in the air when feeding, they need no landing platforms on the flowers they visit.

Hummingbirds have a poor sense of smell but see color well. The flowers they prefer are bright red or orange and supply plenty of nectar in their deep, narrow blooms. Flowers pollinated by flies, which are attracted to decaying matter (where they tend to lay their eggs), are generally dark green, purple, or brown—colors that resemble the rotted material flies prefer. The flowers that bats feed from have large openings for their snouts and strong parts that the animals can grip onto with their claws.

Why do some flowers smell like perfume?

Different chemicals in plants and flowers—called essential oils—give them their special scents. Flowers have fragrances so they can attract the creatures they need for cross-pollination. Some of the insects and other animals that feed from flowers have keen senses of smell. Bees, for instance, have sensitive odor detectors in their antennae, so most bee flowers are scented. Flowers that open only at night are often strongly scented, to help the creatures that feed from them —like moths —find them in the dark.

Not all flowers have pretty scents, though. Some flowers actually smell like rotten meat or other decaying matter in order to attract flies. Flies usually lay their eggs in decaying materials because that's what hatched fly larvae (the immature stage of a fly) feed on; therefore, flies are drawn to plants that look and smell (to the fly, anyway) like garbage. Bats that feed on plants are also attracted to flowers that have what we would consider unpleasant scents.

What is **nectar**?

Nectar is a sweet liquid made in special glands called nectaries in flowering plants. Located deep within a flower, at the base of its petals, nectar is an important part of the diets of many insects and animals. The most important gatherers of nectar are honey bees, which bring it back to their hives to make delicious honey.

Do all flowers **close at night**?

Many flowers close at night (or when the weather is cold). They start to shut as sunlight begins to fade. Studies have shown that the temperature inside a closed flower, where a plant's important reproductive structures and pollen are located, can be several degrees warmer than the surrounding air outside. In some flowers, the warmth attracts pollinating insects, who spend the night there! In the morning, when sunlight returns, flowers open again, ready for insects and other animals to feed from them and spread their pollen. Some plants are even known to close their leaves at night.

Wildflowers grow in many different environments—maybe even in your own backyard.

Some flowers remain closed during the day and open at night, like the evening primrose. Such flowers follow that schedule because the creatures that feed from and pollinate them—like moths and bats—are nocturnal, or active only at night.

What plant has the **biggest flower**?

The largest flower in the world has a rather unpleasant name and an equally unpleasant scent: the stinking corpse lily, or Rafflesia arnoldi. This rare and endangered flower grows in the jungles of the southeast Asian islands Borneo and Sumatra. The flowers are orange-brown in color with large white speckles. They can measure three feet across and weigh up to 25 pounds (11 kilograms). Because the stinking corpse lily is a parasite plant—which means that it gets its nourishment from other plants—it has no stem or leaves. The flower's seeds attach themselves to jungle vines and burrow into the vines' tissue, where they germinate and grow. Eventually a blossom pushes through the vine and grows to huge proportions.

What is a **wildflower**?

Wildflowers are flowering plants that grow in the wild, in their native habitats. Most of the flowers that people plant in their gardens or keep in their homes are cultivated, which means they have been grown with the help of people rather than occurring on their own in nature.

Over the past several hundred years, gardeners and scientists have worked to gradually improve the plants that they grow. To improve a plant species, people work to germinate (or grow plants from) only the seeds that came from the best plants (discarding the seeds of weaker, less attractive plants). Further improvement comes from hybridization, or cross-breeding. In this process, a plant that has beautiful flowers but no scent might be combined with a different plant that has dull flowers but a lovely fragrance; the hoped-for result is a plant that combines the best of both plants' features, producing pretty flowers that smell nice. This kind of change occurs very slowly, over long periods of time.

But the plants that people began with were plants that grew wild. Some plants grew in one part of the world, while others only grew in another part. As people began to travel more, however, they collected plants not native to their homelands, bringing them back to raise at home. Many of the plants that we buy for our gardens today originally came from far away and are the products of the breeding efforts of generations of plant experts.

Wildflowers are perfectly suited to their environments because they have not been transported from foreign lands. They have also not been changed by plant breeding, and they exist in their original state. Wildflowers grow in many different environments, like fields, swamps, and forests, and even in your own backyard.

THE DARK SIDE OF PLANTS

What is a **weed**?

Strictly speaking, a weed is simply a plant growing where it is not wanted. Weeds usually grow easily and spread, and they often interfere with the growth of more desirable plants. Weeds don't usually have nice features, like pretty flowers or tasty leaves, to make them more appealing to people or other animals. They are frequently hard to get rid of, growing back from the smallest bit left in the ground. People's opinions vary greatly about which plants are weeds. In the United States, for instance, most people consider dandelions weeds and spend a lot of time and effort trying to get rid of them. In France, however, they are grown as a crop, with their leaves used in salads and their roots processed to make a coffee-like drink.

How do plants cause **hay fever**?

The male reproductive cells of many plants are encased in a hard grain called pollen. Wind carries the pollen of many trees and grasses from one plant to another. When these male reproductive cells unite with female reproductive cells in plants of the same species, fertilization and seed-making takes place. Unlike plants that are pollinated by insects or animals, wind-pollinated plants have to produce huge numbers of pollen grains because wind pollination is a less reliable method of fertilization. During certain parts of the year, the air is filled with such pollen grains, which are fine and dry for easier wind travel. Billions of spores, microscopic reproductive cells produced by other types of plants, like molds, also fill the air.

Some people are allergic to all these tiny airborne plant particles. They cause inflammation and extra fluid production in the eyes, nose, and throat, resulting in symptoms like itchy, watery eyes, stuffy noses, coughing, and sneezing. The condition is known as hay fever, though it doesn't usually involve hay or cause a fever. People who have seasonal hay fever get these symptoms in the season of the year when the specific pollen they are allergic to is released. In spring, hay fever may be caused by tree pollens. In summer, grass pollens may be the culprit. Ragweed plants bloom in the late summer and fall; their pollens are the most common cause of hay fever.

Why are some plants **poisonous**?

Plants can't run away from "predators"—animals that will eat them—so some have developed other methods of defense. Many plants have some poisonous parts. The leaves of a rhubarb plant are extremely dangerous to eat, for example, though its stems are quite harmless and tasty. Scientists believe that plants often have one poisonous part to keep predators away, while other parts remain harmless and safe for animal pollinators.

Why does **poison ivy** give people **rashes**?

A very irritating oily substance called urushiol is in all parts of a poison ivy plant, as well as in its itchy cousins, poison oak and poison sumac. The plants are found across North America, especially near streams and lakes. The oil itself is harmless, but once it interacts with substances on human skin, it can be interpreted by the body as an unwanted foreign invader. The body's immune system then kicks in and tries to get rid of it—this response is an allergic reaction. About 70 percent of all people are allergic to the plants and will develop itchy red bumps, blisters, and skin swelling a short time after they come in contact with them. Once the rash occurs, it can spread from one part of the body to another and sometimes lasts many days. Contact with these poisonous plants can happen directly, when a person touches them, or indirectly, when he or she touches clothes, tools, or animals that have the irritating oil on them. Very sensitive people can even get a rash from the smoke of burning poison ivy, oak, and sumac.

The best way to keep from getting an itchy rash is to avoid the plants that cause them. Avoidance is especially hard with poison ivy, which is a creeping, crawling vine

Some plants, like this cactus, have prickly parts that help protect them from predators. *Robert J. Huffman/Field Mark Publications © 2001*

that lives among other plants (poison oak and sumac are more bushlike). Learning what poison ivy looks like helps: the vine has smooth leaflets arranged in clusters of three, which are red in early spring, change to shiny green in summer, and then back to red in autumn. Poison ivy sometimes has gray berries, too.

If you know that you will be visiting a place where poison ivy grows, wear pants and long sleeves and even gloves. Afterwards, your outfit should be washed as soon as possible—separate from other clothes—with hot water and strong soap. If you accidentally touch a poison ivy plant, wash your skin with soap and water right away and then use rubbing alcohol to make sure that all of its irritating oil is gone. If you get a rash anyway, try not to scratch, which will only make it worse. Most people get relief from such rashes with anti-itch medications like hydrocortisone (which reduces the swelling and keeps your body from reacting to the plant's oils). See a doctor if the rash covers your face or a large area on your body.

Why do some plants have **thorns**?

Plants have no means of escaping from hungry animals, so they develop ways to defend themselves. Some plants have poisonous parts, while others have thorns and other sharp growths to defend against animals that would want to eat them. Animals that approach such a prickly plant are painfully snagged, which discourages them from coming closer.

If plants **make their own food,** why do some **eat insects**?

Carnivorous, or "meat-eating," plants do make their own food through photosynthesis. But they also capture small prey, most frequently insects, for the minerals that they provide. Usually carnivorous plants, like Venus flytraps, grow in swamps and marshes where the minerals that plants need for growth (especially nitrogen) are in short supply. Minerals from the bodies of insects caught in their leaves allow carnivorous plants to grow in these otherwise unsuitable places.

The Venus flytrap has jaw-like leaves that can snap shut on visiting insects.

Carnivorous plants usually attract insects with nectar or with a pleasing smell or color. Many have sticky leaves or slippery pouches that trap insects once they land there. The Venus flytrap has pairs of jawlike leaves that snap shut when attached trigger hairs are disturbed by a visiting insect. Once insects are trapped, carnivorous plants produce special chemicals that digest them. Scientists have identified nearly 500 species of carnivorous plants.

Can carnivorous plants be **harmful to humans**?

While some science fiction books and movies have portrayed giant carnivorous plants with an appetite for human flesh, such plants do not exist in the real world. Insect-eating plants are much more likely to be harmed *by* humans than to cause harm *to* humans. These plants capture small insects, digesting them using chemicals that are too weak to have any affect on people.

PLANTS IN EXTREME ENVIRONMENTS

How can **desert plants** live **without water**?

No plant could live in a true desert, where it never rains. But the places where cacti and other desert plants grow do get rain once in a while—even if it's only every couple of years or so. When it rains, desert plants quickly take up the water through their roots, storing it in fleshy leaves and stems. That stored water allows them to survive until the next rain comes.

The roots of desert plants are either very deep, drawing from hidden underground water, or widespread and shallow to best gather the water that hits the ground. Their leaves and stems usually have a heavy, waxy coating to help keep moisture in. The tiny pores, or stomata, on their leaves—through which carbon dioxide, oxygen, and water pass—are located in pits instead of on the surface to further minimize moisture loss. Some desert plants even keep their stomata closed during the blistering heat of the day and open them in the cool of the night—the reverse of what most plants do.

Cactus plants are particularly well adapted to their hot, dry surroundings. Over millions of years the leaves of cacti became so small—to reduce water loss—that on many only sharp spines remain. Their thick stems or branches now do the work that leaves ordinarily do—making food through photosynthesis. Often the stems of a cactus are ribbed, allowing any morning dew to run down and be absorbed by the plant's roots. The ribs also allow the plant to expand and contract according to the amount of water it has stored inside. After a good rain, up to 90 percent of a cactus's weight may be water.

How can plants like seaweed **grow underwater**?

As long as they get enough sunlight to carry out photosynthesis, plants can live at various depths in oceans or other bodies of water. The stems of most underwater plants usually hold them upright so they can grow toward the light that filters down through their watery homes. When the countless animals that live in seas and lakes breathe, they provide water plants with the carbon dioxide they need for photosynthesis. As underwater plants release oxygen during photosynthesis, you can sometimes see it bubble to the surface (in the same way that bubbles appear when people breathe out underwater).

Seaweeds are odd underwater plants because they don't have true roots, stems, or leaves. They are really just larger forms of single-celled algae, the simplest type of plant that exists. Many seaweeds have "fronds" that look like leaves and "stalks" that look like stems. Some even have "holdfasts" that do the work of roots, attaching them to rocks or seabeds. But these special parts don't do different jobs, like they do in most plants. All parts of a seaweed plant absorb water, carbon dioxide, minerals, and sunlight for photosynthesis.

Algae are very important plants. Water covers much of the world's surface, which means algae cover much of the world's surface too. All plants release oxygen as part of photosynthesis, and the large quantities of this simple plant make algae a major source of the oxygen we breathe. One of the most common types of seaweed, known as giant kelp, forms underwater forests in the oceans, providing shelter, food, and oxygen for countless sea animals. Some of these plants have fronds up to 200 feet (61 meters) long and grow up to 75 feet (23 meters) below the sea surface! (A type of red seaweed can grow even deeper—up to 200 feet, or 61 meters, below the surface.) Some seaweeds are eaten by people—mostly in the East—and they are used to make things like fertilizers, cosmetics, and medicines.

What is **hydroponics**?

Hydroponics is a method of growing plants in nutrient-rich water instead of soil. People have grown plants using hydroponics for about 50 years. This method is useful in places that have poor soil or for producing special plants for research. Growing conditions can be more closely controlled with hydroponics than out in the field: crops are not bothered by weeds or insects in their protected, watery environments, and their water and mineral needs are perfectly met in the large tanks in which they grow. Without soil, plants can also be grown closer together. One problem with hydroponics, though, is that plants often have trouble supporting themselves when their roots aren't in soil, which can keep them from reaching full growth. Sometimes the roots of hydroponic plants are put in sand or gravel to fix the problem, or the plants are supported by wires. In the future, if people live in space stations—or on other planets—they will need to use hydroponics to raise food and to recycle carbon dioxide and oxygen.

SPORE-BEARING PLANTS

What are **spores**?

Complex types of plants—conifers and flowering plants—reproduce by way of seeds. These seeds began as tiny spores. The spores in the female reproductive parts of the plant produce an egg cell, while the spores in the male reproductive parts produce sperm cells enclosed in a pollen grain. When the pollen grain is carried (by wind or insects, for example) to a plant's female parts, one of the sperm cells joins with the egg cell, and a seed is formed. That seed contains everything necessary (with the help of water, the right soil, and sunlight) to make a new plant, and once seeds are scattered, they can germinate, or grow into a plant.

Simpler types of plants—like mosses and ferns—reproduce by scattering spores rather than seeds. These plants produce spores in sporangia, or spore cases. Once the spores are mature, they are released and scatter, sometimes carried by wind and water until they reach suitable places for new plants to start. Once spores germinate, they produce tiny plants called gametophytes, which look nothing like the parent plants they came from. Gametophytes produce sex cells and then unite with each other to create the next generation, plants called sporophytes (which do resemble their parents). During the sporophyte stage, the plant produces spores, which eventually fall to the ground, scatter, and begin the process all over again.

Spores are in the air all around us, though they are so small that we can only see them with a microscope. But we know they are there because some of them grow into the molds and mildews that show up around the bathtub or on certain foods that are left on the counter for too long.

What are **ferns**?

Ferns are green, leafy, spore-producing plants that can be found all over the world, though they prefer warm, wet, shady regions. With more than 10,000 species, ferns are a large and diverse group of plants. Gardeners love them for their delicate beauty and their easy maintenance. Ferns range in size from tiny, one-inch (2.5 centimeters) varieties to treelike plants, the tallest of which is New Zealand's black tree fern, which can grow as tall as 65 feet (20 meters). While the leaves of a fern, called fronds, live only about a year or two, the stems and roots of these plants can live a very long time, up to 100 years. Fern species are some of the oldest land plants; scientists believe they have been around for more than 350 million years.

What are **mosses**?

Most of us have seen moss growing in a soft, green carpet at the base of a tree in the woods. Like ferns, mosses can grow all over the world, but they thrive in damp, shady areas. Both plants require moisture to reproduce—during the reproductive stage, the male sex cells need water to swim to the female sex cells so they can fuse and create new plants. Most mosses are small, but one tropical species can grow to heights of 27 inches (69 centimeters).

Lacking true roots, mosses connect to the ground or trees with tiny, rootlike structures called rhizoids. Mosses can hold tremendous amounts of water, which has made certain varieties very useful to the environment (and some Native American Indians took advantage of moss's absorbency by using it for diapers). Mosses help prevent flooding, and gardeners use a type called peat moss to keep soil moist and rich with nutrients.

Are **mushrooms** plants?

Fungi, which include mushrooms, molds, and mildews, are not really plants. They have no real roots, leaves, or stems, and contain no chlorophyll with which to make their own food (that's why they aren't green and don't need sunlight). Fungi feed

Mushrooms are fungi, a group that also includes molds and mildews. *Robert J. Huffman/Field Mark Publications © 2001*

mostly on dead plant and animal matter, which helps keep the environment clean and enriches the soil. Some fungi feed on live plants and animals, though, often harming their hosts. A fungal disease called rust, for instance, can completely ruin the wheat crop it has infected.

Mushrooms are the visible parts of certain fungal (basidium) growths that live underground, where they feed on dead and decaying matter. When these fungi are ready to reproduce they send up mushrooms, fruiting bodies that carry spores for reproduction. Spores form on the gills of a mushroom underneath its cap. Within a few days they shoot out and scatter, and the fruiting body dies. Some of the billions of spores released will develop into new fungi. Autumn is the best time to spot mushrooms and other fungal fruiting bodies.

What is a **toadstool**?

A toadstool is simply a mushroom, the reproductive part of certain fungal growths that has an umbrella or cone-shaped cap on a straight stem. Because mushrooms often grow in cool, moist, dark places (where most toads like to live) and because they are shaped like little stools, the name "toadstool" arose to describe them. Usually the term toadstool is used when talking about a type of mushroom that is not suitable for eating or is poisonous. The practice of calling such mushrooms toadstools may have come from the fact that some toads emit poisonous fluid through their skin.

How can you tell if a **mushroom** is **poisonous**?

Many types of mushrooms are good to eat. The fruiting bodies of other fungi—like truffles and puffballs—are also tasty. But there are many mushrooms that are poisonous, and it is very hard to tell the harmful from the harmless. So you should never pick and eat a mushroom. Only an expert, who has studied the different types, can tell the difference for sure.

People have been eating mushrooms for thousands of years. Because they contained some protein and minerals, they were an important source of food at times when fruits and vegetables were not available. Now they are grown commercially, like other food crops.

What is the **deadliest mushroom**?

The most poisonous mushroom is the death cap toadstool (Amanita phalloides). It is commonly found where beech and oak trees grow. Even a small piece of it can kill, usually within 6 to 15 hours. Unlike some poisonous plants, the poison of the death cap toadstool is not destroyed by cooking.

TREES

What are the **two** main **groups of trees**?

Trees can be classified in many different ways, but the two main groups of trees are conifers (or softwood) trees and broadleaf (or hardwood) trees. Conifer trees bear seeds in cones and have needle-like or scale-like leaves. Most conifers are evergreen, which means that they keep their leaves throughout the year. Pines, spruces, and giant redwoods are examples of conifer trees. Broadleaf or hardwood trees have broader leaves and flowers that produce seeds, though sometimes the flowers are so small and plain that they are hard to notice. Most broadleaf trees are deciduous, which means that, in climates that have changing seasons, they lose their leaves in the fall (in tropical climates, they keep their leaves all year long). Maples, oaks, and palms are examples of broadleaf trees.

The wood that makes up the trunk and branches of conifers is generally softer and lighter than those of broadleaf trees, making softwood easier to work with in building and manufacturing. This fact, along with the conifer's quick growth, has led to a commercial industry where softwood trees are planted and raised in man-made forests. One-fourth of the world's forests, in fact, are not natural, but have been created for commercial use.

Why do trees have **bark**?

The cells that make up plants have walls—made mostly of a material called cellulose—that vary in thickness. In young, flexible plants, cell walls are thin and elastic. As a plant reaches full size its cell walls have grown several layers, making it more rigid. A plant's firm cell walls help give it its shape. Even after plant cells die, their firm walls can help support a plant.

A plant as big as a tree needs a lot of support. The cells that form a tree's bark—covering its trunk and branches—have extremely tough walls. Outer bark is really a thick shell of dead cells that protect softer, living tissues inside. Outer bark keeps a

tree from losing too much water, which could happen easily in a plant so large. It also keeps many insects and other damaging things like fungi from reaching a tree's living center. Bark can protect a tree in very cold or very hot weather too.

The living, inner bark of a tree is made of long, stiff-walled xylem cells, arranged like tubes or pipes, which transport water and minerals from its roots. Located inside that bark is a spongy wood center make of similarly arranged, thinner-walled phloem cells, which distribute the tree's food supply that has been manufactured in its leaves. The strength, weight, and hardness of the woods of different trees depend on the size of their cells and the way they are arranged together. Certain chemicals in woods give them their different scents, colors, and other characteristics.

Conifer trees, like the pine tree pictured here, bear seeds in cones and usually have needle-like leaves.

How can you tell **how old** a tree is?

When a branch or the trunk of a tree is cut, you can see a series of rings inside. If you count each ring, you can tell how many years the tree has lived. Each year a tree grows a new layer of wood just below its bark, making the tree's trunk wider and wider as time goes by. The rings inside a tree often vary in size; in some years a tree has more of the things that it needs—like water—to produce food, which allows it to produce more new tissue. In a year with very little water, on the other hand, less new tissue would be produced, resulting in a smaller ring.

What is **sap**?

Sap is a term used to describe all the fluids that travel through complex types of plants, fluids that move through transportation systems made of special xylem and phloem cells. Sap is water with substances like minerals or sugar dissolved in it. Some plants, like maple trees and sugar cane, have so much sugar in their saps that they are raised commercially to make syrup and sugar. Other plants have specialized saps that are hard or sticky, like latex, which is used to make rubber. The sticky gums and resins produced by many trees are thought to protect them from damaging insects and to seal any holes or tears that might occur in their barks.

Each year a tree grows a new layer of wood just below its bark, making the tree's trunk wider as time goes by. *Robert J. Huffman/Field Mark Publications © 2001*

Why do evergreens have **needles instead of leaves**?

The needles of conifers, or evergreens, are really specially shaped leaves. They have the same features that normal leaves have: tiny holes or stomata through which carbon dioxide and oxygen pass; the green substance chlorophyll that allows food-making through photosynthesis; and special transportation cells that move food, water, and minerals to wherever they are needed. Conifer leaves are small, narrow, and have a thick surface, though, to limit transpiration, or water loss. Evergreens usually live in dry places where it is very cold for much of the year. Their special leaves allow them to live in the far north or high in the mountains, where the ground is often frozen. (These trees' typical conical shape—with narrow, pointed tops and drooping branches—also helps prevent damage during heavy snows.) Conifers live in places with hot, dry summers, too, like around the Mediterranean Sea in Europe and in the Middle East.

If evergreens **keep their needles** all year long, why are there so many **on the ground**?

A conifer doesn't keep each of its needle-like leaves forever. The needles usually have a three- or four-year life span, after which they are shed. A conifer is different from a deciduous tree in that it loses its leaves gradually, rather than all at once. So a conifer always looks green. The same thick outer covering that keeps evergreen needles from losing water in their often dry environments also keeps them from decaying quickly once they are discarded. That is why you see so many dry needles on the ground under mature evergreens—it takes a long time for these needles to decompose, especially compared to the leaves that fall off deciduous trees.

What are **pine cones**?

The cones found on pines and other conifer plants are reproductive structures. Small male cones produce millions of grains of pollen that are carried by the wind to sticky female cones, where fertilization takes place and seeds begin to grow. Shortly after they release their pollen, male cones die, their work done. Soft and green at the time of fertilization, female cones gradually become larger, brown, and woody. This change makes room for and protects the growing seeds within its scales, which—unlike those of flowers—don't have hard pod coverings of their own (conifer seeds are described as "naked"). After a couple of years, when its seeds are mature, a female cone will open and release them into the wind. The female cone may then fall from the plant, its work also done.

Which **tree** is the **tallest**?

Along the coast of northern California and southern Oregon, where the climate is cool and moist, live some of the largest and most ancient trees in the world. They are sequoia trees, commonly known as redwoods because of the color of their bark and wood. There are two kinds of these conifers, which have scale-like leaves. The giant redwood (*Sequoia sempervirens*) is the tallest tree on Earth. It can grow up to 385 feet (117 meters)—about as tall as a 37-story building! Its trunk can measure up to 25 feet (7.6 meters) in diameter. Many are more than 2,000 years old. The other giant sequoia (*Sequoiadendron giganteum*) isn't quite as tall, but it is wider and heavier. It can grow up to 325 feet (99 meters) and have a trunk with a diameter up to 30 feet (9.1 meters). With the biggest of these trees weighing an estimated 2,500 tons, they are considered the largest living things in the world, even bigger than blue whales. They have also been around longer than giant redwoods, with many almost 4,000 years old.

Because the wood of sequoias is strong, beautiful, and decay-resistant, many of these rare and ancient trees have been cut down in past decades and used for building. Replacing such trees is difficult, as they can take up to 500 years to reach maturity. But now they are protected in some 30 national parks. If you go to the central West Coast of the United States you can visit these special forests. You may even be able to drive your car through tunnels that have been carved out of the trees' huge trunks.

How **long** can trees **live**?

It was long thought that the giant sequoias (*Sequoiadendron giganteum*) that grow along the middle Pacific coast of the United States were the oldest living trees in the world. Some are nearly 4,000 years old. But a few decades ago it was discovered that

The giant redwood is the tallest tree on Earth. It can grow up to 385 feet (117 meters) tall.

another conifer tree that grows in North America is even older: the bristlecone pine tree, found in Nevada, Arizona, and southern California. The oldest known living tree of this kind is 4,600 years old.

Why do some trees **lose their leaves** in autumn?

Broadleaf trees like maples and oaks are called deciduous trees because they lose their leaves in autumn. The loss of their leaves prepares these trees for the lack of water in winter; cold, dry air has little moisture in it, and snow can supply water only when it melts. In addition, the frozen ground makes it difficult for a tree to draw up water through its roots. In spring and summer, gases pass and moisture escapes through thousands of microscopic openings, or stomata, in the leaves. Without its leaves in the winter, a tree can conserve as much water as possible.

In autumn, as the days get shorter and the nights get colder, leaves are sealed off from the branches on which they grow, and water and minerals can no longer travel to them. Photosynthesis stops then, and the leaves gradually fall to the ground. The tree goes dormant (which is like going into a deep sleep) without its active food supply. It rests and stops growing, using food stored earlier to survive until spring arrives.

Why do leaves **turn colors** in autumn?

In autumn, when leaves are sealed off from the branches on which they grow, and water and minerals can no longer reach them, photosynthesis stops. Once leaves are sealed off, their food-making chlorophyll—the substance that gives them their green color—breaks down, and other colors that were in the leaves all along (masked by the abundance of green chlorophyll) appear. Colors like yellow and orange show up then, courtesy of the pigment carotene, which also makes carrots orange.

Some of the beautiful fall colors result from pigments formed by chemical reactions that are triggered by the unique weather conditions in the fall—cooler temperatures at night and shorter days spark the production of anthrocyanin pigments, which give leaves their red and purple tones. Autumn temperatures also produce red colors by reacting with glucose, a type of sugar trapped in the leaves after photosynthesis has stopped.

Changes in the weather affect the brightness of the leaves' colors and the length of time those colors can be seen before the leaves drop off the trees. When temperatures are low—but not to the point of freezing—more anthrocyanin will be produced, giving leaves a brilliant red color. Cloudy and rainy days can also result in brighter, bolder fall colors.

Why do some plants **die in winter,** while others don't?

Plants that grow in temperate zones, where there are changes of seasons, have to be able to go dormant or rest when conditions—like short days and cold temperatures—

become unfavorable for growth. Many trees and shrubs do this by shedding their leaves in the fall, halting photosynthesis and reducing moisture loss. A great number of flowering plants (known as herbaceous perennials) die down to ground level, sheltering new buds in the ground until spring arrives.

Autumn, with its shorter days and cool nights, begins a survival process in plants called "hardening off." Lacking conditions for new growth then, a plant uses its energy to build up more food in its cells. This buildup, in turn, pushes water out into surrounding spaces, where it will do little damage when it freezes. Plants without this ability to harden their tissues die once freezing temperatures arrive. We call plants that die in winter—leaving only their seeds to grow again in spring—"tender" plants, or annuals, because they complete their life cycles within a year. "Hardy" plants, or perennials, are capable of surviving many winter seasons, continuing to grow year after year.

PLANTS AS PROVIDERS

What is the **difference** between a **fruit** and a **vegetable**?

A fruit is the part of a plant that has developed from a flower and contains seeds. Fruits are generally fleshy, sweet, juicy, and colorful. Scientists think that fruits developed in order to spread seeds: fruits attract hungry animals, who carry the swallowed seeds in their digestive systems until they expel them in waste, far from the plants on which the fruits grew. Many of the plant foods that we think of as vegetables— because they are not particularly sweet—are really fruits, because they contain seeds. Tomatoes, peppers, pumpkins, and even nuts are all technically fruits.

Fruits are divided into four types: fruits with seeds embedded in their flesh, like oranges and watermelons; fruits with pits or stones inside, like cherries or peaches; fruits with seeds in a central core, like apples and pears; and dry fruits, like nuts, grains, beans, and peas. (Dry fruits are the seeds themselves—you can eat sweet peas or fava beans, or you can plant them in the ground to grow more.)

Vegetables are simply other parts of plants that are eaten, like roots, stems, and leaves. Carrots and sweet potatoes are roots. Asparagus is a stem. Cabbage and spinach are leaves. Eating fruits and vegetables provides us with valuable vitamins and minerals.

Which plant grows the **largest fruit**?

A plant known as the jackfruit, which grows in the countries of India and Sri Lanka, is thought to produce the largest fruits in the world. One fruit can weigh up to 50

Fibers from these cotton bolls can be picked and then spun into yarn or thread.

pounds (22 kilograms)! They are oval, yellow, and prickly on the outside and have sweet or sour brown pulpy flesh on the inside. The flesh can be cooked or eaten raw.

Can **flowers** be **eaten**?

Believe it not, people have been eating flowers for centuries. The broccoli and cauliflower that we eat are actually clusters of flowers. Artichokes are also flower heads. Even some blossoms that look more like regular flowers—pansies and roses, for instance—have a long edible history.

Flowers can taste sweet, minty, or bitter. They give a special flavor—or even a pretty look—to many foods. But it is very important to know which flowers (or parts of flowers) can be eaten, because lots of plants are poisonous. Even if you know it isn't poisonous, it's better not to eat blooms that you find growing outside because you don't know if they've been treated with chemicals (pesticides) to control insects. Safe, edible flowers can be found in food stores. Or you can grow your own from seeds that come in specially labeled packets that tell you the flowers will be okay to eat.

How is **fabric** made from plants?

Since ancient times, people have been using the fibers of plants to make cloth. Cotton, which comes from the cotton plant, and linen, made from the flax plant, are the most important of these.

The seeds of shrublike cotton plants are surrounded by long, fluffy white fibers. The seeds and fibers are enclosed in capsules, or bolls. The bolls are picked either by hand or machine, and then the fibers are separated the from boll and from the seeds. The fibers are then spun into yarn or thread strong enough to weave into cloth. Weaving is done on looms, which are frames or machines that interlace yarns or threads together. Different types of cotton plants produce fibers with different qualities, with some grown for their sturdiness and some for softness. For centuries, cotton has been grown in many parts of the world, and the cloth and objects made from it have provided valuable trade between countries. But because cotton grows best in mild climates with plenty of rain, the United States is now the biggest producer of cotton.

To make linen, the stems of tall flax plants are soaked until they are partially decomposed. Their long fibers are then removed and used to make yarn or thread that is woven into fabric. Until the widespread use of cotton for clothing (beginning around 1800), people generally wore linen clothes. Linen has been used for so long that examples of it have been found in Egyptian tombs more than 3,500 years old! Although linen is stronger and finer than cotton, it is harder to make because its fibers break easily. Linen is made in many parts of the world, with Ireland being its biggest producer.

How is **medicine** made from plants?

Beginning in ancient times, people discovered—through trial and error—that certain plants could treat diseases, heal wounds, or stop pain. This valuable information was passed down from generation to generation. Today companies that make drugs either raise these special plants and extract their healing substances to put into medicines, or study the plants and make chemical substitutes in laboratories. Currently, at least 25 percent of all the drugs that doctors prescribe still use extracts that come directly from plants: a substance called digitalin that is found in the leaves of the flowering foxglove plant, for instance, continues to help people with heart problems, and the dried sap of the seed pod of the opium poppy plant is still used as a powerful painkiller. New plants with healing properties continue to be discovered in unexplored places like the rain forests, but—sadly—large portions of these habitats have been and continue to be destroyed.

HOW THINGS WORK

TRANSPORTATION

How do **airplanes** fly?

A large jet plane—complete with hundreds of passengers—weighs several hundred thousand pounds. How can this huge and heavy machine get off the ground in the first place, let alone stay aloft for thousands of miles? Airplanes function according to a complex mix of aerodynamic principles—theories that explain the motion of air and the actions of bodies moving through that air.

Airplanes get their power from engines. Small planes generally use piston engines, which turn propellers that push aircraft through the air in the same way that boat propellers push vessels through water. But bigger planes use jet engines, powered by burning fuel. These engines expel great amounts of air that thrust them forward and up.

Airplanes are able to lift into the air and stay there because of the shape of their wings. An airplane wing is flat on the bottom and curved on the top. When a plane's engines push it forward, air divides to travel around its wings. The air that passes over the larger curved top moves faster than the air that passes under the flat bottom. The faster-moving air on top becomes thinner and has lower pressure than the air below, which pushes the wing up. Uneven air pressure caused by the shape of an airplane's wings, then, creates a force called lift, which allows an aircraft to fly.

The force of moving air is also used to steer an airplane. Steering is done through a system of moveable flaps—working much like boat rudders—that are located on the plane's wings and tail. When set at an angle, they push at flowing air that pushes back, turning or tilting an airplane. To descend, for instance, a pilot lowers a plane's tail flaps, causing airflow to direct its nose downward. Turning requires changing the direction of wing flaps and the tail rudder.

233

Airplanes get their power from engines, but they are able to stay up in the air thanks to aerodynamic principles.

An airplane must be in constant motion—its wings slicing through rushing air to create lift—in order to stay up; moving air is also required to steer it. In other words, a plane cannot fly without the power of its engines thrusting it through the air. In order to get enough lift to rise into the air on takeoff, an airplane has to travel along the ground first at great speed.

What is a **sonic boom**?

As long as an aircraft is moving at a rate slower than the speed of sound (about 1,120 feet, or 340 meters, per second, which is known as Mach 1), the air that it disturbs is evenly distributed around it. But as an aircraft approaches Mach 1, the air molecules in front of it become crowded together. The impact made when an aircraft flies through them—called breaking the "sound barrier"—causes shockwaves that reach our ears as a thunderous sonic boom. The aircraft leaves the waves behind as it enters supersonic flight.

A supersonic airplane is shaped quite differently than a regular, "subsonic" plane. It is usually shaped like a dart, with a long pointed nose and wings that swing back and hug the plane body. This slim shape causes less friction as it races through the air. The close-set wings also stay within the shock waves the plane creates, which is necessary to maintain control of the aircraft. While the special wings of supersonic planes don't provide as much lift as those of regular planes, the aircraft get the lift they need for takeoffs and landings by traveling at very high speeds.

How do air traffic controllers **know where planes are** in the sky?

Air traffic controllers use radar—invisible bands of energy called radio waves (which are similar to visible light waves)—to detect where airplanes are located in the air. They are the same type of waves as those used in broadcasting but with higher frequencies. Radar waves, which travel in a straight line and at a constant speed, are sent out in all directions through antennae. When radar waves meet distant objects like planes, they are reflected back to receivers. Controllers can tell how far away the objects are located by the speed at which the reflected waves return. Radar receivers process the return signals electronically, using them to visually plot planes on a screen that represents the sky. With radar, controllers can tell how high and fast a plane is flying and in what direction it is heading. While large commercial airplanes have their own radar devices on board to report their altitudes (distance from the ground) and to warn them of obstacles in their paths, smaller aircraft do not. Air traffic controllers keep all planes around an airport at a safe distance from one another, and they direct takeoffs and landings. Controllers can even help a plane land in heavy fog by watching its flight on their radar screen and radioing directions to the pilot.

Because radar can detect the position, motion, and even the size and shape of very distant objects, it is used for many other purposes. These purposes include ship navigation, storm detection and weather forecasting, mapmaking, and space exploration.

How do **helicopters** fly?

Although a helicopter doesn't have wings like an airplane, it uses the same principle of lift to rise and maneuver in the air. The blades of a helicopter's propeller-like top rotor are shaped just like a plane's wings—flat on the bottom and rounded on the top—and are likewise adjustable. Instead of rushing forward through the air like a plane does to gather enough lift to fly, a helicopter moves only its (three to six) rotor blades, which are attached to a central shaft driven by an engine. The rotor blades slice through enough air—creating the changes in surrounding air pressure that produce lift—to achieve flight.

Adjusting the angle at which the rotor blades are set helps control a helicopter's lift and manner of flight. Because the angle of the rotor is adjustable, too, a helicopter has far greater maneuverability than an airplane: besides moving up, down, and forward, it can fly backwards and hover in the air.

One problem with a helicopter's design is the spinning force of its main rotor. As the rotor blades of a helicopter turn, its shaft pushes back on the craft, trying to spin it in the opposite direction. The helicopter would spin out of control if it were not for an equal, counteracting force. This force is supplied by a second, smaller rotor located vertically on the craft's tail. Acting like a propeller, the thrust from this rotor pushes the tail in the direction opposite the twisting force of the main rotor. A helicopter pilot can adjust the thrust of this tail rotor in order to turn his or her craft. Some large

235

helicopters that carry heavy loads have two top rotors, which supply twice as much lift. In such cases there is no need for a tail rotor because each horizontal rotor spins in an opposite direction.

How do **rockets** blast off?

A rocket has a simple heat engine. It uses quick-burning fuels, known as propellants, in a combustion chamber, which has an open end at the bottom. The hot gases produced from the burning fuel expand and push in all directions, but they can escape only at the open end, and they do so with great speed and force. The difference in pressure between the closed front and open back of the chamber pushes the rocket forward. The size of a rocket blastoff depends on the amount of gas it produces and the speed at which it is released. Weapons like large missiles and space ships use rocket engines to power them. (The Chinese are believed to have used the first rocket-type weapons—pieces of bamboo filled with gunpowder—about one thousand years ago.) Most engines require oxygen (supplied by air) to burn the fuels that power them. Rocket engines, however, need to be able to operate in airless outer space, so they can't rely on oxygen normally found in the air. Rocket fuel is usually a mixture that includes oxygen in liquid form.

How do **boats** float?

The weight of an object pulls it down into water. It displaces or pushes water aside. But if the object's density (its weight in relation to its size) is less than the density of the water it displaces, it will float. That principle explains why a heavy wooden raft can float in water, while a small stone will sink to the bottom: one spreads its weight over a large area, while the other's weight is concentrated.

Boats, which are hollow, float because of this principle. The air inside them makes them less dense than they appear. Large ships that transport heavy material, though, have less air inside when they are carrying a big load. Such ships must be careful about weight limits and have load lines on their hulls that show how low they can ride in the water and still maneuver safely. Weight limits vary with the kind of water the boats are traveling through: they can carry more weight when in saltwater seas, which are denser than freshwater, and in cold water, which is denser than warm water.

Boats need a power source to move them forward in the water. In small vessels this power can be provided by people, who use oars to paddle along. Muscle power can't move boats very fast or very far, though. The wind can be used, too (as long as it's blowing), to move boats equipped with sails. But for a large boat that needs to go a long distance, the most reliable source of power is a motor-driven engine.

Depending on the size of the boat, a gasoline engine, diesel engine, or steam engine can do the job. Nuclear power is even used to run some boat engines, like

When a submarine needs to come to the surface, compressed air is blown into its ballast tanks.

those found in submarines. Motors rotate boat propellers, which have large twisting blades that radiate around a central hub. These blades push water backwards, and the boat moves forward as the disturbed water pushes back. Rotating propellers also create lower water pressure in the space in front of them, which sucks them forward, along with the vessel to which they are attached. (Using these same principles of movement, propellers can also power aircraft.) A boat is steered by a rudder, which is a flat, upright, movable piece of wood or metal that is attached to its stern, or rear. When turned, the rudder changes the direction of the water around it— which pushes back—forcing the stern, and gradually the rest of the boat, to change direction, too.

Because boats must push aside the weight of the water through which their hulls are moving, they do not travel very fast. Water that is pushed one way always pushes back, causing resistance. Boats that are meant to go fast, like speedboats, are designed to ride as high in the water as possible, to minimize water drag. Their hulls are shaped to rise out of the water when they are running at top speeds.

How do **submarines** sink and rise?

The body of a submarine is uniquely constructed. Under its strong outer hull are huge ballast tanks that surround its working core. The tanks can be filled with and emptied of seawater and air, which allows the submarine to sink or rise in the water.

When a submarine travels on the surface, its ballast tanks are filled with air, which makes it less dense than the seawater it displaces, and it floats. But when a submarine needs to submerge or dive below the surface, its ballast tanks are flooded with seawater. This action makes the submarine sink; now equal in density to the water that surrounds it, it can move about below the surface. Motor-driven propellers are used to move the vessel along (its streamlined shape creating as little water resistance as possible), and swiveling fins located on its sides, called hydroplanes, direct it up and down. When a submarine needs to return to the surface, compressed air stored in tanks is blown into the ballast tanks. This air forces out the seawater, and the vessel begins to rise, aided by the hydroplanes. Once again lighter than the seawater it displaces, the submarine is able to float on the surface.

How do submarine pilots know where they are going when they are underwater? If they are not too far below the surface, a periscope is used. This tall, rotating, tube-shaped instrument can be raised above the water's surface to view surroundings, using a series of mirrors and lenses inside to relay images. Beyond that, submarines use sonar (sound waves) to make echo soundings of their surroundings. Transmitted sound waves are reflected off objects or the ocean floor; the time it takes for these sound waves to be reflected back indicates how far away things are located. The echoes are then converted into electrical signals that appear on a display screen, which gives a picture—similar to that of an airport's radar screen—of surrounding waters.

How is **sonar** different from **radar**?

Sonar (short for "*so*und *na*vigation *r*anging") and radar ("*ra*dio *d*etection *a*nd *r*anging") work in much the same way to locate distant objects. In both cases invisible waves are sent out and reflected back once they hit something solid. The time it takes for the waves to return to their point of origin tells how far away an object is located.

Radar uses a certain type of light wave known as a radio wave to locate objects. Like all light waves, radar travels in a straight line and at a constant speed: at 186,000 miles (299,274 kilometers) per second, which is the speed of light. Sonar uses sound waves to locate objects. These waves, too, travel in a straight line, but at varying speeds, depending on what they are traveling through. Sound is caused by the vibration of an object, which in turn vibrates surrounding molecules that make sound waves in a kind of chain reaction. Sonar detection is mainly used underwater, where light waves do not travel well. In water, sound waves move about four times faster than they do through air because water is denser and has more molecules that can vibrate. But even at 4,600 feet (1,400 meters) per second, sound waves travel much more slowly than light waves. They also can't be used in outer space, which is airless and has essentially no molecules at all.

How do **trains** run?

A train is a series of unpowered cars pulled along tracks by a locomotive, or engine. The locomotive is run by a motor—either electric or a diesel-electric combination—that provides the power that turns its wheels, moving the engine and the cars attached to it. A single locomotive can pull dozens and dozens of cars; some trains reach more than a mile in length. Electric motors are used only for trains that run over the same track for short distances. They receive electricity from wires that run above the track. Trolleys and streetcars are types of electric trains. (A subway train is powered by electricity delivered through a third rail on its tracks.) Unlike electric engines, diesel-electric engines can provide the amount of power needed to propel locomotives that travel long distances and pull great weights. Burning diesel oil powers a generator that creates electricity; the electricity powers motors that turn the wheels. For many decades, before diesel oil was used, locomotive engines were powered by superheated steam, made by burning coal or wood in large furnaces.

How do elevators work?

An elevator is any device that moves things or people from one level to another. They are especially important in tall structures like skyscrapers, where climbing stairs to get to top floors would be very difficult. The car of an elevator, in which people ride, is attached to guard rails inside a tall, empty space called a shaft. It is moved by a steel cable that is attached to a large weight that counterbalances it. An electric motor raises and lowers the cable, changing the positions of the car and weight as the elevator moves from floor to floor. (Usually posted inside an elevator are numbers that indicate the car's weight limit; an elevator motor cannot do its job if a car is a lot heavier than the weight that balances it.)

The first elevators in use were not especially safe because once in a while a cable would break, and a car, pulled by gravity, would come crashing down. Safety devices were soon added, though, to keep such disasters from occurring. (American inventor Elisha Otis invented the first "safety" elevator in 1853.) Additional ropes attached to cars and powerful metal "jaws" that grip guard rails keep elevators from falling if their main cables break. Other safety devices keep elevators from moving when their doors are still open and from traveling too fast. Automatic switches in the shaft allow an elevator to hurry past unwanted floors, or to slow and stop when a chosen floor is reached, unlocking its doors to admit and release passengers.

How do **escalators** work?

An escalator is a continuously moving stairway. It takes people from one floor of a building to another, just like an elevator. But it can transport many more people than an elevator can in the same amount of time (between 5,000 and 8,000 per hour).

An escalator is run by an electric motor located at the top. It turns a large, geared drive wheel that moves a chain—with steps attached to it—in a continuous loop above the floor and below. A large return wheel guides the chain at the bottom of the escalator. So a set of escalator stairs runs under the set you travel on, which pop up for more riders. Rubbery handrails, which also move in a continuous loop, are connected to the drive wheel as well and give riders a good grip as they travel along.

What causes **escalator steps** to **fold flat** when they get to the top and the bottom?

The secret has to do with hidden wheels—connected to each step—that run along rails. Each stair has two wheels on each side. Wheels connected to the front of each stair run along one rail, and wheels connected to the back of each stair run along another. When escalator rails run alongside each other, their stairs have a normal shape. But the rails change position in relation to each other as they approach the top and bottom of an escalator, and the stairs are gradually pulled flat.

COMMUNICATION

How does **television** work?

Television works through a series of complicated processes. It starts with a television camera, which takes pictures of scenes. Photo cells inside the camera change the pictures to electrical signals. At the same time, a microphone records sounds that are occurring during the scenes. A vibrating magnet in the microphone changes these sounds into electrical signals, too.

Some television shows, like news reports, are recorded live, which means that they are broadcast to homes as they occur. But most of the television programs that we watch are recorded, which means that they are put on videotape and sent out later. The electrical signals of sound and pictures are stored as magnetic signals on videotape, which are converted back to electrical signals when played.

Before a program is broadcast, its electrical picture and sound signals are run through a device called a television transmitter. With the help of strong magnets, the transformer turns the electrical signals into invisible bands of energy called radio waves (similar to visible light waves), which can travel great distances through the air. They can travel directly to outdoor television antennae, which catch the waves and send them to television sets that change them into pictures and sounds again. Cable companies send electrical picture and sound signals through cables directly to homes.

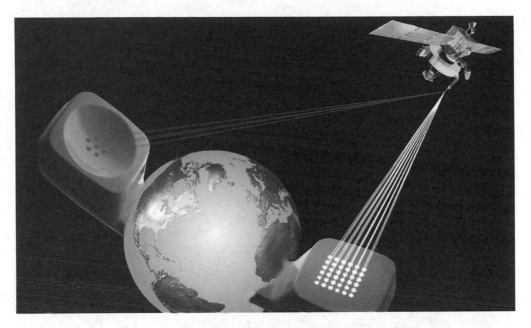

Communication satellites that orbit the world make things like long-distance phone calls fast and clear.

When broadcasting to faraway places, communication satellites that orbit the world are used to bounce or return the waves back to Earth, extending their travel distance. Satellites are necessary because radio waves move in straight lines and cannot bend around the world.

When an antenna or satellite dish receives radio waves, it changes them back into electrical signals. A speaker in a television set changes some of the signals back into sound. The pictures are reproduced by special guns at the back of a television set that shoot electron beams at the screen, causing it to glow with tiny dots of different colors. Viewed together, the dots look like a regular picture. The individual pictures that make up a scene are broadcast and received—one after another—at a pace so quick that it looks like continuous action is occurring on the screen. The entire process happens very fast because television stations and broadcast towers are all around and because radio waves travel very quickly, at the speed of light. Radio programs broadcast talk and music across the airwaves using the same technology.

How do **telephones** work?

All sound is made by the back and forth movement, or vibration, of objects. When an object vibrates, it makes the molecules around it vibrate too, causing a ripple of motion known as a sound wave, which can travel through air, water, and solid materials. A telephone has vibrating parts—a disc in the mouthpiece and one in the ear-

241

piece—that turn voice sounds into electrical signals that can travel along telephone wires and then turn back into sound again.

Phones are usually connected to wires because they run on electricity. When you pick up a phone, a low electrical current allows you to dial the series of numbers that will connect you to the phone of a friend, for example. Each number on the phone has its own special electrical signal, and when the right numbers are combined, they can exactly identify your friend's phone line. A local telephone office receives this information when you dial and sends your call in the right direction. Call signals to places close by travel along wires or cables buried underground or strung high in the air between supports. But when the person you call is very far away, the electrical signals sent from your phone are changed into invisible waves of energy called microwaves, which can travel long distances through the air. These waves are sent through space to communication satellites that orbit the world, which bounce them back to Earth, extending the waves' travel distance. An antenna at a receiving station near the home of your friend picks up the waves and changes them to electrical signals once more. They travel by cable to the telephone office that services your friend's neighborhood, where his or her number is identified. A signal is then sent to your friend's phone to make it ring. The entire process from dialing to ringing takes just a few seconds!

When your friend answers the phone, a microphone in its mouthpiece contains a plastic disc that vibrates, turning his or her message into electrical signals that travel along the same path as before. A speaker in the earpiece of your phone receives the electrical signals, which vibrate another plastic disc that changes them back into sound. Two circuits—from microphone to speaker—are created, and you can talk back and forth with your friend. The next time you use the phone, think of the remarkable process that makes it possible!

How do **cellular phones** work?

Cellular phones have exploded in popularity in a relatively short period of time. Cell phones first became available to consumers in the early 1980s, but the technology that made them small and truly portable evolved gradually over the next 10 years or so. By the beginning of the twenty-first century, millions and millions of people in countries all over the world were using cell phones on a daily basis. And it isn't just adults who enjoy the benefits of completely mobile phone capabilities: in the United States alone, more than 20 percent of teenagers have a cell phone. That translates to at least one in five American teens.

Before cellular phones, people like police officers or taxi drivers could communicate from their cars using two-way radios. All of the radios in one city transmitted signals via a large, central antenna located on top of a tall building. With all callers sharing one antenna, the number of calls that could be made at any one time was very limited. The cellular system takes care of that problem by dividing each city into many small cells (a large city can have hundreds). Each cell has its own tower (which contains an antenna as well as transmitters and receivers that send and receive signals). Each tower can handle numerous callers at a given time, and their small size and weaker signal (compared to the radio antennae) means that their signals don't interfere with those of nearby towers.

When you call someone using a cellular phone, your phone is sending and receiving signals via radio waves, invisible bands of energy that work like light rays. In other words, your cell phone is a fancy, high-tech radio. After you dial a friend's number, your phone must find the closest tower by searching for the strongest signal. Once that signal is located, your phone transmits certain information—like your cell phone number and serial number—that help your service provider (the company your parents pay each month for cell phone service) make sure you are one of their customers. Then the mobile telephone switching office (MTSO) finds an available channel where your conversation can take place. The MTSO then completes the connection (all of this happening in a few short seconds) and you are chatting with your friend—without wires or cords to hold you down. If you are sitting in the back seat of the car while talking, and your mom is driving you from one end of town to the other, your call will be automatically switched from one cell to the next without any pause in your conversation.

How does a **tape recorder** work?

A tape recorder uses a magnetic language to record and play back music, words, and sounds. It does this by way of a plastic tape coated with tiny iron particles that are arranged in a haphazard way. Sound that enters a tape recorder's microphone is turned into electrical signals. These electrical signals, in turn, are changed into magnetic signals by an electromagnet, located in the recording head. When a recording tape rubs against the head as it winds from one spool to another, its metal particles are magnetized and rearranged in patterns that correspond with the different sounds being recorded.

When a tape is played back, the reverse process takes place. When rubbed across a playing head, the iron particles of a tape send magnetic signals that are converted into electrical signals. These signals are then changed by the tape recorder's speaker into sound. The videocassette player (VCR) that you use to record television shows and play movies has a similar magnetic language. All the information that makes up sound *and* pictures can be stored on a videotape in magnetized metal particles, arranged in complicated patterns. Videotapes are much wider than cassette tapes because they carry so much more information.

How do **computers** work?

A computer, like all digital machines, changes writing, images, and sound into a special numerical language. It is a binary (or two-part) language that has just two numbers: 0 and 1. These numbers are called "binary digits," or bits for short. In a digital machine, the numbers take the form of electric signals. With a 1 the electricity is switched on and with a 0 it is switched off. Information of all kinds, then, is turned into electrical on-off signals arranged in countless individual patterns. These patterns can be stored, sent along digital pathways, or converted back into forms that we can use and understand with extraordinary speed and accuracy.

Bits enter a personal computer from the keypad, mouse, microphone, and scanner. They are received and sent out by the modem, as well as stored in various memory devices. The computer screen, printer, and speakers convert the bits into forms of information that we can use.

How does the **Internet** work?

Just as telephones are connected by a worldwide phone system, home and work computers can connect with a global computer communications network known as the Internet. Each computer that is linked to the system has its own Internet address, as individual as a phone number. Home computer users buy the services of an Internet provider, which is an organization with powerful computers that link all its subscribers to the Internet; many large organizations and companies have computers that link them directly to the network. Internet users can visit the World Wide Web, which is a global network of Web sites providing information, entertainment, products, and other services.

People can use the Internet to send electronic mail, known as e-mail, to one another in just a few seconds. Once you type a message into your computer to send to your cousin, let's say—who lives miles from you across the country—it travels through the wires of your phone line as a series of electrical signals (or, for some people, the signals travel through the same cables that bring them cable television). These signals travel to a station run by your service provider, where a big computer sends them to an Internet routing center. Located all over the world, routing centers—linked to organizations and Internet providers—send the countless computer communications that come to them each second along the quickest possible routes to their destinations. A giant computer there reads the address on your e-mail and sends it farther: depending on the distance it must travel, it may continue along phone lines, be changed into light signals that can travel with great speed along thin glass strands called fiber-optic cables, or be converted into equally speedy invisible bands of energy known as radio waves and transmitted to a communications satellite that will bounce it back to Earth to a ground station located close to where your cousin lives.

Once your message reaches the routing center nearest your cousin, it will be sent to the station of his or her service provider. From there it will be sent along regular phone lines to his or her computer. And all of this happens in a matter of moments.

How does **mail** get from **one place to another**?

Once you mail a letter, a complex process that requires the efforts of many people and machines—sometimes located in different parts of the world—begins. Perhaps you put your letter into one of the mailboxes found at various locations in your community (these conveniently located boxes mean you don't have to make a trip to the post office each time you want to mail a letter). Mailboxes are visited by mail carriers a few times each day to pick up their contents. The mail collected by carriers is taken to a local postal sorting office, where it joins all the other letters that have been mailed in the area that day. High-speed machines take over then, preparing your letter to reach its destination.

Mail is dumped onto a moving (conveyor) belt that brings it to a machine that separates it by size. Another machine checks to make sure that all the mail is properly stamped, and then it cancels, or prints over, the stamps so that they can't be used again. A postmark is also printed on each envelope, which tells the time, date, and place from which the letters have been mailed.

A machine reads the zip codes written in the addresses of letters, which tell exactly to which part of the country—or the world—they are headed. (Postal services around the globe work together to distribute mail and most have similar code systems.) Postal workers process by hand the letters that have missing or unreadable zip codes. The zip code machine prints a bar code—a machine-readable series of lines, more reliable than written numerals—on each letter, and a second sorting machine reads and separates them by destination. Mail is grouped by city and country. Local mail is prepared for delivery the next day. Other mail travels by truck, express train, or plane, depending on where it is going.

Once mail travels close to its destination, it is unloaded at another postal sorting office. A bar code–reading machine scans the letters again, separating them further for delivery to districts, neighborhoods, and streets. The letters are sent to local post offices, where carriers are given the mail for their delivery areas. Routes may include homes, shops, and office buildings. Carriers who work in farm country—where people live very far apart—may have to travel many miles to deliver the mail each day.

How are **newspapers** made?

People usually read newspapers to get information about current events, things that are happening at the present time or have just occurred. So when the people that work for a newspaper learn about something that would make a good news story, they move quickly. Reporters are immediately sent out to gather as much information about the situation as possible and photographers take pictures that add visual information. When they return to the newspaper office, the reporters type their story into a computer, and camera film is developed into photos in a darkroom.

The photographs are put into the computer with a device called a scanner. Increasing numbers of photographers use digital cameras, which means their photos do not have to be first developed on paper. They are automatically in digital, or computer-ready, format and can be transmitted over phone lines or via satellites just like e-mail or other electronic files. Once the photos are in digital format, the printed story and the pictures that illustrate it are arranged together. The story may take up part of a newspaper page or may extend for a few pages. Designers arrange all the stories and photos that make up a newspaper into visually appealing, easy-to-read pages on the computer screen. They are then printed out on pieces of clear film.

Next, the film print of each newspaper page is laid on a light-sensitive metal plate. When it is exposed to a flash of bright light, shadows of the film's letters and pictures are left on the plate. The shadows are permanently etched or marked into the plate when it is soaked in acid, which eats some of the metal away. What is left is a perfect copy of the film print of the newspaper page, with its words and pictures appearing as grooves in the metal.

The newspaper page is now ready to be printed on paper. The metal plate is first wrapped around a roller on a motor-driven printing press and coated with ink. After being wiped clean, ink still stays in the grooves. When paper (in big rolls) is passed under the roller, it is pressed into the grooves, and perfectly printed pages appear. This process is repeated for each newspaper page. As you can imagine, printing plants are enormous, with some presses standing three stories tall. These expensive machines (costing tens of millions of dollars) can print and sort up to 70,000 copies of a newspaper per hour. Once the press is done printing and sorting, the newspapers are bundled for delivery the next day to homes and newsstands.

Long before computers and motor-driven presses, printing was done by hand with wooden blocks of letters and figures dipped in ink and pressed onto paper. It is believed that this method of printing was invented in China around the year 700. A hand-operated printing press—with moveable type or letters—was first used in Europe in the mid-fifteenth century. (Johannes Gutenberg printed the first book, a Bible, in what is now Germany, in 1455.) Until that time all books and other manuscripts had to be written out by hand!

How does a **lie detector** work?

Lie detectors, or polygraphs, have been featured in countless police dramas on television and in the movies, and they are usually portrayed as foolproof methods of determining whether a person accused of a crime is lying or telling the truth. A person taking a polygraph is hooked up to several sensors that measure things like heart rate, blood pressure, breathing rate, and perspiration, or sweat. The results measured by the sensors are recorded as jagged lines on a piece of paper that moves through the polygraph machine.

The tester begins by asking the subject questions he or she knows the answers to, like the subject's name, the day of the week, or the color of an article of clothing. From the answers to these questions the tester can see what the subject's normal heart and breathing rates look like. Then the tester begins to ask the serious questions, about the crime that was committed, for example. The idea is that if a person is lying, his or her heart will beat faster and he or she will sweat more, and these changes will be recorded as higher peaks in the jagged lines. Many people believe that an experienced reader of polygraph tests can accurately tell if the person being tested has lied. Others insist that such tests are highly inaccurate and easy to beat for those who know how.

IMAGE MAKERS AND PICTURE TAKERS

How does a **copy machine** work?

Most photocopiers are machines that use static electricity and powder, rather than ink, to print copies on plain paper. Once you place the page you want reproduced onto the glass plate on top of the copy machine and close its lid, a strong light inside sweeps across the page. With the help of a lens the image from your page is reflected on the outside of a turning metal cylinder or drum below. Invisible positive charges of static electricity create an image on the drum. Dark parts of your image are more strongly charged than light parts.

Negatively charged black powder called toner is dusted across the surface of the drum, sticking most to wherever the positive charges are strongest. Then the drum rolls across a blank piece of paper, and the powder is transferred to its surface. In order to make the powder stick, though, it must be melted onto the paper. This melting occurs when the paper passes through heated rollers. Your copy is now complete and slides out of the machine.

This "dry ink" method of copying works well because images instantly stick to the drum and are just as quickly removed, enabling the photocopier to be ready for immediate reuse. The process is repeated—from beginning to end—whether you want more than one copy of your page or need to copy a new page altogether.

What is **static electricity**?

All matter is made of tiny particles called atoms. Inside an atom are even tinier particles: electrons that move in orbit around a center, or nucleus, made of neutrons and protons. An electron has a negative electric charge and a proton has a positive one. Usually an atom has the same number of each, which keeps the atom neutral or uncharged. But sometimes electrons leave their orbit, attracted to other atoms that lack an electron and are positively charged. The movement or flow of electrons from one atom to another produces the form of energy called electricity. When electrons are moved by a force through a conductor—like a wire—the flow of energy they create is known as current electricity. The work that this form of electricity does can be seen when we turn on a light bulb or watch a television show.

Static electricity is a form of electricity that does not flow: it is electricity at rest. Objects carry positive electric charges when some of their atoms have fewer electrons than they should, and they carry negative electric charges when some of the atoms have more electrons than they should. An easy way to produce static electricity is to rub two objects (made of certain materials) together: this transfers electrons from one item to another, giving each a positive or negative charge. Positively and negatively charged objects are attracted to each other like magnets—because each wants to shed or acquire electrons. When static electricity becomes powerful enough, so many electrons jump from one thing to another that they cause a visible electric spark, which you will feel as a little "shock" if one of the things the electrons jump to is you! (Loose electrons can attach to atoms in the surface of your skin.) Lightning, in fact, is really just a giant spark that results when static electricity builds up in a cloud during a thunderstorm.

How does a **camera** take pictures?

When you press the picture-taking button on a camera, you open the shutter and let light inside for a fraction of a second. The light passes through a lens that focuses it on film, leaving a record there of what the camera "saw" during that button-pressing instant. The film is coated with light-sensitive chemicals that save the impression, but it usually has to be placed into a bath of other chemicals to make an image appear and remain permanently. The film is developed into negatives, on which appear images that look very different than those that were photographed: dark shades appear light, light shades appear dark, and colors are the opposite of what they should be. But when light passes through these negatives onto special photo paper, which is also developed using chemicals, the images that appear are normal again—exact copies of the photographed scenes. With "instant" cameras, developing chemicals are contained inside, treating the film right away. A picture pops out on photo paper, its image forming while you wait.

How do **X rays** work?

X rays are similar to visible light in that both are forms of electromagnetic energy, which travels in waves. But X rays have much shorter wavelengths than light, so they are invisible. Just as light can pass through some things, like glass, X rays can pass through certain materials. They can pass through your skin, muscles, and organs, for example, but not through dense things like your bones (which contain heavier atoms). When you have an X ray taken, the waves are projected through you onto a film or

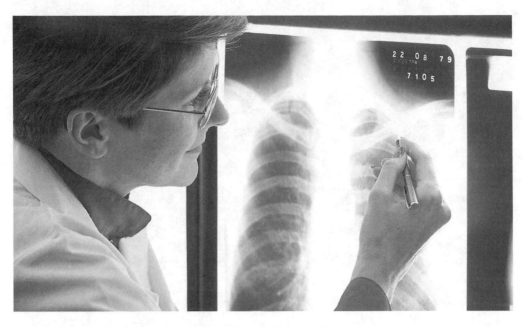

X rays pass through skin, muscles, and organs, but not through dense things like bones.

plate that is coated with special chemicals. Most X rays are stopped when they hit a bone, but pass through other body parts, which appear dark on the X ray after it is developed. Bones stand out light and clear. When organs like the stomach or intestines need to be X-rayed, the patient drinks a special liquid that stops the rays. That liquid coats the organ, and a picture can be taken.

Doctors take great care to minimize the number of X rays given to any one patient because the radiation can damage living tissue. But sometimes the ability of X rays to destroy cells is beneficial; many cancer patients have undergone radiation therapy in an effort to kill diseased cells in tumors.

LIGHTS AND LASERS

What makes a **shadow**?

Visible light spreads out in waves as it leaves its source. These waves travel in straight lines through the air until they hit an object. The object will absorb some of the waves and reflect some back into the air. (Light waves will not be able pass through most materials, unless they are clear, like glass.) Behind any object that has stopped the light waves is a dark spot, or shadow, which is simply a space where no light is.

249

Objects that interrupt light waves create a dark spot, or shadow, which is simply a space where no light is.

There are no shadows in dark rooms because no light waves are traveling through them. And on overcast days you won't see shadows outside because the Sun's rays are absorbed and scattered in all directions by the clouds in the sky; not enough direct light waves make it to Earth to cause shadows. Why does your shadow change shape during a sunny day? It has to do with the location of the Sun and the angle of the light waves that hit you. When the Sun is high in the sky, the angle of its light waves in relation to you produce a short, squat shadow. When the Sun is low in the sky (early or late in the day), it produces a long, giant-sized shadow. One way to think about this concept is to pretend you could draw a line from the Sun that skims the top of your head and ends on the ground behind you. When the Sun is right above you, that line will end very close to your body (and so will your shadow). When the Sun is low during evening hours, that line (and your shadow) will end farther behind you.

How does a **light bulb** work?

Electricity runs through a thin, coiled wire, or filament, in a light bulb. The filament is made of a metal called tungsten, which can reach very high temperatures before it melts. This high melting temperature is a good thing, because when electricity runs through the filament of a light bulb, it reaches a temperature of about 4,500 degrees Fahrenheit (2,482 degrees Celsius). As the filament becomes white-hot, it glows, or becomes incandescent. That glow is the light of an electric bulb.

Wires that carry electricity usually allow it to flow through easily. But when wire is very thin—like in the filament of a light bulb—electrical currents have to force their way through, causing friction, which causes heat, which, in this case, results in incandescence.

Instead of air, light bulbs are filled with a gas called argon. Air has oxygen in it, which all things need to burn. If the super-hot filament of a light bulb were exposed to air, it would burn out instantly, instead of giving hundreds of hours of light. So why does a light bulb eventually "burn out," then?

A light bulb doesn't really burn out. But during each intense heating, some of the tungsten in the filament vaporizes, breaking off into tiny particles that float in the argon. This process causes the filament to weaken in spots and eventually to break. The discoloration that you see on the inside surface of a worn-out light bulb is not caused by burn marks, then, but by a thin coating of evaporated tungsten.

Electricity and a filament, a piece of thin, coiled wire, are responsible for the light of a bulb. *Robert I. Huffman/Field Mark Publications © 2001*

How do clocks and other things **glow in the dark**?

When a substance is exposed to light, it absorbs light energy. The molecules of most substances usually release this excess energy—in the form of light and heat—but do it so quickly that the process can't be seen. Some substances, like calcium sulfide, however, are able to store a portion of the light to which they have been exposed, releasing it a bit at a time. This characteristic is called phosphorescence. Other substances can be added to phosphorescents to increase the amount of time that they can store light, because the ability usually fades over time. Glow-in-the-dark toys and paint used on clock and watch dials are made of phosphorescent materials. While their slow-releasing light is not detectable during the day, it is very clear at night, when all is dark. Without light exposure, though, phosphorescent things won't work, because they can't store light energy to release.

What is a **laser**?

A laser (which is short for "*l*ight *a*mplification by *s*timulated *e*mission of *r*adiation") is a device that produces laser light. Laser light is more powerful that ordinary light

251

because all its rays have the same wavelength and move together, allowing them to be focused in a narrow beam with great precision. (The rays that make up regular light are made of several wavelengths that spread out in all directions once they leave their source.) A laser beam can be focused on so small an area that it can put 200 holes on the head of a pin!

Laser light beams vary in strength, depending on the materials and amount of energy used to make them. Some—made of invisible infrared rays—can create so much heat that they can cut through metal. Because laser beams can be controlled with such precision, these same infrared rays can be used instead of scalpels to perform the most delicate surgeries. Lasers that produce visible light beams are equally useful, both in scientific work and in our everyday lives. Because laser beams can measure great distances with such accuracy, for example, they have been reflected from mirrors placed on the Moon to record our exact distance from it. Telephone and computer signals are sometimes changed into laser light so that they can travel with great speed through glass fiber-optic cables. Low-powered light lasers read the bar codes on the labels of products we buy at stores and scan the patterns etched on compact discs to give us music.

How does music come from a **compact disc**?

Not too long ago, music was recorded on a phonograph record, which was the first invention that made a permanent record of sounds that could be played back. Sound vibrations—like a voice singing or an instrument playing—were changed by a microphone into electrical signals that directed a sharp needle to cut a wiggly groove into a spinning plastic or vinyl record. A record player, with its needle riding lightly in the groove of a revolving record, could reproduce the electrical signals and change them back into sound through its speakers.

Today, compact discs (CDs) are used instead of phonograph records to record music. Less than five inches across, CDs can hold more music than long-playing (LP), 12-inch records. This capacity is possible because a CD spins very fast as its signals are read, up to 500 revolutions per minute (LPs make about 33 complete turns per minute). The spiral track of a CD is also very fine—thinner than a human hair—which allows more music to be fit onto its smaller surface.

On the bottom side of a CD is a thin metal sheet. Tiny round depressions called pits—which represent sound—fill its spiral track. Just as needles were used to cut grooves into phonograph records, chemicals eat away the metal on CDs to create these pits. A beam of laser light is used instead of a record player needle to change a CD's pitted track back into sound. Unlike ordinary light, which spreads out in all directions once it leaves its source, laser light can be focused with great accuracy. It moves along the track of a CD, and sensors detect the pattern of shiny flat parts (which reflect light back) and pits (which don't). These on-and-off flashes of reflected light turn into electrical signals. A computer in a compact disc player, which has an enormous memory that stores every possible combination of on-and-off patterns, converts the signals to musical notes with different pitches and volumes in the player's speakers. And then the music plays! Unlike phonographic sound, which could be impaired by scratched records, dull playing needles, or wobbly turntables, the sound from compact discs is remarkably true to life because such problems don't affect the efficiency of laser beams.

A DVD (which stands for digital versatile disc) uses very similar technology to a CD, only DVDs can hold much more data (about seven times more than a CD). In recent years their outstanding quality have made DVDs increasingly popular. They can hold a full-length movie as well as many added features, like subtitles in multiple languages, commentaries from directors, extra scenes that were deleted from the final version of the movie, and more.

Why do most things bought in stores have **bars and numbers** printed on them?

The groups of lines and numbers that you see on the packaging or labels of most items in a store are called the Universal Product Code (UPC). Widely used in the United States, the series of bars holds a coded message that allows a computer to exactly identify the name and size of each product and the company that makes it. The numbers accompanying the lines give the same information, but the bars can only be read by a machine, while the numbers can be read by store employees.

When you buy an item in a store, a worker passes the item's bar code in front of a reading device. A beam of laser light scans the bar code, and its unique light and dark pattern is changed into on-and-off electrical signals. These signals travel to a computer, which identifies the item and sends information about it to a main store computer or to one located in the business's main office (to help keep track of the store's stock of that item, for instance). The computer is also connected to a cash register, which can print the item name and price on a receipt. UPC symbols have made it easier for retailers to keep track of merchandise and to learn what kinds of items customers want to buy. It saves purchasers time in the check-out line, helping store employees ring up items quickly and accurately.

How do **mirrors** work?

A mirror can be any smooth, shiny surface that reflects, or bounces back, light. But most mirrors are made of sheets of glass, the backs of which have been coated with thin layers of reflective materials or metals, including silver.

We see all things because light waves reflect off objects and into our eyes, creating images that are recognized by our brains. You can see yourself in a mirror because light rays reflected from your body bounce off the mirror's shiny surface and back into your

A mirror effect can be seen on any smooth, shiny surface that reflects light, including a lake.

eyes. But this double reflection creates an odd effect—everything appears reversed. When you hold a book up to a mirror, for instance, the printing appears backward.

In the same way, this double reflection of light allows you to see yourself in a glass window or on the surface of still water. But the reflection will not be as clear as one produced by a mirror, because some of the light waves that are reflected from you will be absorbed by the glass or water instead of bouncing back. If the wind disturbs the surface of your watery mirror, the water will absorb even more light. And the smooth areas—now small and scattered—will produce parts of a reflection so broken up that it will be too unclear to recognize.

How does a **magnifying glass** work?

A magnifying glass is a convex lens, which means that it is much thicker in the middle than around its edges. This shape bends the light waves of objects viewed through it, causing us to see them in unusual ways. When you hold a magnifying glass close to an object, its light waves are widened before they are focused on your eyes, causing the object to appear very large. But when you hold a magnifying glass out and view a distant object with it, the item appears smaller and upside down. This effect is due to the image being beyond the focus of the lens. The more curved a convex lens is, the greater its ability to bend light and magnify. Microscopes (which allow us to look at things that are too small to be seen with our eyes) and binoculars and telescopes (which make far away things look bigger and nearer to us) also use convex lenses.

HOT AND COLD

Why do **metal** things feel **cold**?

When heat is transferred from one material to another it is called conduction. Metal is a good conductor of heat, while nonmetals like wood and plastic are poor conductors. The temperature of any metal object in a room is about the same as the air that surrounds it. Your body, on the other hand, has its own internal furnace, which keeps it running at a temperature of about 98.6 degrees Fahrenheit (37 degrees Celsius). When you touch a metal object that's surrounded by air cooler than your body, the object quickly conducts heat away from your fingertips, which makes

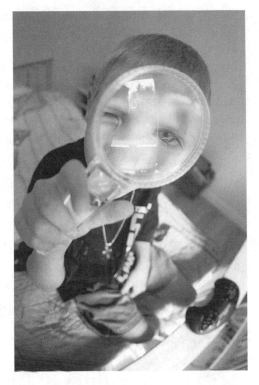

A magnifying glass bends light waves, causing us to see objects in unusual ways.

them feel cold. The sensation travels to your brain, which perceives that the metal object is cold. (If you hold a small metal object, like a penny, in your hand for a long time, it will absorb enough of your body heat to feel as warm as you are.) The opposite is also true: if you touch the hood of a car that's been sitting in a sunny driveway on a warm day, the metal will conduct heat to your fingertips, and the hood will feel hot to you.

How does a **thermos** keep cold things cold and hot things hot?

A thermos is also called a vacuum bottle because it uses a vacuum—a space that has no air in it—to keep heat from escaping from hot things inside; it also keeps heat from getting inside to make cold things warmer. The vacuum is located in a thin space between the thermos liner and its outer wall, where it stops the movement of heat to and from the outside air. A vacuum works in a thermos because it is empty of air (and molecules) and therefore has no conductivity. (Heat is caused by the motion of molecules.) Because the opening of a thermos is also tightly sealed with a stopper or lid made of a nonconductive material, no heat can escape or enter there, either. Hot food stored in a thermos can keep its heat for many hours; in the same way, cold food can remain cold because the vacuum insulates it from the warm air surrounding the thermos.

The linings of thermoses used to be made of glass, which is a good insulator. The linings were also coated with silver, which made them shiny and reflective. Such mirrored liners worked very well—they were able to efficiently bounce back the invisible rays of heat energy (radiation) given off by all hot things. But there was one problem: glass thermos bottles broke easily. Today, most thermos containers are made of metal or plastic, which generally don't work quite as well. Also, because vacuums in thermoses aren't perfect—they contain some air—and because their lids don't seal perfectly, they cannot keep cold things cold and hot things hot forever.

How does a **refrigerator** keep food cold?

When a liquid evaporates, or changes into a gas, it absorbs heat from the things around it. (That principle explains why you feel cooler when you sweat: the liquid perspiration removes body heat as it evaporates into the air.) The opposite occurs—a gas gives off heat—when it changes into a liquid. These two principals are used in most refrigeration systems.

Refrigerators are cooled by a special fluid (refrigerant) that is easily changed into a gas, or vapor, and then back into a liquid again. Compressing the refrigerant (squeezing it into a smaller space than it would normally occupy) makes it take on its liquid form, and it is pumped through evaporator tubes inside a refrigerator. As it changes back to a gas there, it absorbs heat from the food and air inside, cooling the refrigerator's interior. The warmed vapor is pumped outside the refrigerator (by a compressor) and through condenser tubes, where it releases heat into the air as it turns into a liquid again. That heat is the warm air you feel at the back or bottom of a refrigerator. The cycle continues as the refrigerant travels in and out, carrying heat away and keeping food cold. A thermostat set at a certain temperature turns an electric motor on and off; the motor circulates the refrigerant, keeping the right amount of coolness inside the refrigerator. Air conditioners work in a similar way.

How does a **toaster** work?

Inside a toaster are thick wires arranged in panels that heat up and toast your food. When you push down the lever that lowers your bread, it catches on a hook inside, turning on the heater. While your bread turns brown and crispy, a special metal switch inside the toaster gets hot, too, and bends. After a certain amount of time it bends so much that it pushes on a bar that releases the lever from the hook, and the toasting stops. This action also releases a spring, which pushes the lever up again—and your toast pops up.

All metals expand when they are heated. But how does the metal switch in a toaster bend? It bends because it is made of two metals that are joined together, something called a bimetal switch. One metal (usually brass) expands quickly when heated, while the other expands much more slowly. This difference causes the switch to bend toward the low-expansion metal. Bimetal switches are used in other appliances that switch electricity on and off to keep their temperatures even, like irons and refrigerators. The thermostat that regulates the temperature of your home by turning your furnace and air conditioner on and off also uses a bimetal switch.

How can a microwave oven cook food so fast?

Unlike other ovens, which cook food with heat waves made from burning gas or electric currents, microwave ovens use special bands of electromagnetic energy called microwaves (similar to light waves) to cook food. While heat waves gradually work their way inside food to cook it, microwaves can travel right through food in an instant. In a microwave oven a device called a magnetron produces a beam of microwaves that pass through a spinning fan, which sends the waves bouncing in all directions. As they travel through food their energy is absorbed by molecules of water. The water molecules vibrate at the same high speed as the microwaves (2.45 billion times per second!) and rub against other molecules. All this movement and friction causes a great deal of heat, cooking the food inside and out. Microwaved food is cooked through a process similar to steaming, which explains why it doesn't turn brown. But some microwave ovens have traditional heating elements to make food look more appealing —giving it the outer color that we expect in cooked food.

Certain materials allow microwaves to pass through (meaning they aren't heated by the waves) while other materials absorb the waves and still others reflect them, or bounce them back. For this reason it is important to be careful about the containers and coverings we use in microwave ovens. Microwaves pass through glass and plastic wrap, for example, which are safe to use, as are paper products and most sturdy plastics. But metal containers and coverings like aluminum foil are reflective. Such surfaces keep food from absorbing microwaves, allowing the waves to bounce around so much inside an oven that it may break.

Why do **burning things** make **smoke**?

During a fire, the air around it becomes heated. The heated air sweeps up water vapor (molecules of water that float in the air) and tiny specks of the fuel (the material being burned) into a dark cloud of smoke. The more incompletely something burns, the more smoke it produces, because more particles are left to be swept up into the air. Smoke gradually spreads out and drifts away, with gravity pulling the heaviest bits back to the ground. When a fire first starts to burn, there is usually a lot of smoke, which decreases as more of the fuel is burned completely.

257

Smoke detectors take advantage of the fact that fires cause a lot of smoke in their early stages. The detectors sense the small particles in smoke before a fire really starts to burn. An optical smoke detector uses a light beam and light sensor that sounds an alarm when smoke particles get in the way of the beam. An ionizing smoke detector can sense even smaller particles; they disturb a low electric current inside, which sets off an alarm.

How does a **fire extinguisher** work?

In order for something to burn, high heat and oxygen are needed. All fuels have their own particular temperatures at which they begin to burn when exposed to high heat (called their flash points). Removing heat or oxygen from fuel will put out a fire.

Water is frequently used to extinguish fires. Large supplies of water can be found almost anywhere, an important condition when dealing with large fires, like those in burning buildings. Water works in two ways to put out a fire. First, it sharply reduces the temperature of the burning material. Second, it covers the material, keeping oxygen-filled air from reaching the material.

But water can't put out oil fires. Because oil floats on the surface of water, an oil fire's oxygen supply can't be cut off by water. Other substances—liquids, gases, or powders that don't burn—must be used to smother the fire and remove its oxygen supply.

Most fire extinguishers are filled with carbon dioxide, a heavy gas that prevents burning. When released, the gas forms a type of snowy foam that both covers and cools a fire. Powdered sodium bicarbonate (what we know as baking soda) is also used in extinguishers, usually for use on oily chemical fires. It quickly melts in heat, forming a crust that keeps oxygen out. (If you don't have a fire extinguisher on hand you should always throw baking soda on a cooking fire that involves grease; water will only spread the fire by causing splattering.) Because the substance in a fire extinguisher must cover a large area very quickly, it needs to be released in a powerful spray. The extinguishing substance is stored inside the tank under high pressure, which drives it out of a nozzle with great force once it is released.

ENERGY

Why are **dams** built?

Dams, which are structures that hold back water, have been built since ancient times. They are usually made of earth, rock, brick, or concrete—or a combination of these things. They are constructed to control the flow of water in a river, and they are built for a number of reasons.

Dams can be used to prevent flooding, create electricity, or store water.

One reason is to prevent flooding. Heavy rains in high country may cause water levels in a river to rise. As the river flows downhill, it may overflow its banks, flooding communities located downstream. A dam can prevent this by stopping or slowing rushing water, allowing it to be released at a normal rate.

Dams are also frequently used to store water for general use and farming. When a river's flow is restricted by a dam, water often spreads out behind the dam to form a lake or reservoir in the river valley. That water can then be used as needed, preventing water shortages and crop damage during long periods of dry weather.

A great number of dams today are used to make electricity. Such hydroelectric dams are built very tall, to create a great difference in the height of the water level behind and in front of it. High water behind a dam passes through gates in the dam wall that allow it to fall to the river far below. As the water falls, it flows past huge blades called turbines; the turbines run generators that make electricity. One of the world's largest and most productive hydroelectric dams is the Hoover Dam, located on the Colorado River between Nevada and Arizona. Built in the 1930s, it is 726 feet (221 meters) high and 1,244 feet (379 meters) long. Its reservoir (Lake Mead)—the world's largest—supplies water to several states, allowing huge regions of naturally dry terrain in southern California, Arizona, and Mexico to flourish. Many modern dams are used for all three purposes: flood control, water storage, and hydroelectric power.

How does **nuclear energy** work?

We usually make heat energy by burning fuels—oil, gas, coal, or wood. In large quantities, such energy can be used to heat water, and the resulting steam can be used to run generators that make electricity. Burning fuel (combustion) is a chemical reaction that converts one form of energy into another: it recombines elements from the fuel and the oxygen in the air into things like ash, smoke, and waste gases, as well as heat.

A fission-generated nuclear reaction produces heat in a different way: it breaks apart elements themselves, turning them into waste products with less mass, which creates a great amount of energy. The tiniest particles of matter—atoms—of heavy elements like uranium or plutonium provide the fuel for nuclear reactors. At the center of each atom is a nucleus, which is made up of even tinier particles called protons and neutrons. A nucleus is held together by a powerful force, and breaking up the nucleus releases that force. A nuclear reaction starts when fast-moving neutrons strike the nuclei of fuel atoms, causing them to break into smaller nuclei. These in turn release neutrons that break up more fuel nuclei. All this movement produces great heat, which can be used to make steam to run electric generators.

The good thing about fission-generated nuclear energy is that very little fuel is needed to produce huge amounts of energy. (Two pounds of nuclear fuel could produce as much energy as 6.5 million pounds of coal, for instance!) The challenging part is that the process must be *very* carefully controlled. If it isn't controlled, the chain reaction behind it could create so much energy and heat in a fraction of a second that the result would be an enormous explosion. This explosion is exactly what occurs in nuclear weapons. (In a nuclear reactor, control rods that absorb neutrons are moved in and out of the core to control the process.)

A nuclear explosion is especially damaging because it releases harmful gamma rays known as radiation into the environment. This by-product of nuclear fission is another problem connected with nuclear power. Nuclear reactors are encased in thick layers of steel and concrete to keep radiation from escaping. And because leftover nuclear fuel is highly radioactive, it must be carefully stored far away from people for decades or even centuries before it is safe again. Transporting and disposing of dangerous waste is another challenge presented by nuclear power; most recently used fuel is sealed in safety containers and buried deep underground.

The nuclear process that we get our power from is called fission, where atomic nuclei that break apart produce great energy and heat. But nuclear power can also be created by a process called fusion, where atomic nuclei join together. Scientists are still working on creating a satisfactory fusion reactor. The Sun produces its great energy and heat through the nuclear fusion of its hydrogen gases.

HOME LIFE AND SCHOOL DAYS

AROUND THE HOUSE

Do all people **live in houses**?

Nearly all people in the world live in some kind of shelter. But a great many of these shelters look very different from the kinds of buildings we think of as homes. House types differ around the world because climates, local building materials, and ways of life vary greatly. In southeast Asia, for example, where many people live on the banks of large rivers that frequently overflow, houses are built on stilts. In South America's rain forests, tribes of indigenous, or native, peoples build huts with thick domed roofs made of palm leaves that keep the heavy rains out. People that live near marshy rivers sometimes use the heavy reeds that grow there to build their houses, and people who live near large forests often have houses made of wood. People who live in hot countries sometimes build their homes from bricks that are sun-dried blocks of mud. In many of these places, modern building materials are available, but the region's traditional shelters are still made because local materials are far cheaper.

Some people take their homes with them. Such people are known as nomads and their portable homes are usually tents made of sturdy poles, ropes, and fabric. Nomads usually live off the land by raising livestock or hunting. They are constantly on the move, in search of food or grazing land for their animals. Their tents, which are easy to set up and take down, are carried along on their journeys. People who live in deserts, like the Bedouins of the Middle East, are frequently tent dwellers. But hunting bushmen in Africa's Kalahari Desert carry huts made of sticks and grass around with them for use as shelters at night.

Most of the world's people don't have shelters with the features that we think are essential for comfort and safety in a home, like electricity and running water. A surprising 80 percent of the population live in what we would call substandard housing.

Huts like this one are used as homes by many people in places like South America and Africa.

What are **chimneys** for?

Since ancient times people have built fires to stay warm. When fires were built in small dwellings, an opening was needed through which smoke and other by-products of burning—like the dangerous gas carbon monoxide—could escape.

In places where house were made of combustible, or easily burned, materials like wood and thatch (dried grasses), fires had to be built outside to protect such dwellings from going up in flames. But even under those circumstances, people eventually figured out a way to make indoor fires safely. They built stone hearths in the middle of their houses, well away from walls, and made holes in their roofs so that smoke could escape. These hearths came to be located in more convenient places once people learned how to build stone fireplaces topped with stone chimneys that channeled smoke safely out of dwellings, high above their roofs. Stone fireplaces could be safely built into the walls of any type of shelter.

While our houses are now usually kept warm by central heating systems, we still build fires in fireplaces for temporary warmth and for their beauty and the cozy feeling they give. Stone or brick hearths and chimneys are still needed to protect house walls and roofs from fire. Even houses without fireplaces have chimneys because most furnaces make heat by burning fuel. The poisonous by-products of this combustion usually flow out of a house by way of a chimney, keeping the air indoors healthy and safe to breathe.

Why does our **house** make **funny sounds at night**?

All matter—gases, liquids, and solids—expands when heated and shrinks when cooled. This principle explains some of the funny and unexpected sounds that your house makes at night. During the day, the Sun's rays warm the materials your house is made of—like the wooden frame that supports its roof and walls—and they expand. Heat from the Sun may also make the interior of your house warmer and even shine on some of its furniture. When night comes, the temperature outside can drop 30 degrees or more as Earth turns away from the Sun. Things like house-building materials and furniture become cooler, too, shrinking and slipping a little, which can sometimes cause creaking and groaning sounds. The noises are particularly noticeable at night because your home and neighborhood are so much quieter than they are during the day. Some of the funny noises you hear at night may also be sounds that are going on all the time—like the motor that runs your refrigerator or a dripping faucet—that you just don't notice when you are busy and a lot of things are going on around you. But in the stillness of the night, when you are trying to fall asleep, you can suddenly hear them all, loud and clear!

Where does our **clean water** come from?

Rain is the source of the water we use. It collects in rivers and lakes and in human-made gathering places called reservoirs, or it sinks into the ground, where it is pumped back to the surface by wells. Water usually has to be "treated" before it is safe for drinking and general use: it has to be free of harmful bacteria and chemicals, as well as substances that make it look or taste bad.

Water is pumped from lakes, rivers, or reservoirs through huge pipes to water treatment plants. There it is filtered to remove large pieces of debris, like twigs and dead fish. Two special chemicals—aluminum sulfate and lime—are then added; these make the small particles of dirt left in the water cling together in tiny lumps called flocs. Pumped into a sedimentation tank, the water is allowed to settle, with its flocs gradually sinking to the bottom for removal.

Ready for more filtration, the water is run through layers of stone and sand that remove fine particles of dirt. Bacteria are then added to eat any microscopic creatures that may still be present. A chemical called chlorine is added to kill the bacteria once their job is done. Other chemicals may be added to make the water "softer"—so that it works better with soap for washing—or healthier; fluoride, for example, is often added to prevent tooth decay.

Once treatment is complete, water is sent through huge tubes to storage places— tanks or covered reservoirs—where it is ready for use. It is pumped into communities through big pipes located just underground called water mains. These mains supply homes and businesses with water through smaller pipes that attach to faucets and other outlets. In order to meet the needs of communities, treatment plants can produce many millions of gallons of fresh water everyday. Next time you fill a glass with water, think about the incredible journey it took to arrive there.

Where do things go when they're **flushed down the toilet**?

When there were far fewer people in the world, things like used water and waste were transported from homes and businesses by sewer pipes to large bodies of water, where they were released. Sewage disposal then consisted of allowing waste to mix with the freshwater or saltwater, which would dilute it. Now, with so much waste in our highly industrialized and overpopulated world, sewage must go through treatment processes in order to keep the waters of the world safe. The decomposition, or breaking down, of waste (by bacteria) uses up a great deal of oxygen, and if decomposition of sewage were to occur in a river or lake, the animals and plants that live there wouldn't have enough of the gases—oxygen and carbon dioxide—they need to live. Certain waste products, like human and animal feces, also carry harmful bacteria that can cause infectious diseases when they are concentrated in large amounts and people have contact with them.

So when you flush your toilet, or let dirty water run down your drain, the waste is on its way to a sewage treatment plant to protect you and the environment. It travels down pipes in your home to larger sewer pipes that run underground, some so large that waste flows through them like a river. (Sometimes collected groundwater and rainwater empty into sewers, too.) Along the way to the treatment plant, waste from other homes and businesses in your community join the flow. (In some communities, where homes and businesses are—or once were—located far from one another and a sewer system is impractical, waste is often emptied into large septic tanks that are buried near each property underground. Much of the waste in a septic tank is decomposed by bacteria, but every so often, these tanks must be emptied and cleaned.)

When waste arrives at a sewage treatment plant, it is filtered through a large metal grill. This grill traps large objects that can't be processed. Small stones and sand are also filtered out. Once cleaned and dried, these materials can be used for building work and road repair. Now a smelly, soupy mixture, the sewage that's gone through the grill is put into an enormous tank where solid particles eventually fall to the bottom. This muddy sludge goes into a special processing tank where bacteria feed on it and break it down into harmless material. During this decomposition a gas called methane is produced; it is burned to boil water and produce steam, which provides the power that runs the pumps in the sewage treatment plant. Treated sludge, which is nutrient-rich, can be used as manure.

Once separated from sludge in the settling tank, waste liquid is pumped to filter beds, where it is cleaned. This cleaning is done by allowing the liquid to drip through layers of stones that are covered by bacteria, which eat any waste that remains. Clean water results and is pumped back into rivers, lakes, or the sea.

The electricity we use is made by huge machines, or generators, in power plants like this one.

Where does our **electricity** come from?

All matter is made of tiny particles called atoms. Inside an atom are even tinier particles: electrons that move in orbit around a center, or nucleus, made of neutrons and protons. An electron has a negative electric charge and a proton has a positive one. Usually an atom has the same number of each, which keeps the atom neutral or uncharged. But sometimes electrons leave their orbit, attracted to other atoms that lack an electron and are positively charged. The movement or flow of electrons from one atom to another produces the form of energy called electricity.

The electricity we use is made by huge machines, or generators, in places called power plants. An energy source is needed to run the generators: heat from burning coal, oil, or natural gas, or from the fission of nuclear fuel, is used to boil water for the steam required to turn the turbines, or giant blades, that start the generators. Heat-based energy is known as thermal power. Rushing water from giant man-made dams or waterfalls (hydropower) can also do the job. Although not widely used, the force of the wind and the heat of the Sun can be used to power generators to make electricity, too.

With the help of a giant magnet, a generator creates a flow of electric charges, or an electric current, that runs through copper wire. But in order for this electricity to travel great distances, to homes and businesses far away, its voltage—the force that pushes a current along—must be raised. To accomplish this, the electricity passes through a device called a transformer. Travel-ready but now too powerful and danger-ous to use, electricity is sent out from a power plant through huge cables that need to

267

be buried safely underground or stretched high in the air between tall support towers. When the electricity reaches its destination, it is run through another transformer that reduces its voltage so that it is again suitable for normal use. It then travels to homes and businesses, through large wires attached to meters that show how much electricity is used at each location, so that the power company that runs the plant can be paid for it. Smaller wires run through the floors and walls of a home—bringing electricity to every room. These wires are attached to safety devices called fuses or circuit breakers, which stop the flow of electric current if, for any reason, it should rise to dangerous levels (which may cause overheating and fire). Devices that are powered by electricity, like lights, televisions, and toasters, can be connected with the current running through a home by the flip of a switch or by being plugged into outlets or sockets.

Why do I have to clean my room?

Your parents have the big job of taking care of your home, and it's a lot more work than it may seem. But you can help out by taking care of your room and your own things. Everyone needs to work together in a family to make things run smoothly.

It's important to pick up your toys and clothes and other things and put them back where they belong after you use them. This cleanup keeps them in good shape so they won't be stepped on and ruined, or cause you to trip and fall; you will also be able to find them the next time you need them. When you take care of your things, it shows that you are responsible and will treat future possessions with the same care (which helps when you want something new).

At a certain age, most kids are asked by their parents to take care of their rooms further by dusting and vacuuming. Such additional responsibilities are a part of growing up. If you lived outside, a big gust of wind would be all that you needed to get rid of the dust! But because your room is in an enclosed space, the dust that builds up there has to be removed in other ways. Keeping your room clean and dust-free helps your lungs by giving you cleaner air to breathe. It cuts down on allergies, too, because a lot of people are allergic to dust mites, tiny creatures that live among dust. And dusting and vacuuming make things like carpeting and furniture look nice and last longer.

What is **dust**?

Dust is made up of particles of all sorts of things. In places where people live, a great deal of dust comes from flakes of dead skin, which are being shed all the time. Dust mites, tiny microscopic creatures that feed on this dead skin, make up dust, too (including their waste and tiny skeletons). Particles of the environment contribute to dust as well: grit from the sidewalk, salt from the sea, dry earth, pollen from plants, smoke from burning materials. And Earth gets 10 tons of dust from outer space everyday, from the millions of meteors that burn up as they enter our atmosphere.

How does a **vacuum cleaner** pick up dirt?

A vacuum cleaner is run by an electric motor that turns a fan at an extraordinarily high speed —about 25,000 revolutions, or full turns, per minute. This spinning creates an area in front of the fan that has lower air pressure than normal—a partial vacuum (from which the appliance gets its name).

Surrounding air rushes into the partially empty space caused by the whirring fan, carrying small particles with it as the vacuum cleaner runs over dirty surfaces like carpet and furniture. The air usually passes through a suction head or attachment and then a filter, where dirt and dust are trapped in a collection area that can be emptied. The rush of air continues through the fan, which blows it out of the vacuum cleaner.

When all family members pitch in, household chores get done more quickly.

Why do **clothes** need to be **washed**?

If you want to look clean and smell nice your clothes must be washed frequently. Most clothing is made of tiny threads that are woven together. As you go about your day, dirt and odors get trapped in the weave of your clothes and can only be removed by washing. Clothes must be jiggled and swished around quite a bit in water—as is done in a washing machine—to best remove dirt and odors from their tiny hiding places. Detergent is added to water to help the process: it can break up oily dirt into smaller pieces that can be whisked away, and it can surround other dirt particles and pull them away from fabric.

269

Washing machines are run by electric motors that turn large blades inside a big drum or tub that is filled with water. The blade turns back and forth, pushing soapy water and clothes around. (A front-loading machine has no blades, but the drum turns and tumbles the clothes to get them clean.) A washing machine automatically gets rid of dirty water and rinses the clean clothes before wringing water out of them, making them nearly dry. Before washing machines, people had to use muscle power and a great deal of time to loosen dirt from the weave of clothes. They did this by stamping on wet clothes with their feet, or beating them against rocks, or rubbing them on bumpy washboards to get them clean.

Why do I have to do **household chores**?

Running a household is a lot of work. Your parents do most of the chores required to take care of your family's food, clothing, house, and yard, especially when you are young. But as you become older, your strength and skills increase, and you can help out.

Household tasks are called chores because they usually aren't fun to do. You can probably think of plenty of activities that would be more entertaining than cleaning your room or mowing the lawn. But these things have to be done by somebody, and it is only fair that everybody in a family does his or her part. And when all family members pitch in, household chores get done more quickly, and everyone has more time to do the things that they like. So when you do household chores, you are really showing that you care about your family. Also, taking on such additional responsibilities is a part of growing up, preparing you for the time when you will have to do those jobs by yourself.

What is an allowance?

An allowance is an amount of money usually given each week to a child by his or her parents. Kids can use this money to pay for their personal expenses, for things like special snacks, toys, or activities with their friends. In some families, parents do not give their kids allowances, and children just ask their parents when money is needed. But allowances are useful, because they help teach kids how to manage money. Children learn how to control their expenses by staying within their weekly budgets. And children can learn to save—if they want to buy something expensive—by holding on to a portion of their allowances each week.

Generally, as children grow older, they become better at handling money; they also have more expenses. So older children usually require larger allowances. In some families, allowances are considered payment for doing household chores, and they increase when children grow older and do more work around the house.

How can I get a **bigger allowance**?

One way to get a bigger allowance is to prove to your parents that the amount you are getting now is not enough to cover your expenses. Keep track of your spending for a week by making a list. Show this to your parents when you tell them about the increase you think you should have. Explain why your expenses have changed—that the price of movie tickets has gone up at your neighborhood theater, for example. If you want to save money to buy something expensive, tell them that, too. Or maybe you feel that you have grown old enough to handle more of your own expenses, like buying your own clothes. Whatever your reasons for needing a bigger allowance, present them as clearly and calmly as you can. Give your parents time to think it over and you might have good results.

Why do **houses** usually have **lawns** around them?

Houses have lawns around them for several reasons. The stretches of green grass look pretty, and they are good, safe places for children to play when they are outside. Also, lawns frequently mark the boundaries that separate one person's property from another.

Long ago, only the rich could afford to have lawns. Other people had to use all of their land to raise crops so that they had enough to eat. So a lawn became a status symbol, a sign to others that its owner had enough wealth to "waste" a portion of his or her land on grass (which was merely pretty, not producing anything that could be eaten or sold). That way of thinking may still be at work today: the average American lawn could produce about 2,000 dollars' worth of fruits and vegetables if it were planted. But instead of using land as a way to *save* money, American homeowners do exactly the opposite, spending several hundred dollars and countless hours each year on maintaining their lawns. Many people value the beauty of a well-cared-for lawn, however, admiring the effect of a homeowner's hard work.

Dr. John Falk, who works for the Smithsonian Institution in Washington, D.C., has conducted studies to prove his own interesting theory about why people like lawns. He thinks that because most of our history as humans was spent on the grassy savannas (large grassy areas with few trees) of East Africa, our desire to live around lawns is biological, or passed on through our genes from our prehistoric beginnings. Falk thinks that people naturally prefer the familiarity and safety (because the approach of predators can be seen) of flat, grassy land over any other kind of environment. And his experiments seem to prove the theory true: Falk showed people from all over the world pictures of different terrains—desert, rain forest, coniferous (evergreen) forest, deciduous (leaf-shedding) forest, and savanna—and most chose the grassland as the place where they would like to live.

What happens to our **garbage** after it's collected?

A garbage truck probably comes to your neighborhood once a week to pick up your family's trash. On other days garbage trucks are at work in other parts of your city. Sometimes trash that can't be reused or recycled is taken away to an incinerator plant,

271

where it is burned into ash. Most often garbage is taken to a landfill, a huge hole in the ground commonly known as a garbage dump. Both methods of disposal cause problems. Burning garbage creates waste products that enter the air, causing pollution. Landfills use up precious space (there are more than 9,000 in the United States) and are so ugly and smelly that few communities want one located near them. Transporting trash to distant landfills is troublesome and expensive. The best way to handle garbage is to make less of it—developing habits that are not wasteful—and to reuse and recycle the trash that we can't avoid making. Americans produce about 230 million tons of garbage each year.

In order to get as much garbage as possible into a landfill, it is crushed and tightly packed into its space. At the end of each day, new trash is covered with a layer of dirt to keep germs from spreading and to keep creatures like rats and flies away. Pipes have to be inserted into landfill sites to allow the escape of gases that are produced when garbage decomposes. If this wasn't done, the gases could explode. Once garbage nears the top of a landfill, the hole is sealed off and covered with tons of dirt. Over time, when decomposition has stopped and all dangerous gases have escaped, the spot can be used for other things. One northern community, for example, built a great sledding hill on top of its landfill.

What happens to **garbage that is recycled**?

Many communities have trash recycling programs to try to reduce the amount of garbage that must go to landfills. Certain types of trash—things made of materials like metal, glass, plastic, paper, and cardboard—can usually be processed and reused. Once cleaned and sorted, metal cans, for instance, can be melted down and poured into molds that make new cans or parts for things like cars and kitchen appliances. Glass jars and bottles are cleaned, too, and sorted into colors—clear, green, brown, and more. They are then smashed into tiny pieces that can be used to make bricks and paving materials, or they are melted down and poured into molds to form new jars and bottles.

Plastics cause the biggest garbage problem. All sorts of containers and other products are made from plastic, but only some types can be recycled. Plastic doesn't rot or decompose like many other kinds of trash, which means that when it goes into a landfill, it is there to stay for a very long time. When many plastics are burned, they produce dangerous chemical vapors that pollute the air. The kinds of plastics that can be recycled are cleaned, melted, and poured into molds to make new plastic objects, like pipes, insulation, and office equipment.

Because so many trees are cut down every year to make paper for books, magazines, newspapers, and other products, it is important to recycle paper items so new paper can be made from them. During the recycling process, wastepaper is chopped into very fine pieces, mixed with water, boiled, and made into a thick soup called pulp. This pulp may be washed and bleached to make it white or left a natural color. Pulp is

Recycled metal cans like those stacked here can be made into new cans or into parts for things like cars and kitchen appliances.

then spread out onto large screens that allow water to drip through. Next, giant rollers squeeze the pulp, removing more water. Once the new paper is dry, it is wound onto huge spools and later cut into sheets of paper. Other paper products like cardboard boxes are made in similar ways. Wood fibers and other plant materials are also used in paper-making.

PLAYING IT SAFE

What should I do when I **meet a stranger**?

Most of the strangers you encounter are decent people who treat children with respect and would never think of hurting them. But there are dangerous people who do harmful things to children.

How do you know which is which? The problem is that you can't always know. Sometimes hurtful people can fool kids into thinking they are gentle and helpful: they may have pleasant faces and friendly voices, and they may say nice things. So it's important to follow personal safety rules with all strangers.

What can you do to stay safe when you are outside or away from home? Here are some basic guidelines: Play with at least one other kid and in familiar places. Don't go near a car with a stranger in it, even if the person says he or she has a gift for you, or needs your help to find a lost pet, or is asking for directions. Think about it this way: if an adult really needed help, he or she would ask another adult, not a kid. Don't accept a ride home from school or anywhere from someone you don't know, even if that person says your parents asked him or her to pick you up, and even if that person knows your name. Basically try to avoid situations where you are alone with an adult you don't know unless it is a person your parents have arranged for you to meet with, like a doctor or a counselor. If a stranger approaches you, tell that person to please not speak to you because you don't know him or her. If the stranger continues toward you, start yelling and run away. If you need help, your best bet is to go to a public place like a store, a library, or especially a police station. Afterward, be sure to tell your parents about your experience with the stranger.

What should I do if another kid is **being a bully**?

If you're on a playground and you see a kid hurting or making fun of another kid, your first impulse might be to turn around and pretend you didn't see it. But imagine how that bullied kid is feeling, and you'll know that the right thing to do is to try to put a stop to it. Sometimes, if the bully is a bigger kid and is being rough, the best thing to do

274

is to find a teacher or another adult and tell that person what's going on. Or, if the situation doesn't feel like it could threaten your personal safety, the best thing you can do is to stand up for the kid being bullied. Kids who make fun of others usually expect to get a laugh from their friends, and if you show the bully that his or her teasing isn't funny and that you support the person being teased, it could end the teasing right there.

Lots of kids have been picked on by a bully, for many different reasons. If you've been the target of a bully, you know it can be very scary and upsetting to be teased, hit, or threatened. Sometimes it helps to simply ignore what the bully is saying—most bullies do what they do to get a reaction from those they tease, and if they get no reaction at all, it's a lot less fun for them. It usually helps to have friends around, too. A kid walking alone is more vulnerable than a group of kids, and if you are bullied when your friends are with you, it might help you feel brave enough to stand up to the bully. Even if you don't *feel* that confident, sometimes just *acting* confident can go a long way. If you hold your head high and tell a bully to stop calling you names, you may just surprise that bully into silence. One approach to avoid is responding to bullying with violence. It will probably only make matters worse.

Even though it may feel awkward or embarrassing, it might help to tell your parents or a teacher what you're going through. At the very least, they can make you feel better by explaining why bullies behave the way they do and by reassuring you that what the bully says about you has nothing to do with who you really are. And at the most, adults can help keep you safe if you're being threatened.

What should I do if someone **asks for my name** when I'm **online**?

The Internet is an amazing place where you can find information on all kinds of things. You can chat with friends, e-mail long-distance pen pals, and read what other people are saying about things you're interested in. But just as you shouldn't talk to strangers when in the outside world, you should also use caution when chatting in the cyber world. Unfortunately, there are people surfing the Web who present a threat to kids. They may be adults posing as another kid or somehow lying to you about who they are and what they want. To be safe, never give anyone you don't know personal information about yourself online—including your name, address, or phone number. And never agree to meet a person you've chatted with online, even if that person seems friendly and harmless. Let your parents know if a stranger is sending you e-mail or instant messages.

It's also important to ask your parents first before registering at a Web site. Many sites offer special benefits if you register as a member, which involves providing your name, e-mail address, and sometimes home address, phone number, and other information. While some sites protect your privacy and only use that information to send you things you want, others sell your information to advertisers or organizations. As a result of registering at a Web site, your family may end up getting lots of unwanted e-mail, regular mail, and phone calls from companies trying to sell you things. And even if you find a great deal online for something you really want, never give out your parents' credit card information unless they say it's okay.

What should I do if I **find a gun**?

Studies have shown that hundreds, perhaps even thousands, of children and teenagers are accidentally killed by guns in the United States each year. Millions of American kids have access to guns in their homes. People use guns all the time in movies and television shows, and the action scenes in these shows make guns look exciting and powerful. What these shows can't really convey is the massive, painful destruction an exploding bullet causes when it hits a person's body.

While many kids understand that, in real life, guns can be very dangerous and can cause great harm, most still find guns fascinating. If an adult is supervising and your parents have given their approval, it's okay to look at and even touch an unloaded gun. But if you are alone or with other kids and you come across a gun, remember that it is not a toy and should not be handled. Guns should never be pointed at another person, even if you intend it as a joke. If you find a gun in your own house, a friend's house, or elsewhere, as tempting as it might be to play with it, remember the damage that guns can cause and leave it alone. If you're away from home, leave right away and tell your parents what happened. Your parents may be upset and worried that you found a gun, but they will be very glad that you told them about it because then they can help you stay safe.

NEIGHBORHOOD TRANSPORTATION

How does a **bicycle** work?

A bicycle is a simple device that increases the power that you have in the muscles of your legs, taking you faster and farther than you could ever run. When you push the pedals of your bike around once, the pedal sprocket—the wheel with teeth to which the pedals are attached—goes around once, too. But it pulls a chain along, one that is connected to a much smaller sprocket (with fewer teeth to grip each link of the chain) in the center of your bike's rear wheel. This smaller sprocket moves around a number of times for each single turn of your pedals, moving your bike wheels a lot faster than you're moving your feet!

Some bicycles have several "speeds," which means that they have a number of gears (called derailleurs) that vary the rate at which their wheels turn. These extra sprockets are located at the pedals and rear wheel of a bike, where levers move the dri-

A bicycle increases the power you have in your legs, taking you faster and farther than you could ever run. *Robert J. Huffman/Field Mark Publications © 2001*

ving chain sideways, from one to another. A special spring system keeps the chain tight when it changes from a larger to a smaller sprocket. Although you might think that a rider would always want the wheels of his or her bike to move as fast as possible for each pedal turn, that is not always the case. When going uphill, for instance, a rider can get more force out of a wheel that turns fewer times, making the task easier.

Brakes can quickly stop the rotating wheels of a bicycle. On some bikes you can stop by pedaling backwards, which activates a braking mechanism (coaster brake). On other bikes, you activate the brakes by squeezing levers located on the bike's handlebars. While a person's leg strength is far greater than the strength in his or her hands, a hand brake uses a set of three levers that increase the original squeezing force, making it strong enough to stop a speeding bike. A compressed hand brake pulls a cable connected to two metal arms with rubber pads that grip a bicycle tire rim, causing enough friction to stop it. After a quick stop, feel the brake blocks on your bike—the friction makes them hot.

Why are **men's and women's bicycles built differently**?

The crossbars on bicycle frames give them added strength. On a man's or boy's bike the crossbar extends straight across the top of the frame, just below the seat. On a woman's or girl's bike the crossbar is attached to the seat tube at an angle, far below the seat. Because of this structure, women's bikes are not nearly as sturdy as men's bikes.

277

When bicycles were first built, women didn't wear pants; they always wore skirts or dresses. The low crossbars on their bikes allowed them to get on, ride, and get off with dignity—without showing their underwear! The design of bicycles for women and girls, then, is based on a long-standing tradition and still offers the advantage of easier mounting and dismounting. But today, women and girl bicyclists wear pants or shorts when riding and can easily use bikes designed for men. As a matter of fact, serious female bicyclists who do a lot of riding or travel through tough terrain and need bikes with sturdier frames buy those made for men.

Why do **bicycle tires lose air** so fast?

Early bicycle tires were made out of solid rubber. (Before that, iron covered the edges of wooden bicycle wheels.) Solid rubber tires made bicycling a bumpy experience because they were unable to provide any cushioning on rough roads. When the air-filled rubber bicycle tire was invented, it made riding a lot more comfortable.

But along with the comfort of air-filled tires came the frequent task of filling them up. The rubber that is used to make bicycle tires is thin and porous, which means that it has tiny microscopic pores, or holes, through which air can escape over time. Air that is pumped into bicycle tires is pressurized, meaning it is compressed into a much smaller space than it would ordinarily occupy. Without pressurized air inside, a bicycle tire would not have its firm shape. Air under high pressure, like all gases, moves or migrates to surrounding areas that have lower pressure, traveling even through fairly solid materials. So air in a bicycle tire naturally tries to escape through the valve stem that is used to fill it and the inner tube that holds it. So even bicycles that don't undergo the wear-and-tear of frequent use eventually end up with flat tires.

Why do little kids **ride tricycles** instead of bikes?

The triangular shape of a tricycle, with its three wheels spread apart, is much more stable than a regular bicycle, which balances on two aligned wheels. (The "tri" [three] and "bi" [two] before "cycle" refers to the number of wheels each vehicle has.) Tricycles suit young children well; with larger heads and undeveloped muscles, little ones lack the coordination and balance needed to ride regular bikes. But as soon as they can learn to pedal, children can ride a tricycle, turning leg power into wheel power.

A tricycle is built for stability and not for speed: its pedals are attached to a sprocket in the center of its large front wheel, which moves around once for each completed pedal turn. So the larger the front wheel of a tricycle, the faster it will go—but it cannot be so large that young legs cannot reach the pedals! This design makes a tricycle unlike a regular bike, which has chain-driven sprockets that move its wheels a lot faster than its rider's feet. Tricycles are also easier for little ones to steer and turn because they are pulled forward by the movement of their front wheels; regular bikes are powered by their rear wheels.

Did you know that early bicycles had pedals attached to their front wheels, just like tricycles? To give them greater speed, bike designers kept enlarging the front wheels, some of which measured up to 64 inches (163 centimeters) across. Known as "high-wheelers," they were quite dangerous to ride—bicyclists couldn't touch the ground with their feet when they stopped, and they often fell forward over their handlebars when they hit bumps. (A high-wheeler was also hard to balance because it had only one rear wheel, not two.)

What are the **reflectors** on my bicycle for?

Reflectors help protect you when you are riding your bicycle in the dark. When a car approaches you the light waves produced by its headlights hit your reflectors and bounce back into the eyes of the driver, making him or her aware of where you are and helping that person drive past you carefully. Reflectors are located at the front and back of your bike, as well as on your pedals. That way you can be seen regardless of the direction in which you are heading.

Reflectors are usually made of hard colored plastic with a backing of reflective material. The inner surface of the plastic is cut into many tiny angles, kind of like the sides, or facets, of a diamond. These bounce light waves around inside before they are reflected away, which explains why reflectors are so startlingly bright.

When you ride your bike at night it is also a good idea to wear reflective clothing, with strips of material or tape attached that bounce back light. Light-colored clothing will also make you more visible. And if you have to bicycle in the street, travel along the right side of the road, in the same direction that traffic goes. Be especially careful when cars approach, because their drivers may still not see you, despite your reflectors.

Why must I always **wear a helmet** when riding a bike?

While riding bicycles is a lot of fun, it is important to remember that bikes are not just toys. They are machines that can sometimes be involved in accidents that result in injury. So all bike riders—as well as inline skaters and scooter riders—must follow certain rules, for their own safety and the safety of others.

Bicyclists have to follow some of the same traffic laws that people who drive cars do, like stopping at stop signs and obeying traffic lights. But bike riders also have their own special set of safety rules. They have to make sure that their bikes have reflectors in order to ride safely at night. They can't let other people ride with them—like on bicycle handlebars—because that threatens their balance and could lead to accidents. One of the most important of all bicycling safety rules is wearing a protective helmet.

Head injuries are the leading cause of death in bicycle crashes. About 300 children die in bike accidents each year. Another 17,000 to 18,000 children in bike accidents suffer brain injuries that sometimes cause very serious, and even lifelong, problems.

So it doesn't matter where you will be riding, or for how long—you should always wear your helmet. Accidents are called accidents because they are unexpected and can happen at any time. If your friends don't wear helmets when you bicycle together, teach them by your wise example. In the United States, bicycle helmets save one life everyday and prevent one head injury from happening every four minutes.

HOUSEHOLD PETS

Why do dogs **bark**?

Dogs bark to communicate with other dogs and with humans. Dogs are descendants of wolves, which are social animals that live in packs, and they share many of the behaviors that define the complex relationships that exist within such animal groups. Few domestic dogs live together in packs (though they often consider their human family their group), but they still use complicated behaviors that involve smell, sight, and hearing to communicate.

A dog has many scent-producing glands that it uses to communicate. The scent that a dog leaves behind (in its urine, feces, and paw prints) can reveal its sex, age, and even its mood to other dogs that come sniffing by. A dog uses its posture, facial expression, and ear and tail position to communicate with other dogs, too. And it uses its voice to communicate by whining, growling, howling, or barking.

A dog usually whines or whimpers when it is in distress: when it is hungry, cold, or in pain. Growls indicate that a dog is angry and ready to fight. Howls and barks usually show excitement. In the wild, wolves and other canines use howling and barking to call together the pack for a hunt, for feeding, or to warn against danger.

When wolves were tamed, or domesticated (between 12,000 and 14,000 years ago), the less dangerous ones were kept to act as guard dogs, to help in hunting, or to herd other domesticated animals. Barking was a useful trait, a handy alarm system that let their human masters know of approaching intruders, prey, or predators. This desirable trait was bred into new dogs. This means that the owners would arrange for two dogs who barked a lot to mate, producing a litter of pups with a tendency to bark often. Then those pups would be bred with other pups who liked to bark, and so on. Over time, domesticated dogs came to use their barks to communicate with their owners. Today, your pet dog barks when it's excited, needs attention, or wants something. It uses its bark to communicate much more than it would if it were living in the wild.

Why don't dogs get **hoarse** when they **bark a lot**?

It seems like some dogs can bark and bark for hours. Yet they never seem to get hoarse or lose their voice (bark) like people do when they talk, yell, or sing too much. Veterinarians (animal doctors) think that is because a dog's voice box, or larynx, is not as complicated as the larynx of a human, who needs to make a wide range of different sounds to speak. So the stress that results from excessive barking doesn't do nearly as much damage as overusing a human voice does.

Why do dogs **wag their tails**?

We usually think that a dog wags its tail to show happiness. But tail-wagging in dogs is a little more complicated than that. A dog communicates a lot of information by the movement and position of its tail. If the dog wags its tail while holding it high and stiff, that animal feels threatened and is preparing for a fight. If the tail wags slowly and is held low, the dog is feeling insecure but friendly. But a tail that is held high and swings gracefully back and forth shows that the dog is confident, relaxed, and happy. Even the position of a nonwagging tail has a lot to say. A dog reprimanded for bad behavior often tucks its tail between its legs, showing its distress or fear.

Why do dogs **pant**?

When people get hot, millions of tiny sweat glands, located deep in their skin, produce sweat, or perspiration, which evaporates into the air and cools them. Dogs, however, have very few sweat glands. So they pant or breathe hard to cool off, which works in a similar way. Panting produces a strong flow of air that blows away moisture from a dog's lungs and mouth. The evaporating moisture takes some of the dog's body heat away with it. Just like a sweating person, a panting dog usually needs a good drink of water to maintain body fluids and keep the cooling process going when conditions are hot.

How do **dog years** compare with **human years**?

It has long been thought that one dog year equals seven human years, but many people believe another formula gives a more accurate picture: At age one a dog has the equivalent of 15 human years; at age two it has the equivalent of 24. After that, each additional year counts as four years. The average life span of a dog is 12 years, which, according to that formula, equals 64 human years. Large breeds tend to have shorter lives than this and small breeds tend to live longer (the record is 20 years).

Why do cats **purr**?

It is generally believed that cats purr to show contentment, but no one knows for sure. Cats are born with the ability to purr; kittens make the tiny rumbling sounds when they are nursing. Scientists think that purring starts out as a form of communication between a mother cat and her kittens. The purrs let the mother cat know that her babies are happy and feeding well, and she may purr back in response. Later, cats continue to purr when they are in a contented mood or as a friendly greeting.

But scientists aren't exactly sure *how* cats purr. Many think that it comes from the vibration of blood in a large vein in a cat's chest, caused when surrounding muscles repeatedly squeeze and release the blood vessel. Air in a cat's lungs and windpipe increase the sound of the vibrations so that it can be heard (though sometimes the purring of a cat is silent and can only be felt). Other scientists think that cats purr when membranes called false vocal cords, located in a cat's throat near the real ones, start to vibrate.

Why do cats' eyes shine at night?

In the wild, cats frequently hunt in twilight and at night. They can do this because they have special vision that allows them to see well in dim light. They have mirror-like tissue in their eyes (called tapetum lucidum) that reflects light back to their retinas—where visual images are formed—helping them to see better than most animals when light is scarce. When you see the glowing eyes of a cat at night you are seeing light reflected from this special tissue. House cats have the same excellent vision as their wild cousins and may still hunt at night, when prey animals like mice and rats are most active. While cats don't see colors particularly well, they can spot motion quickly, which is more important for an animal that hunts at night.

Because cats have eyes that use light very efficiently, only small amounts of light are needed to see during the day. That explains why a cat's dark center pupils—which let light into the eyes—are only narrow slits when light is bright. At night a cat's pupils look more like those of other animals, large and round. A cat can see six times better than we can in dim light.

Why do cats have **whiskers**?

The whiskers of a cat are part of its sense of touch. The long stiff hairs are called vibrissae, and, just like our own hairs, they are connected to nerves at their roots that send information to the brain. A house cat usually has 12 whiskers on either side of its nose, as well as a few above its eyes, on its cheeks, and behind its front legs.

These long, sensitive whiskers are particularly useful at night, when many cats are most active. They can give a cat information about surroundings that it can barely see. Whiskers can help a cat feel the distance between objects, letting it know if it can pass between them. Some scientists think that cat whiskers are so sensitive that they can feel the air move around objects, keeping a cat from bumping into them or helping it to travel safely over uneven ground.

The long, stiff whiskers of a cat are part of its sense of touch.

Do cats really have nine lives?

No animal has more than a single life. But cats do seem to survive dangerous situations that would likely hurt or kill other animals. Most remarkable cat survival stories involve the animals falling from high places. Cats love to perch on top shelves or at windowsills to get a good view of their surroundings. Their narrow, flexible bodies and great sense of balance allow them to climb into some pretty unusual places. They rarely fall from their high perches, but when they do, they usually end up with little or no damage. One reason for this is that cats have the ability to twist and turn themselves around in midair, landing on all four feet. Also, their flexible muscles and skeletons help their bodies absorb the impact of falls without getting hurt. Some cats have survived long falls from the windows of high-rise buildings without a scratch. Their natural characteristics seem to give them more lucky chances than other animals—hence the saying that cats have nine lives.

How do **cat years** compare with **human years**?

The formula to figure out the age of a cat in human years goes like this: at one year old a cat has the equivalent of 20 human years and each additional year counts as another four. The average life span of a house cat is between 12 and 14 years, which equals between 64 and 72 human years.

Can pets **see** what's on **television**?

When dogs and cats look at the television, they don't see the same things that you do. They can see little or no color and can't identify objects that appear on the flat screen. But they are attracted to the movement that they see on television. Action on the screen probably stirs their hunting instincts, making them think they are watching small, scurrying prey. Dogs and cats may also show interest in some of the sounds that come from television shows. A dog barking on TV may make your pet dog bark back, or a ringing doorbell in a TV show might prompt your dog to get up and go to the door.

SCHOOL DAZE

Why do I have to **go to school**?

So much of what you need to know to live successfully as an adult does not come naturally—it has to be learned and studied and memorized. Children learn to speak naturally, for example, by listening to those around them, but reading and writing must be

Kids need to go to school to ensure that they learn the kinds of things that will help them do well as adults.

specifically taught. The complicated process of learning the alphabet and the sounds it represents, putting letter sounds together to make words, and learning the meaning of words in order to read and write are skills that only come with special effort. Knowing how to figure out problems that involve numbers, and learning how the world is run or how nature works are important things to learn, too.

Your parents might be able to teach you these things, but they would need many hours each day to do it. Most parents need to work outside the home and wouldn't have the time to give proper instruction (though some kids are "home schooled" by their parents instead of going to school). In the United States, a public school system provides years of free education for all children. Teachers—who are specially trained to know what children should learn, and how, and when—are the people who do the job.

In past centuries, when most people worked on farms or in simple factory jobs, formal schooling (that done in a classroom) was not as important. But today, jobs frequently require complicated skills and complex knowledge. To ensure that all children learn the kinds of things that will help them do well as adults, state governments now require that all children to go to school for a certain number of years (usually to the age of 16). So that's another reason you have to go to school—it's the law. Kids who skip school a lot find themselves in court. (Children who go to private schools or whose parents have received special permission to teach them at home are exceptions.)

Do **all children** go to school?

A lot of children around the world learn to read and write and do arithmetic in places that don't resemble the school that you go to. A temple, a tent, or a building on stilts may serve as a classroom for some children living in very different places around the world. In poor places that have no money to build schools, children may learn their lessons outdoors. In isolated places like the Australian outback or Alaskan wilderness—where families live hundreds of miles apart and far from cities and towns—children may get their lessons from teachers over two-way radios—or, in recent years, over the Internet.

And not all children go to school as we know it, learning lessons from a teacher. Reading, writing, and arithmetic may not be important skills for some children to learn. A child living in the bush in Africa, for instance, may have little use for mathematics but will need to know how to identify animals tracks and make bows and arrows for hunting. Parents or other adults will train the child until the skills are learned, acting as teachers. So while not all children learn what they need to in a typical classroom, most learn the skills that are important to their way of life. Children learn all sorts of things inside and outside classrooms.

Why isn't there school **during the summer**?

Our 10-month school year—from September through June—developed when most
people still lived and worked on farms. Parents needed their children to help out at

home during the growing season, so there was no school in the summer. The 10-month school year became a tradition.

Even now, when most people no longer live and work on farms, the traditional school year has remained, and other traditions were built around it. A summer vacation from school became a tradition, too, allowing children to go on special trips with their families. The summer tourist industry depended on family vacationers in order to make money (and on students to do the work with summer jobs).

But studies have shown that the two to three months that children have off in the summer can cause problems. A lot of learning is forgotten over the long summer, and a lot of time is wasted relearning it during review time when school begins in the fall. Because our society is no longer an agricultural one—and because almost all institutions operate throughout the year—many educators have been looking into the idea of year-round schools.

There are about 2,700 year-round schools in the United States today, and studies show that most of their students learn more than those who attend traditional schools. Continuous education appears to be better than "interrupted" education. Children at most year-round schools attend the same number of days—180—as children at regular schools. But instead of a long summer break, they have shorter, more frequent breaks throughout the year. These breaks, called intersessions, are often used by students who need extra help or who want to learn more about things that especially interest them. The number of year-round schools is growing, which may indicate the start of a new tradition

Why do I have to do **homework**?

Sometimes there are not enough hours in the school day to get everything done or to learn all that needs to be learned about a subject. Then you have to use your time outside of school to finish the work. When you don't do homework, you are only hurting yourself by not learning—or practicing—what you need to know. (Homework is not just something you do to make your teacher happy.) Completing school assignments and doing school projects outside the classroom can teach you important skills, too, like how to manage your free time, work independently, or use resources in a library.

Why is **kindergarten** important?

In the United States, public schooling begins with kindergarten, when a child is about five years old. Kindergarten is a half day of classes in an elementary school. While most of the activities in kindergarten are play activities—like singing, storytelling, and drawing—children are also learning basic skills through these activities that they will need throughout their lives. These skills include listening to directions, using their time well, and working in cooperation with others. Kindergarten helps children

287

adjust to school slowly, going only a few hours each day. It bridges the gap between the age when kids spend their days playing (at home, or in daycare or nursery school) and the more formal learning that will begin once a child enters the first grade. A German educator name Friedrich Froebel opened the first kindergarten in 1837. Its name is German for "garden of children."

Why are some kids **better students** than others?

Some children do better in school than others for many reasons. All kids have different talents and abilities, and some of these just show up better in school. Some children may be naturally better at reading and writing and working with numbers, and at storing and using information. Most schoolwork requires these skills, so kids who are strong in these areas are likely to be better students. Other children, whose special talents may lie in music or art or sports, may not do quite as well. Still, most kids have enough ability to learn the basic skills taught in schools, things that they will need to know to get along well in the world once they graduate.

But remember that schoolwork does take effort—you can't learn if you don't work at it. A student can almost always become better by caring more and trying harder, even if it requires asking for special help. Good students usually come from families that consider education important, and they put a lot of time and effort into their studies.

What should you do if all your efforts in school bring disappointing results? Don't be ashamed and don't give up! The most important thing is not how much you learn, or how fast you learn, but that you *continue* to learn and do your best.

What are **learning disabilities**?

Learning disabilities are disorders that keep people from understanding or using spoken or written language in typical ways. Learning disabilities are not due to physical handicaps like blindness or deafness; rather, the disorders have to do with problems in the brain and the way it perceives things. About six percent of all children in the United States have some sort of learning disability. The most common of these are dyslexia—where the brain has trouble understanding words, sometimes reversing the order of letters and words—and attention deficit disorder (ADD)—which is marked by an inability to concentrate. Special teaching methods have been developed that help such children learn successfully despite their disorders. This teaching is done either in the regular classroom, in special classes, or at a specialized school, depending on the severity of the disorder.

It is important to identify learning disabilities early, before affected children express their frustration in bad behavior or start thinking of themselves as "stupid." Most people with learning disabilities simply need help learning things in different ways, or at a different pace, from other kids. A great number of people with learning disabilities have above-average intelligence. Many go on to lead very successful lives. It is believed that inventor Thomas Edison, political leader Winston Churchill, and scientist Albert Einstein all had learning disabilities.

What is meant by **I.Q.**?

I.Q. stands for intelligence quotient, and it is supposed to be a measurement of how naturally intelligent a person is. Intelligence tests are not designed to show how much a person has learned; rather, they are meant to measure a person's *ability* to learn. This ability is something that doesn't change much as a person grows older, even though he or she may pick up a lot of new facts and skills. Scientists think that each person is born with a certain amount of intelligence or mental ability. Still, how well a person uses his or her natural intelligence has a lot to do with the person's desire to learn and the learning environment in which he or she grows up.

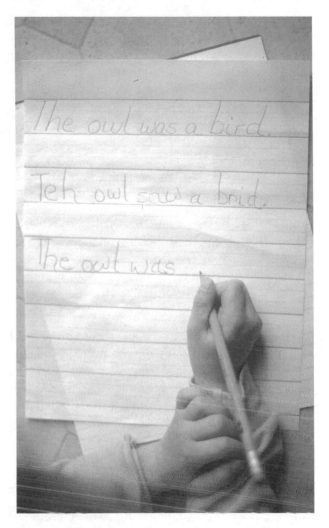

Dyslexia is a learning disability that causes the brain to sometimes reverse the order of letters and words. *Robert J. Huffman/Field Mark Publications © 2001*

I.Q. tests measure things like the ability to use words, the ability to see how things relate to one another, and the ability to store and use information. But a lot of intelligence experts think that I.Q. tests are unfair, because they can't help but test a person's *learned* knowledge in the phrasing of the questions. Depending on where you grew up or what language is spoken in your home, you may not be familiar with certain words used in some questions. And if you have trouble understanding what's being asked of you, it can be difficult to demonstrate your ability to think and reason.

The term "intelligence quotient" comes from a mathematical equation used to score intelligence tests. A person's mental age—which is determined by how many questions he or she answered correctly on such a test—is divided by his or her actual age. Then that number is multiplied by 100 to give an I.Q. score. A person whose mental and actual age are the same will have an I.Q. that is 100, which is average.

Remember that intelligence is just one thing that contributes to a person's ability to succeed in life and be happy. Special talents, hard work, creativity, and character are just as important.

Who made up our **system of numbers**?

From earliest times, people have had to keep track of things by counting. Historians believe that people used their fingers and toes, and then notched sticks, and finally number systems to help them count and measure things. The system of numbers that we use is known as a base-10, or decimal, system because it advances in segments of 10 ("dec" means 10). It is believed that such a system is based on finger counting. Two of the most widely used number systems—Arabic and Roman—are decimal systems.

We use the Arabic system of writing numbers. Europeans learned it from Arabs, who in turn developed it from the number system used by Hindus in ancient India. But other types of decimal number systems had developed simultaneously in different parts of the world. As early as 4000 B.C., Babylonians (who lived in the region that is now Iraq) wrote numbers from left to right and grouped them in 10s. Ancient China, too, used a decimal number system. The numeral zero was added to the Arabic system later; it was first used in India and China around A.D. 600.

How many **numbers** are there?

Numbers are unlimited, or infinite, which means that you could go on counting them forever. One man, Edward Kasner, asked his young nephew, Milton Sirotta, to come up with a name for the huge number he was working with, which was a 1 with 100 zeroes after it. The boy called it a googol. While the googol is the largest number with a name, there are numbers much larger than googols, so big that you could never write all their zeroes down during your lifetime.

Why do we **measure things differently** than most people in the world?

Different systems of measurement are used in the world today, with the two most important being the metric system, or International System of Units (SI), and the English Units of Measurements. From ancient times, people have always used various units to measure the weight, volume, and length of things: a certain number of plant seeds might make up a unit that measured weight, for instance—and then that unit could be used to measure other things besides seeds. The measurement of a body part might have been used to create a unit that showed length. The length of an inch, for example, came from either the width of a man's thumb or the distance from the tip of a man's finger to the first joint. The yard came from the length of a man's arm—from nose to fingertip—and the foot from the size of a man's foot. But until these units were standardized, with a set unit of weight or length agreed upon, measurement was unreliable, because seeds and people come in all sizes. As late as the eighteenth century, the same measurement units varied from place to place.

But French scientists began a movement around that time to have a single, precise measurement system used by all countries throughout the world. They called it the International System of Units, and it is based on the metric system, where all measurement units are multiples of 10. The meter is the standard unit of length, and the kilogram is the standard unit of mass, or weight. Bit by bit, this system of measurement was officially adopted for use by all the countries of the world, except for the nations of Liberia, Myanmar (also known as Burma)—and the United States. (Many people believe the United States should switch to the metric system, but the complicated process of changing from one measurement system to another usually takes a number of years.) In the United States, most people still use an older and more complicated measurement system called the English Units of Measurements. That standard unit of length is the yard and the pound is the standard unit of mass, or weight. Measurements can be changed from one system to another using mathematical equations or a conversion chart. While the metric system is being used more and more in the United States, particularly in the scientific community, there has still been no official move to adopt it.

How did **writing** begin?

People communicated through speaking long before they began writing. Historians think that writing, a visible record of language, began around 4500 B.C. in Mesopotamia, located in the area that is now Iraq. People there (probably Sumerians) used wedges to make marks on wet slabs of clay that were later dried or baked to hardness, making a permanent record. Their system of writing—which consisted of symbols that represented words or syllables of words—is called cuneiform.

At about the same time the ancient Egyptians began to use a similar writing system called hieroglyphics. Pictures and symbols represented ideas and words or parts of words. Egyptians also wrote on clay tablets or carved hieroglyphics on the stone walls of monuments and tombs. They also painted them on paperlike materials made from river grasses (papyrus) or other plants; few of these more delicate examples have survived. (The Rosetta Stone, found in Egypt in 1799 and carved in three languages—including hieroglyphics—gave scholars the key to understanding ancient Egypt's picture language.)

Later, the Maya people of Central America invented their own hieroglyphic writing system. None of these written picture languages are true alphabets, the symbols of which represent all the sounds of a language. The ancient Greeks created the first true alphabet around 1000 B.C. (The word alphabet comes from the names of the first two Greek letters: "alpha" and "beta.") All complex civilizations have some form of writing.

Where did our **alphabet** come from?

An alphabet is a system of writing in which symbols or letters represent all the sounds of a language. Because ancient Egyptian hieroglyphics sometimes used symbols to represent language sounds, they are considered the root of true alphabets.

Our alphabet came from the ancient Romans (who based theirs on that of the ancient Greeks). Modern English uses a modified form of this Latin alphabet. The written languages of Western Europe, Africa, and the Americas, as well as scientific writing, all use the Roman, or Latin, alphabet. It has 26 letters, and is written from left to right.

How many **different alphabets** are there?

There are about 46 different alphabets in use today. Modern English and languages of Western Europe, Africa, and the Americas use a modified version of the Latin alphabet, which was developed by the ancient Romans. The Cyrillic alphabet, which is used by many countries in Eastern Europe—like Russia, Serbia, and Bulgaria—is based on the ancient Greek alphabet. Modern Greek, Hebrew, and Arabic all have their own alphabets. (Hebrew and Arabic are written from right to left.)

Some writing systems that are in use today are not true alphabets. A true alphabet is a system of writing in which symbols or letters represent all the sounds of a language. The Indian Devanagari alphabet is the source of many types of Asian writing; some of its symbols represent syllables of words instead of individual sounds. Japanese uses similar syllabic features. It also shares features with China's nonalphabetic system of writing, where each of its many symbols or characters represent a different word or idea. (Modern Japanese and Chinese are written from right to left, too, though they were once written from top to bottom in vertical columns.) As you can imagine, these writing systems are especially challenging to learn. China's writing system is so complex, in fact—with several thousand characters—that it has kept much of that country's population from becoming fully literate (able to read and write).

How do **pencils write**?

Since ancient times people have drawn or written by taking solid pieces of colored material, like earth or chalk, and rubbing them across surfaces, where they stick and leave marks. Graphite, a soft form of the element carbon that performs this function very well, is the dark writing material that you see inside most pencils (not the ele-

Egyptian hieroglyphics, one of the world's first writing systems, used pictures and symbols to represent ideas and words.

293

ment lead, though such pencils are often referred to as lead pencils and the graphite inside them described as lead). Wood is used as a protective outer covering to keep the inner lead of a pencil from breaking and to keep the hands of its users clean. After you write for a while, you rub enough graphite particles off onto paper to make it necessary to sharpen your pencil, grinding away the wood to show more of the lead again.

Pencils have been used to write and draw for a very long time, since the sixteenth century. At the beginning of the nineteenth century, pencil makers discovered that they could control how dark or light a pencil lead would write by mixing certain amounts of clay with the graphite, which was crushed into a powder. More clay would make the lead harder, capable of producing fine lines for delicate work. Less clay would produce a soft, dark lead best suited for the drawing and shading of artwork. Today, when you buy a pencil, the number that is usually printed near its end tells you how hard its lead is (with a higher number indicating greater hardness). The lead of a colored pencil contains no graphite; it is a mixture of white clay and dyes, or pigments.

Today pencils are made on assembly lines by machines. First, crushed graphite and clay are mixed and shaped into thin leads, like spaghetti. Then they are cut to pencil size and dried before they are baked to make them hard. Next, they are laid in grooves on a thin wooden board, and another grooved wooden board is glued on top of it. Each pencil is then sliced and shaped. Pencils are usually round or hexagonal (six-sided), which keeps them from rolling off of desks. In the final step, the outside of pencils are painted to give them a hard, smooth, non-splintery surface.

How do **erasers remove writing**?

When you write with a pencil you are rubbing its lead across a surface—usually paper—leaving marks. The marks are really tiny bits of the pencil lead, or graphite, that have stuck to the paper. The surface of an eraser (which is made of rubber or a similar material) is both soft and sticky. When it is dragged across pencil marks, the lead sticks to it. Conveniently, during rubbing, an eraser's surface breaks off in bits, too, which gets rid of the areas where the pencil marks have stuck. The eraser surface remains clean and ready for more work, while the shreds of it that are black with lead can be brushed away. Only special erasers can remove ink, which sinks into paper instead of sticking to its surface. These erasers are made with sand in them to make them more abrasive, because they need to rub away some of the paper in order to remove the ink marks. Erasing crayon marks doesn't work very well because the wax from which crayons are made stick well to paper but not to erasers. Usually trying to erase crayon leaves a smeary mess.

What is **literacy**?

Literacy is the skill of being able to read and write fairly well. Unlike speech, reading and writing do not come naturally; they have to be learned. Most people who live in industrialized or "developed" countries can read and write because everyday activities there depend on it. "Developing" countries in places like Asia and Africa—with very different ways of life from the industrialized nations—have low literacy rates because most people there can get along without the skill. (Some tribal languages don't even have a written form.) Almost 30 percent of adults in the world (people 15 years or older) cannot read and write, or are illiterate. Even in such wealthy, highly developed nations as the United States, many people don't know how to read and write.

What is a library?

A library is a collection of reading materials (and sometimes music and videos, too) that is kept available for people to use but not to buy. The first public library was established in Greece in 330 B.C. for use by certain members of the population. The first *circulating* library, which allowed materials to be taken out by paying members and returned after use, was begun by Benjamin Franklin in Philadelphia, Pennsylvania, in 1732. But not until the late nineteenth century could the general population borrow books from public libraries for free.

Today, taxes paid by people who live in cities and towns provide most of the funding for local public libraries. So, in a way, that makes you and everyone else in your community joint owners of your local library and of all the wonderful books, videos, CDs, and other resources that it has in it. What better reason could you have for taking good care of the library materials that you use? It makes sense to treat them with the same respect that you would your own possessions or those of a friend. It's also important to return borrowed library material on time, so that another library user can have his or her turn using it.

How are **books** made?

Once a book has been written and edited, it must be typeset, printed, and bound—and today those tasks are performed mostly by machines. The typesetter follows the instructions of the book designer, taking a regular-looking electronic document (like something you might create on a home computer for a school report) and formatting it so it looks like a book page—with type in all different sizes and styles. After the book has been proofread—checked for mistakes—the typesetter either prints out the pages onto a special kind of paper that can be photographed or creates a special computer file containing the whole book (including pictures). The second method, called electronic prepress, eliminates several steps for the printer and has become far more common in recent years.

Regardless of the method used for delivering the book to the printer (whether on camera-ready paper or a computer disk), the printer must create several large negatives (like the ones you get back with your pictures when you've had film developed at the drugstore). Each negative contains several pages of the book. These negative sheets, called flats, are placed over a thin metal plate that is sensitive to light, like the paper that photographs are printed on. When exposed to light, the images from the negatives—the words and pictures of the book—appear on the metal plate, which is now ready to accept ink and print the pages of the book. The metal plate is loaded onto large cylinders (tubes) and covered with ink, which only sticks to the parts of the plates that have the letters and images. Then large sheets of paper are rolled through the cylinders, which press the ink onto the paper. Once the ink has dried, machines fold the sheets of paper many times over, pinching, pulling, and creasing them. Each large sheet, once it's been folded up by the machine, forms a section of the book, called a signature, and all the sections of the book are then put together and readied for binding.

The final step of making a book involves either gluing or sewing all the signatures together, attaching the cover, and trimming the pages so all the book's edges are perfectly even. The book is now ready to be shipped to a bookstore or library where it can be read and enjoyed.

What is the most **widely read book** in the world?

The world's best-selling book is the Bible. During the past two centuries alone, it has sold an estimated 3.88 billion copies. The Bible, made up primarily of the Old Testament and the New Testament, is the holy book of Christianity, the most widely practiced religion in the world today. The Old Testament, which covers events before the birth of Jesus Christ, constitutes the Jewish Bible.

MY FAMILY AND FRIENDS

FAMILY MEMBERS

Why do men and women **marry**?

Throughout the centuries—and in different parts of the world—men and women have married for a variety of reasons. It used to be common for young people to marry the person their parents chose for them, and some cultures continue to practice arranged marriages. Throughout most of the world today, however, a man and a woman usually marry because they love each other and want be together and care for one another for the rest of their lives. Adults often want to have children together and raise them in a family. While people don't have to be married in order to have children, many people feel more comfortable raising a family as part of a married couple. When a man and a woman marry they make their permanent partnership public. After a marriage ceremony, they are connected by a legal contract, or agreement—a marriage license--that can only be dissolved by another legal decree known as a divorce (though death legally ends a marriage as well). Marriage grants a couple a new legal and social status, changing such things as the way they pay taxes and the amount they pay for health insurance. (Many employers, for instance, extend an employee's health insurance benefits to that person's wife or husband and children; if two people live together and have children but are not married, the employee's family often cannot participate in the company's health plan.)

Will I be a **parent** someday?

Deciding whether or not to have children is something every adult has to decide for him or herself. Statistics of married people in the United States indicate that you have a good chance of becoming a mother or father someday—more than half of all married couples in America have children. (Of course, it isn't necessary to marry to become a parent, but many people do.) The average American family has two children, though some families have one child and others have more. If a man and a woman cannot have a baby for health reasons, they may be able to adopt a child whose own biological mother and father cannot take care of him or her, and raise the child as their own. It really makes no difference where a child comes from when it comes to being a mother and a father. Lots of people can produce babies physically, but it is the caring for and the worrying about and the endless love for their children that truly make people mothers and fathers.

Why do husbands and wives divorce?

Husbands and wives divorce when they can no longer live happily together. It is usually a sad thing, because when people marry they expect to be with their partner for the rest of their lives.

But over the course of a marriage things happen and people change and the happiness that the couple was so sure of in the beginning sometimes disappears. When couples with children get divorced it is even more unfortunate because more people are affected. Many children feel bad when their parents divorce because their family will not be the same. After a divorce, they generally do not see one of their parents as much as they did before. Still, just because the feelings between a mother and a father change doesn't mean that their love for their children changes in any way. It's important to remember that divorce is something that happens between a husband and wife—it has nothing to do with the kids. Many children feel that if they adjust their behavior somehow their parents will want to stay together, but divorces are not caused by anything kids do.

Who decides **which of the divorced parents** their **children will live with**?

Because a marriage is a legal partnership, its dissolution, or end, takes place by a judgment of a court. The court, then, awards custody of children after a divorce. The judge that presides over the court makes this decision, ideally keeping the best interests of the children in mind. A judge's involvement is especially important when parents can't agree over who should be the main caregiver for their children and provide their main home. But in the best cases, both parents and children decide together how they would like custody to be awarded, and they let the court know their preferences. Sometimes joint custody is the solution, which means that the parents share responsibility for the kids and the children divide their time equally between their mother and father and their separate homes. Most of the time, however, one parent becomes the custodial parent and the children live with her or him, while the other parent has visitation rights, which means that he or she can see the children at certain times, like on weekends or during summer vacations.

What is a **single parent**?

A single parent is either a mother or a father who raises her or his children alone—without being married or in a long-term, committed relationship. This situation usually happens because the parent divorces or the parent's husband or wife dies. But some people decide ahead of time to raise a child without the help of a partner. For at least a part of their lives, almost half of the children in the United States are raised by a single parent. While many people picture the typical family as two parents and their kids, that view of the family doesn't match up with the way numerous people are raised today. Some people have two parents who live together, some people's parents are divorced, some only have one parent. And some kids are raised by grandparents or aunts and uncles, or by foster parents who take care of them when their biological parents can't. A family can be defined in many ways, and the most important thing is to be raised by people who love and support you, rather than trying to fit in with anyone's definition of a "typical" family.

What is a **homosexual**?

A homosexual is a person who has romantic and sexual feelings for someone of his or her own gender. Men who love men in this way are referred to as gay, and women who similarly love women are known as lesbians. Some people are attracted to both men and women; these people are called bisexual. Just like heterosexual people—who are romantically and sexually attracted to the opposite sex—homosexual and bisexual people share love and companionship with their partners. Like other people, they work hard at their jobs, pay taxes, and participate in their communities. Some create families together. But because they are not like most people when it comes to sexual orientation, gay men, lesbians, and bisexual people are often criticized for their lifestyles. Many people view anything other than heterosexuality as unnatural and abnormal, and they want to deny gay, lesbian, and bisexual people the basic rights and respect that all people deserve. Lots of people have false ideas or prejudices about homosexuals and are afraid of them. For some people, these prejudices and fear cause them to treat gay, lesbian, and bisexual people unfairly or even violently, which is against the law.

What is a **widow**?

A widow is a woman whose husband has died but who has not remarried. She may or may not have children. Similarly, a man whose wife has died but who has not remarried is called a widower. (You may be familiar with the word because of the poisonous black widow spider, which lives in North and South America. It gets its name from the fact that the female may eat the male after mating—making herself a "widow.")

Identical twins have the same genes, making them look amazingly alike.

What is a **stepmother** or **stepfather**?

If your dad marries someone else after divorcing your mom, what is his new wife's relationship to you? She is your stepmother (and if your mom marries someone else after divorcing your dad, that man is your stepfather). You could also have a stepmother or stepfather if one of your parents died and the other remarried. While stepparents usually come to love and care for their stepchildren as though they are their own, it can be difficult for the kids to accept this new adult in their lives. It means living by a new set of rules, getting used to someone else's cooking, or even having new siblings if your stepparent has kids from a previous relationship. It's important to remember that nobody expects a stepmother or stepfather to replace your "real" mom or dad. And it's also important to remember that adjusting to a new family takes time, and probably lots of arguments, before things start to feel normal. But after a time the new family, while different from the old one, will feel more like home.

What is a **sibling**?

A sibling is a brother or sister. Most brothers and sisters share the same mother and father. But sometimes siblings have the same mother but different fathers, or the reverse—the same father and different mothers. Siblings that have one parent the same as you and one different are said to be half-brothers or half-sisters. You may have siblings who have a different mother *and* a different father from you. Those siblings are considered stepbrothers and stepsisters. It doesn't really matter how you are related to your brothers and sisters, though. They are still an important part of your family and can be wonderful to have around.

What are **identical twins**?

When the sperm from a man fertilizes the egg cell of a woman, a baby begins to grow in the woman's body, developing in her uterus, or womb. Through the joined sperm and egg, the man and woman each contribute half of the genes that will give the baby its inherited characteristics, like eye color and height. Once in a while, before the baby begins to grow, the fertilized egg, or zygote, splits in two, forming two separate zygotes that develop independently. When this happens two babies start to grow inside their mother. The babies will be identical twins, which means they will have the same genes, be of the same sex, and look amazingly alike.

Can a **boy and girl** be **twins**?

Usually a woman's ovaries—the reproductive organs that produce the eggs—release just one egg each month. If that egg is fertilized by a man's sperm, then a baby eventually begins to grow in the uterus of the woman. Once in a while, however, two eggs are released at the same time. Both eggs may become fertilized by two different sperm, and then two babies will grow. The babies will develop at the same time, and they will be born together as twins. But unlike identical twins, these fraternal twins—as they are called—will not have identical genes. Because they have developed from different eggs and sperm, fraternal twins can be as different as any two siblings can be (they just happened to share their mother's uterus). Fraternal twins can consist of one boy and one girl, or two girls, or two boys. They may look alike, but they may not. They may grow up to have similar interests, or they may pursue very different paths.

What is a test-tube baby?

Sometimes, a man and a woman who want to have a baby have trouble conceiving. Many factors can contribute to a fertility problem, and sometimes medical science can help fix it. One solution to infertility is something called in vitro fertilization. With this method, a woman's eggs are fertilized with a man's sperm outside the woman's body. Fertilization takes place in a laboratory, in a glass dish (not really in a test tube); once fertilization occurs there and the fertilized eggs begin to grow, they are placed inside the woman's uterus to develop further. Eventually a baby is born (sometimes multiple babies are born if more than one of the fertilized eggs attaches to the uterus and develops fully). Kids who originate from this method of fertilization are no different from other kids—they are simply children who began their lives outside their mothers' bodies.

Why can't **babies** do **anything**?

Try to imagine what it is like to be born. One minute you are floating in a warm, dark, quiet world where there is nothing to see, not much to feel, and where you don't even have to eat or breathe on your own—it's all done for you, with nutrition and oxygen reaching you through a special tube called an umbilical cord that connects you to your mother. Then all at once you arrive in an unknown world, as strange as any planet in outer space. Suddenly, air touches your skin and feels warm or cold. Loud sounds, and light, and strange-looking creatures and objects surround you. You have to breathe at once in order to survive. You experience hunger for the first time and will soon have to learn how to eat, too.

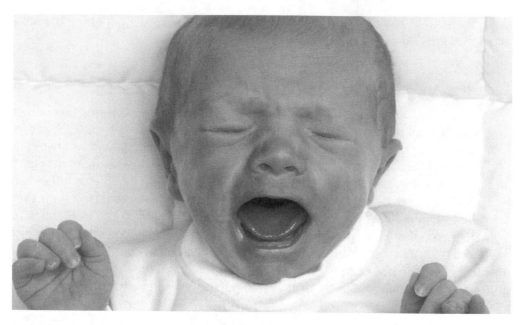

Newborn babies can't talk, eat on their own, or move around very well—they're totally dependent on their parents (and siblings!).

It takes a long time for a newborn to learn about his or her new world. Human babies are born with instincts and reflexes that help them survive, just like other baby animals, but they have no knowledge or experience about the complex world of people into which they arrive. So don't be impatient with babies—they have everything to learn.

Making the learning process twice as hard is the fact that human babies are not fully developed when they are born. In nature, less complex life forms like insects, for instance, can move about and get their own food as soon as they are hatched. But the young of higher forms of life—and humans are at the top—take many years before they are physically mature. People grow until they are between the ages of 18 and 20 years old (with body changes occurring very quickly in the early years), and—because the human brain is so complex—mental growth continues throughout a lifetime. During much of their lives, then, children must be fed, cared for, and taught by adults.

So when newborns start out, their bodies aren't even ready for the demands of their new world. They can't see very well at first, especially things that are far away. They don't know how to use their arms and legs much; for a while they can't even grasp things with their hands. The digestive systems of newborns are immature, too, and babies don't have teeth; unable to eat solid foods, they depend on breast milk or baby formula for all their nutrition, and sometimes they can't even keep that in their stomachs, spitting up a lot. Most frustrating of all—for everyone, including the baby—is the fact that babies are unable to talk at first, and the only way they can communicate their feelings or needs is to cry.

302

What is an **only child**?

An only child is a child who has no brothers or sisters. For a long time, parents—and experts on raising children—worried that only children would not be as well adjusted in adulthood because they had no brothers or sisters to relate to and share things with as they matured. Some people feared that as adults, only children would be antisocial and selfish. But studies have shown that none of this is true; as only children grow up, they share their lives with young friends and relatives. Lots of only children become well-adjusted adults, and many become high achievers.

What does **adopted** mean?

Sometimes children cannot be raised by the women and men responsible for their births—their natural, or birth, parents. This situation arises for many reasons: the parents may be too ill or may have died, or they may feel that they are too young or too poor to raise children properly. Happily, many couples, or single women and men, want to raise the children of such parents as their own. When a child is legally adopted, the law recognizes that the new parent or parents and the child are connected in the same ways that natural children are connected with their parents, sharing the same rights and duties. (Once a child is adopted, his or her birth parents lose all legal control over that child.) What the law doesn't state—but what every adopted child knows—is that the love shared with an adoptive parent is the same too.

Can **adopted children** find their **birth parents**?

In many adoption cases, the identities of a child's birth parents are kept secret. This practice is meant as a protection for all individuals involved. It allows the natural parents to go on with their lives without having contact (which could be very painful) with the child or children they gave up. The adoptive parent or parents and adopted child can build a new life together and form loving bonds without the interference of a natural parent. But as adopted children grow up, some feel a strong need to get to know their natural parents, particularly their mothers, and to learn the circumstances surrounding their births. In many parts of the United States, an adopted person who is at least 18 years old can find out some information about his or her birth parents—things that wouldn't give away the parents' identities, like medical history, ethnic origin, and religion—from hospital and adoption records. An adopted person can also locate his or her birth mother through a "reunion" agency, but only if the parent has put her name on a list to be contacted. (Locating a biological father can be more difficult—if the father was not involved in the life of the birth mother when she put her child up for adoption, she may not have given the agency any information about him.)

303

What is an **aunt**?

An aunt is the sister of your mother or father. She can also be the woman who marries your mother or father's brother. If your mother and father have many brothers and sisters, you can have a lot of aunts! Sometimes a woman who is not related to you but who helps, advises, and encourages you as an aunt would, is affectionately referred to as your aunt.

What is an **uncle**?

An uncle is the brother of your mother or father. He can also be the man who marries your mother or father's sister. You may also know a man who is not related to you—a close family friend who loves and encourages you, for example—that you refer to as your uncle.

What is a **cousin**?

A first cousin is the child of your uncle or aunt. The term cousin can also refer to other family members to whom you are not as closely related.

GETTING ALONG

What is a **best friend**?

A best friend is a special pal who generally likes to do a lot of the same things you like. You tend to have more fun with your best friend than with other friends, and you can tell him or her more of your feelings, even secrets, because you trust that person more than anyone else. And your best friend feels the same way about you, sharing important ideas and feelings. It seems like your best friend understands you better than any other person you know. You care about each other a great deal. You share your good times and bad times with a best friend, and that person does the same with you.

Why do I have to **be nice** to people?

With billions of people crowded onto one planet, it is critical that we treat each other with basic decency and respect so we can get along with one another. One basic rule of behavior, called the golden rule, has helped people do this, century after century. That rule states that we should treat others in the way we would like to be treated ourselves. If you want people to be nice to you (and who doesn't?), then it is wise to be nice to them. Courteous, kind behavior not only makes the people you're dealing with feel good, it can make you feel good too. You've probably noticed that being nice is contagious, spreading good feelings to lots of people; not only that, but you'll find you get what you want a lot more often when you're behaving pleasantly than if you're whining or ordering people around. Imagine if each person made the effort to be more respectful and thoughtful—the whole world would run a lot more smoothly.

Why can't I **take things** that aren't mine?

People can only get along together when they show care and respect for each other. Likewise, people must show care and respect for the property of others. History has shown us—through its wars and invasions—what chaos can be created when people take by force what isn't theirs.

Everyone has personal possessions that mean a lot to them. When you take something that belongs to someone else without asking (or without paying for it), it is considered stealing, and it is wrong. (Grown-ups who do serious stealing end up in jail.) No matter how much you want something, it is never okay to steal. Just think how bad you would feel if someone took something special that belonged to you.

A lot of times you can borrow something that belongs to another person if he or she gives you permission. Take good care of the item, then, and don't forget to return it! Also be prepared to replace the item if you lose or ruin it. That is part of the deal when you borrow something. And remember, you can't expect other people to share their things with you if you don't share your things with them. When you are generous, others tend to be generous back. Sharing with one another is a great way to use and enjoy more things than you could own yourself, and everybody benefits.

What is a lie?

A lie is a statement that isn't true. It is told on purpose, to make others believe something that is false. Sometimes people tell what are called "white lies," which are generally told to avoid hurting someone's feelings. If your grandma asks if you like her cookies, for example, you might say yes even though they tasted like cardboard. While your motives may be pure, it's still best to tell the truth in as gentle a way as possible, or, in the cookie example, to redirect the conversation by pointing out something your grandma makes that you really do like. Most people would rather know they can count on you to give an honest answer than suspect that you might be saying something just to make them feel good.

Why **shouldn't I lie**?

Because people live together and depend on each other for their care and safety, it is important that they tell the truth to one another. Lying can cause bad things to happen, and a famous story dramatically illustrates this idea.

The story describes a boy who lived in a village that was sometimes threatened by wolves. One day he thought he saw such a beast and cried, "Wolf! Wolf!" The villagers

305

Best friends share secrets, go through good times and bad times together, and rely on each other.

ran to the boy's house with pitchforks and other weapons to protect him from the wild animal. But the boy was mistaken—there was no wolf—and the villagers were glad that he was safe. The people returned to their homes.

The boy liked the attention that his cries had brought, however, and thought that he would give the alarm again. He cried "Wolf!" a second time, and again the villagers came running. Again they were glad that the boy was safe, but they told him that he should be more certain the next time before calling them. The boy cried "Wolf!" a third time and the villagers still came, but not as fast as before. By the time he had called a fourth and fifth time, the people of the village knew that the boy was a liar. They no longer answered his calls, which turned out to be a very bad thing: when the wild beast finally did come one night, the villagers assumed the alarm was false and did not come to rescue the boy who cried wolf.

Lying breaks the basic rule of conduct that helps people get along in the world: treating others in the same way in which you would like to be treated. When you lie, it shows that you care more about yourself—and about what the false information can do for you—than about other people, who may face problems because of it. Imagine what your life would be like if people frequently lied to you. You would make all sorts of mistakes and be in a constant state of confusion, not knowing what was true and what was false. The world would be a crazy place if people couldn't trust one another to tell the truth.

It is especially tempting to lie when telling the truth will get you into trouble, but remember this: lies are usually discovered, which only makes matters worse. All people make mistakes, but lying about what you've done makes the situation far worse. It shows that you can't be trusted. People who are truthful about their mistakes are admired because it takes courage and a great deal of maturity to admit when you're wrong. You will find that when you own up to your misdeeds, your parents or teachers will appreciate your honesty and be much more forgiving than if you had lied about it and later been found out. People appreciate others who are honest because they know those people can be counted on.

Is it okay to **tell a secret** that someone else told me?

A big part of listening to someone's secret is promising not to tell anyone else. Doing what you promise is a way of showing that you can be trusted. When you tell someone else's secret it usually indicates that you care more about yourself than about the person who shared the confidence with you. That behavior breaks the basic rule of conduct that helps people get along in the world: treating others the same way in which you would like to be treated. Before you tell someone's secret, think: How would I like it if someone told *my* secret? Because people depend on each other for so many things, it is important that they do what they say. How could the world run smoothly if no one kept his or her word?

Once in a while, though, you have to tell a secret in order to protect someone (including yourself). If a friend tells you confidentially that he or she is doing something harmful, for example, then you have to break your promise of secrecy and tell a grown-up, who will know what should be done about the situation. In such a case, the safety of other people is more important than your promise of trust. How do you know when to keep a secret and when to tell? A good rule to follow: if a secret makes you feel bad, scared, or confused, share it with an adult you trust.

Why can't I **yell or hit** when I'm mad?

It certainly isn't wrong to feel mad about things that happen. You can't help but get mad when your brother breaks your favorite toy or when someone cuts in front of you when you're standing in line. Life is full of all sorts of things that we think are unfair or that upset us. But yelling and hitting is not the answer. When you yell or hit someone, it is likely that he or she will yell or hit back. Someone could get hurt, and the situation gets worse, not better. If everyone yelled and hit when they got mad, the world would be an awful place.

Stop and count to 10 when you get mad. That way you can get control of your feelings. Then you will be able to think more clearly, and thinking—not just quickly reacting—is what changes bad situations. Maybe your brother feels terrible about breaking your toy but can't say he's sorry because you're punching him. Instead, tell him how sad you feel and give him a chance to apologize. It was probably an accident—after all, nobody's perfect. (Chances are you've broken something that belonged

307

to someone else, too.) And if you and your brother use your brains instead of your raised voices and fists, maybe the two of you can think of a fair solution.

Sometimes even when you talk reasonably to the person who has made you mad, he or she still doesn't respond in a nice way. It is hardest then to control your feelings. But ask yourself, is the situation worth a fight? Sometimes, if your rights are being abused, or you are being treated in a dangerous way, you need to get the help of a grown-up. But a lot of the times, the situation is really not important enough to get mad over. Does it really matter, for example, if the person who cut in front of you in line gets into the movie theater before you do? Remember, as much as you wish you could, you can't control how other people act, especially not with yelling and hitting. But what you can control in a given situation are your own feelings and behavior.

Why do I have to take a **"time out"** sometimes?

To help us survive, our bodies and minds are set up to respond a certain way to situations that we think are threatening. We react physically to such situations first, and we think later. This response was very useful in the lives of prehistoric men and women when they roamed the planet and faced physical dangers constantly. When a wild animal attacked, for instance, a cave dweller fled or drew his or her weapon without stopping first to think about the danger he was in.

In the modern world, we find ourselves in very few situations that threaten our lives. But our bodies still react to things in the same instant, physical way. When troubling situations occur, our feelings come first before our thinking takes over. When someone does something we don't like, or that upsets us, our first reaction is to act on our feelings, which might include yelling or hitting. A person can get pretty worked up physically, which doesn't allow him or her to listen to the thinking messages that are also going on inside.

When an adult makes you take a "time out," it takes you away from the upsetting situation. Your body and feelings can settle down then, and you can start to think. It is normal and natural to react strongly to things that put your body on alert, but as you get older, you will begin to recognize that most situations don't require a "caveman" response. You will be able to control your feelings better and use thinking to guide your actions.

Why do I have to say **I'm sorry** after behaving badly?

Everybody makes mistakes, even grown-ups. Mistakes are a big part of learning to be a better person. If you behave badly—breaking rules and hurting other people—it is important to show that you realize the mistakes you've made and the harm you've done, and that you will try to do better next time. Saying "I'm sorry" brings that message to the person you've hurt or disappointed and often makes him or her feel better. And even though it's very hard to apologize, you may find it will make you feel better, too.

When someone has hurt or disappointed you and comes to apologize, try to forgive him or her quickly. Remember, that person is learning how to be a better person, just like you.

Why am I **punished** when I've done something wrong?

Try to remember that when you are punished it is not because you are bad. You are being punished because you need to learn that there are better ways to handle your feelings and control your actions when upsetting situations occur. When you are young it is hard to do this; to help keep you from hurting yourself or others, grown-ups make rules for you to follow. Some rules—like those about sharing and taking turns, for instance—are meant to help everyone get along and treat each other with thoughtfulness and respect. Other rules—like those about wearing a helmet while riding a bike, let's say—are meant to keep everyone safe. So rules exist for good reasons, and it is wise to follow them. Punishments—which are unpleasant—are meant to remind you that breaking rules results in negative consequences, and maybe next time you will think harder when tempted to do something you're not supposed to do.

Who decides what is right and wrong?

When you are young, it is mainly your parents, but also teachers and other grown-ups close to you, who decide what is right and wrong. They are the ones who make the rules that they believe will keep you safe and help you learn how to become a good person and get along in the world. Adults make the best teachers because they have experienced a lot of different situations while growing up themselves, and they have learned lessons from those experiences that they can share with you. Grown-ups are wiser than children, who have lived just a short time in the world. But, as you continue to mature, you will have your own experiences and learn your own lessons. You may begin to question certain rules, and your ideas about what is right and wrong may change. This development is a normal part of growing up, the point at which you start to become the independent and unique person you are meant to be.

Still, no matter how much you change, it is important to remember that some rules of behavior will always remain the same. One rule is to treat yourself with care and respect. Another is to treat others with the same thoughtfulness and respect with which you would like them to treat you. When you grow up, you will have to follow the rules of law and government in the country in which you live. Many of these rules are based on respect for the rights of others.

Why do I have to be a **"good sport"** when I lose a game?

Games or competitions always have winners and losers. When you agree to play a game you have to prepare yourself for the fact that you may not win. Accepting a loss is hard, because winning a game gives you a wonderful feeling of being the best. Who wouldn't want such a feeling?

But not everyone can be the best on a particular day or even at a particular game or sport. Every person is unique and has his or her own strengths and talents. Just because you are not the best at some activity doesn't mean that you can't participate in it—and even have fun! And as you continue to play that sport or game, your skills will probably improve. If you can see the game as a way to improve your own skills and to have fun, you may even be able to admire (and learn from) the talent of the person who beats you and congratulate him or her. After all, it's only a game.

So remember that when you play a game, the object is to participate well: play fairly, with respect for your teammates and opponents, and with your best effort. It is also important to show good behavior following the game, whether you win or lose. If you can do that, then you are demonstrating good sportsmanship. Being a good sport is actually much more important than being a winner.

Why are **"please"** and **"thank you"** magic words?

Most human beings live with other people all their lives. You grow up in a family, learn along with classmates in your school, and participate with your friends and neighbors in activities in your community. You are a citizen of a country, which is one of many that make up the world. People have always lived together and over the years have developed something called manners, or etiquette, that help make all this togetherness—of so many individuals—a little easier. While these rules of conduct have changed from century to century and vary from place to place, they are all based on the idea that a person should treat others like he or she would like to be treated. People who have good manners are said to be polite. Polite people are appreciated because they have respect for others.

"Please" and "thank you" are not magic words like "abracadabra," which a magician says as he pulls a rabbit out of a hat. But they are special words because they make dealing with other people go more smoothly. People depend on one another for all sorts of things. We have to ask for help or permission all the time. Saying "please" shows that your request also comes with respect for the person you are asking. People are usually more willing to fulfill the requests of those who treat them with respect. Similarly, after someone gives you something or assists you, it is polite to say "thank you" to show your appreciation. Someone whose actions are appreciated will be more likely to help out or be generous again. So you can see how being polite can help people get things done. The words "please" and "thank you" make the world a more thoughtful and generous place.

Why do we need **table manners**?

It does seem that there are more rules about eating at a table with others than just about anything else. Put your napkin in your lap. Don't take huge bites. Don't talk

When you agree to play a game you have to prepare yourself for the fact that you may not win. *Robert J. Huffman/Field Mark Publications © 2001*

with your mouth full. Ask for something to be passed to you instead of reaching for it. Don't start eating until everyone is seated and food has been offered all around. How can a person remember so many rules? And why are there so many in the first place?

Meals bring people into very close contact with each other. When you're sitting so near to one another, you can't help but notice everyone's behavior. Table manners were developed to make the dining experience as pleasant as possible, focusing on safety and consideration for others. Believe it or not, when you examine each rule separately, it actually makes sense. You shouldn't take big bites, for instance, because you could choke if you have too much food in your mouth. You shouldn't talk with your mouth full because that too increases the risk of choking, and because other diners will be able to see your half-chewed food, which is unpleasant. Reaching for things far away on the table could lead to knocking something else over along the way, including someone else's drink, for example, creating a real mess. The good reasons for different table manners go on and on. Maybe if you think about the reasons behind the rules, it will be easier to remember and follow them.

Why do **hugs and kisses** make me **feel good**?

Human beings are the only animals who communicate through language, a complicated system of vocal symbols that our complex brains allow us to learn after we are

311

Hugging and kissing are ways to share love and caring through touch.

born. But like other animals, we also communicate through our bodies and senses. Our organ of touch is our skin, covering the outside of our bodies. (Nerve endings under the surface of skin give us our sense of touch.)

Hugging and kissing are ways to share love and caring through touch. When you were born, well before you knew language and could understand caring words, you were learning about love through your sense of touch. As a newborn, when everything was frighteningly new, you immediately experienced the comfort of touch when you were held in your mother's arms, feeling the warmth of her body and the beat of her heart, sensations familiar to you when you were inside her womb. You were held close when you first learned about food and about how good it felt to have milk in your empty stomach. Your parents' caring hands kept you clean and dressed in dry clothes when you could not yet do those things for yourself. So, from your earliest days, you learned that someone's touch usually made you feel comfortable and safe.

Loving and caring about special people in our lives is a feeling inside that is hard to describe in words. But hugs and kisses make it easy to show that love—and their message is clear. Giving hugs and kisses feels as good as getting them. (Because the lips have an extra supply of nerve endings, kissing is an especially intense way to touch.) The human need to share affection through touch is something we all experience throughout our lives.

312

What should I do when **someone's touch** makes me **feel bad**?

Sharing a hug or kiss with someone starts with loving feelings inside. When you don't have those feelings, hugging and kissing should not be expected. You have a right to say no to touching or being touched by someone. A person's control over his or her own body is personal and private—no matter how old he or she is—and should be respected by all.

Although most grown-ups you know are nice people who care about and respect children, there are a few who do things to harm kids. One bad thing they may do is treat children in a sexual way—which is behavior that should only take place among grown-ups who have a special love relationship. It is never okay for a grown-up to treat a child like this, under any circumstance. It is against the law.

If someone ever touches your body in a way that invades your personal privacy, you should tell a trusted grown-up at once. Sometimes telling someone about it is hard to do, though, because you may have confused feelings about the situation. Maybe the touching gives you an uneasy feeling, but the attention it brings makes you feel special. Maybe you get treats or presents if you agree to touch or be touched, and you like those, too. And sometimes you might feel afraid because you know that if you tell what's going on, a lot more trouble will start.

Still, touching between people should be a happy thing. If it makes you feel confused or bad, then you know it isn't right. If for some reason the adult that you go to for help doesn't believe your story, tell it to someone else. Keep on telling until the person who is touching you has been stopped. Molesting a child is an awful thing, so a lot of people will be very upset when they find out about it. Just remember that nobody is upset with you and that you are not responsible for the bad things that were done in any way. Children are taught to trust adults and to do what grown-ups tell them. Adults who abuse the trust of children in this terrible way are completely to blame.

DEATH AND DYING

Why do people have to **grow old**?

Growing old is part of being a living thing. Every plant and animal must go through a cycle of life that involves a beginning, a middle, and an end. Actually, as soon as we are born we begin aging or growing older. But when we talk of growing old we think of the physical changes that occur when bodies cannot grow and repair themselves as they once did. At about age 30 the signs of aging start to appear, though for most people the physical changes aren't really obvious until many years later.

The time that each person spends on Earth is an important part of the cycle of life and has an impact on future generations.

As people age, skin may begin to sag and wrinkle, and hair may turn thin or gray. Over time muscles become less strong and flexible, and bones may become more brittle and breakable. Blood may not flow through the body as well as it once did, which slows the activity of the brain and the senses. The immune system becomes weaker and does not fight off sickness as well as before. People experience these changes at different ages, but all will grow old as they near the end of their life cycle. It may seem sad that a person has grown old and cannot do all the things they once did, but try to look at it this way: When people grow old, that means they have been lucky enough to avoid things like accidents and diseases that could have cut their lives short. And better yet, regardless of the physical changes of old age, many people remain healthy and lead full and happy lives.

Why do people **have to die**?

All living things must die. It is a part—the final part—of the biological cycle of life. A flowering plant, for instance, springs from a seed, grows, blossoms, produces seeds for the next season, fades, and dies. Similarly, an animal is born, grows and matures, reproduces, ages, and dies. Old plants and animals must make way for new plants and animals, through which the cycle of life can continue. If plants and animals did not die, eventually there would not be enough food, water, or space in the world for life to flourish. Even dead plants and animals contribute to the cycle of life, for their remains enrich the soil for the next generation of living things.

New generations of plants and animals are needed to ensure the survival of life on our planet. The world's environment is constantly changing, and new plants and animals—with unique characteristics resulting from the combined genetic contributions of their parents—may be better equipped to survive under the evolving conditions. This process of change and improved survival, which has taken place gradually over millions of years (ever since life began), is called evolution.

Just like all plants and other animals, people also experience this biological cycle of life. A person is born, grows into physical maturity during adolescence, perhaps has a family in adulthood, ages, and then dies. At death, the cycle of life is completed as that individual makes way for following generations. But because people are such special beings, they can live on in so many other ways—besides in the genetic makeup of their offspring—after they die. A great painter or writer, for example, can live on in the work that he or she has left behind for others to enjoy. A politician may leave behind new laws that improve the lives of many. A parent or friend may live on in the minds and hearts of his or her loved ones, thanks to the experiences and affection that were shared and the memories left behind. The time that each person spends on Earth, and every contribution he or she makes, however small (like planting a tree to make the world a little healthier), is an important part of the cycle of life and has an impact on future generations.

Will **I die** someday?

Because all living things must die when they complete their life cycle, and because no person has ever escaped death, it is certain that you will die someday. But because medical science has eliminated or brought under control many of the diseases that once kept people from reaching old age, it is likely that you will live a very long time. Today, the average life expectancy of a man living in the Unites States is around 74 years; the average American woman will reach about 80 years of age. And because medical science continues to improve health care—and is studying old age and trying to find ways to minimize its effects—the average life span is expected to climb higher still.

For people fortunate enough to live in a wealthy, industrialized nation (like those in North America and Western Europe), their chances of living a longer life are improved by those countries' high-quality living conditions, food supply, and medical care. Your genes, inherited from your parents, also play a role in your life span. In addition to determining things like your hair color and height, your genes can also affect your ability to avoid certain diseases or conditions. Finally, your behavior and lifestyle have a lot to do with how long you'll live: eating right, getting enough sleep, exercising, and seeking regular medical care can all contribute to a longer life.

What happens **when people die**?

When death occurs, blood—which carries oxygen to all the cells of the body—has stopped circulating. This stoppage may be caused by damage to the heart, which is the

315

muscle that pumps blood throughout the body, or by damage to the brain, which gives the signals that direct the heart to do its pumping. (Other circumstances, like severe accidents, also stop blood flow.) But whatever the reason, once blood stops bringing its life-giving oxygen to the body's billions of cells—the building blocks that make up the human body—the death of those cells starts to occur. When the brain, which is the body's command center, goes without oxygen for about 15 minutes, all cells there die. While machines can help our lungs breathe or our hearts pump blood, no machine can assume the complex functions of the brain. Without a brain, we cannot live. Soon after a person dies, an official document called a death certificate is filled out and later filed as a record with the local government. It includes such information as time, place, and cause of death.

Does it hurt to die?

Nobody who has died has been able to come back to tell us about it, so it is impossible to know whether dying hurts. But people who have had "near-death" experiences—those whose hearts have stopped, for instance, but were later restarted—have only good things to report. Most tell of a peaceful sensation of floating above their bodies. A number also describe traveling through a tunnel toward a beautiful light or having loving meetings with friends and relatives who have died before them. Scientists know that when a person is in a state of very low oxygen—often a condition that precedes death—he or she experiences feelings of euphoria, or great happiness. So as far as we know, the act of dying is not painful at all.

What is often painful for dying people is the thought of leaving behind their family and friends. They may also be sad at the thought of never again doing the things they love about life, like watching sunsets, or gardening, or going to the movies. In addition, they may be afraid because they are uncertain about what awaits them after death.

Still, many sick people welcome death. The same wonders of medicine that have allowed people to reach old age have also enabled them to live through long, and sometimes painful, illnesses. Often, death is seen as a welcome end to pain, both for the ill person and for the family and friends who have watched their loved one suffer. People with strong religious faith, too, may fear death less because they believe they will journey to a better place.

Can people who die **see and talk with living people** after they are gone?

Although for centuries living people have reported seeing and talking to people who have died, there is no scientific proof that this can be done or that visiting with "ghosts" is possible. Although some people claim they have special skills allowing them to contact and receive messages from the deceased (such people are known as spiritualist mediums), their communications—usually conducted during meetings called séances—have generally proven to be fake.

Sometimes, though, people who have recently had a loved one die feel that they can sense that person's presence with them; they may even talk to the deceased. It is likely that these sensations arise out of very powerful feelings of loss and vivid memories of the loved one. For many people, believing that a physical connection continues after death lessens their sorrow. It is one of many ways through which people keep alive the memories of those who have died.

What do we do **after a person dies**?

Throughout human history and in places around the world, people have done many different things with their dead. The ancient Egyptians, for instance, took great care when preparing the bodies of their dead rulers; it was believed that their leaders were immortal and would need their bodies in another world after death (the afterworld). In a process that took several months, ancient Egyptians carefully preserved dead bodies through a process called embalming. They wrapped the bodies with layers of linen, wax, and spices. Some of these mummies still exist today, some 6,000 years later.

In the United States today, most people are buried in coffins. Funeral ceremonies take place so that people can honor the deceased and give comfort and support to his or her family and friends. Music, prayers, and eulogies—speeches remembering and praising the dead person—are often a part of these ceremonies. A funeral usually ends when the deceased is taken to a cemetery, a place where bodies are buried in the ground. A headstone or marker listing the person's name, birth and death date, and other information is left at the burial spot, which family members and friends may later visit and decorate with flowers in memory of their loved one.

Why do people **cry** when someone dies?

Crying is a way of expressing sadness. It helps people who have lost someone close to them to express their grief and sorrow. (Talking about the dead person also helps.) People cry because they will never again see the person who has died and they know they will miss that person. If the death is unexpected, the tears may also be caused by feelings of shock and anger. During the period immediately following a person's death, when the loss of that loved one is felt most sharply, grieving people are not comforted by the fact that dying is a natural and necessary process that happens to all living things. As time passes, however, they begin to accept the loss of their loved one, and the pain of that loss becomes easier to bear. Thinking of the person after some time has passed brings less sadness and maybe even some pleasure as good times with the loved one are remembered.

Where do **people go** after they die?

Because no one has come back to our world after dying, it is not possible to know for sure what happens to people after death. Nearly all the religions of the world believe that some kind of existence continues after life on Earth stops, that a person's soul or spirit continues to exist—in a way we can't really imagine—even after his or her body is dead. In fact, a lot of religions teach the belief that our life on Earth is a stage or time of preparation (or a test by which we're judged) that leads to a final, perfect state of existence that we will share with God in a spiritual realm after we die. Many people who don't subscribe to religious beliefs about an afterlife think that people simply end when they die, that once the physical body has died, all awareness and existence ceases.

What is **heaven**?

According to many religions based on Judaism and Christianity, heaven is a state of existence where a person's spirit is at last united with God forever. In a number of Christian religions, heaven is believed to be the reward for people who have lived good lives according to certain rules of thought and behavior that God has made known through scriptures (sacred writings, like the Bible) and through the teachings of churches and religious leaders. (Those who have not followed these rules, it is believed by many, go to a place of punishment known as hell.) Many Christians believe that at the end of the world their human forms will be resurrected in a perfect state—just as the body of Jesus Christ was, when he arose from the dead on Easter morning—and join their souls or spirits in heaven for eternity. This idea has led to the concept that heaven is an actual place—located above—with physical characteristics. Over the centuries, through pictures and writings, people have tried to create images of heaven, imagining a place of perfect happiness perched atop fluffy white clouds. It has often been portrayed as a place full of things that would bring happiness on Earth, possessing, for instance, pearly gates and streets of gold.

What is **hell**?

In many Christian religions, hell is the place of punishment where people go after death if they have not lived good lives and followed the rules of thought and behavior set forth by God in scriptures (sacred writings, like the Bible) and in the teachings of churches and religious leaders. Hell is believed to be a horrible place because it is the opposite of heaven; hell is a place where a person's spirit will forever be deprived of the presence of God. To never know the joy of God's presence, believers feel, is so painful that it is compared to burning in Earthly fire forever, one of the most awful things that can be imagined. Just like with heaven, people have tried over the centuries, through paintings and writings, to create images of hell, a place of enormous suffering. And as heaven is thought to be located above, hell was given an opposite location down below. Satan, or Lucifer—who, according to the Bible, was a favorite angel of

Many people picture heaven as a place existing above us, amidst sunbeams and white, fluffy clouds.

God's until he disobeyed Him —is the ruler of hell. In many Christian religions, Satan and his wicked angel followers (devils) are thought to be the cause of evil in the world, always tempting people to be bad. Many non-Christian religions also teach of a place like hell where people who have led bad lives on Earth must go after they die. Even the ancient Greeks and Romans (who lived before the development of Christianity) believed in an underworld, a place where people traveled to after death. Good and bad people lived in different places in this ancient underworld.

Are **angels** real?

In many religions, angels are powerful spiritual beings who live with God but who sometimes become involved in the lives of people on Earth, often bringing God's messages to them. According to the Bible, for instance, the angel Gabriel appeared before the Virgin Mary and announced that she would become the mother of Jesus Christ. In the Muslim religion, Gabriel revealed to the Prophet Muhammad the words of Allah (God), which were recorded in the Koran, the sacred book of Islam. Angels are not believed to have physical bodies, but they may look like people when visiting Earth. Over the centuries, artists have portrayed them in many ways: neither men nor women, angels have human forms (appearing as babies, children, or adults) and are winged for travel to their heavenly home. In a few religions, like Roman Catholicism, it is believed that each person on Earth has a special angel who watches over him or her and gives protection from the temptations of the devil; such a being is called one's

319

guardian angel. The answer to the question of whether angels are real, then, is a matter of faith.

Who is **God**?

It is believed by many people that God is the perfect spiritual being who has always existed and who created everything. (Although having no physical form and therefore no gender, God is usually referred to as a male.) Believers feel that God made the universe and all that is in it. God is thought by many to be all-knowing and all-powerful. In many religions, it is thought that the souls of people who have led good lives on Earth join God after they die.

While many of the world's most widely practiced religions—Christianity, Islam, Judaism—teach of the existence of a single supreme being (called God in Judeo-Christian religions and Allah in Islam), some religions teach that there are many gods. Hinduism (practiced by many people in India and elsewhere) teaches that there are many gods, but all are part of one divine being, called Brahman.

Some people feel that God is everywhere and part of everything—the universe itself, and all life, and all natural occurrences, are divine. Others, called atheists, do not believe a supreme being exists in any form.

ODDS AND ENDS

FOOD TRIVIA

Who invented the **sandwich**?

A sandwich is a piece of meat or other food that is placed between two pieces of bread. It is named after John Montagu, the fourth earl of Sandwich (a place in England), who invented this way of eating in the eighteenth century. Hooked on gambling, he couldn't take the time to stop playing and eat a regular meal. He asked to have his meat brought to him between two slices of bread so the cards wouldn't get greasy, and he ate this meal, dubbed a sandwich, right at the gaming tables.

Why do some fruits and vegetables **turn brown** after you cut them?

Some fruits and vegetables, like apples and potatoes, have chemicals in them that turn brown when they mix with oxygen in the air. A chemical reaction called oxidation causes the brown coating on the cut surfaces of such fruits and vegetables. This coating actually preserves the rest of the fruit or vegetable—at least for a while—by forming a protective coating that keeps oxygen from getting at the rest. By brushing the cut surface right away with lemon juice, you can keep oxygen from getting to the flesh of a fruit or vegetable and stop it from turning brown altogether.

What makes popcorn **pop**?

Believe it or not, most hard popcorn kernels have tiny bits of water inside. When these kernels are heated, the water gradually expands and turns into steam. At a certain point, the increasing steam can no longer be contained inside each kernel and explodes through the hard coating, causing a pop. The steam also cooks the starchy material inside kernels, turning it into the fluffy stuff we know as popcorn. Why don't some kernels pop? Such duds probably don't have enough water inside to pop them.

Why do **doughnuts** have holes?

A doughnut is a little cake fried in oil that has a hole in the middle. Since ancient times, almost all cultures have had some type of fried cake. It is believed that American author Washington Irving (who wrote the stories *The Legend of Sleepy Hollow* and *Rip Van Winkle*) came up with the name "doughnut" when he described the balls of fried, sweetened dough made by Dutch settlers in colonial New York as "dough nuts."

Carbon dioxide gas causes the bubbles in your soda pop.

A sea captain named Gregory Hanson is given the credit for inventing the hole in the doughnut. Legend relates that one night while Hanson was eating a fried cake and piloting his ship, a storm arose. Needing both hands free to steer, he jammed his cake over a spoke of the ship's wheel—and the doughnut was created. The captain was so pleased with his invention that he ordered the ship's cook to put holes in the fried cakes from then on.

What's the advantage of having holes in doughnuts? From a baker's point of view, it makes it easier to cook the cake more evenly, because the heat of the hot oil can penetrate from the outside and from the inside. Without their holes, doughnuts would sometimes end up with uncooked middles. And if a baker tried to fry a holeless cake a little longer to get the inside done just right, the outside would often be overcooked.

What makes soda pop **fizz**?

Soda pop gets its fizz from carbon dioxide, a harmless gas that makes up part of the air we breathe. It is mixed into soda pop to make it light and fun to drink. When a soda bottle or can is sealed, the gas can't escape and stays mixed with the beverage. But when soda is opened or poured into a glass, carbon dioxide—which is much lighter than the liquid—rushes to the surface in the form of bubbles and escapes into the air after bursting. Sometimes the bubbles rise so fast, bringing soda pop with them, that they make a frothy, fizzing foam. Soda pop "goes flat" when it has been left in an open container for a long time and has lost all of its bubbles, or carbonation.

What do the letters on **M & M candies** stand for?

During the 1940s, when M & M candies were first introduced, two men headed the company that made them. Mr. Mars and Mr. Murrie ran the M & M Candies Company (which has since become Mars, Inc.), and they put the initials of their last names on the colorful treats. The letters used to be printed on the candies in black, but since 1954 the "m"s have been white.

What makes holes in Swiss cheese?

Enzymes (complex proteins), special bacteria, and molds are added to milk to make cheese. These different additives give cheeses their distinctive looks and tastes. The bacteria that are used to make Swiss cheese remain active for an especially long time. These bacteria turn milk sugars into gas long after the cheese has developed its firm outer covering or rind. Because the gas can't escape at that point, it gathers in pockets as the cheese continues to ripen inside, creating bubbles, which look like holes when the cheese is sliced.

Why do most cereals make **crackling noises** when you pour milk on them?

Most cereals are made by baking grain mixtures (made from rice, corn, wheat, or oats) that have been formed into bite-sized pieces. During the baking process these pieces expand, causing tiny holes or cavities to form on their surfaces. When milk is poured onto cereal, it flows over these holes and traps air inside. As the milk starts to soak into the cereal, it forces the air out and fills up the tiny holes. So, the crackling noise you hear coming from your bowl is actually air being released from your cereal.

When were **knives, forks, and spoons** first used?

While knives have been used as tools, weapons, and even to help in food preparation—to carve up large pieces of meat, for example—it wasn't until the Middle Ages (a period ranging from roughly A.D. 500 to around 1500) that people began regularly using knives to get food from their plates to their mouths. Since forks weren't in use yet, people in that era used knives with narrow blades and pointed ends to spear their food and then eat it. (Historians have pointed out that these weaponlike utensils gave the dinner hour the potential for serious violence.) In the late 1600s table knives became blunter and wider, a shape that made them more useful in catching the food that sometimes fell off forks and spoons.

People have been using spoons for centuries, and these helpful scoopers were probably among the first eating tools developed by early humans. In prehistoric times spoons were made of curved pieces of shells or wood. During the Middle Ages royal and wealthy citizens used spoons made of precious metals like gold and silver; common folks had to make do with tin or pewter spoons.

People in China and other Asian countries have been eating with chopsticks for about 5,000 years.

As eating instruments, forks are the latecomers in the utensil world. While the ancient Greeks used two-tined forks to stabilize food they were carving and serving, and table forks were used by the wealthy in the Middle East and other countries in what is now Eastern Europe, the concept of table forks did not become widespread in Western Europe until the sixteenth and seventeenth centuries. At first, people didn't understand the need for a fork—they had spoons and knives and, of course, their hands, to pick up food. But forks came to be popular symbols of social status among the wealthy, and eventually the general population came to accept their use as well.

Another kind of utensil—chopsticks—came into being around 5,000 years ago in China. Historians believe chopsticks evolved from twigs people used to grab pieces of food out of large cooking pots. Over time, these twigs were carved into sticks that worked well when picking up small pieces of food. By A.D. 500, chopsticks had spread to other Asian countries, with some differences among them in style and size.

What did people use before **toothbrushes** were invented?

Early in human history, people used anything that they could find to keep their teeth clean. Usually a thin, sharp object, like a stick, was used to pick out food left between teeth. Chewing on the end of certain sticks would fray the wood, making a kind of brush, which could then be rubbed across the teeth. (Even today, members of primitive tribes chew sticks to keep their teeth clean. The constant chewing produces more saliva than usual, which helps wash food away.)

324

Later, people found that if they rubbed abrasive elements, like salt or chalk, across their teeth, they could get rid of grime. They also used water and pieces of rough cloth to clean their teeth. Toothpicks made of all kinds of materials also became popular. Rich people had jeweled toothpicks made of gold and silver. Toothbrushes for the wealthy, with fancy handles and hog bristles, came into use in the eighteenth century. Only much later, when cheaper, wooden-handled toothbrushes were made, and the importance of good dental hygiene became known, did most people start to regularly use them.

CLOTHING

How did **clothing develop**?

People first started wearing clothing to keep warm and dry and to protect themselves against the blazing sun, scratching plants, and attacking animals. Early men and women used animal furs as clothing, wrapping them around their waists and shoulders. But since ancient times, clothing has also been a means of expression, a way in which people have let others know more about themselves. Even in prehistoric times people used dress to indicate which group they belonged to, their status or position within their group or tribe, and as an expression of their customs and religious beliefs. Early men and women used strings of beads or stones, feathers, and other ornaments to make themselves look special and different from one another.

Early on, people found that by scraping animal hides and treating them with fats they could make them softer and more flexible. This allowed the skins to be cut, sewn, and shaped into better-fitting clothing. Thin strips of leather drawn through holes in the hides kept the pieces together. Finer sewing could be done once sharp needles that could pierce the skins were developed (starting about 50,000 years ago); these were usually carved from wood or bone.

Then people began to make cloth. Cloth is material made from threads that are woven together in a crisscross pattern. About 10,000 years ago, people first made cloth out of animal hair that was spun into thread. When the short hairs of an animal were overlapped and twisted together, long strands could be made, which were then woven into fabric. People in ancient Asia used the hair of sheep, camels, and goats to make cloth. In other parts of the world people used the hairs of different animals—of mountain creatures like llamas and alpacas in South America, and of horses, buffalo, and moose in North America—to make their cloth. And it could be colored by using dyes made from certain plants and even animals. In ancient Greece, for example, a rich red dye was made from the skin of the tiny kermes worm.

Ancient Egyptians were some of the first people to make cloth, beginning around 5000 B.C. Instead of using animal hair, the Egyptians wove together the long fibers of

325

flax plants to make lightweight linen, perfect for their desert climate. Historians think that they got the idea for weaving from fishermen, who made nets by tying threads together in a special way—with weights attached to their ends to keep them tight, straight, and free from tangling.

As centuries passed, clothing continued to be used to express the identity and status of its wearer. The clothes of farmers and tradespeople like blacksmiths and carpenters, for example, remained simple and sturdy, meant to last a long time; their clothing styles were also loose, making them easy to work in. But wealthy people could afford fine fabrics from faraway places, and they had the luxury of thinking about the way their outfits were shaped and decorated. They could show their higher social status by wearing clothing styles that were sometimes wildly impractical—things that would never be worn by someone who performed manual labor for a living. In the fourteenth century, for instance, long pointed shoes were in fashion, some with 20-inch toes that had to be stuffed with moss to keep their shape. A farmer certainly couldn't work in his fields in shoes like that. Immense hanging sleeves and corsets that pinched waists in to make them smaller—worn by both men and women—are other examples of impractical and uncomfortable fashions.

Why do clothes for men and women have their **buttons on different sides**?

Most people (about 90 percent) are right-handed, and it is easiest for them to button their clothes from left to right, which is the way that men's buttons are arranged. Why, then, are the buttons on women's clothing arranged in an opposite way, for fastening from right to left? Although no one knows for sure, it is believed that the tradition for arranging women's buttons began long ago, when buttons where considered very fine ornaments, made of silver, gold, and jewels. Women who could afford many fine clothes with beautiful buttons usually had maids who dressed them. It was easier for maids, who were usually right-handed, to help with their mistresses' clothing if the buttons that faced them were fastened from left to right.

Of course, today, nearly all women dress themselves, and it would make sense if all clothes buttoned with the ease of the right-hander in mind. But the tradition of button arrangement is so old and women are so used to fastening them a certain way that the situation is unlikely to change.

Why do women in some countries wear **veils**?

A veil is a piece of cloth that is usually worn to hide a person's hair or face. Women have worn such veils since ancient times—mostly in Middle Eastern countries—primarily for the purpose of keeping men from looking at them. Many women of the Muslim faith still wear veils of some type when they are out in public. In some Muslim countries, only a woman's eyes are allowed to show. Although Westerners (people from North

America and Western Europe) may find these veils symbolic of women's restricted freedoms in many Muslim societies, Muslim women wear them to honor long-held traditions of modesty and to show respect for their religion and the men in their lives.

Why did soldiers once wear **armor**?

Since ancient times, soldiers have worn special clothing or armor to protect themselves during warfare. Hard materials like leather, wood, shells, and even woven reeds were used to give soldiers extra protection against enemy arrows. Metal started to be used for armor about 3,500 years ago, by warriors in the Middle East. By the time of the ancient Greeks, about 1,000 years later, soldiers were well protected, wearing large pieces of metal on their chests and backs, shin guards, and metal helmets, and they carried metal shields.

Soon armored clothing, garments with metal strips and plates attached, began to be made for soldiers. Then chain mail, a type of metal cloth, was developed. Made of small metal rings linked together, chain mail was much more flexible than metal plates, but could not withstand the force of larger weapons, like lances. So full suits of armor made of steel plates, hinged at the knees and the elbows, came into use around the fourteenth century. Soldiers were covered with steel from head to toe, with heavy metal helmets covering their faces, heads, and necks. A warrior could see and breathe through small slits or openings in the helmet's visor, a movable metal flap that could be lifted up. (Only important or wealthy warriors could afford this kind of elaborate armor.) Suits of armor weighed so much that the soldiers or knights who wore them usually couldn't move around in them very well; they wore such armor mostly when they fought on horseback. Even the horses sometimes wore armor.

As the methods and weapons of warfare changed, clumsy personal armor was no longer useful. It became far more important for soldiers to be able to move quickly and easily. Today's soldiers usually wear cloth uniforms and steel helmets. But armor is used on war vehicles like tanks, naval vessels, and aircraft. The bulletproof vests that police officers use are also a type of armor.

Why do soldiers **salute** one another?

It is believed that the tradition of saluting—raising the right hand to the forehead—got its start many centuries ago, during the time when knights fought in full suits of armor. When two knights met, they had to raise the visors on their metal helmets to identify themselves and to see if they were friends or enemies. The motion associated with lifting the visor continued when two fighting men met, even when soldiers no longer wore armor. This behavior turned into the salute. The salute became a sign of recognition and respect, used especially by military men and women when in the presence of a military superior—someone who ranks above them.

327

Full suits of armor made of steel plates, like the one pictured here, came into use around the fourteenth century.

What do the patches on the **uniforms of soldiers** mean?

For as long as there have been large armies, the personnel of those armies have been divided into various ranks. For such organizations to work effectively, some people have to be in charge and others have to follow their orders. One way to quickly determine who is in charge is to look at the differences in uniform, particularly the patches and other ornaments on sleeves and shoulders. The patches on a soldier's uniform tell his or her rank, reflecting the importance of that person's position in the armed services. A beginning soldier might have a patch with a single stripe. As a soldier gains experience and earns promotions, the number of stripes will increase, a symbol that reveals to other soldiers his or her advanced rank. The uniforms of military officers have metal bars, stars, or eagles (depending on the branch of the military). Some enlisted personnel (people who aren't officers) wear chevrons, or stripes in an upside-down "V" shape.

Some of the medals and patches on a soldier's uniform also symbolize accomplishments, with medals honoring acts of bravery and outstanding service.

Why do people wear uniforms?

Some jobs require special clothing or uniforms. Sometimes these special clothes are meant to protect workers or the people they work with. An emergency room doctor, for instance, may wear special clothes to protect herself from blood and infectious agents as well as to protect patients from the germs and impurities that may be present on ordinary clothing.

Most often, though, special clothes or uniforms are worn so that workers can be easily recognized by other people. Occupations that require uniforms are frequently service jobs, where workers help or perform services for other people. Workers in stores and restaurants frequently wear uniforms so that customers know who to ask for help or service. Uniforms help police officers do their jobs better, because people recognize them and go to them for help or give them the cooperation they need to maintain the law. On the battlefield, soldiers wear uniforms to identify which country they are from, signaling whether they are friends or enemies.

Are there people in the world who **don't wear any clothes** at all?

Yes, believe it or not, there are people in the world who don't wear any clothing at all. Tribes of primitive people still exist in places like the Pacific island of New Guinea and—especially—in the Amazon region of South America. Some of these tribes' members have never met modern men and women and know nothing about the industrial world. These native, or indigenous, people live much like people did in prehistoric times, eating what grows naturally in their jungle homes and hunting with bows and arrows. In the warm, humid climates in which they live, they have no need for protective clothing (and in some cases don't have the skills or tools to make cloth). Because of their lack of contact with people from other places, they are not familiar with the idea of modesty or the practice of covering the body with clothes, which is a behavior that most people learn quickly when they are growing up. Being naked is as natural to these primitive peoples as wearing clothing is to us.

In our modern world, there are also people—known as nudists—who enjoy not wearing clothes because it gives them a feeling of freedom. While these men and women wear clothing most of the time as they go about their regular lives, they sometimes get together in special, isolated places with others who enjoy the practice, too.

KEEPING TRACK OF TIME

Why are there **365 days** in a year?

A long time ago (thousands of years, in some cases), when ancient societies recognized the need to record events and plan future happenings, calendars came into being. In colder climates, a calendar reflected the changing of the seasons and the movements of Earth around the Sun. A solar, or sun-based, calendar, with some modifications made by different regions and religious groups, is in use in most of the world today. In warmer climates, where seasons passed without dramatic climate changes, calendars were based on the actions of the Moon. Such moon-based, or lunar, calendars still exist in a few places.

In the system of solar calendars, the length of a day is determined by the approximate amount of time it takes Earth to rotate once on its axis (about 24 hours). The length of a year is measured by the time it takes Earth to rotate around the Sun (365 days, 5 hours, 48 minutes, and 46 seconds).

In 45 B.C., Roman emperor Julius Caesar instituted what came to be known as the Julian calendar. The Julian calendar was based on a solar year, with a year consisting of 365 days, 6 hours. The year was divided into months that were either 30 or 31 days long (except for February, which has 28 days). Caesar also decreed that the year would begin with January 1; previously the year had begun on March 25, coinciding with the beginning of spring in the Northern Hemisphere.

It turned out that the Julian calendar (still in use in some parts of the world), in estimating that a year is 365 days, 6 hours, was off by almost 12 minutes. After several hundred years, those minutes added up, and the Julian calendar was about a week off course from the movements of Earth around the Sun. In 1582 another major calendar reform took place, this time instituted by Pope Gregory XIII. The Gregorian calendar, used in the United States and most other countries of the world today, made further adjustments to align it more closely to astronomical movements.

Why do we have **leap years**?

Calendars are fairly fixed things: each year has the same number of months and days, and the days follow a seven-day rotation going from Sunday to Saturday. But the movements of Earth do not conform exactly to the time designations humans have imposed. For example, the calendar used in much of the world, the Gregorian calendar, says that a year has 365 days. In fact, it takes Earth about 365.25 days to go around the Sun. That extra one-quarter day must be accounted for in the calendar or, eventually, the calendar and the seasons of the year would no longer be aligned. To correct this problem, an extra day is added to the calendar every four years. In such years, called leap years, February has one extra day, or 29 days. When the Gregorian calendar was devised, astronomers realized that even adjusting the calendar to add one day every four years would still not make it match exactly the movements of Earth. So they decreed that when that fourth year falls in a century year (one with two zeros at the end) that is not divisible by 400 (like 1700 or 1900) there would not be an extra day.

What do **B.C.** and **A.D.** mean?

B.C. stands for "before Christ," while A.D. is short for the Latin phrase "anno Domini," which means "in the year of the Lord" (some mistakenly believe those letters to stand for "after death"). These designations, established around A.D. 523 by a monk named Dionysius Exiguus, mark the year of Jesus Christ's birth as the beginning of the Christian era. Everything that happened before Jesus Christ was born is labeled as B.C., and everything after is considered to be part of the Christian era and is labeled as A.D. The years before the birth of Christ count down (or are counted backwards) to his birth, ending in 1 B.C.. The Christian era begins with the year A.D. 1 (there was no year zero).

Fairly soon after Dionysius's system was put in place, discoveries were made that showed he had miscalculated the year of Jesus Christ's birth. But in spite of his error, his system remains the standard in use around the world.

This system of counting years is based on the Christian religion, and yet it is used even in countries that have citizens of other religions. Many people prefer that nonreligious terms should be used, with the abbreviations B.C.E., or "before common era," replacing B.C., and C.E., or "common era," replacing A.D. But the usage of B.C. and A.D. are still far more common than any alternatives.

When did the **twenty-first century** begin?

As the end of the year 1999 approached, people all over the world began preparing for huge celebrations to mark the end of the twentieth century and the beginning of the twenty-first. This changeover was particularly significant as it also began a new millennium, or one-thousand-year period. Many people pointed out, however, that the new century and the new millennium would begin not on January 1, 2000, but on January 1, 2001. The first year of the Christian era was not the year zero; it was the year 1 A.D. Therefore, the first century, or one-hundred-year period, ended at the beginning of the year 101. Fast-forward 20 more centuries, and the twenty-first century (and the third millennium) officially began on January 1, 2001. That information didn't stop people from throwing gigantic parties on December 31, 1999; it just meant that the following year could provide an additional excuse for gala celebrations.

How did the months of the year get their names?

The months of the year in the Gregorian calendar, used by most of the world, originated with the ancient Romans, who named the months after gods and goddesses, important emperors, and in some cases the month's position on the calendar. For example, January is named for Janus, a Roman god. Janus had two faces, one looking into the past and the other into the future. August commemorates the Roman emperor Octavian, who was known as Augustus Caesar. The names for September through December were all taken from the words for numbers; September, for example, was at one time the seventh month in the calendar, and its name came from the word "septem," meaning "seven."

Why are the **number of days** in a month different?

In ancient times, when calendars were first put into place, the year—measured by the cycle of changing seasons—was divided into months. The lengths of the months varied slightly from one culture to the next, but the basic length—from 28 to 31 days—was consistent across many cultures. That number of days was based on the cycle of the moon, which lasts about 29 and one-half days and is easily noticed by just observing the moonlit sky. The months could not all have the same number of days because the number of days in a year, approximately 365, is not divisible by 28, 29, 30, or 31.

In the time of Roman emperor Julius Caesar, who instituted the Julian calendar in 45 B.C., it was decided that all months would have 30 or 31 days, except February, which at that time had 29 days. Why did February get short-changed? Before the Julian calendar, the new year began in March, and perhaps simply because February was the last month of the year, it was seen as the logical choice for having the fewest number of days.

One version of calendar history relates how February came to have 28 days. After Julius Caesar's death, the month that was then known as Quintilis was renamed July in his honor. During the reign of Julius's successor, Augustus Caesar, the month that then had the name Sextilis was renamed in honor of the new emperor as August.

While July had 31 days, August only had 30, and in order to make his month as long (and as important) as Julius's month, Augustus took a day from February and added it to August. From then on August had 31 days and February 28 (except on leap years, when it once again has 29 days).

Why are there seven days in a week?

Scholars are not sure why it was decided that a week is seven days long. There are many different theories. The beginning of the Bible states that the world was made in six days, and on the seventh day God rested. This biblical source, however, does not explain the seven-day week established in societies that did not know of or follow the teachings of the Bible.

One widely held theory explains that in ancient times, many civilizations all over the world believed that each day was governed by either the Sun, the Moon, or one of the five planets that were then known. Because each of the seven astronomical bodies ruled one day, there were seven days in a week.

Before the seven-day week became widely accepted, many societies based their week on the amount of time between market days. If it was decided that farmers needed nine days to accumulate and transport their goods to the marketplace, and the market day was the 10th day, then the week was 10 days long.

How did the **days of the week** get their names?

In the English language, some of the days of the week take their names from the celestial bodies that, according to ancient beliefs, ruled that day. So the day ruled by the Sun became Sunday, the day ruled by the Moon became Monday, and the day ruled by the planet Saturn became Saturday. The remaining days of the week take their names from figures in Anglo-Saxon or Norse mythology. Tuesday is named for the Anglo-Saxon god of war, Tiu (which is Mars in Roman mythology). Wednesday is named for Woden, the Anglo-Saxon name for the chief Norse god Odin. Thursday gets its name from Thor, the god of thunder in Norse mythology. Friday is named either after Freya, the Norse goddess of love and fertility, or Frigg, the wife of Odin and the representative of beauty and love.

Why do we have different **time zones** throughout the world?

At one time, every region of the world had its own system for measuring time. Traveling from one locality to another could be very confusing. Adding to the confusion is the fact that, even if every place measured time in the same way—with each day being 24 hours, each hour being 60 minutes, etc.—the fact that Earth is constantly rotating means that when it's midday in Chicago, Illinois, it's early evening in London, England.

The rotation of the planet means that we can't have just one time zone for the whole world. If that were the case, then noon would be the middle of the day in some places, the evening in other places, and the middle of the night somewhere else. In some places, the Sun would go down at 7 P.M., but that same hour thousands of miles to the east would be the time the Sun was rising.

In the late 1800s participants at an international conference figured out a way to divide the world into different time zones to account for Earth's movements. In one day, Earth makes one rotation on its axis. It moves 15 degrees every hour, so after 24 hours it has come full circle, or 360 degrees. Scientists therefore decided to divide the planet into 24 sections of 15 degrees each. They used the imaginary longitudinal lines, called meridians, that run between the North and South Poles. The starting point is a place called Greenwich, a London suburb; the line running through Greenwich is called the prime meridian. Every 15 degrees to the west of Greenwich is another hour earlier than what is known as Greenwich Mean Time (or GMT), and every 15 degrees to the east is another hour later. So if it is noon in Greenwich, in one time zone to the west it is 11 A.M., and in one time zone to the east it is 1 P.M.

While the longitudinal lines are straight and fixed, the lines dividing actual time zones have been changed a bit to accommodate the people who live there.

How many time zones are there in the **United States**?

The continental United States (meaning the 48 states on the North American continent, which excludes Hawaii and Alaska) is divided into four time zones. From east to west, they are: eastern, central, mountain, and Pacific. Each of these time zones is one hour apart, with times being successively earlier as you move west. So if it's 3 P.M. eastern time, it's 2 P.M. central time, 1 P.M. mountain time, and noon Pacific time.

The Alaska time zone is one hour behind Pacific time, so when it's noon in California, it's 11:00 A.M. in Alaska. Hawaii's time zone for part of the year is one hour behind Alaska. Hawaii does not participate in daylight saving time, however, so during that period (from April to October), when most of the U.S. states have set their clocks forward one hour, Hawaii stays at standard time and is two hours behind Alaska.

What is the **International Date Line**?

Travel around the world either east or west from the prime meridian in Greenwich, England, and when you've crossed to the opposite side of the globe you will have arrived at the International Date Line (IDL). This imaginary line runs from the South Pole to the North Pole at 180 degrees longitude, passing through the Pacific Ocean and zigzagging around countries located there (so no country is split down the middle by this "line").

Starting from Greenwich and moving east, each time zone is one hour later than the last. A funny thing happens at the IDL, however. When you cross the IDL going east, it is suddenly a whole day earlier. And while traveling westward from Greenwich takes you back one hour with each new time zone, crossing the Date Line in that direction takes you *ahead* one whole day. While not part of international law, the IDL is agreed upon by countries all over the world.

Imagine if two travelers began at Greenwich and went across the globe at the same speed, one going east and one going west. The eastbound traveler moves his watch *ahead* one hour every time he reaches a new time zone. The westbound traveler sets her watch *back* one hour with each new time zone. By the time both travelers have reached the other side of the globe, they have passed through twelve time zones (in opposite directions). They reach the IDL at the same time, but for the eastbound traveler it would be, say, 8 P.M. on Wednesday, while for the westbound traveler it would be 8 P.M. Tuesday. Twenty-four hours separate them, yet they are only a few feet apart. If the eastward traveler crosses over the International Date Line, however, he will suddenly move a whole day back, to 8 P.M. Tuesday.

Why do we have daylight saving time?

Daylight saving time (DST) came about as a way to adjust clocks during the summer months, when days are longer, to make better use of the daylight hours. Countries began making such clock adjustments during World War I (1914–1918) to save on the fuel needed for artificial light. If people could adjust their clocks so that it got dark at 9 P.M. instead of 8 P.M., then they could turn their lights on one hour later (or not at all if they simply went to bed when it got dark). These energy savings have continued today—since it gets dark later in the evening, people don't turn on lights until later in the day. And in the summer, the Sun rises very early and is usually up when people awake, reducing the need to turn on lights first thing in the morning. In the fall, as the days begin to get shorter, we go back to standard time, which means that the Sun sets—and rises—at an earlier time of day. As the days get shorter, the amount of time between sunrise and sunset shrinks, so that in the heart of winter daylight arrives later in the day and departs earlier than in the spring and summer months.

In the United States, daylight saving time, as decided by Congress, begins at 2 A.M. on the first Sunday in April and ends at 2 A.M. on the last Sunday in October. When DST begins, people move their clocks forward one hour; when it ends in October, clocks are moved back one hour. If you have trouble remembering which direction the clocks should go at which time of year, just think of the expression "spring forward, fall back." Many other countries in the world observe some form of daylight saving time, though the exact starting and ending dates differ.

What do A.M. and P.M. mean?

The abbreviation "A.M." stands for the Latin phrase "ante meridiem," which means "before noon"; "P.M." stands for "post meridiem," which means "after noon." Meridian

335

(the English spelling), which used to mean "midday," refers to an imaginary line that would appear if you could draw a line from the North Pole to the South Pole. The terms came into use in ancient Rome, when the movements of the Sun were used to measure time. At three points during the day—when the Sun rose, when the Sun set, and when the Sun was directly overhead at midday—it was easy enough for the Romans to determine the time. So they divided the period of daylight into two parts—the period of time before midday (A.M.) and the period of time after (P.M.).

AMERICAN SYMBOLS AND GOVERNMENT

Why was the **Statue of Liberty** built?

The Statue of Liberty, officially named *Liberty Enlightening the World* and sometimes referred to as "Lady Liberty," was built in the late 1800s as a symbol of the friendship between France and the United States. France had supported American efforts to gain independence from England in the 1770s, and the United States had returned the favor during France's revolution of the 1780s and 1790s. A joint effort between the two nations, the statue was designed and built in France, while the 154-foot (47-meter) concrete pedestal was the responsibility of the Americans.

Intended as a gift to celebrate the 100-year anniversary, or centennial, of American independence (which happened in 1776), the statue was designed by sculptor Frederic Auguste Bartholdi. He had help from many engineers and designers, including Alexandre Gustave Eiffel, the man who designed the Eiffel Tower in Paris, France. Lack of funds in both countries slowed down the construction of the statue, and it wasn't actually completed until 1884, eight years after the centennial. It took nearly a year for the statue, which was broken down and divided among more than 200 crates, to travel across the Atlantic Ocean to the United States, and it was another whole year before the pedestal was completed. Finally, on October 28, 1886, the Statue of Liberty was officially dedicated in front of a crowd of thousands.

Made of copper and steel, the statue, which depicts a woman who represents the concept of liberty, stands just over 151 feet (46 meters) tall, plus the height of the pedestal. To give an idea of just how big the statue is, bear in mind these statistics: Her index finger is 8 feet (2.4 meters) long; her nose is 4.5 feet (1.4 meters) long, and the width of her mouth is 3 feet (.9 meters). Lady Liberty holds a torch in one hand, symbolizing enlightenment, or freedom from ignorance. The other hand holds a plaque that bears the date of American independence, July 4, 1776.

The Statue of Liberty in New York Harbor has welcomed millions of immigrants to the United States.

Why is the Statue of Liberty such an **Important symbol** of the United States?

The Statue of Liberty stands for many of the nation's most cherished ideals: freedom, equality, and democracy. Perhaps most important to the millions of immigrants for whom the statue was one of their first sights of the United States is the ideal of opportunity—the chance to begin a new life, in a new land. While their lives in the United States were frequently difficult, for millions of immigrants America offered the chance to escape from grinding poverty and abusive governments in other lands.

Standing in the midst of New York Harbor, the point of entry into the United States for so many immigrants arriving on ships from other countries, the Statue of Liberty has been a powerful symbol of opportunity for more than 100 years. A poem called "The New Colossus," written by Emma Lazarus, was mounted on the statue's pedestal in the early 1900s. Its famous lines include these words that Lazarus imagined Lady Liberty to be saying: "'Give me your tired, your poor, / Your huddled masses yearning to breathe free, / The wretched refuse of your teeming shore; / Send these, the homeless, tempest-tost to me, / I lift my lamp beside the golden door!'"

Why is the **bald eagle** the official national symbol of the United States?

In 1782, six years after the end of the Revolutionary War, leaders of the newly independent United States were designing a national seal, an image that would appear on official documents and elsewhere. Eventually these men settled on the bald eagle for the

337

Great Seal of the United States. The bald eagle was chosen in part because it was believed to be found only in North America. The bald eagle was also admired for its strength, its noble appearance, and the freedom of its life spent soaring through the sky. While the eagle became an important American symbol when it was adopted for the U.S. seal in 1782, it wasn't until 1787 that it officially became the national emblem. The bald eagle has been used for the official seals of many states, and it has appeared on stamps, currency (or paper money), and several coins, including the quarter.

The bald eagle's head is covered with white feathers. So why is it called the *bald* eagle? Because one meaning of the word "bald" that is not commonly used anymore refers to white markings. Due to excessive hunting, environmental pollution, and loss of habitat, the bald eagle population became dangerously low at one point, prompting the U.S. Congress to pass a law protecting it. Bald eagles were once listed by the U.S. Fish and Wildlife Service as an endangered species, meaning they were close to being extinct. Thanks to the laws protecting it, these birds have rebounded a bit. They are now listed as threatened, which means they are not as close to being extinct as they once were, but their numbers are still few (only about 50,000 in the United States), and it is illegal to hunt them.

What do the **stars and stripes** on the United States flag mean?

When the first United States flag was adopted in 1777, it had 13 alternating red-and-white stripes (seven red, six white) and, in the upper left portion, 13 white stars on a blue background. The number 13 was chosen because that was the number of original states that formed the United States. For several years after that design was adopted, a new stripe and a new star were added each time a new state joined the Union, but in 1818 Congress decided to keep the number of stripes at 13 and simply add a new star for each new state. The U.S. flag has several nicknames: the Stars and Stripes, the Star-Spangled Banner, and Old Glory.

At the time the U.S. flag was designed, the stars and stripes (and the colors of each) were given no specific meaning. The ideas for the design most likely were based on other countries' flags. In 1782, when the national seal was designed and the flag was incorporated into it, national leaders decided that each color and symbol should have a meaning. As reported in the book *Our Flag,* published by the U.S. House of Representatives in 1989, it was decided that red symbolized "hardiness [strength] and valour [bravery]"; white symbolized "purity and innocence"; and blue represented "vigilance, perseverance, and justice." It has also been said that the stars are symbols of the heavens, and the stripes represent rays of light coming from the Sun.

How did we get the **United States national anthem**?

In September 1814, the United States and Great Britain were in the midst of fighting what is known as the War of 1812. The British had taken over Washington, D.C., and planned to attack Baltimore, Maryland. A few American citizens, including a lawyer and poet named Francis Scott Key, approached the British fleet, which was anchored in Chesapeake Bay, to request the release of an American who had been taken prisoner. The British agreed to let the prisoner and the others return to American shores, but their return had to wait until the British were done attacking Fort McHenry, which was defending Baltimore.

Throughout the night of September 13–14, Key heard the explosions of the battle, anxiously awaiting morning to see whether the Americans had won the battle. In the early morning light, Key could see that Fort McHenry's enormous American flag was still waving, indicating that the Americans had been triumphant. Relieved and inspired by the sight, Key composed a poem called "Defence of Fort M'Henry." Its opening lines recalled his first glimpse of the flag that morning: "Oh, say can you see, by the dawn's early light / What so proudly we hailed at the twilight's last gleaming?" Key may have had a popular tune in mind when writing the poem. That tune, called "To Anacreon in Heaven," had been an English drinking song, but it soon became linked with Key's poem, and the title of the new song became "The Star-Spangled Banner."

"The Star-Spangled Banner" (which actually has four verses, though usually only the first is sung) spread quickly throughout the country and became extremely popular. It was played at important ceremonies and military functions for many years before being officially declared the national anthem by Congress in 1931.

What kind of **government** does the United States have?

While many people describe the form of government in the United States as a democracy, it is technically defined as a federal republic; "federal" means that the individual states have some power but that a central national government has authority over them. Republics and democracies are, in fact, very similar, and in some cases, interchangeable. In a republic, the people have the power to elect leaders who govern according to a set of laws (in the United States the Constitution and the Bill of Rights lay the groundwork for all laws that follow). That definition is very close to that of a kind of government called constitutional democracy; in that type of government, people exercise political power by electing leaders. These leaders, and the citizens of the country, are bound by a set of laws that guarantee certain freedoms, like the right to speak freely or practice any religion. While the U.S. government may be defined as a republic, many of its governmental processes are democratic in spirit.

What are the **three branches** of the United States government?

When the U.S. Constitution was written in 1787, the people writing it (referred to as the framers of the Constitution) were very concerned with maintaining a balance between the power of the government and the freedoms of the citizens. The framers divided the federal government into three branches—the executive, legislative, and judicial. Each branch has its own separate, unique authority (known as the separation of powers), and each branch is limited by the powers of the other two. This system of checks and balances ensures that no single branch of government has all the control.

The executive branch, which is led by the president, also includes the vice president and the cabinet. The cabinet includes the attorney general and such departments as defense, treasury, labor, and agriculture. The legislative branch—called Congress— is responsible for making laws. This branch consists of the Senate and the House of Representatives. The elected officials in these houses can introduce and debate legislation, but—as an example of checks and balances—the bills passed in the Senate and House of Representatives can't become laws until they are signed by the president. The president can veto, or reject, a bill, but if enough people in Congress (at least two-thirds) vote to override that veto, the bill can become a law without the president's signature. The judicial branch, headed by the Supreme Court and also including the U.S. Courts of Appeals and U.S. District Courts, explains the laws passed by the legislative branch and interprets whether these laws follow the principles laid out in the Constitution. The court system performs extremely important functions, resolving arguments between citizens and determining the guilt and possible punishment of people accused of crimes.

Why do people **go to jail**?

One of the jobs of a government is to maintain order among its citizens. It does this by making rules known as laws. Every country has its own unique set of laws, though there are striking similarities among the legal systems of many nations. Numerous laws involve the protection of people and their property. In democratic societies like the United States, government representatives are elected by the people to write new laws and vote on their passage. Federal law governs all residents of the country, but state and local governments can make their own laws, as long as they don't conflict with federal laws.

People who break laws are punished by the government. Laws would be useless if they were not enforced and lawbreakers went unpunished. Ideally, U.S. laws are applied equally to all citizens—rich or poor, black or white, male or female. Many lawyers, judges, and police officers strive for such equality, though sometimes people harbor prejudices against certain kinds of people or certain ethnic groups without even knowing it. Flaws do exist in the justice system; sometimes, for example, wealthy people who can afford to hire a team of expensive, savvy lawyers get special treatment in the form of lighter punishment or no punishment at all. But many of the people who have sworn to uphold our nation's laws try to do so with fairness and compassion, regardless of the accused's race, ethnicity, or economic status.

In the United States, several laws have been written to protect the rights of someone accused of committing a crime: he or she is considered innocent until proven guilty in a court of law. Someone suspected of a crime is usually arrested and taken into custody by a police officer. Sometimes (in federal cases, for example), the case is presented before a grand jury (a group of citizens who examine the accusations made). The grand jury files an indictment, or a formal charge, if there appears to be enough evidence for a trial. In many criminal cases, however, there is no grand jury. While awaiting trial, the accused may be temporarily released on bail (which is an amount of money meant to guarantee that the person will return for trial instead of leaving the country) or kept in a local jail. Trials are usually held before a judge and a jury of 12 citizens. The government presents its case against the accused person, or defendant, through a district attorney, and another attorney defends the accused.

There are strict rules about what can be used as evidence in a trial. Any evidence taken by police as a result of an illegal search of someone's home, for example, cannot be used against the defendant during the trial. If the defendant is judged innocent, he or she is released. If he or she is found guilty of committing a crime, the judge decides the punishment, or sentence, using established guidelines. The lawbreaker may have to pay a fine or go to prison or both.

DISABILITIES

What is a **disability**?

The word "disabled" usually refers to a person who has a physical or mental handicap that keeps him or her from doing certain tasks—or makes performing them unusually difficult. Most physical disabilities, like blindness or paralysis, are easily noticed, but many mental disabilities are harder to detect. Mental disabilities can include diseases like schizophrenia, which causes severe disturbances in people's thoughts and emotions. Another category of disability is learning disabilities, like dyslexia, which is a learning disorder that makes reading very difficult because the brain reverses the order of letters and words.

A disability can be the result of a disease, an accident, or of genetics, which means that it is a condition that a person is born with. A lot of times disabled people can learn new ways to do things or use special machines or specially trained animals to help them work around their disability. Many disabled people prefer the term "differently abled," a description that doesn't divide people into categories like "normal" and "disabled," but addresses the idea that every person has different abilities.

In ancient and medieval times, people were frightened of and cruel to those with disabilities. Because those disabilities were not understood, the disabled were ignored

A disability can be the result of a disease, an accident, or genetics, which means that it is a condition a person is born with.

or abused. Even today, many people feel uncomfortable or awkward around disabled people—staring at them, treating them differently, or even behaving unkindly. Classifying disabled people as "different" makes it easier for some people to behave in a disrespectful way toward them, but it's important to remember that all people, regardless of whether they have the use of their legs or eyes, or whether they learn quickly or slowly, deserve to be treated with decency.

Why are some people **blind**?

Blindness is complete loss of sight. It can happen when certain parts of the eyeballs, the optic nerves (which carry visual signals from the eyes to the brain), or the sight centers of the brain are damaged. Such damage can occur as a result of injuries or diseases. A person can also be born with eye or brain abnormalities that cause blindness. In many cases, particularly in very poor countries, infectious diseases and poor diets can also cause blindness. A lack of vitamin A, in fact, is the leading cause of blindness worldwide. With basic medicines and proper nutrition, such cases could be prevented.

For every one person in the United States who is totally blind, there are four others who are visually impaired or "legally blind." These people have some ability to see, but they see so poorly—even with eyeglasses—that they cannot do things that require good vision, like driving a car.

How do people who are blind **get around**?

People who are blind rely on their other senses—smell, touch, hearing, taste—to help them manage in the world. Blind people have to memorize identifying features, like sounds and smells, of the places that they often go. They also have to pay close attention to where things are located in their homes in order to get around safely, always putting objects in the same places after use so that they can be found again.

Some blind people use canes or guide dogs to get around. A white cane indicates that the person using it is visually impaired. Blind people tap their canes on sidewalks, floors, and streets. They learn to identify the locations of things—like steps, walls, or doors—simply by the different sounds that their cane taps make. Various high-tech devices have been invented, including laser canes, that use sound or light waves that bounce off objects and send signals to the user about where these objects are located, what they might be made of, and how big they are. Guide dogs, or seeing-eye dogs, are specially trained to lead blind people about. The dog and the person work as a team, with the dog following commands that help the blind person go about her day. The dog, in turn, signals the person when she is approaching a curb or when it is safe to cross a street.

How can blind people **read books**?

Many blind people read specially printed books using the Braille system, developed by a French boy named Louis Braille in 1824. Braille, who became blind when he was three years old, was only 15 when he modified a code used by the military for reading in the dark. Braille's new system involved raised dots that stood for letters, numbers, punctuation symbols, and words. There are 63 characters in the Braille code, each one a unique combination of one to six raised dots. Once blind people have learned the Braille "alphabet," they can read Braille books by lightly touching the book's pages with their fingers.

Some people who become blind later in life (after having learned to read) prefer to use a system that incorporates the alphabet they are familiar with rather than learning Braille. A device called the Optacon can be used with regular books; it enlarges and raises each letter, which the blind person can then feel with her fingers and "read." Another way for blind people to discover the content of a book is through "talking books," which are recordings of entire books—novels, schoolbooks, and so on—that can be played back on cassette or compact disc players. Optical scanners are another way to translate printed materials into sounds— these computers scan a page from a book or magazine, and a computer-generated voice reads the material aloud.

Why can't some people **hear**?

The inability to hear, or deafness, can occur for many reasons. Some types of hearing loss result from something blocking sound as it travels from the outer ear to the

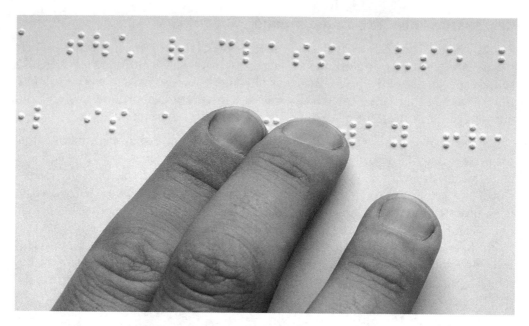

There are 63 characters in the Braille code, each one a unique combination of one to six raised dots.

eardrum and the tiny bones in the middle ear. Other types of loss arise from damage or defect to the inner ear or the auditory nerve, which is the nerve that carries sound signals from the inner ear to the brain. Deafness can happen as a result of disease, including severe ear infections, or it can be inherited, with the deafness being apparent at birth or sometimes showing up years later. Injuries and accidents also account for many cases of deafness. Extremely loud noises, like those that come from an explosion, can cause deafness, though that loss of hearing is sometimes temporary. People who work in noisy factories or those who are frequently exposed to very loud music can also develop hearing loss over time. Many people gradually lose some or all of their hearing when they reach old age, but some of those types of hearing loss can be overcome by wearing a hearing aid, which makes noises like speech or music louder.

How do people who are deaf **communicate**?

Deaf people have numerous ways of communicating with each other and with hearing people. Many deaf people use sign language, which is a system of hand signals that correspond to letters, words, and ideas. When deaf people must communicate with hearing people who don't know sign language, sometimes they are accompanied by an interpreter, a hearing person who knows sign language. The interpreter relays the hearing person's speech to the deaf person by sign language, and then reads the deaf person's signs and speaks aloud those words to the hearing person. Some deaf people

344

also become skilled at lip reading, in which they understand other people's speech by watching the way their mouths, faces, and bodies move when they are talking.

Deaf people who live on their own rely on special devices in their homes to alert them to danger or the arrival of visitors. Many smoke detectors, telephones, and door-bells can be equipped with light signals, vibrating devices, or, for those with some hearing, very loud rings or buzzers. Dogs can also be trained to perform such func-tions; these "hearing-ear" dogs alert their deaf owners whenever the phone rings or the alarm clock goes off. Deaf people can communicate by phone with the help of a Telecommunication Device for the Deaf (TDD). These machines, which must be used at both ends of the conversation, translate spoken words into written words; the peo-ple on the phone can then read their conversation rather than hearing it. Enjoying television is also possible, with the help of a closed captioning device. Many television programs are broadcast with captions—the text of every word spoken on the show—that run along the bottom of the screen. With a special device attached to the televi-sion, these captions become visible for those who can't hear what's being said.

Why do some people use **wheelchairs**?

A person may use a wheelchair for many different reasons. Many people in wheelchairs suffer from partial or complete paralysis, which is the loss of control over the move-ment of some part of the body. Paralysis can result from injury to the nervous system, including the brain or spinal cord, or damage to the muscles that control movement. It can also be caused by certain diseases that affect the nervous system, including mul-tiple sclerosis. Some people use a wheelchair not because they are paralyzed but because an injury or disease— like arthritis or scoliosis—has made walking extremely painful or difficult. Many older people, suffering from a stroke, a broken hip, or per-haps simply the weakness and frailty that sometimes accompany old age, must use a wheelchair to get around.

There are many different kinds of wheelchairs, from the manual types that are propelled by moving railings attached to the wheels, to electric wheelchairs that are operated by hand controls that resemble the joysticks used in video games. Some peo-ple prefer a motorized cart, or scooter, with either three or four wheels. These carts are generally smaller and easier to maneuver than typical wheelchairs.

While wheelchairs have the potential to give disabled people much more freedom of movement, that freedom would be useless without things like ramps at building entrances and wheelchair-accessible bathrooms. Thanks to the Americans with Dis-abilities Act (ADA), a law passed in 1990, public buildings and transportation (like buses) must have facilities to accommodate people in wheelchairs. The ADA also makes it illegal for employers to discriminate against disabled people. Young people with disabilities are protected by the Education for All Handicapped Children Act of

1975, which specifies that all children, regardless of disability, have the right to a free and accessible education.

Can people in wheelchairs **drive cars**?

Depending on the severity of the person's disability, driving a car can be an option for people in wheelchairs. Cars can be modified so that the accelerating and braking are done with hand controls. Other modifications, like ramps or motorized lifts, assist the person in getting in and out of the car.

SUBSTANCE ABUSE AND ADDICTION

What is **substance abuse**?

Substance abuse means taking drugs (other than those prescribed by a doctor for a specific illness) in amounts that are dangerous or that prevent a person from doing everyday things, like going to school or work. The substance being abused can be alcohol, marijuana, pills called tranquilizers that make people feel very tired and relaxed, household products that are inhaled, or a number of other drugs. Drug abuse happens all over the world, to all kinds of people, young and old. It frequently causes terrible damage to the person's body, to relationships with family and friends, and to career or education. In some cases, substance abuse leads to death, because the person taking the drugs gets involved in an accident or because he or she overdoses, or takes enough of the drug to cause the body to completely shut down.

What is **addiction**?

In many cases, substance abuse leads to addiction, which means the person taking the drug is dependent on it to feel pleasure or to not get sick. There are two different types of addiction. One type is called psychological addiction, which means the person taking the drug gets hooked on the pleasurable feelings associated with that drug. A physical addiction, on the other hand, means that the person has built up a tolerance to the effects of the drug, requiring more of the drug more often to achieve the same high. Eventually the addicted person must take massive quantities of certain drugs to feel anything from it at all, and those quantities can sometimes reach deadly proportions. If an addicted person stops taking the drug, he or she will go through what is called withdrawal. That means the body has adjusted so much to having the drug in the system that the person feels sick without it. Withdrawal symptoms include fever, restlessness, vomiting, diarrhea, and severe dehydration.

Some drugs are more addictive, or habit-forming, than others. Cigarettes, for example, contain nicotine, which is a highly addictive drug. Many cigarette smokers have a desire to quit but have a very difficult time doing so.

Why do people **do drugs**?

People may begin taking drugs out of a desire to rebel against their parents or society, or because they long to experiment with new feelings and experiences. Many people take drugs to escape from problems with family or at school. For most people, drug use begins because they like the way they feel when they are under a drug's influence, or high. Different drugs have different effects—some are stimulants, which means they give an energy boost and create a feeling of excitement. Others are depressants, which means they slow down the body's systems and produce a calm, relaxed feeling. But no matter how a drug makes you feel, it can't get rid of the things in your life that made you feel like escaping in the first place. In fact, drug use usually makes matters worse— drugs reduce your ability to cope with difficult emotions on your own, and they will make problems you might be having in school or with your family even worse.

While many people refuse to see the harmful effects of drugs, particularly when they first begin taking them, the fact is that every drug has the potential to be harmful, and many drugs can cause death. Drug habits are expensive, and they frequently cause unpleasant personality changes in the user, which results in strained relationships with family members and friends. Many people make the mistake of believing that the more accessible legal drugs, like cigarettes and alcohol, are not as dangerous as illegal drugs. But legal drugs can have serious consequences: if a person consumes very large quantities of alcohol, even if it's his or her first time drinking, it can result in a coma or even death. Many young people wrongly believe that inhaling household chemicals produces an easy and safe high. But inhalants, by coating the lungs and preventing the absorption of oxygen, can also kill—whether it's the first time or the fiftieth. One danger common to nearly all drugs is that, while under the influence, your judgment is impaired and you are more likely to do something that could harm yourself or others.

What does **alcohol** do?

A short while after a person takes a drink of beer, wine, or liquor, the alcohol in that drink will be absorbed into the bloodstream and transported to the brain and the rest of the body (the rate at which that happens depends on the person's size, the concentration of alcohol in the drinks, and how much food is in his or her stomach). Alcohol interferes with the messages normally passed from nerve cells to the rest of the body—a drunk person can't hear, see, smell, taste, or feel as well as a sober person, and drunk people are less sensitive to pain. Alcohol is a depressant, which means it slows down brain function. That slowing gives people a relaxed feeling, but it also

347

means that the senses are dulled and reaction time is slower. With alcohol in their blood, people are less coordinated and lose some control over their muscles—many drunk people have trouble walking without staggering. A particularly dangerous effect of alcohol is the resulting lack of inhibitions, or inner restrictions over behavior. While most people wouldn't drive into oncoming traffic while sober, it might seem like a fun thing to do when drunk. People are more likely to get into fights, drive dangerously, and generally put themselves into risky situations when they are drunk. And because alcohol is a depressant, it will only increase the feelings of sadness or loneliness that drive some people to drink in the first place. For people under the legal drinking age (21 in the United States), alcohol can also cause problems with the police; anyone under age 21 caught with alcohol or under the influence of alcohol can face legal penalties.

Why do people **smoke cigarettes**?

People smoke cigarettes for the same reasons they do any kind of drug—they like the way it makes them feel. Cigarette tobacco contains nicotine, which is a stimulant that produces an energetic, happy feeling in some people. It can also make people feel relaxed, and for some it decreases appetite. Lots of people start smoking because they want to fit in with a certain group of friends, or because they like the image they present when they light up a cigarette. But while smoking is legal (for those over the age of 18), it has been repeatedly proven to be highly addictive and extremely harmful.

In addition to nicotine, cigarettes contain numerous harmful chemicals, like tar and the poisonous gas carbon monoxide. Some minor (but highly unattractive) side effects of smoking include bad breath and permanently discolored teeth and fingers. But these problems pale in comparison to the major health risks of smoking. Cigarette smoking is believed to be the cause of 90 percent of all cases of lung cancer, and lung cancer causes more deaths each year than any other kind of cancer. Smoking causes many other kinds of cancers too, as well as heart disease and numerous other ailments. If women smoke while pregnant, it can cause problems for the health of the fetus. And babies who live in households where people smoke are at an increased risk of dying from Sudden Infant Death Syndrome, or SIDS. Hundreds of thousands of people die each year in the United States from smoking-related illnesses—and if those people had never picked up a cigarette in the first place, those illnesses could have been prevented.

What is **second-hand smoke**?

Second-hand smoke is the smoke inhaled by people who are not themselves smoking but who are near others who are smoking. In the early 1990s, the United States Environmental Protection Agency declared that second-hand smoke can cause cancer and other diseases in people who have never actually smoked a cigarette themselves. As the dangers of second-hand smoke became widely known, many laws were passed in the U. S. to protect nonsmokers from having to inhale another person's smoke. Some of these laws prevent people from smoking in public or government buildings. Non-smoking sections in restaurants have grown larger and larger, with some restaurants banning smoking altogether. As recently as 10 years ago, many people could smoke while sitting at their desks in a large office. Now such behavior is unheard of, and smokers usually have to go outside to have a cigarette.

ENVIRONMENTAL ISSUES

What is **pollution**?

Pollution refers to excessive amounts of waste, much of which contains harmful poisons, that are released into the environment—air, water, and soil. Pollution is usually caused by people; more specifically it is caused by the waste produced by the cars we drive, the factories that make the things we buy, the power plants that produce the gas and electricity we use, and even the farms that grow the food we eat.

Pollution has been a problem ever since large numbers of people occupied a relatively small space. During the 1800s and 1900s, however, as the world became increasingly crowded, and more and more factories were built, environmental pollution became a serious issue.

Air pollution is caused primarily by the burning of fuel. Gas-powered transportation methods—airplanes, cars, boats, and trains—are the biggest culprits. The amount of fuel required to heat and cool homes and other buildings also contributes huge amounts of air pollution. Air pollutants damage Earth's atmosphere and harm plants and animals (including humans).

Water pollution comes from a variety of sources. Any factory that makes things—toys, tires, steel—creates waste products as well. This waste, filled with toxic chemicals, is often released into bodies of water, including lakes, rivers, and oceans. Other harmful water pollutants include sewage, which is human and animal waste. Most sewage is somewhat filtered in septic tanks and treatment plants, but some raw sewage still gets released into water. The chemicals used to control pests and fertilize plants on farms also ends up in lakes and rivers when rainwater drains from the farmland to the bodies of water. Ships carrying massive quantities of oil have also been responsible for polluting the water; if those ships break apart, the oil spills into the water killing birds and fish and damaging the shoreline. The world's oceans and rivers can break down some pollutants into forms that are either harmless or beneficial to

Pollution is caused by the waste produced by cars, factories, power plants, and even farms.

aquatic life. But when pollution levels become too high, the plants and animals living in the water suffer.

Land pollution comes primarily from garbage. Some types of garbage—paper, plastic, some metals, glass, and so on—are recyclable, meaning they can be processed and reused. Some garbage is biodegradable, which means it will naturally break down into tiny particles that can be reused by the environment. Vast quantities of the garbage we produce, however, is not easily broken down or recycled. Garbage is usually dumped in landfills, and as some things slowly decay, a harmful gas called methane is released into the air. Another source of land pollution are the chemicals used on farms; some of those chemicals are washed into bodies of water, and some are absorbed by the ground where they can harm various forms of plant and animal life.

What can be done to **minimize pollution**?

Wherever there are a lot of people, and wherever there are industries, there will be pollution. It cannot be eliminated. But it can be reduced, and many laws have been passed in the United States and elsewhere to help accomplish that. These laws help establish pollution standards, requiring industries to release fewer pollutants into the air and water. But several obstacles remain: Some industries have successfully lobbied lawmakers to be less strict about pollution controls. Many industries are reluctant to cooperate with the laws that have been passed, stating that the required changes are too expensive. And federal agencies lack the funding to enforce the existing laws, so many companies ignore the tighter standards about how much polluting they can do.

In spite of these obstacles, there is much that can be done to clean up our air, water, and land. Some car companies have begun building cars that burn fuel more cleanly or that operate on a more environmentally friendly mix of gas and electricity. Producers of gasoline can make adjustments to the fuel so that fewer harmful emissions are released when it is burned. Sewage treatment plants, if they install the right equipment, can remove nearly all the waste before dumping what's left in bodies of water. Factories can treat their waste to neutralize or remove much of the harmful chemicals before dumping. Alternative energy sources—harnessing the power of water or the Sun, for instance—can be used to supplement the gas and oil that is used now. Landfills can be constructed so that underground pipes carry away the dangerous methane gas, using it to provide power. They can also be covered with dirt, grass, and trees to create a playground or a park. Farmers can use fewer chemicals, relying instead on organic farming methods (free of man-made chemicals).

Individuals and families can also play a part in reducing pollution. Taking part in community recycling efforts and using biodegradable items to create compost (which can then be used in the garden) helps reduce each family's weekly amount of garbage. Families can also make an effort to use less water and electricity. And choosing to buy organic foods supports the farmers who have decided to avoid harmful chemicals.

What is **smog**?

Smog, which originally was named by combining the words "smoke" and "fog," is a type of air pollution. Smog was so named because it can form when moisture in the air combines with smoke particles. The smoke particles come from factories burning coal. This kind of smog has been a problem in London and other cities in Great Britain.

Another kind of smog, called photochemical smog, is generally what people mean when they refer to this kind of pollution. Photochemical smog occurs when sunlight combines with the fumes from cars and factories in big cities. This combination produces a chemical reaction, resulting in gases called oxidants. When the weather conditions are right—very little wind, or a layer of warm air settling on top of a layer of cool air—smog can accumulate and hover in the air. The Los Angeles, California, area is especially famous for its high levels of smog. (The conditions are ripe for a smog problem in Los Angeles: there are a lot of cars, producing a great deal of exhaust; the city is located in a valley, where smog tends to accumulate; and it is surrounded by mountains, which means little wind gets in to break up the smog.)

The oxidants produced in photochemical smog pollute the air, damage plant life, and, in extreme cases, causes people to get sick. It has even been responsible for deaths. Over a four-day period in 1952, the smog in London became so heavy and thick that people could barely see what was in front of them. By the end of that period,

4,000 people had died from lung ailments produced by the toxic chemicals. In the United States, in the town of Donora, Pennsylvania, 20 people died and thousands more became sick when smog levels reached a dangerous high. Laws attempting to reduce levels of air pollution have made some improvements, but the huge number of cars, factories, and power plants in industrialized nations like the United States continue to produce high levels of air pollution.

What is ozone?

Ozone is a sharp-smelling gas that is a form of oxygen. There is a layer of ozone in the upper atmosphere, about 15 miles (25 kilometers) above Earth. That layer helps protect us from the harmful ultraviolet rays of the the Sun. Without the ozone layer, too many of those rays would get through, making it difficult for plants and animals to live. During the 1970s, scientists became aware that certain chemicals, called chlorofluorocarbons, or CFCs, were making the ozone layer thin and even causing some holes. CFCs were used in aerosol cans, air conditioners, and refrigerators. By the mid-1990s, the United States and many other countries had banned the use of CFCs.

Ozone also exists in the lower atmosphere. But while the ozone in the upper atmosphere is beneficial, that in the lower atmosphere causes air pollution. When sunlight interacts with the fumes from cars and trucks, ozone is the main ingredient of the smog that is produced. In large amounts, ozone can cause headaches, itchy eyes, and lung problems in people. It can also harm other animals and plants, and it damages rubber tires and the outside surfaces of buildings.

What are the **greenhouse effect** and **global warming**?

A greenhouse is a glass structure built for plants. The glass walls and ceiling allow the light from the Sun to enter but prevent the Sun's heat from leaving, providing the kind of warm climate greenhouse plants need. Certain gases in the atmosphere act in much the same way as the glass panels of the greenhouse, letting sunlight shine through to the ground and trapping the heat produced by that light.

The greenhouse effect happens naturally, without human interference. But by introducing large amounts of greenhouse gases into the atmosphere, human beings have turned a natural occurrence into a potential problem. With the industrialization of the 1800s and 1900s, the amount of greenhouse gases increased tremendously. Some greenhouse gases, like carbon dioxide, are produced by burning such fuels as coal, natural gas, and oil. The amount of carbon dioxide in the atmosphere has increased by about 25 percent in the last 200 years. Plants absorb some carbon dioxide, but much of it rises to the atmosphere, contributing to the greenhouse effect. Other gases that contribute to the greenhouse effect are ozone and methane.

If too much heat is trapped in the atmosphere, it may eventually make Earth's climate warmer. This effect, known as global warming, may seem harmless enough (and if you live in a place with harsh winters, it might even seem like a good thing), but the delicate balance of life on Earth can be severely disrupted by a change in the planet's climate. If the temperature of Earth's surface increased enough, it could melt the polar ice caps (the massive, thick ice formations at the North and South Poles), raising the level of the oceans and possibly flooding coastal areas. Climate changes can also affect weather patterns—changing rainfall and snowfall amounts and making storms more severe—and the lives of plants and animals.

What is **acid rain**?

Some of the gases released as waste products from factories, cars, and power plants mix with water vapor in the atmosphere to produce acid rain (or sleet or snow). Rain is slightly acidic anyway, but when mixed with such chemicals as sulfuric acid and nitric acid, it can reach dangerous levels. Acid rain can damage soil, crops, and forests as well as eat away at the outer surfaces of buildings. In some places, acid rain that has fallen into lakes and rivers has caused severe harm to the animals and plants living there. Acid rain has affected many parts of the United States and Canada, as well as countries in northern and western Europe and parts of Asia. Because the wind can carry pollutants great distances from their source, many areas have suffered devastating effects of acid rain without being responsible for the chemical waste that caused it.

What are some of the different **energy sources**?

The main energy sources used around the world today are oil, coal, and natural gas. These sources of energy are called fossil fuels, so named because they come from the fossilized remains of plants and animals that lived hundreds of millions of years ago. Coal, for example, comes from fossilized plants and trees. A long time ago, as plants and trees died, their remains became buried under the weight of layers of mud or new plants, and they eventually turned into stone. That stone can be cut out from deep, underground coal mines and burned for energy. Fossil fuels are used primarily for transportation—airplanes, cars, trains, and so on—and for heating and cooling houses and other kinds of buildings. Fossil fuels provide a large percentage of the energy consumed around the world, but they are nonrenewable resources, meaning that there is a limited amount of each of these types of fuel, and when they are gone, no more can be produced.

Because there is a limited supply of fossil fuels, scientists are continuously exploring other sources of energy that have an unlimited supply. These renewable energy sources are cleaner and have much less of an impact on the environment than nonrenewable sources like fossil fuels. Such sources include the Sun (solar power), water (hydropower), and wind. The heat of the Sun can be captured with solar panels and

353

used to heat homes and offices. It can also generate electricity, which can then be used for a variety of purposes. Flowing water can also produce energy. Usually hydropower plants use a dam on a river to collect water in a reservoir, or large pool. When that water is released to flow downward, it passes through a device called a turbine, which has blades like a giant fan. The force of the water spins the turbine, which then activates a generator, which produces electricity. Turbines are also used to convert the power of wind into electricity. These turbines, with blades like a propeller, are mounted on a tall tower. The wind spins the blades, and, as with hydropower, the spinning of the turbine causes a generator to produce electrical power. Another renewable energy source is called geothermal energy, which uses the heat from just below Earth's surface. This heat can be converted into electricity or used to directly provide heat for buildings. There are many advantages to renewable energy sources, but scientists have yet to solve problems associated with producing these kinds of energy inexpensively and transporting that energy to distant areas.

Another important energy source is nuclear energy. Nuclear energy comes from either splitting the nucleus of an atom (called nuclear fission) or combining atomic nuclei (called nuclear fusion). The nuclear energy produced today comes from fission. The process of splitting atoms produces a massive amount of energy that can be used in many different ways. But nuclear fission has some serious disadvantages. The process creates large quantities of hot water that must be cooled, using expensive machines, before being dumped into lakes or rivers. (If water is dumped while still hot, it can cause something called thermal pollution: the hot waste water raises the temperature of a body of water, disrupting the balance of life in that water and even killing some fish and other creatures.) Nuclear fission also produces radioactive waste, which is dangerous to the environment and must be stored safely for long periods of time. The threat of an accident involving a leak of radioactive material is always present at a nuclear power plant.

What is **Earth Day**?

During the 1960s information about problems with the environment—chemicals killing fish in waters, air pollution damaging the atmosphere and endangering the health of all creatures, the widespread destruction of forests and other natural areas— began to concern people all over the world. A country's senator named Gaylord Nelson wondered why environmental issues were so disturbing to citizens but didn't seem to be on the government's list of problems to correct. A massive war protest movement, led by regular citizens against the United States' involvement in the war in Vietnam, gave Nelson an idea: why couldn't there be one day set aside for the entire nation to focus on environmental issues, learn about ways to improve the situation, and protest against the government's unwillingness to act?

After months of hard work and lots of publicity, the first Earth Day was celebrated on April 22, 1970. Twenty million Americans gathered at different places from coast to coast to hear speeches, participate in community-wide cleanup efforts, and, perhaps most important, to demonstrate to the government that the environment is a major national issue. One of the most impressive points about Earth Day is that it was (and still is) what is called a grassroots effort. This means that all the activities in the thousands of communities around the country were planned and organized by the people living in those communities. The idea was started by someone involved in government (Senator Nelson), but Earth Day happened because huge numbers of citizens got involved and decided to make a difference.

Ever since then, April 22 has been the date for celebrating Earth Day—a time when the whole country (and now many countries all over the world) could participate in educational activities that celebrate Earth and come up with new ways to preserve our natural resources and clean up the messes that have been made in our water, air, and land.

DINOSAURS AND FOSSILS

What is a **fossil**?

A fossil is the hardened remains or an imprint of a plant or animal that lived a very long time ago. Some fossils are thousands of years old, others are several hundred million years old. Most plants and animals died and then decayed without ever leaving a trace. But some were buried— under mud, rocks, ice, or other heavy coverings—before decaying. The pressure of these layers over thousands of years turned animal and plant remains into rock. Usually fossils preserve the organism's hard parts—the bones or shells of an animal and the seeds, stems, and leaf veins of plants.

Sometimes the fossil is the actual animal part, like a bone or tooth, that has hardened into rock. Some fossils, called trace fossils, show the imprint of parts of the animal or plant. Occasionally these imprints act as a mold, and the sediment that fills the imprint hardens and becomes a cast of, for example, a dinosaur footprint. Sometimes bones or trees are preserved by minerals that seep into the part's pores and then harden, or petrify, that part. Arizona's Petrified Forest contains numerous examples of giant trees that were petrified millions of years ago.

In some cases, an entire animal is preserved in ice, hardened tree sap (called amber), or in dry, desert areas. In these instances, as with woolly mammoths found in Alaska and elsewhere, the whole animal—hair, skin, bones, internal organs—is preserved much as it was when it died thousands of years earlier.

355

Trace fossils like this one show the imprint of parts of an animal or plant. *Robert J. Huffman/Field Mark Publications © 2001*

How can scientists tell the **age of fossils**?

Scientists can learn many things about the conditions on the planet and ancient animal behavior from fossils. They can learn whether an area was once covered by lush forests, for example, or they can determine that some dinosaurs traveled in herds. They can also tell, in many cases, how long ago the fossilized plant or animal lived. One way to narrow down a fossil's age is by seeing what layer, or strata, of rock it appears in—the deepest layers contain the oldest fossils, while the top layers contain the most recent fossils. If they know the history of other fossils found nearby, specifically when these other animals lived, then they can determine the approximate age of newly found fossils.

In some cases, scientists can pinpoint the age of a fossil by measuring something called a radioactive isotope. An isotope can be thought of as a version of a chemical element, like hydrogen or carbon, that has a slightly different atomic makeup than other versions of that element. For example, one isotope of hydrogen has one particle, a proton, in the nucleus. Another isotope has two particles, a proton and a neutron. Both are hydrogen, but they are different types of hydrogen. A radioactive isotope is one that is unstable and gives off some radiation. Over time, radioactive isotopes decay, forming a different chemical element altogether. For example, uranium eventually changes into lead. Scientists know how long it takes for various radioactive isotopes to decay. They discuss this time in terms of the isotope's half-life, or the amount of time it takes for half of the isotope to decay. If a radioactive isotope has a 1,000-year half-life, then half of it will have decayed in 1,000 years and all of it will have decayed, or turned into another element, in 2,000 years. So let's say a scientist measures the amount of a radioactive isotope in a chunk of rock, knowing that this element will have completely transformed into another element after 2,000 years. If the scientist finds very little of the isotope and a great deal of the element it turns into, then he or she knows that the rock—and the fossil found in it—is almost 2,000 years old.

How long ago did **dinosaurs live**?

Dinosaurs first appeared about 230 million years ago, during the Triassic Period. Their large size and vast numbers meant that they dominated animal life on Earth for millions of years. Dinosaurs became extinct around 65 million years ago, at the end of the Cretaceous Period. The earliest human beings lived about 2 million years ago, millions of years after the last dinosaur had died.

Earth was much different when dinosaurs roamed the planet. Several hundred million years ago, instead of there being seven continents, or large land masses, there was just one giant mass of land that was surrounded by ocean. This land mass gradually broke apart into separate continents. Areas that are now covered with tall buildings or mountain ranges were once beneath the sea, and scientists believe the climate was fairly warm throughout the year. By the end of the era in which dinosaurs lived, temperatures had cooled and distinct seasons had developed.

What did dinosaurs eat?

Dinosaurs came in many different shapes and sizes, and they also had a variety of diets. Most dinosaurs ate plants, with the very large dinosaurs eating leaves from the tops of trees and smaller ones eating plants and bushes growing close to the ground.

Some dinosaurs were meat-eaters, with most hunting other animals for food and some being scavengers who ate the flesh of dead animals they encountered. The hunters preyed on plant-eating dinosaurs and even on each other. Smaller meat-eating dinosaurs fed on other animals, like insects, lizards, and mammals. Evidence suggests that some dinosaurs hunted in packs, while others lived solitary lives.

How big were the **largest dinosaurs**?

Information about dinosaurs changes all the time as new bones are found and new evidence about their surroundings becomes available. Each year, scientists discover around seven new types of dinosaurs. The dinosaur now considered the largest could be pushed out of first place by another creature soon to be discovered.

The largest dinosaurs belong to the group called sauropods. These giant plant-eaters include the Apatosaurus (pronounced "uh pat uh SAWR uhs"; used to be called

357

A model of the Apatosaurus, one of the biggest dinosaur species that ever roamed the planet.

Brontosaurus) and Brachiosaurus (pronounced "bray key oh SAWR uhs"), which weighed around 80 tons (that's 160,000 pounds, or 72,640 kilograms) and stood 50 feet (15 meters) tall. Among the longest of these dinosaurs were the Seismosaurus (pronounced "SYZ muh sawr uhs") and Supersaurus. The Seismosaurus may have been as long as 150 feet (45 meters), while the Supersaurus may have stretched to nearly 100 feet (30 meters). A newly discovered dinosaur, called Paralititan, is thought to have been close to 100 feet (30 meters) long, weighing close to 70 tons (140,000 pounds, or 63,560 kilograms). The upper bone of its forelimb (front leg) is 6 feet, 7 inches long (close to 2 meters). The Argentinosaurus, thought to weigh as much as 100 tons (200,000 pounds, or 90,800 kilograms), was uncovered in the late 1990s in Argentina, which was home to many of the world's largest dinosaurs.

These gentle giants were once thought to live in watery, swampy regions, but recent evidence suggests that most of them were forest dwellers who ate leaves from the tops of trees. They had enormous bodies, very long necks, relatively small heads, and thick, tree-trunk-like legs, much like an elephant's legs. They moved very slowly and didn't have many ways to defend themselves, but their tremendous size kept most predators away.

Which dinosaurs were the **smallest**?

When most people think of dinosaurs they picture the huge ones, like the giant plant-eating sauropods or the large carnivores (meat eaters) like Tyrannosaurus rex. But some dinosaurs were actually very small. The smallest of them may have been the Compsognathus (pronounced "kahmp SAHG nuh thuhs"), which was only about as big as a chicken.

What were some of the biggest **meat-eating dinosaurs**?

For many years Tyrannosaurus rex (whose name means "king of the tyrant lizards") reigned as the biggest and meanest of the carnivorous dinosaurs. At 40 feet (12 meters), and with a head nearly 5 feet (1.5 meters) long and teeth 6 inches (15 centimeters) long, T. rex was definitely not a dinosaur you'd want to meet face-to-face. But some dinosaur bones discovered in the early 1990s show that T. rex was not the biggest carnivorous dinosaur ever to have terrorized the planet. Giganotosaurus (pronounced "JY ga NO toe sawr uhs") was slightly longer at nearly 42 feet (12.6 meters) long. It lived about 30 million years before T. rex. Scientists believe there are other ferocious meat-eaters that were even larger than the Giganotosaurus.

Why did dinosaurs become **extinct**?

Scientists do not know for sure why dinosaurs became extinct. They have many different theories, some of which explain the extinction as something that happened gradually over a long period of time. Other theories suggest that a single catastrophe caused the dinosaur population to die off rather suddenly. And some scientists believe the dinosaur population had been gradually getting smaller and then was finished off by some dramatic event.

Some who believe gradual changes brought about the dinosaurs' end suggest that, as more and more mammals appeared, the dinosaurs had trouble competing with them for food sources. And these mammals may have eaten dinosaur eggs in such large numbers that fewer and fewer baby dinosaurs were born. Some experts believe that widespread disease killed off dinosaurs. Many suggest that gradual climate changes—from continuously warm, mild weather to seasonal variations with hot summers and cold winters—affected the dinosaurs. Scientists are not sure whether dinosaurs were warm-blooded or cold-blooded (and there may have been some of each). If they were cold-blooded, meaning that their body temperature changed depending on the temperature of their surroundings, it would have been difficult for such large animals to survive extreme temperatures. Smaller cold-blooded creatures can burrow under the ground, for example, to escape both heat and cold. But most dinosaurs were simply too large to do that.

The scientists who believe that dinosaurs became extinct after a major catastrophe point to evidence that suggests a huge asteroid, perhaps several miles wide, hit Earth. The impact of such an object would have created enormous clouds of dust and other debris. The heat of impact would have started fires over a great area. Between the dust

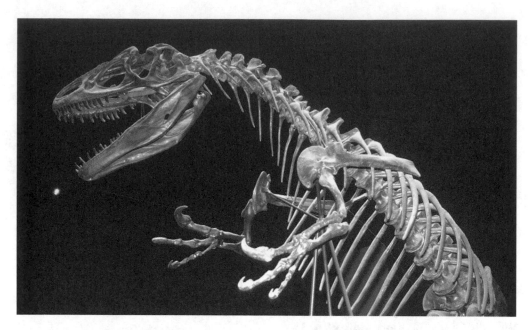

Some scientists believe that dinosaurs became extinct after a huge asteroid, perhaps several miles wide, hit Earth. *Robert J. Huffman/Field Mark Publications © 2001*

clouds and the smoke from the fires, sunlight would have been blocked, maybe for several months. A lack of sunlight would have caused a dramatic drop in temperature, and much plant life would have died. Without plants, the plant-eating dinosaurs and many other animals would have died; without the plant-eating dinosaurs and those other animals, the meat-eating dinosaurs would eventually die as well.

Some scientists argue that not all dinosaurs became extinct. The striking similarities between modern birds and some kinds of dinosaurs have led some people to believe that birds are living descendants of dinosaurs.

AMAZING SCIENCE

What is a **clone**?

To understand cloning, we must first understand a few things about cells. All living things, from the simplest to the most complex, are made up of cells. Cells are specialized to perform a variety of functions—there are muscle cells, skin cells, nerve cells, and so on. Cells group together to form tissue, and tissues group together to make organs like the heart, liver, and kidneys. An organism grows and develops through a process called cell division—one cell divides into two, then each of those two divides again, and so on until eventually, in the case of human beings, trillions of cells have been produced to make up a complete living person. All cells in multicellular organisms contain a nucleus, which acts as the command center of the cell. The nucleus contains all of the organism's genetic material, including the DNA, or deoxyribonucleic acid, which determines whether a rose will be red or yellow, whether a person will have curly hair or straight.

The word "clone" can refer to a group of cells that share the same genetic material or to two or more complete organisms that are genetically identical. That means that the clone is an exact copy of one of its parents (whereas we are made up of the combined features of both our parents). Cloning does occur naturally—simple organisms like bacteria, for example, reproduce asexually, which means new organisms come from only one parent and share that parent's genetic material. When humans and other animals produce identical twins, those twins are clones of each other (though not of either parent).

But the kind of cloning we hear about in school or on the news is engineered by scientists. Scientists have been conducting experiments for years in an attempt to create a complex organism that is a clone of another organism. While they had some success over the years cloning frogs and salamanders, nothing captured the world's attention like the breakthrough scientists made at the Roslin Institute in Scotland in 1996. After 276 failed attempts, a group of scientists led by Ian Wilmut successfully cloned a sheep (named Dolly), the first mammal ever to be cloned. The process used to create the cloned sheep, called somatic cell nuclear transfer, began with an egg cell from one sheep. The scientists destroyed that egg cell's nucleus and then injected the nucleus from the cell of another sheep into the egg cell. With a little encouragement from electronic stimulation, the donated nucleus fused with the egg cell, and the new cell began to divide. The cluster of cells was then implanted into the uterus of the sheep that had provided the egg cell, and five months later Dolly was born—an exact replica not of the sheep that had carried her in the womb but of the sheep that had supplied the nucleus.

While cloning mammals is very controversial, some scientists argue that it could have many benefits. Under the right circumstances, cloning could be used to increase the population of animals that are listed as endangered species. Cloning also has advantages to livestock farmers, who could use the technology to breed only high-quality animals that produce the most milk or the finest wool.

Will **people be cloned** someday?

The breakthroughs in cloning technology made by the Roslin scientists—and several other scientists since then who have successfully cloned mice, monkeys, and cows—

361

have raised new hopes (and fears) that the technology to clone a human being is within reach. Some scientists believe that the first successful cloning of a human being will happen before the end of this century's first decade. The method to clone a human will most likely be the same as that used to clone Dolly the sheep.

The cloning of mammals—and the possibility of cloning a person—has sparked many arguments about whether it's right or wrong to conduct such experiments. While some argue that cloning can yield tremendous benefits, others worry that the technology is ripe for abuse. Many politicians and scientists have called for a worldwide ban on human cloning until further research can be conducted. Some countries have agreed and instituted such a ban.

Why is cloning so **controversial**?

The possibility of cloning human beings arouses curiosity and excitement in some people and deep suspicion and fear in others. Scientists and doctors have long intervened in the creation of new life, such as using various fertility treatments to help people have babies who otherwise couldn't. But these techniques require doctors to assist in the process that happens in nature—the merging of a sperm cell from a man's body with an egg from a woman's body. Cloning bypasses that process altogether, using one person's cells to create a new human being that will be identical to that person. That level of scientific involvement in the creation of human life makes many people uncomfortable.

Supporters of cloning technology argue that there are numerous benefits to human cloning. Many scientists believe that cloning can lead to important breakthroughs for people with incurable diseases. This type of activity, called therapeutic cloning, has as its goal the creation of certain kinds of cells rather than the duplication of a complete person. In such experiments, a human embryo (the group of cells that, if implanted into a uterus, would grow into a baby) would be produced through cloning so that the embryo's stem cells, special cells that can develop into many different kinds of cells and tissue, can be extracted (destroying the embryo in the process). Stem cells can then be used to grow new tissue to replace a sick person's damaged organs or to cure diseases that otherwise would be fatal. Some scientists wish to pursue cloning technology to create babies for people who are unable to have children (and who wish to produce a child that shares their genetic makeup rather than adopting a baby).

Many people have deeply felt concerns about cloning, particularly human cloning. They fear that this relatively new science is still too risky and unpredictable; experiments with cloning a human might result in serious defects or health problems for the cloned subjects. Even Ian Wilmut, the scientist who led the team that produced the cloned sheep Dolly, has strongly objected to experimenting with human cloning before further research is done. Many people object to cloning on religious grounds, arguing that life is sacred, and only God—not scientists and doctors—can create new life. Others worry that the ability to clone a person might be abused by some who would spend a great deal of money to create a genetically perfect child, selecting certain traits and discarding others. Many people are disturbed by the thought that some people might use cloning technology to "replace" a loved one who had died.

For More Information

Books

The American Medical Association Family Medical Guide. New York: Random House, 1994.

Ardley, Bridget, and Neil Ardley. *The Random House Book of 1001 Questions and Answers*. New York: Random House, 1999.

Arnold, Caroline. *Cats: In from the Wild*. Minneapolis: Carolrhoda Books, 1993.

Baron, Connie. *The Physically Disabled*. New York: Macmillan, 1988.

Black, David, and Anthony Huxley. *Plants*. New York: Facts on File, 1985.

Burnie, David. *The Concise Encyclopedia of the Human Body*. London: DK Publishing, 1995.

Chiarelli, Brunetto, and Anna Lisa Bebi. *The Atlas of World Cultures*. New York: Peter Bedrick Books, 1997.

Cribb, Joe. *Money*. New York: Knopf, 1990.

Dow, Lesley. *Incredible Plants*. New York: Time-Life, 1997.

Farndon, John. *What Happens When . . . ?* New York: Scholastic, 1996.

Feldman, David. *Why Do Clocks Run Clockwise? And Other Imponderables*. New York: HarperCollins, 1988.

Fogle, Bruce. *The New Encyclopedia of the Dog*. London: DK Publishing, 2000.

Ford, Brian J. *The Random House Library of Knowledge First Encyclopedia of Science*. New York: Random House, 1993.

Guinness World Records 2001. New York: Bantam, 2001.

Gundersen, P. Erik. *The Handy Physics Answer Book*. Detroit: Visible Ink Press, 1999.

Halley, Ned. *Farm*. New York: Knopf, 1996.

The Handy Science Answer Book, 2nd ed. Detroit: Visible Ink Press, 1997.

Hickman, Pamela. *Starting with Nature: Plant Book*. Toronto: Kids Can Press, 1996.

James, Elizabeth, and Carol Barkin. *Social Smarts: Manners for Today's Kids.* Boston: Clarion Books, 1996.

Knox, Jean McBee. *Death and Dying.* Broomall, PA: Chelsea House, 2000.

Langone, John. *National Geographic's How Things Work: Everyday Technology Explained.* Washington, D.C.: National Geographic Society, 1999.

Leach, Penelope. *Your Baby and Child: From Birth to Age Five.* New York: Knopf, 1997.

LeShan, Eda. *What Makes Me Feel This Way?: Growing Up with Human Emotions.* New York: Macmillan, 1974.

Lyons, Walter A. *The Handy Weather Answer Book.* Detroit: Visible Ink Press, 1997.

Macaulay, David. *The New Way Things Work.* Boston: Houghton Mifflin, 1998.

The New York Public Library Amazing Space: A Book of Answers for Kids. New York: John Wiley and Sons, 1997.

Oxlade, Chris. *Houses and Homes.* Danbury, CT: Franklin Watts, 1994.

Parker, Steve, and Giovanni Caselli. *The Body and How It Works.* London: DK Publishing, 1992.

Rosenberg, Matthew T. *The Handy Geography Answer Book.* Detroit: Visible Ink Press, 1999.

Silverstein, Alvin, and Virginia Silverstein. *Dogs: All About Them.* New York: William Morrow, 1986.

Things Around Us. New York: Time-Life, 1988.

The Universe (First Facts series). New York: Kingfisher, 1994.

Visual Encyclopedia of Science. London: DK Publishing, 2000.

Waldbauer, Gilbert. *The Handy Bug Answer Book.* Detroit: Visible Ink Press, 1998.

Wood, Robert W. *The McGraw-Hill Big Book of Science Activities: Fun and Easy Experiments for Kids.* New York: McGraw-Hill, 1999.

Web Sites

ASPCA Animaland. [Online] Available http://www.animaland.org/index.asp (last accessed September 24, 2001).

DiscoverySchool.com. [Online] Available http://school.discovery.com/ (last accessed September 24, 2001).

Enchanted Learning. [Online] Available http://www.enchantedlearning.com/Home.html (last accessed September 24, 2001).

Guinness World Records. [Online] Available http://www.guinnessworldrecords.com/ (last accessed September 24, 2001).

Infoplease.com. [Online] Available http://www.infoplease.com/index.html (last accessed September 24, 2001).

Kidport Reference Library. [Online] Available http://www.kidport.com/RefLib/RefLib.htm (last accessed September 24, 2001).

KidsHealth. [Online] Available http://kidshealth.org/index.html (last accessed September 24, 2001).

Marshall Brain's How Stuff Works. [Online] Available http://www.howstuffworks.com/ (last accessed September 24, 2001).

Nowak, Ronald M. *Walker's Mammals of the World*. [Online] Available http://www.press.jhu.edu/books/walker/w-contents.html (last accessed September 24, 2001).

"Science Q&A." *The Learning Network: The New York Times on the Web*. [Online] Available http://www.nytimes.com/learning/students/scienceqa/index.html (last accessed September 24, 2001).

Index

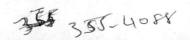